"I've read *The Art of BART*. I didn't agree wit] didn't understand every word, many of which re(erudition or oriental spiritual awareness than I currently possess. But I learned a very great deal from it, and I believe there is a lot of original thinking behind it.

"Most major advances in scientific and psychotherapeutic thinking have come from one passionately engaged person believing in something new, trying it out, beginning to gather evidence for it, and then sharing. Dr O'Malley's professional career and interests have given him a distinctive viewpoint and perspective in mental health, within a focal aperture, which is still relatively youthful in the psychotherapeutic world. It is a courageous book, as there will no doubt be many in the conflating worlds of neurobiology, psychology, psychiatry, and psychotherapy who, as Dr Iain McGilchrist might well put it, will address this book from their rationale, 'black or white,' left brain hemisphere instead of their intuitive, 'open to the new,' right one.

"Mental ill-health is now widely accepted – to represent a huge and growing proportion of all ill health; to have a knock-on effect in causation of related physical ill health through psychosomatic interaction; to account for more lost UK working days than any other cause; and to cost the UK NHS a rapidly growing amount to treat while only beneficially addressing a relatively small proportion of the latent demand now estimated to exist within the UK population.

"The book is carefully referenced and draws attention to the seminal work of others leading in the field of neurophysiological and neuropsychological interaction, including current leaders in their field like Shapiro, F., Porges, S, Panksepp, J., Ogden, P., and McGilchrist, I. In addition, Dr O'Malley brings together aspects of both Western and Eastern healing traditions to show a historical global direction of travel towards a unified understanding of the way human beings respond to developmentally chronic and/or subsequently acute traumatic stress.

"Dr O'Malley proposes more than a scholarly comment. He adds a novel therapeutic approach, requiring new bio resonating equipment that he has designed, commissioned, and tested, bringing together the worlds explored with such very recent success using EMDR, SF-EMDR Psychotherapy, and Polyvagal Theory. With it he has obtained effective clinical improvement in the mental health of many of his patients, of all ages. Publication of this work is his critical step in opening it up to professional scrutiny, and further critical research by interested others, towards his hope that many more people may benefit from it."

Peter Eldridge,
Counsellor, Psychotherapist, Supervisor, and EMDR Therapist Fleet,
Hampshire, UK

Sensorimotor-Focused EMDR

Sensorimotor-Focused EMDR combines two hugely influential and effective therapies, EMDR therapy and sensorimotor psychotherapy, to provide a new approach. In doing so, the book supports the widely held view of psychotherapists that in trauma the primary store of neurological information is somatic rather than cognitive.

Many therapists trained in EMDR find that additional resources are needed for patients who present with symptoms of complex trauma and dissociation. This is because EMDR is primarily a top-down approach based on CBT, with the addition of bilateral stimulation (BLS) in visual, tactile and auditory modalities. By contrast, *Sensorimotor-Focused EMDR* takes a body-based and bottom-up approach that seeks to resolve trauma by reprocessing information at multiple levels – in the gut-brain, the heart-brain and the head-brain, as well as in the endocrine, immune and nervous systems.

Fully revised since *The Art of BART* (2015), the book looks at the latest advances in neuroscience, including research into the effectiveness of psychotherapy and the mysteries of consciousness and the development of mind. It also looks at the role of newly discovered organs, the mesentery and the interstitium, and provides clear anatomical evidence for the communication of biophotons in energy channels known as the primo vascular system.

SF-EMDR is the only therapy that fully integrates Western theories of affective neuroscience with Eastern observations on activation of chakras, pranas and energies, and in doing so it offers strong potential for enhanced outcomes and optimized performance for patients.

Arthur G. O'Malley qualified as a doctor in Trinity College Dublin in 1990. He worked as a consultant psychiatrist in the NHS from 2004 and has been in full-time private practice since 2018. A fellow of the Royal College of Psychiatrists since 2011, he has presented widely on trauma, neglect, the brain, attachment and personality disorders, autism spectrum conditions, depression, anxiety, and ADHD.

Sensorimotor-Focused EMDR

A New Paradigm for Psychotherapy and Peak Performance

Arthur G. O'Malley

R Routledge
Taylor & Francis Group

LONDON AND NEW YORK

First published 2019
by Routledge
2 Park Square, Milton Park, Abingdon, Oxon OX14 4RN

and by Routledge
52 Vanderbilt Avenue, New York, NY 10017

Routledge is an imprint of the Taylor & Francis Group, an informa business

British Library Cataloguing-in-Publication Data
A catalogue record for this book is available from the British Library

Library of Congress Cataloging-in-Publication Data
A catalog record has been requested for this book

ISBN: 978-1-138-34622-2 (hbk)
ISBN: 978-1-138-34623-9 (pbk)
ISBN: 978-0-429-43740-3 (ebk)

Typeset in Times New Roman
by Swales & Willis Ltd

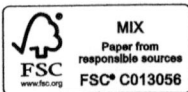

MIX
Paper from
responsible sources
FSC
www.fsc.org   FSC® C013056

Printed and bound in Great Britain by
TJ International Ltd, Padstow, Cornwall

In memory of my father Arthur who died surrounded by family in 1993 age eighty-two and my sister Grainne who lost her battle with Crohn's disease in 1996 at the age of forty-two. And for my sister Suzanne and mother Joan who died in 2015. May their guiding light continue to shine and may they rest in peace.

Contents

Figures

About the author

I have worked for the UK National Health Service as a child and adolescent psychiatrist from 2004 until 2017 and became accredited as an EMDR consultant in 2008. I have been a member of the UK and Ireland EMDR association since 2002 and was a member of the European Conference organising committee for the London Conference and the Child and Adolescent Committee. I have presented at our AGMs in Glasgow, Manchester, Dublin, and at the European conferences in Paris and London. I have presented widely in the fields of trauma, neglect, and the developing brain, attachment disorders, personality disorders, emotional dysregulation in ADHD, and ASD diagnosis and management.

I have an interest in infant and maternal mental health and am a member of the North West Regional Steering Group. The report "Improving outcomes and ensuring quality" was published in April 2011. It is a guide for commissioners and providers of perinatal and infant mental health services. I have jointly set up a parent–infant mental health clinic in Halton General Hospital. This is designed for parents of infants where there are significant difficulties in the parent–infant relationship. The trauma-focused approach includes SF-EMDR psychotherapy for both psychotherapy and peak performance. Infant mental health is addressed using the Watch, Wait, and Wonder dyadic psychotherapy approach (WWW). This book expands on my previous model to incorporate an SF-EMDR–focused approach using EMDR for psychotherapy, optimal functioning, and eventually peak performance for clients and patients.

I have been actively supervising therapists towards accreditation as both Practitioners and Consultants in EMDR. I worked as part of a multidisciplinary CAMHS team at the Thorn Road Clinic. In January 2011 I was elected to the fellowship of the Royal College of Psychiatrists. I organised a conference on trauma-focused therapies (17 June 2011), which was held in Manchester Conference Centre and hosted by the Association for Child and Adolescent Mental Health.

I presented my therapeutic approach at the annual conference of the International Society for the Study of Trauma and Dissociation in November in Canada and the Bowlby Centre in London in 2011. My first one-day workshop on the

Art of Bart was presented at the Brunei Gallery in SOAS, London in November 2013. I introduced attendees to the concept of Bilateral Affective Reprocessing of Thoughts as a dynamic form of psychotherapy at the second one-day workshop held in the Welcome Centre, Coventry, for the West Midlands branch of ACAMH. Since 2015 the concept of SF-EMDR has been developed to provide clinicians with a range of therapeutic options to enhance their therapeutic client relationship.

Acknowledgements

I would like to thank my wife Maura and our children Sorcha, Oisín and Clíodhna for their support and encouragement during the arduous process of writing this book. I would like to thank Sorcha O'Malley for her superb artwork in creating many of the enclosed drawings. Steve Pratt during one of our many supervision sessions first encouraged me to write down my ideas. He and his wife Carol have been a constant source of support. It was from this seed that the idea for a book blossomed. Jeff Hughes and Cathy Hamer gave me the opportunity in their St Helen's home to deliver my first presentation of my therapeutic approaches. They have continued to be a support throughout the process. To all the friends who took the time to read early drafts. Special thanks to Peter Eldridge who provided meticulous notes to accompany his very helpful comments. To Nick Poole for looking after me when I lost consciousness and who in many ways has kept me on the path when it seemed easier to stray from it. To Andrea and Colin Willan for always being there when needed. For Krys, Sandie, and Sarah; who have shown the enduring qualities of friendship. Fran S. Waters from the US encouraged me to submit an abstract on BART to the International Society for the study of Trauma and Dissociation (ISSTD). I was able to present at their annual conference in Montreal, galvanising my determination to see this work reach a wider audience. My sisters Maire Mc Loughlin and Una Wan were always excited by the work and keen to hear of the latest instalments. When I presented my work to an audience in Sheffield, Sian Morgan from the Humanitarian Assistance Programme of the UK and Ireland EMDR association invited me to be the guest lecturer for a one-day workshop to raise funds for the HAP organisation. The day was facilitated by Mark Brayne and attended by seventy-five delegates. I received an overwhelmingly positive response. This was vindication for my ideas as I was leaving myself open to criticism by promulgating a novel approach to therapy. I was reassured by speaking to David Grand, a psychologist based in New York. He trained like me in EMDR. He then went on to teach Natural Flow EMDR before stumbling on brainspotting, which he has been teaching around the world for ten years. New discoveries are emerging about information processing in the human nervous system on a regular basis. It is up to each therapist to integrate this knowledge and apply it to the benefit of his or her clients and patients.

My family in Ireland remain a source of strength, none more so than my mother Joan. Her wisdom stems in part from the upheavals in society experienced since her birth in 1921 at the time of the Irish Civil War. She died on 4th July in keeping with her lifelong independence. I would like to thank Pat Scully from Rédacteurs Ltd for editorial assistance and Denis, whose case history is part of the book. Ania Partakis helped prepare this transcript while Rod Tweedy and Constance Govindan from Karnac Books have held my hand along each step of the publication process. I am indebted to their professionalism. Finally, I would like to thank my patients and supervisees who always provide an opportunity for learning and growth.

Preface

This book arose from a need to analyse and synthesise the fields of psychotherapy, peak performance and neurobiology. Knowledge in these areas has mushroomed over the last ten years. The next decade has been designated by Europe as the start of the human brain project (HBP). The goal is to develop a computerised model of the brain to test out and model brain diseases and their treatments. *Sensorimotor-Focused EMDR: A New Paradigm for Psychotherapy and Peak Performance* presents a new paradigm in psychotherapeutic research and practise. This is one integrating medicine from the East and West, merging chakras with the endocrine nervous and immune systems and allowing the information-processing neural networks of the gut-brain to communicate with those of the heart and head. Moving on from the model proposed in 2015 the refined sensorimotor-focused EMDR, for psychotherapy and peak performance, integrates the latest research on quantum consciousness and information and energy processing at the level of the body and mind, to stimulate positive change both psychologically and psychiatrically.

This book:

1. Introduces a new concept around integrating information processing.
2. Helps therapists treat traumatic stress more effectively.
3. Discusses the role of quantum field therapy in the evolution of psychotherapy.
4. Enables psychotherapists to move their clients and patients towards the achievement of their goals and objectives, optimal functioning and ultimately peak performance.

Chapter 1

Concept of intuition and introduction to **SF-EMDR** for both psychotherapy and peak performance

Introduction

It was during my childhood in Northern Ireland in a town called South Armagh that the "troubles" started. I was only six. We lived over a drapery shop on the main street in a rural village called Newtownhamilton. Soon the region became known as bandit country, and a large joint RUC–British Army base was established in the heart of the town, less than one hundred metres from our house. In 1970, while leaving the kitchen, I was suddenly blown onto the floor by the force of an explosion, which had gone off without warning. What amazed me was the fact that I had no conscious awareness of what had happened. As I gingerly got up and realised the walls were still standing, I gradually came to comprehend what had happened. This was the first of over forty explosions, rocket attacks, shootings, and incendiary devices that the town's residents experienced over the years. The personal nadir for our family was when my parents and some workmen were held hostage while the IRA planted booby-trap explosive devices in our house and hardware shop. The British Army, in a controlled explosion, later razed this to the ground while our whole family was evacuated. One week later, my older brother was over from England on holidays. While walking over the rubble, he spotted a wire. The alarm was raised, as he had just stumbled over an unexploded bomb. We were again evacuated while the army bomb disposal squad made the device safe.

I relate this to explain where my interest in trauma resolution came from. When I specialised as a child psychiatrist, I started to investigate and train in trauma-focused therapies. These included:

- Trauma-focused cognitive behaviour therapy. However, many of my patients were "unable to think" and in a state of speechless terror. They needed a different approach. I like to conceptualise this as targeted functional core-belief therapy. Isolating the key core belief is vital for successful trauma-focused treatment.
- Eye movement desensitisation and reprocessing therapy (EMDR). I became an EMDR Europe accredited consultant in 2008 when very few child and adolescent psychiatrists had trained in this approach. In 2013, I renewed

my accreditation as a consultant in EMDR for a further five years. I found this technique very useful for my patients. However, children's eye movements are immature, and they are often unable to track across the midline. I therefore used tactile and auditory bilateral stimulation to good effect. However, part of the jigsaw was missing concerning preverbal traumatic memories. This was partially addressed by attending training delivered by the wonderful paediatrician from California Dr Joan Lovett, and summarised in her book *Small Wonders*. She recounts how she was several years recovering from a road-traffic accident. This caused her to re-evaluate her life and dedicate her career towards helping families with babies born prematurely and in incubators in neonatal intensive care as well as other traumatised infants. I used this training along with colleagues to deliver a parental and infant mental health service in the NHS. However, it was clear to me that these techniques did not address the instinctive responses of the body.

- I spent one year training in SM psychotherapy at the training institute based in Lincoln. This approach was developed by Pat Ogden (2006), who published the book *Trauma and the Body: A SF-EMDR Approach to Psychotherapy*. During the practical sessions of the training, I realised that my SF-EMDR trauma memory could be accessed as easily as my episodic and semantic memories. I knew this would lead to more effective psychotherapy when combined with the other techniques.
- This led to the dynamic model for psychotherapy and peak performance called bilateral affective reprocessing of thoughts or BART. It is a form of psychotherapy with universal application.
- I have recently commenced a series of podcasts with the trauma therapist Roland Bal. Although from Holland he is based in Barcelona and treats clients internationally via Skype using a combination of somatic and cognitive techniques. Using somatic experiencing, clients are encouraged to get a felt sense of their traumatic experience. These will be made available via artomalley.com and rolandbal.com.

In this book, I will outline the art and science behind the technique. I started my life's journey in 1962 and now, fifty years later, in the words of Victor Hugo, "there is nothing more powerful than an idea whose time has come."

Background to SF-EMDR for psychotherapy and peak performance

Sensorimotor-focused EMDR has evolved into SF-EMDR for psychotherapy and peak performance. The first component represents various forms of bilateral stimulation from continuous auditory stimulation at the level of the mastoid processes – just behind each ear – to peripheral tactile stimulation using zappers applied at various frequencies. The second component represents access to the person's affective experience. Third, in ways that will be explained, repeated iteration of emotions, sensations, and feelings are reprocessed so that, finally, new thoughts emerge (recognition). This allows the patient to strive psychotherapeutically towards peak performance, which is the goal or target of therapy.

The relationship between the patient and the therapist depends on a lot of intuition for its effectiveness in helping to establish a therapeutic alliance. Intuition derives from the Latin term *intueor*; which itself comes from *intuitus*, meaning to look upon, to contemplate, and *tueor* I look (hence tutor and tuition).

This is a key goal of SF-EMDR psychotherapy and its activation via bilateral cerebellar stimulation. It is also the mechanism whereby the mind perceives either the agreement or disagreement of several ideas. It is how we become aware of the truth of things immediately, without reasoning and deduction. In a "sense," it is assumed in the body's experience (the technique of SF-EMDR psychotherapy is grounded in acknowledging this experience).

There is an increasing awareness of the need to move from chaos towards coherence in the lives of our patients and clients, and this can be represented by the integration of gut, heart, and head-brains. Cohere comes from the Latin words *co*, "for" and *hoero*, "I stick together." The organs of the body must stick together, i.e. be in close contact for information to flow freely and to form a connection or cohesive mass. In a coherent state, we optimise energetically: emotionally, mentally, and physically. The heart, head, and gut-brains synchronise and operate efficiently when they are internally coherent. This is accelerated by SF-EMDR psychotherapy when used both as a trauma therapy and for peak performance. In the body's neural networks, about 85 to 90 per cent of neural fibres travel from the body to the brain, especially via the different components of the vagus nerve. These dominate our decision-making, creativity, and emotional state. During traumatic stress, this information can be blocked anywhere along the affected neural pathway.

The basic premise underpinning the mechanism of action of SF-EMDR psychotherapy is that information is processed in three ways:

1. Reactively by the gut-brain;
2. Emotionally by the heart-brain; and
3. Analytically by the head-brain.

The human nervous systems can be conceptualised as the gut-brain, which first registers sensations and feelings as a "gut reaction or instinct." This is followed by the heart-brain or sympathetic and parasympathetic nervous system. These sensations are felt in the chest, often relate to emotions of loss, and delayed grief. The central and peripheral nervous systems work together to analyse this information, which leads to the production of thought and speech in the head-brain. This is the final stage of logical and objective thought and rational analysis (Figure 1.1).

It is the linking of these separate processes that is unique to SF-EMDR psychotherapy. For example, it is by recognition and inhibition of the sensation of butterflies in our stomach during reprocessing that we can ultimately achieve our objectives by engaging heart-brain and head-brain reprocessing capabilities.

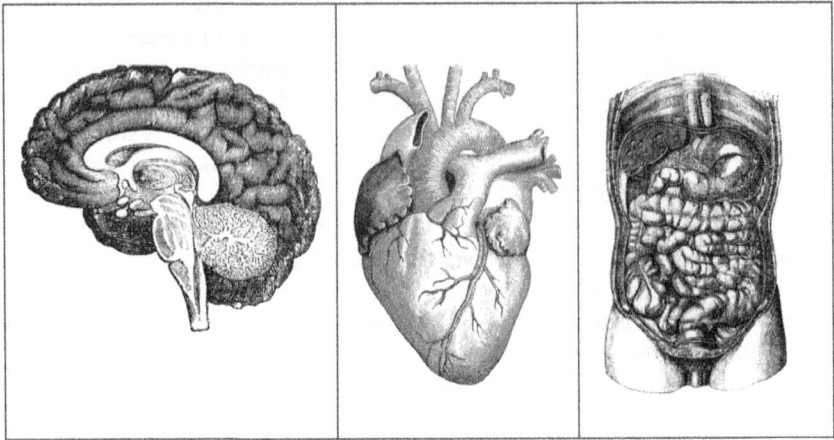

Figure 1.1 The physical brain, heart-brain, and gut-brain. (a) Head-brain. (b) Heart-brain. (c) Gut-brain. Morphart Creations/ Hein Nouwens/ Morphart Creations/ Shutterstock.

The bilateral activation at the level of the mastoid processes resonates at the level of both cerebellums. This information appears to further access processing in the temporal, occipital, and parietal lobes. Finally, patients often report a tingling sensation in their frontal lobes. This appears to coincide with a release of energy from both the third eye and forehead chakras, correlating anatomically with the pituitary and hypothalamic glands. The techniques underlying this process are explained further in Chapter 8.

The anatomical connections in patients can be illustrated as follows:

The local circuit neurons in the heart are involved in the coding of long-term memory in the hippocampus. The heart's functional memory via these heart neurons processes intuitive or heartfelt feelings in the heart-brain. They also link directly with the gut-brain and head-brain networks (Figure 1.2). This builds on the widespread cultural belief that feelings registered at a heart level are as powerful if not more powerful than those of the gut-brain and head-brain.

Connections between the brain in the gastrointestinal tract (gut-brain) and the brainstem (head-brain) are illustrated in Figure 1.3. This is highly significant in anxiety resolution. There are layers of protection for the intrinsic neurons of gut plexuses from the contents of the gut mucosa. When the neural plexi afferents from and efferents to the head-gut and heart are all connected, then the maximal flow of information occurs. This appears to be possible using SF-EMDR psychotherapy. The head-brain links up with the other systems via the sympathetic and parasympathetic nervous systems. The dorsal motor nucleus of the tenth cranial or vagus nerve has its origin in the brainstem and synapses in the muscle wall of the gastrointestinal tract

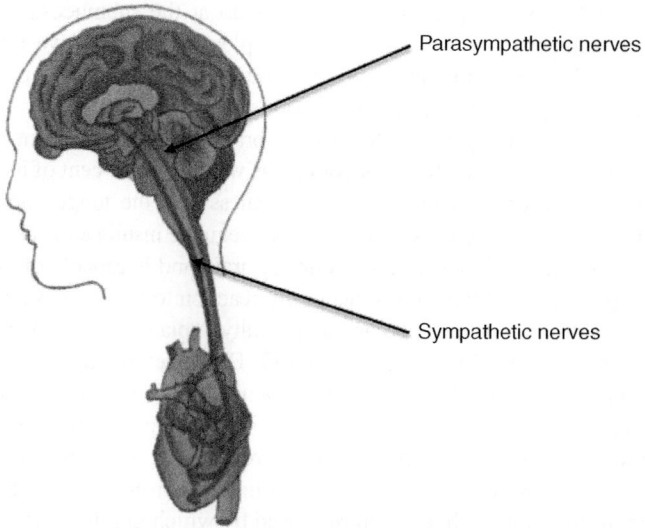

Figure 1.2 The heart–brain interaction and connections with the head brain.

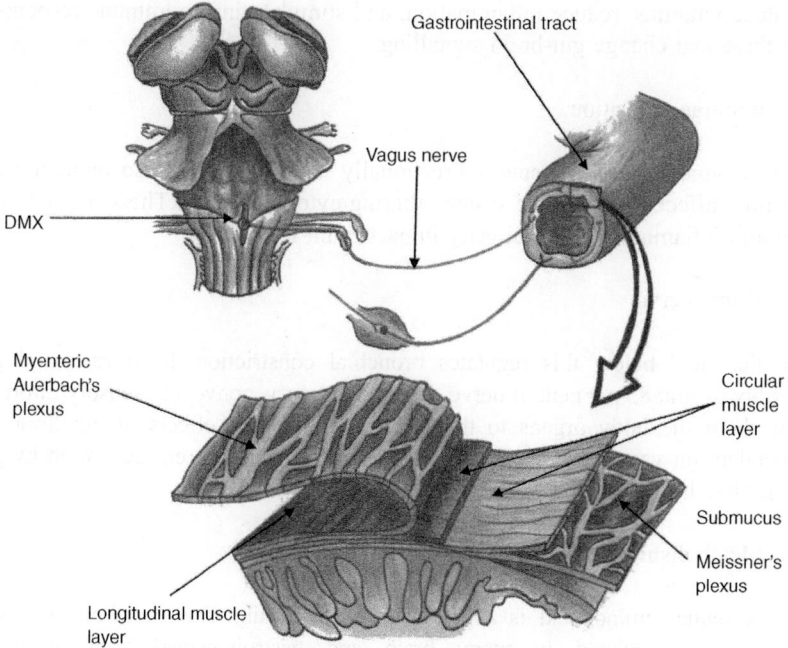

Figure 1.3 The gut-brain connections with the brainstem.

(GIT). The black arrow shows a magnified section of the GIT containing the intrinsic neurons of the gut plexus. There are longitudinal and circular muscle layers comprising of Meissner's plexus in-between them at the submucosa layer. These only contain parasympathetic fibres. Auerbach's plexus also lies between the circular and longitudinal layers at the muscularis propria layer. It has both sympathetic and parasympathetic input from the central nervous system.

The Enteric Nervous System (ENS) or gut-brain has thirty different neurotransmitters and 90 per cent of the body's serotonin as well as 50 per cent of its dopamine. It also has taste receptors which sense "sweetness" on the tongue and levels of glucose in the bloodstream. These taste receptors regulate insulin and are an excellent example of how the ENS really acts as our gut-brain and is capable of independent action. The processing of the gut instinct or gut reaction to incidents is a prerequisite for the SF-EMDR therapeutic approach and is fully explained in Chapter 8.

Research by John F. Cryan and Timothy G. Dinan reveals how the gut microbiota communicates with the CNS through neural, endocrine, and immune pathways. This provides scientific evidence for an influencing role in the regulation of anxiety, mood, cognition, and pain. The microbiota are integrated into the illustrated gut–brain axis and impact on the brain in states from satiety to stress.

A range of mechanisms have been proposed by which gut flora affect the CNS:

• Altering composition of the gut flora.

They can compete with dietary ingredients such as growth substrates; they can produce vitamins, reduce inflammation, and stimulate innate immune responses. All these can change gut-brain signalling.

• Immune activation.

The immune system interacts bidirectionally with the CNS. Also indirectly the gut flora affects the immune system altering cytokine levels. These are both pro and anti-inflammatory and directly impact brain function.

• Vagus nerve.

As illustrated below this regulates bronchial constriction, heart rate, and gut motility. About 85 per cent of nerve fibres are sensory, conveying sensory information about the body organs to the CNS. Many of the effects of gut flora are dependent on vagal activity. The mechanisms of vagal afferent activation by gut microbiota have yet to be elucidated.

• Metabolism of tryptophan.

This essential amino acid is a precursor of serotonin. This metabolic pathway becomes dysregulated in many brain and gastrointestinal tract disorders.

Inflammatory mediators and corticosteroids activate two critical enzymes involved in the metabolism.

• Microbial metabolites.

Gut flora is essential in the production of bile acids, choline, and short-chain fatty acids. Complex carbohydrates are digested and fermented in the colon by gut microorganisms into neuroactive short-chain fatty acids.

• Microbial neurometabolites.

These neurotransmitters act on the enteric nervous system and may have anti-nociceptive properties.

• Bacterial cell wall sugars.

These may modulate neural signalling or act on afferent axons.

On Monday 1 August 2016, Anne Robinson in *The Guardian* reported that overuse of antibiotics and obsession with cleanliness is damaging microbial gut diversity, worsening such conditions as depression, multiple sclerosis, obesity, and rheumatoid arthritis. Most microbes are beneficial, and the gut-brain weighs in at 1–2 kg, the same as the head-brain. Babies are first exposed to maternal gut bacteria as they travel down the birth canal. Those born by Caesarean section appear to be more prone to illnesses.

Professor John Cryan of University College Cork states that good brain health depends on good gut health. The gut microbiome affects every aspect of brain functioning and human behaviour. It appears that people with high levels of bifidobacteria in the gut withstand psychological stress better than those with low levels. It is also true that diversity of the microbiome is associated with physical strength and cognitive flexibility. Work still needs to be done to find out how gut bacteria send signals to the brain.

The techniques outlined in the head, heart, and gut brains of SF-EMDR psychotherapy provide a pathway for this signalling. Professor Cryan thinks that in the next five years we will learn a lot more about which specific bacteria are essential. It will then be possible to test our personal microbiota and supplement any deficiencies. Over a similar time frame, I am optimistic that SF-EMDR psychotherapy will develop hand in hand with these specific blood tests.

Knowledge of all these mechanisms of interaction of the gut enteric nervous system on the central nervous system lends credence to my hypothesis that reprocessing of the gut's emotional response can help to reduce a dysregulation of the gastrointestinal system. Also continuing reprocessing of distressing sensations concerning trauma at the level of the stomach can be signalled to the heart and brain via the vagus nerve. This will enable digestion and metabolism of these sensations at a cognitive level.

The vagus nerve "wanders" from the brainstem to the bodily organs to calm them down.

The sympathetic nerves travel to the bodily organs preparing them for a fight or flight reaction in times of stress.

Stimulation of the vagus nerve shuts down inflammation at a cellular level. Immune system function is then enhanced throughout the body:

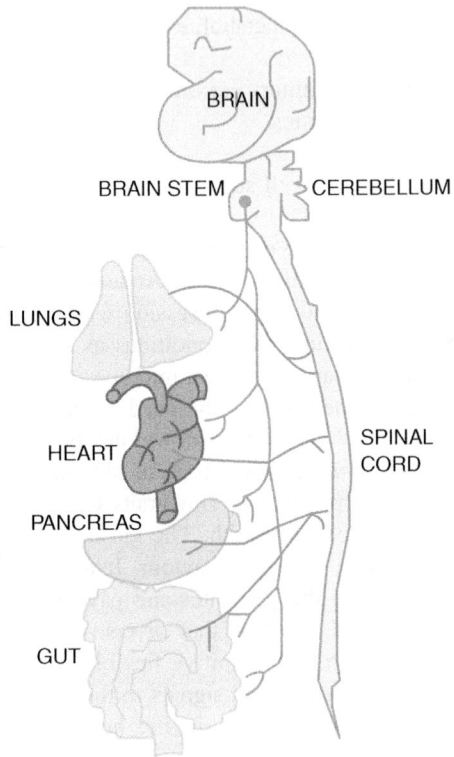

The vagus nerve "wanders" from the brainstem to the bodily organs to calm them down

The sympathetic nerves travel to the bodily organs preparing them for a fight or flight reaction in times of stress

Stimulation of the vagus nerve shuts down inflammation at a cellular level. Immune system function is then enhanced throughout the body

BRAIN

BRAIN STEM — CEREBELLUM

LUNGS

HEART

SPINAL CORD

PANCREAS

GUT

Figure 1.4 The path of the vagus nerve from the brainstem to the lungs, heart, pancreas and gastrointestinal tract via the spinal cord. It is divided into a ventral and a dorsal component.

The vagus or tenth cranial nerve leaves the brainstem and tends to calm down all the organs of the body. The sympathetic nerves have the opposite effect and get the person ready to engage the "fight" response or mobilise the heart, lungs, and muscles for "flight" (Figure 1.4).

The five organs illustrated may represent the five stages of SF-EMDR psychotherapy and peak performance. Creating:

- Activation of the gut instinct or gut reaction at the level of root and sacral chakras;
- Stimulation of the pancreas with the release of insulin and a proposed direct link to anterior inferior and posterior inferior sections of the insular cortex in the cerebrum;
- Energising of the heart chakra and heart organ with reprocessing of loss and grief;
- Inflation and deflation of lungs. This gives rise to the in and out breaths and helps stabilise any functional impairment due to anxiety and rapid breathing or panic attacks; and
- Continuous bilateral stimulation of head-brain so that patient can take on board all of the information reprocessed at lower bodily energy levels.

The techniques of SF-EMDR psychotherapy are designed to boost the immune and endocrine systems and allow for neuronal rewiring (Figure 1.5).

Both cerebral hemispheres and the gastrointestinal tract develop from the neural crest at ten weeks' gestation. Thus, they have the potential to communicate inter-neuronally. It takes both the gut mucosa and the brain four years to develop protective myelin sheaths. Therefore, children less than four are

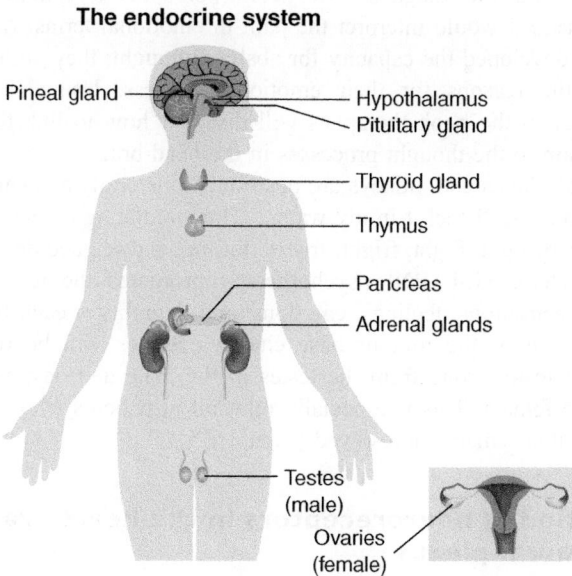

The endocrine system

Pineal gland

Hypothalamus
Pituitary gland

Thyroid gland

Thymus

Pancreas

Adrenal glands

Testes
(male)

Ovaries
(female)

Figure 1.5 Relationship between the endocrine system and SF-EMDR for psychotherapy and peak performance. Alilia Medical Media/shutterstock.com.

especially prone to infections, food allergies, and intolerance and the developing brain is susceptible to abuse and neglect. This is further discussed in Chapter 6.

The heartbeat develops at eight weeks' gestation and sets the basic rhythm experienced throughout life. The heart has its own independent neural network. SF-EMDR psychotherapy enhances the gut, heart, and brain neuronal and energetic communication.

At the head-brain level, SF-EMDR psychotherapy promotes interhemispheric integration. The patient is mindful of feelings and reprocessed thoughts.

The intrinsic nervous system of the heart triggers a heartbeat from the eighth week of gestation. The 40,000 functional groups of autonomous nerve cells in the heart can register heartfelt emotions and sensations linked to loss and traumatic grief. The heart has evolved from; a single tube in fish; two chambers in frogs; three chambers in reptiles; to the four-chambered human heart. With each evolutionary stage has come a greater level of neuronal sophistication.

The pancreas and intestines are part of the gut-brain. They give rise to the patient's gut instinct or reaction. The pancreas produces insulin, which may directly be detected by the insular cortex of the head-brain. The gut's enteric plexus contains 100 million nerve cells. These can function independently to the central and cardiac nervous systems. This is particularly true in children.

Most parents will recognise the scenario: John or Mary does not want to go to school. It is Monday morning, and they are complaining of a pain in their tummy. Concerned, you pay a visit to the doctor. The examination proves inconclusive, and the diagnosis of acute non-specific abdominal pain or ANSAP is made. I would interpret the pain in emotional terms. As a child has not yet fully developed the capacity for abstract thought, they are unable to put into words the reasons for their emotional distress. Using the techniques described later in the book therapists will discover how to link the sensations of the gut-brain to the thought processes in the head-brain.

The adrenal glands and kidneys are positioned bilaterally and can give rise to a patient who says, "I feel it in my water." The circulating adrenaline transmits these feelings of fight, flight, fright, freeze, falling, and feigned death around the endocrine system. SF-EMDR psychotherapy promotes the reprocessing and resolution of sensations, feelings, emotions, and thoughts at each brain level.

The activation of the root or base chakra energies will be related to the processing of testosterone from the testes in the male and oestrogen from the ovaries in the female. This is especially relevant in patients who are victims of sexual abuse that remains unresolved (Figure 1.5).

Composition of neuroreceptors in the heart-brain or cardiac neural plexus

Twenty per cent of heart neurons are receptive, i.e. they detect mechanical pressure in the heart. Chemoreceptor neurons account for the remaining 80 per cent. These are sensitive to hormones and neurotransmitters. This information accumulates in the heart-brain for decision-making at a local level. It connects to brain, gut, skin, lungs, and other visceral organs subsequently.

The patient benefits by paying attention to this bodily information. The heart-brain synchronises with the patient's head-brain, and thalamus. This results in fluent heart rate variability (HRV). Mindful breathing helps induce a harmonious mental state in the patient and regulates HRV helping to calm the patient's dysregulated, emotional state. Quantum coherence leads to the occurrence of synchronised electrical activity emanating from the heart to the thalamus to the frontal cortex. This allows for better focusing and reprocessing of patient reactions, which are appropriate to the situation and within their window of tolerance (Figure 1.9).

Role of the gastrointestinal tract in processing food and emotional reactions and hypothetical link to insular cortex in cerebral hemispheres or head-brain

The gut absorbs and processes food, which increases glucose concentrations in the bloodstream. The pancreas produces insulin (from the islets of Langerhans). The insular cortex in the brain may directly perceive this hormone. It is divided into the anterior insular cortex (AIC) and posterior insular cortex (PIC) and helps to give us insight into our basic gustatory feelings.

Indeed, its phylogenetic origin is from the gustatory cortex, which in mammals enables the processing of taste and leads to the perception of disgust.

A recent review by Kennedy et al. examined the neural pathways connecting the brain to the gut and vice versa. Thus the gut viscera influences brain functioning. Stress, mood, thoughts, and emotion affect gut function via the vagal pathways of the autonomic nervous system. The immune system affects the functioning of the enteric nervous system, which then influences the central nervous system. Other mediators include neurotransmitters and neuropeptides such as serotonin, noradrenaline, and corticotropin-releasing factor. This led to the hypothesis of cognitive dysfunction and stress as important in the aetiology of gut disorders such as irritable bowel syndrome.

Both AIC and PIC components of the insular cortex (IC) have a role to play in the integration of social emotions, from empathy, disgust, and pain to experiences of joy, compassion, admiration, and fairness. The left and right AIC may code for positive and negative affect in the prefrontal cortex (PFC) as suggested by Davidson. This provides further scientific evidence for the benefit of continuous bilateral cerebellar stimulation in the twin approaches of SF-EMDR psychotherapy for resolving trauma and achieving peak performance.

The insular cortex has visceral and sensory neural connections. It encodes body temperature, sensations from the musculature, viscera, and levels of arousal. This leads to a gradual process of interoceptive awareness, which is consistent with the five stages of SF-EMDR psychotherapy. Initial gut instinct such as visceral or somatic bodily feelings is at the genesis of human emotional experience. The integration and appraisal of this information allow the patient to progress to interpretation and action based on their instinctive or conscious experience. Thus, a sensation such as "stomach tension" could be associated with feelings of fear or pleasure. The individual patient is helped by the SF-EMDR psychotherapist to identify the emotional memory linked to the stomach sensation correctly.

The insular cortex plays a critical role in mapping internal bodily somatic and feeling states. Once mapped, they can form the basis for predictions of further bodily reactions to emotional or sensory stimuli directly related to the self.

It appears that painful stimuli map onto the PIC while affective stimuli related to the self, map onto the AIC. I hypothesise that this part of the cortex was named after the pancreas, which produces insulin. It is as if this hormone – which monitors glucose levels in the gut – has a direct neural link to the insular cortex to provide the same role for cortically expressed emotions. Thus, there is an integration of feeling, empathy, and uncertainty in the insular cortex. This is appraised by the cerebral hemispheres as explained in Chapter 12.

The insular cortex has emerged as the key structure in the brain to be activated for trauma resolution according to one of the world's foremost experts on emotion and behaviour, Professor Ray Dolan, of Queen's Square Hospital for Neurology and Neurosurgery in London. It is involved in processing internal bodily signals (interception). In addition, it integrates the patient's mental map with incoming sensory information to create a definitive sense of self.

This is the putative site for registration of gut feelings in the brain. Coherence allows information from the head-brain, heart-brain, and gut-brain to be synchronised and balanced. The autonomic nervous system (ANS), endocrine and immune systems are similarly coordinated. Eventually, the aim is for them all to fire at the same rate. Those that fire together, wire together (i.e. work well interactively). Synergistic adaptive growth ensures that with healthy evolution HRV varies when an emotional stimulus is about to be shown. Thus, four or five seconds before it is actually shown, the prefrontal cortex (PFC) registers this intuitively. The PFC then modulates heart rhythm 250ms later. We become attuned (from sound or stretch) to the heart's rhythm.

Unconsciously stored information is intuitive until it is reprocessed from the body-mind into our consciousness. SF-EMDR psychotherapy accelerates that process in the fourth stage of activating our brain's axons, which are rewired for transmission (cf. stage four of SF-EMDR psychotherapy).

Figure 1.6 shows how the gut has sensory and motor control independent of the peripheral and central nervous systems. The intrinsic and extrinsic pathways are shown.

Doc Childre founded the Institute of Heartmath in 1991 and sought to explore the effect of stress on human body systems. The heart is the most powerful generator of electromagnetic energy in the human body. As such it is uniquely positioned to connect the gut-brain, head-brain, emotions, feelings, sensations, and spiritual awareness. To quote Childre and Rozman: *"Since emotional*

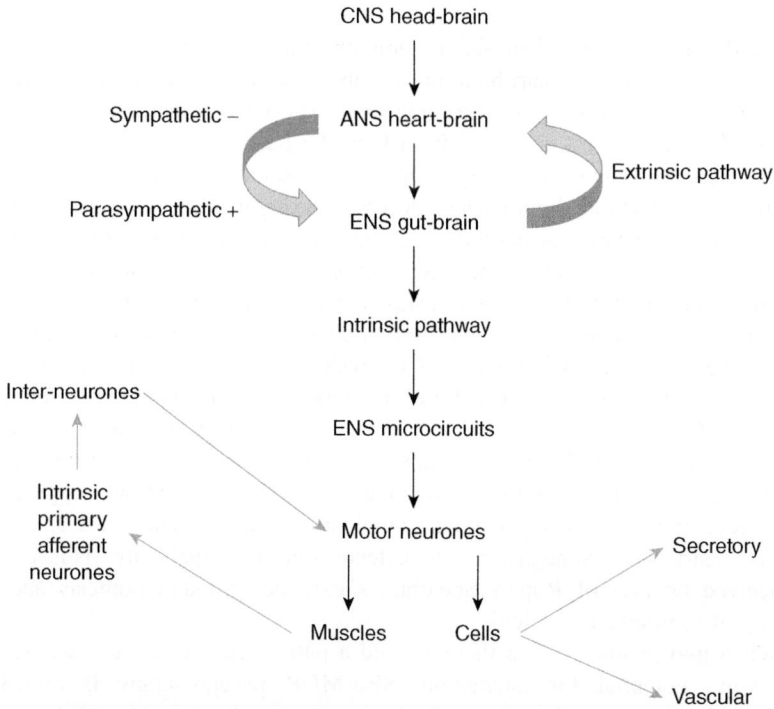

Figure 1.6 Diagram of the head, heart, and gut pathways. CNS = central nervous system, ANS = autonomic nervous system, ENS = enteric nervous system.

processes can work faster than the mind, it takes a power stronger than the mind to bend perception, override emotional circuitry, and provide us with intuitive feeling instead. It takes the power of the heart."

The heart's magnetic field

The magnetic field emanating from the heart is 5,000 times larger than that of the brain and measurable up to several metres from the body.

Augmentation of this magnetic field is a goal of future SF-EMDR psychotherapy. The heart's electrical field is sixty times greater in amplitude than the electrical activity generated by the brain. The heart communicates with the brain and body in four ways via:

1. Nervous system or neurologically;
2. Pulse waves of blood pressure or biomechanically;
3. Hormones or biochemically;

4.   Electromagnetic fields or energetically.

These different forms of heart-brain communication affect how we perceive and react to the world. The heart-brain talks to the head-brain and gut-brain. The gut-brain communicates to both heart-brain and head-brain. Finally, the head-brain digests and replies to the signals from both the heart's nervous system and the enteric nervous system. It is a highly integrated neural network right down to the cellular level. The initial gut reaction accessed during incident reprocessing in SF-EMDR psychotherapy reaches the heart, which acts as a focal point for connection to relevant bodily sensations, feelings, emotions, cognitions, and spiritual insights. Reprocessing of negative feelings leads to the generation of positive ones, for example, compassion. The brain's perception of these feelings is altered. As a result, we feel better. A key goal is the development of a positive psychological change. This is a topic of David Blore's PhD thesis: "In search of the Antonym to Trauma." It is for this reason that the achievement of peak performance is a natural corollary to SF-EMDR psychotherapy. Patients and clients are encouraged to imagine that resolution of persistent traumatic stress opens a window of opportunity to achieve optimal or peak performance in their chosen goals and future templates.

The heart's electromagnetic field extends out from the body. This can be conceived as part of Rupert Sheldrake's extended mind hypothesis and his theory of morphogenetic fields.

When two people – i.e. a therapist and a patient communicate – we get the following potential for interaction. SF-EMDR psychotherapy is aimed at making this a positive interaction for both parties and maximising the opportunities for post-traumatic growth or positive psychiatric/psychological change.

When humans interact, there is an augmented electromagnetic field in the gap between them. This may enhance the prospect of non-verbal or telepathic communication. This shows the potential for enhanced progress in the suitably attuned therapist for the patient. Part of the therapeutic alliance rests on finding a suitable distance between therapist and patient to optimise this resonance. This is taught in both somatic experiencing and somatomotor therapeutic approaches.

Science and psychotherapy

John McLeod described how being a psychotherapist necessitates drawing on diverse sources of personal, practical, and research-based knowledge. However, little of this research directly impacts psychotherapeutic practice. He argues for flexibility around research methods rather than the randomised control trials given pre-eminence by governmental organisations such as the National Institute for Clinical and Care Excellence or NICE. Johnsen and Friborg found in their meta-analysis of CBT that it was less effective in 2014 than it had been in 1977.

Through improving access to psychological therapies, or IAPT, the government has invested £500 million. Longitudinal studies show that initially outcome measures improved but these regressed to pre-referral levels by eighteen months on average. Will the government acknowledge that IAPT appears to have been initiated on a political whim rather than be based on any rigorous scientific study?

I believe that a bottom-up information reprocessing approach is necessary before CBT can be truly effective. Knowledge of body-based psychotherapy is necessary, and clinicians recruited to IAPT teams are not taught these approaches. Scientific knowledge is important for psychotherapy for the following reasons:

1. Because of the need to be publicly accountable in terms of cost-effective investment of taxpayers' hard-earned money when practitioners are employed by the state; and
2. Even the busiest therapists see a small number of cases, and there is limited opportunity to draw conclusions from practice, observe the working of others, or reflect systematically on one's own practice.

There are five key elements that show how science works in relation to psychotherapy.

1. **The social organisation of science.** This creates a context for scientific thinking to emerge. It involves a way of thinking and doing, bringing different communities of scientists together for debate and collaboration. New knowledge would emerge from various worldwide institutions. This can be applied in the form of new technology.

   Elon Musk first proposed his Hyperloop form of transportation in the shape of tunnels under Los Angeles. Now in 2017, he has posted the first picture of a tunnel operating with the capacity to travel at 150 miles per hour. This technology has the potential to be replicated in many cities congested with traffic and offers a timesaving method of transport for scientists, physicians, psychotherapists, and patients.

2. **The logic of refutation.** Karl Popper stated that the proposition that all swans are white could be proven false by a single sighting of a black swan. Similarly, the current almost universal recommendation of CBT by IAPT can be proven false by the effectiveness of EMDR, SF-EMDR, and SF-EMDR psychotherapy. Because the latter are not in NICE guidance they are not used therapeutically. Science is concerned with devising and testing theories, and this is what I have sought in my patients' best interests while adhering to the Hippocratic Oath and the maxim *"primum non nocere"* (first, do no harm). I have sought to connect ideas from different disciplines and philosophical schools of thought from different cultures across the world. By restricting the promulgation of these ideas, the medical authorities are preventing the critical tension and progress that can result from scientific collaboration.

3. **Methodological flexibility.** Valid knowledge does not rely on the method of data collection used. Most of the theories in fields such as astronomy, geology, epidemiology, or evolutionary biology have been tested

with methods other than randomised control trials. In some neuropsychiatry areas, progress has been made through analysis of single unique cases. I would argue that single case studies of benefit achieved using SF-EMDR psychotherapy can contribute knowledge to the field that is generalisable.

4. **Peer Review.** Since *The Art of BART: Bilateral Affective Reprocessing of Thoughts as a Dynamic Model for Psychotherapy* was published in 2015, three major articles on BART psychotherapy have appeared in peer-reviewed journals. These are open access, which will help to make the ideas widely available.

5. **Insulation against political interference.** A significant example of this is the collaboration between the American Psychiatric Association and researchers to distort results of the efficacy of drug treatments and anti-depressant medication (Davies, 2014; Whitaker & Cosgrove, 2015).

Summary

Science is a collective, socially organised system. Science aims to build detailed theories and models of causal processes. Scientific progress requires the effort and imagination of many people over a period in different places. Scientific knowledge emerges through dialogue; openness to feedback is essential. Research is not morally neutral but is always to some extent, shaped by the structures of power and control that exist within society as a whole.

(McLeod, 2017, p. 6)

The influence of politics on research into psychotherapy

Economic benefit, power, and control influence psychotherapy research. There are well-established schools of therapy each supporting livelihoods, professional reputations, and status. Aaron Beck was a founder of cognitive therapy in the 1970s. From an interview given by the Dalai Lama, Beck had a meditative view of psychotherapy, which differs entirely from the mechanistic way CBT is taught today. Two of my key influences are Milton Erickson and Professor Ernest Rossi. I will be discussing the latter's research into the links between quantum field theory and psychotherapy, which links the ideas of key figures in mathematics and quantum physics with the basic rest–activity cycle and neuroscience of the psychotherapeutic relationship.

The pressure is to produce research favourable to the therapy school you are affiliated with. Failure to address this issue over decades has left the profession of psychotherapy vulnerable to external criticism about the effectiveness of competing models of psychotherapy. The drug companies have influenced doctors to prescribe for conditions helping to establish the DSM taxonomy. This has prevented the development of a more appropriate taxonomy which could be widely adopted by psychotherapy and generate scientific hypotheses for research. NICE filters research such that studies from psychotherapy literature are rarely considered. Pharmaceutical companies fund most research where there is no psychotherapy involvement. The use of only considering RCTs by NICE conflict with the principles of flexibility and plurality adopted by mainstream science.

In this book, I have sought to provide a coherent overarching framework based on the work of Erickson, Janet and Rossi. This has now been integrated with the ORCH OR hypothesis of Penrose and Hameroff and the models of change at the level of genomics, proteomics, as well as how a crisis transforms into opportunity with the 90–120 min consultation model. In my experience, this allows for the establishment of new neural networks. There is verification of new information, and the patient feels validated. These fundamental scientific principles underlie all effective schools of psychotherapy and must be subject to rigorous critical testing.

B. F. Skinner believed that causation could be reliably observed one case at a time. Erickson was asked what his model for treatment was. He said that it changes with every patient. He felt it was of critical importance that the unconscious mind of the patient spoke to him and that the verbal content of the psychotherapy exchange was less critical.

In SF-EMDR psychotherapy narrative is used where preverbal trauma is a significant factor. An account is constructed in the format of a bedtime story: a good beginning – "once upon a time," – a middle bit covering the difficult and traumatic episodes of the child's life, and a "happy ending" where the child feels safe and well looked after. This establishes a narrative truth (a coherent account of the child's experiences). These are previously stored at a SF-EMDR level and now become integrated with a verbal account. The increased cognitive awareness allows for a greater degree of understanding. This differs from the historical truth and corresponds to what was observed. Should scientific researchers into psychotherapy have no emotional attachment to the models they were trained in and use? My approach has been to build on what has been achieved and validated by others. This starts with Maslow's hierarchy of needs.

These eight-stage stepped models (Figure 1.7) show the traditional hierarchy of needs according to Maslow and a superimposed hierarchy that maps these needs with their corresponding therapeutic application. The treatment or intervention is designed to address the most significant unmet need first before progressing up the hierarchy. At the most basic level is the need for food, warmth sleep, shelter, air, and sex. These are often because of poverty, homelessness, drug or alcohol addiction, or criminality and imprisonment. A coordinated approach by government NGOs, family support, employment provision, and training may help to give the patient a foot up the ladder where safety needs can be addressed.

Since the recession in 2008, there has been an increase in physical and mental ill-health, and financial and personal insecurity. Again, mental health services

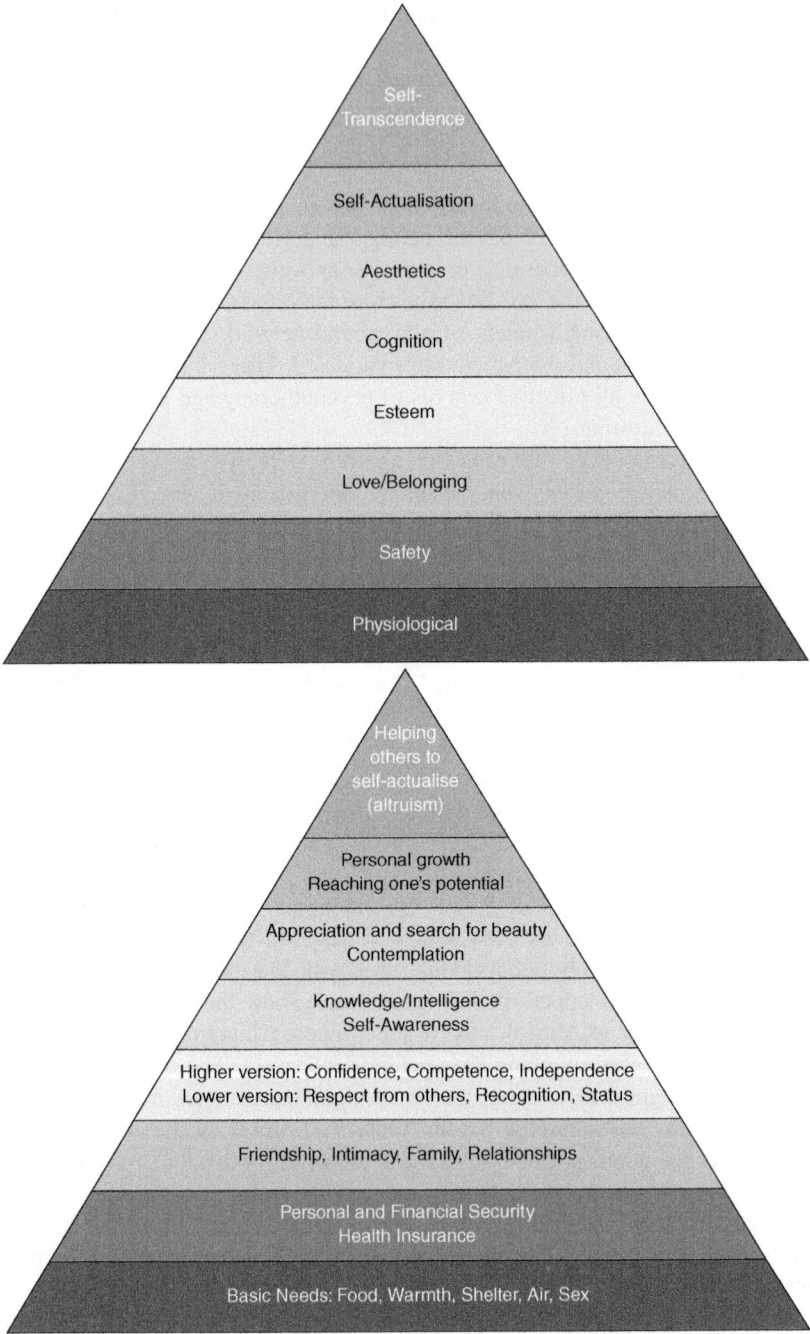

Figure 1.7 Maslow's hierarchy of needs above and expanded therapeutic applications below. These triangles can be superimposed on one another.

alone are not equipped to meet these safety needs. In my experience, there is little coordinated thinking at departmental levels and patients may slip down into the red zone.

We all have fundamental human needs for love and a sense of belonging. This seems to be absent in the 200,000 under-eighteens who rang ChildLine with suicidal ideation and intent. Typically, CAMHS puts a sticking plaster on these cases and seems unable to differentiate non-suicidal self-harm from depression with psychosis, where the risk of completed suicide is highest. The preoccupation with form-filling and risk assessment has been shown not to prevent suicide attempts, and a different approach is needed. The absence of friendships, intimacy, family affection, healthy relationships, and positive peer groups has, I believe, worsened in the digital age of Facebook, Snapchat, Instagram, and with the pressure to be available to others on a constant basis. Psychotherapy has a key role to play in improving self-esteem. At one level this involves respect from others, recognition, status, reputation, and fame. This is the world of celebrity and is promoted by programmes such as "Love Island" and "The X factor." Now teenagers will say that they want to grow up to be famous rather than follow a vocation or other ambition, as would have occurred previously. A more mature form of self-esteem is confidence, competence, and independence and can be achieved in psychotherapy, once the bottom-up processing of the lower needs has been obtained.

Cognition and aesthetics rely on activation of specific areas of the brain. These are namely the prefrontal cortex and visual processing areas, associated with the appreciation of art, music, and beauty. These may correlate with activation of the third-eye chakra and the HPA axis. I will discuss this further in the section on Quantum Bayesian and psychotherapy.

The final goals are self-actualisation and transcendence. These are spiritual goals that vary according to the cultural beliefs, faith, and religious upbringing of the person. There is substantial evidence from communities exposed to conflict that high levels of religious affiliation result in a strong sense of meaning, self-preservation, and low suicide rate. Certain historical iconic figures like Mahatma Gandhi, Martin Luther King, and Nelson Mandela have been attributed this status because of the global legacy and profound impact of their achievements.

Client feedback and tracking: an example of a highly productive line of research

In the 1990s Scott D. Miller and Michael Lambert used outcome measures in real time to give therapists feedback on their clients' progress. This was a major practice innovation. This represents a minimal intervention that can make a big difference. RCTs can be conducted in which the only difference between the study arms was the absence or presence of feedback. When EMDR and CBT are compared in an RCT, it is harder to disentangle distinctive interventions unique to each approach and relative effects of common factors. Also, according to Milton Erickson, each patient is unique and requires an individualised therapeutic approach. However, client feedback is a minimal intervention that can make a big difference.

Better strategies are needed to insulate research from political influence

Organisations such as *WHICH?* magazine and its corresponding website (produced by the Consumers' Association in the UK) could be commissioned to research the effectiveness of psychotherapy. As a non-profit organisation, it would be acceptable to clients' therapists and members of the public. It would be possible to use a citizen-jury system to interpret research evidence and make recommendations (Arriaga, 2014). This would limit the influence of expert committees with vested interests, as happens in some NICE boards. This book is an attempt to synthesise research in psychotherapy and incorporate a neuroanatomical and neuroscience perspective, which has been missing in the past. I would hope that this could mirror the work of Carl Rogers in 1959 when his theoretical synthesis of research and practice of person-centred and experiential psychotherapy had a profound influence. What is now needed is a mind–body theoretical paradigm for psychotherapy research and practice to which all therapy schools could find common ground. Thus, a scientific basis for psychotherapy can explain therapeutic effects on both physical and mental health. I propose to show that the mind–body dualism of René Descartes is no longer valid and has been superseded by a quantum field theory. This incorporates physics, biology, psychology and can be integrated with the psychosocial and cultural genomics of psychotherapy.

As a practical example, it is possible to encourage clients to listen to the language of their hearts. Ask yourself the following questions: if your heart had a voice, what would it say? What would it sense and feel? This technique can also be applied to other organs such as the liver, pancreas, gut, bladder, or spleen. This approach can lead to the survival response being lessened and clients becoming more responsive and intelligent during the therapy session. It is as if they become kinder to their bodily reactions and a more genuine cognitive appraisal is reached, allowing meaning to be made from any symptomatic impairment. There should be a renewal of purpose around research in psychotherapy. There are central roles for the ideas and practices of philosophy, ethics, the arts, culture, and science in influencing the direction of psychotherapy. We need to clearly define the limits of science and help to make practitioners aware of the new science of psychotherapy that is fit for purpose in the twenty-first century.

Schumann (earth) resonances

The Schumann Resonances reported by Cherry occur between the earth and ionosphere and start at 7.83 Hertz. We may send intentions in the form of a radio wave. The particles may consist of neutrinos that can travel faster than the speed of light. It is now believed that they warp in a different quantum or dimension previously undetected by science. As we emit positive neutrino light energy, there is a greater resonance with the earth's geomagnetic energy field, and the atmosphere becomes more coherent (from Latin: *cohere*, to stick together). The earth's magnetic field is changing, and the Institute of Heartmath is recording this through their Global Coherence initiative. By uniting people to speak and feel from the heart-brain a shift in consciousness can occur. The human population can move from a state of instability and disharmony to one of balance, cooperation, and peaceful coexistence. By raising the vibration of one person, then one hundred quantum shifts in consciousness are possible. "The Hundredth Monkey Effect" discusses this possibility. Human thought and aspiration can interact with the wider environment and effect changes at the planetary level of the earth's magnetic field.

There is interaction between Schumann Resonance vibrations in the human brain and geomagnetic atmospheric resonances in planet earth (Figure 1.8). The hypothesis is that our biological systems have been exposed to these waves since the beginning of our evolution. Scientific measurements suggest that the average Schumann Resonance in the ionosphere has increased from 7.83Hz to approximately 11Hz.

It is likely that our biological systems will also start to resonate at a higher frequency. The thrust of SF-EMDR psychotherapy is to start at the lower vibratory energies at the levels of the root and sacral chakra. As reprocessing ascends, the higher chakras are activated and ultimately the brain experiences exposure to a vibratory resonance of 46 Hertz, triggering thalamocortical connections and coherence (Figure 1.9).

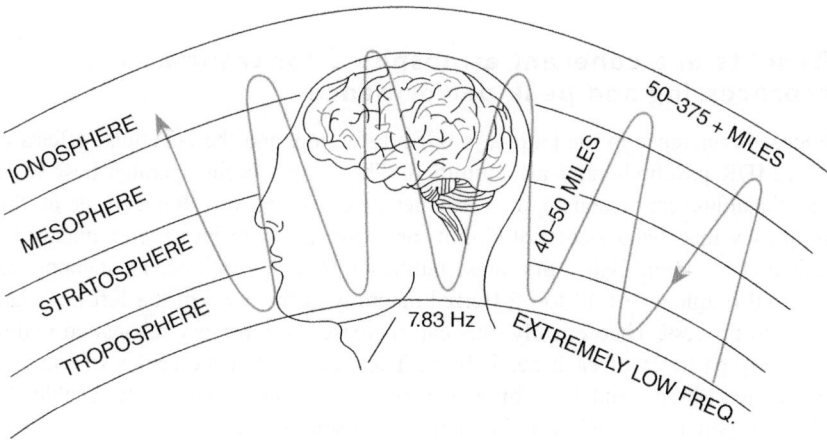

Figure 1.8 Schumann resonance and the planetary ionosphere.

The Schumann Resonance of earth contains seven subtle vibrations. These are 7.83, 14, 21, 26, 33, 39 and 45 Hertz. Are our body's chakra energy points meant to synchronise with these frequencies? My BOKA 10, I believe, is the only bilateral-stimulation machine currently available, which can be set to each of these seven subtle vibrations equivalent to those of earth's Schumann resonances. For psychotherapy I have coined the term ZAPPERS, which stands for:

Zone of
Arousal of
Past &/or
Present
Emotions
Reprocessed
Successfully.

These zappers can be set to coincide with the five stages of SF-EMDR for psychotherapy and peak performance:

• Stage 1 1–9 Hz average 7.8Hz;
• Stage 2 10–19 Hz average 14 Hz;
• Stage 3 20–29 Hz includes Schumann resonances of 21 and 26Hz;
• Stage 4 30–39 Hz includes Schumann resonances 33 and 39Hz;
• Stage 5 40–60 Hz includes gamma wave frequency of 45Hz.

As the patient progresses through the stages of SF-EMDR for psychotherapy and peak performance, they report feeling lighter, consistent with resonance at a higher, more intuitive frequency. They often leave the therapeutic session feeling as if a weight or burden has been lifted from their shoulders.

Benefits of a coherent atmosphere for trauma reprocessing and peak performance

Focused coherence in the patient is self-reinforcing, and the beneficial effects of SF-EMDR psychotherapy are amplified. The human brain operates best when the thalamus can resonate at a frequency of 40 to 60 Hertz. It is at this frequency that thalamocortical circuits are activated with increased capacity for reflective thought. Using the latest multiuser BOKA machine, I can apply an external frequency of 40 to 60 Hertz bilaterally at the level of the left and right mastoid process. Theoretically, this can increase the vibratory resonance within the body particles of each cerebellum. Thus, atoms and molecules of the gut-brain, heart-brain, and head-brain (or body-mind) can coalesce to enable the client or patient to reach a higher state of conscious awareness.

We now know from CERN research at the Large Hadron Collider (LHC) in Switzerland that the elusive Higgs-Boson particles have been discovered and give mass and impetus to this process. ENLIGHT is the European Network for Light Ion Hadron Therapy. Hadron or proton therapy involves multidisciplinary collaboration. Common standards and protocols for treating patients have been developed across twenty European countries. Cross-fertilisation between particle physics and medicine will continue to be essential to improve treatment for susceptible tumours. From the early work of Dr David Servan-Schreiber on improving cancer outcomes by resolution of traumatic stress, we can hypothesise a similar approach will be effective with hadron or proton therapy. SF-EMDR psychotherapy is ideally placed to step into the gap left by other trauma-focused therapy approaches. Crucially it involves continuous resonance of the cerebellum bilaterally at the level of the mastoid eminence.

The mastoid process is chosen for the site of bilateral stimulation using specially adapted headphones. I have found that placing the bilateral auditory signal over the ears interfered with the patient's therapeutic alliance and inhibited their opportunities for direct feedback during SF-EMDR psychotherapy. The mastoid process is derived from the Greek word for "breast." It acts as a point of attachment for the muscles: splenius capitus, longissimus capitus, posterior belly of digastric and sternocleidomastoid. It acts as a focal point of auditory resonance for the cerebellum. This helps to dampen instinctive brain-stem responses and connect to the prefrontal cortex pathways modulating sensations, feelings, emotions, and cognition. Stimulation of these muscles allows for:

- Head extension, lateral flexion, and rotation of the cervical spine;
- Flexion of the head and neck to the same side and bilateral extension of the vertebral column;
- Allowing the jaw to open;
- Lateral flexion and rotation of the head to the opposite side (unilateral contraction); and
- Dorsal head extension (bilateral contraction) and support for inspiration when the head is still.

Role of the thalamus in the brain

This means "inner chamber" in Greek. It surrounds the third ventricle, which contains cerebrospinal fluid and is divided into two walnut-shaped halves with the nutshells positioned horizontally. It now appears to have seven discrete functions:

1. Relay station for somatic sensations apart from the smell and cerebellar motor pathway;
2. Integrating centre for somatic sensory, visual, visceral, and motor in the cerebellum, namely corpus striatum;
3. Regular maintenance of alertness, attention, and consciousness;

4. Emotional reprocessing, hence theory of bilateral affective reprocessing;
5. Pain now conceived as emotion;
6. Regulation of sleep-wake cycle; and
7. Via connections to the mesial temporal lobe, it is believed to be involved in memory recall and familiar memory.

Many of the functions of the thalamus remain poorly defined and understood. It is hoped that the Human Brain Project will further our understanding of this inner chamber. In the great pyramid of Giza, the positioning of the King's chamber and Queen's chamber may represent the pineal gland and pituitary gland respectively.

Schwaller de Lubicz wrote *Le Temple dans L'homme* (The Temple in Man). He theorised that the Triple Sanctuary in the Temple of Luxor (*"lux"* translates into light and *"or"* into gold) corresponded to the human skull and its three endocrine glands or power centres. He claimed that the thalamus was associated with the experience of enlightenment. In SF-EMDR psychotherapy, activation of the sensory thalamus leads to information transfer to the cortex. This is a type of enlightenment.

In *God-man: The Word Made Flesh* (Carey & Perry, 2013), the King's Chamber was the Holy Grail.

Their eyes will become open. The Great Pyramid will reveal to us the sacred claustrum and the Door of Brahm. Before entering the King's Chamber there are the four grooves named the "granite leaf." These may correspond to the four eminences or the colliculi of the corpora quadrigemina in the midbrain.

The superior colliculi act as the visual reflex centre and the inferior colliculi are the auditory reflex centre. They are directly activated by the peripheral bilateral stimulation process, which is integral to SF-EMDR psychotherapy.

In Figure 1.9 (above*)* the arrows show where the sensory information from the thalamus is transferred when rapid eye movements (REM) occur during ninety-minute sleep cycles. I hypothesise that this state of thalamocortical transfer of data as represented by the arrows emanating from the thalamus can be achieved during a two-hour therapeutic SF-EMDR psychotherapy session. Most patients report a profound state of calm at the end of a session and yawn as if they have just had a good night's sleep. The lines coming from the cerebellum illustrate the dampening effect on the brainstem that I hypothesise can happen during the therapeutic session, as both cerebellums receive direct mechanical input via bilateral auditory stimulation.

Role of the cerebellum in human evolution

Chris Stringer, in his book *The Origin of Our Species*, has discussed how the cerebellum plays a role in higher brain functions such as information processing and learning. Initially, around two million years ago, the increased size of the brain was due to an increase in the size of the cerebral cortices. In recent human

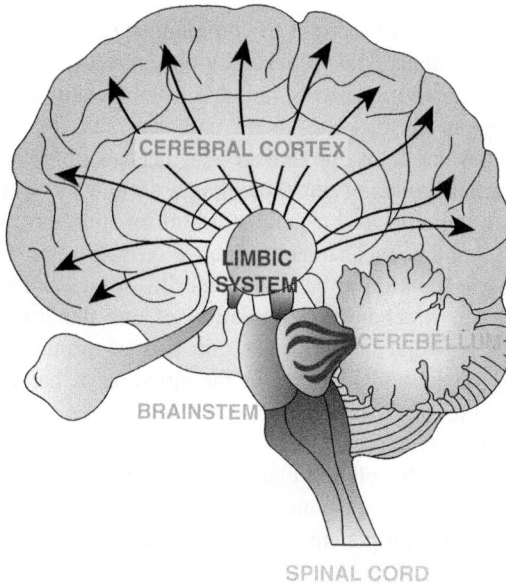

Figure 1.9 The cortex under the influence of an optimally resonant thalamus during sleep. This hypothesis is mimicked during SF-EMDR Psychotherapy and peak performance leading to the potential for thalamocortical binding.

history, the reverse has occurred, with archaeologists reporting that the cerebellum has become larger with the brain overall shrinking in size by ten over the last 20,000 years. It has been hypothesised that the larger cerebellum enables the brain to process information more efficiently. There may also be a connection to the gradual decrease in the size of the connecting fibres between the hemispheres known as the corpus callosum.

This lends support for my direct stimulation of the cerebellum by auditory sound-waves activated bilaterally at the level of the mastoid process. Ananthaswamy is a consultant for *New Scientist* and has written an article in which he postulates that the brain operates, "like clockwork." This reviews the evidence for mechanical influence on the running of the brain that is like the springs and cogs in a finely tuned watch. The hypothesis arose from the observation that a mechanical blow, such as a punch, could render a person unconscious. The brain has traditionally been thought of as a biochemical and electrical organ. Yet, the knockout punch shows that the brain is also responsive to mechanical input. It has been proposed that sound-waves applied to the brain can help to make our thoughts go around more effectively. It has been my experience that using SF-EMDR psychotherapy causes continuous bilateral stimulation of the cerebellum to do just that; helping the brain to run like a well-oiled machine.

The buzz of thought

Traditionally, neurones were thought to communicate only via electrical signals known as action potentials. This is normally propagated from axon to dendritic spine. However, on receiving a nerve impulse when a chemical neurotransmitter binds to its receptor, these spines bend and sway as if also affected by a mechanical sound wave. This movement also acts to progress the transfer of information, potentially making our thoughts go around more effectively. These changes have been hypothesised to help store information during learning about stored memories. Another mechanical influence on nerve transmission has been observed. Forces are transferred between dendritic spines as microtubules store energy like a spring. Mechanical stimulation of one dendritic spine causes a transfer of forces to adjacent ones via this bed of proteins. This has been proposed to help the individual adapt to the situation at hand and tune neural networks so that the brain could hum at a higher resonant frequency. The overall conclusion is that mechanical vibrations in brain tissue, such as the cerebellum, can cause beneficial changes in neural activity. This provides scientific evidence for the mechanism of action of SF-EMDR psychotherapy, which has as a central component continuous bilateral auditory stimulation of the brain.

The brain thinking has been compared to a waterwheel going around and round. When the flow of water into the wheel increases, then more thoughts are secreted or produced. On the other hand, at times when the flow of water is reduced, for example, meditation or sleep, the output of neural activity or thoughts decreases. Depression has been likened to a state where the flow of water stops, the waterwheel grinds to a halt. The patient is unable to think straight or, sometimes, even communicate. From my earlier discussion, there is every possibility that the SF-EMDR psychotherapist will make a difference to the depressed patient's mental state. This can be the subject of future research.

The reprocessing of traumatic memories during SF-EMDR psychotherapy can mimic thalamocortical projections. This is reflected in the verbal feedback from the patient with cerebral sensation, which appears towards the end of a therapy session. As reprocessing ascends past the level of the throat chakra or thyroid gland, patients often report sensations and feelings at the level of the right and left cerebral hemispheres. As reprocessing continues, they point to their forehead as if activating the brow or third-eye chakra. They are then able to reflect on the learning and meaning from experience by engaging with the functionality of their prefrontal cortex. This has relevance to the concept of the Merkaba discussed later. It has been proposed that to achieve the meditative state needed for the Merkaba experience the client or patient must relearn how to breathe through their third eye, which is located at the site of the sixth chakra, or pineal gland.

The most exciting research in neuroscience is pointing us towards the potential for coherent thought when thalamic neurons are exposed to a frequency of 40 to

60 Hertz or a range of gamma band activity. This is believed to facilitate thalamocortical binding.

Influence of the Dalai Lama on meditative practice and neuroscience

From presentations I attended by the fourteenth Dalai Lama in Manchester in June 2012 it was apparent that there is a need for increased conscious awareness and compassion of all like-minded people on earth. This will allow us to better live in harmony with both ourselves and those around us. The Dalai Lama mentioned conversations he had with Professor Aaron Beck, the father of cognitive behaviour therapy (CBT). Professor Beck believed that 90 per cent of a person's negative emotions were due to mental projection. The Dalai Lama said this was similar to the Buddhist belief that reality is influenced by one's projections. He discussed destructive behaviour by cultivating compassion towards them. This process contrasts with being self-centred, which leads to mental unhappiness. When people are selfish, they become oblivious to others and end up creating their own unhappiness, according to the Dalai Lama.

He went on to state that placing the welfare of others at the centre of your life means that your own self-interest is generated as a by-product. The Dalai Lama spoke about how the nature of mind is equivalent to a clear light with space for love. The activation of the chakras discussed in this book is consistent with this Eastern world philosophy. The Buddhist view of enlightenment is to quieten or neutralise the sensorial mind. The goal is to deliberately stop reminiscences on the past and projections about hopes for the future. By remaining in that empty space of present awareness, you will then get a picture of the true nature of consciousness, wisdom, or knowing. The clarity involved in cultivating this mental state means enlightenment will suddenly dawn on you, according to Buddhist tradition. The goal is to seek a deeper understanding of the emptiness of mind by meditating and reflecting on its nature.

The Dalai Lama also sought to explain the environmental conditions present before humanity was aware of consciousness. He stated that particulate matter was already there before the Big Bang. Researchers such as Professor Turok (Leonard, 2010), at the Perimeter Institute in Toronto, Canada, also believe that, and discuss a series of bouncing big bangs, with one coming to an end before the next one starts. In this theory on the origins of the universe, there is a pause between big bangs when only particle matter exists. This shows the compatibility of beliefs between traditional Buddhism and modern theoretical physics. Also, quantum theory is delving into exploring the concepts of dark matter, empty space, and why gravitational forces are so weak. The philosophic and scientific standpoints of east and west are coming full circle and meeting once again in the middle.

This is reminiscent of the parable of the two eagles, one male and one female, who were released from heaven by Zeus. According to legend, both flew around the universe in opposite directions. When they met up, he allegedly pronounced:

"The eagles have landed." A nest was formed, and great wisdom emanated from this location. It became known as the Delphic Oracle and is now a highly revered site from ancient Greece or modern-day Delphios.

The best word to summarise the philosophy of the Dalai Lama is "mindfulness." This philosophy has been adopted by mental health services in the west. It is a vital component in the patients' journey towards wellness. The "compassionate mind approach" and practice of Professor Paul Gilbert are good examples of the infiltration of this approach into the NHS.

The first step to mindfulness is an increase in the individual's level of conscious awareness. You do so by using the staged process of SF-EMDR psychotherapy, using the model for both for trauma resolution and peak performance.

Further aspects of the concepts of consciousness in relation to the experiences of the patient

This also taps into the ideas of archetypes, personality, and collective unconscious first discussed by Sigmund Freud and Carl Jung and illustrated in Figure 1.10.

This is like a ripple spreading from the centre with the overarching influence of the ego. He proposed shadow and archetypal projections into the physical world further expanded in Assagioli's conception of the different strands of consciousness.

Roberto Assagioli developed the concept of psychosynthesis. He saw similarities between this concept and Jung's ideas. The task of therapy is to transform the individual's personality. The goal is to develop the higher psychic functions, such as the spiritual dimension. He said that Jung differentiates four functions: sensation, feeling, thought, and intuition. He believes imagination or fantasy is also a distinct function.

He also placed the will at the heart of self-consciousness or the ego. The debate on consciousness continues to this day and knowledge of past theories will inform future research. The five functions can be likened to the five stages of SF-EMDR psychotherapy.

1. Sensation from the peripheral nervous system;
2. Feeling from the heart-brain and first three chakras;
3. Thought from the head-brain;
4. Intuition from the pituitary gland and higher chakras; and
5. Imagination or fantasy from the pineal gland and the Merkaba.

Interhemispheric connectivity: use of a medical device, body of knowledge activator (BOKA), during SF-EMDR psychotherapy and peak performance

Dr Gerard Karl from Karlware Gmbh in Germany built this machine according to my specifications over the period 2010–2012. The final prototype was delivered after several modifications. This is the first of his machines to calibrate the frequency of

Symbol of the self

↓

Physical world or society, objects and people

↓

Persona/Personae

↓

EGO

↓

Personal unconscious

↓

Shadow

↓

Cultural unconscious

↓

Biological unconscious

↓

COLLECTIVE UNCONSCIOUS

↓

Image of self or God

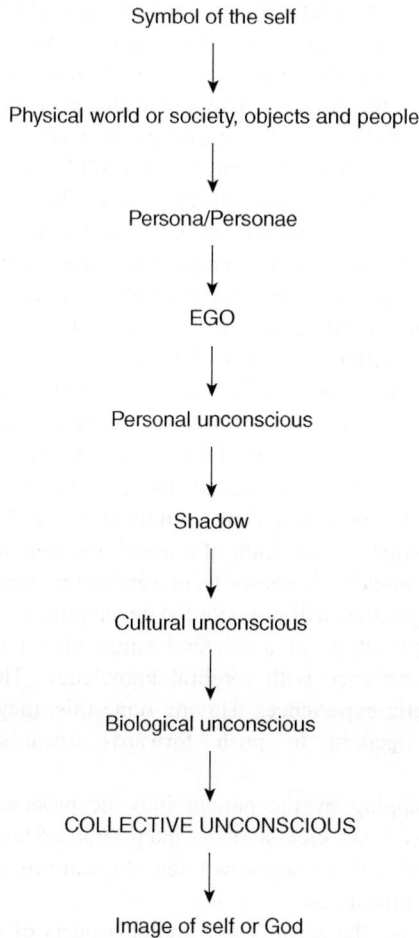

Figure 1.10 Psychic world comprising complexes and archetypes.

bilateral stimulation using multiple tactile and auditory socket outlets. It is electrically operated and can be switched off by a remote-control switch. The machine itself has a position switch with which the frequency in Hertz of bilateral activation is selected. The bilateral stimulation can be applied to the patient either separately or combined. The second position anticlockwise selects the click frequency for bilateral cerebellar resonance in the combined mode, i.e. clicks delivered simultaneously. The third position anticlockwise selects the tactile frequency in Hertz.

The machine surface has five circular switches and three flick switches. The upper left switch controls the speed of the left channel. The opposing right switch controls the speed for both right and left channels. Flick switches set high and low speeds for either separate or combined channels. Speed settings can be set individually. Circular switches adjust vibration intensity and the frequency of vibration for tactile devices. A final switch for the volume of the headphones completes the controls. The digital display on the angled surface of the device gives a readout of the frequency in Hertz. This is the bilateral stimulation applied to the patient. (Range: 0.1 to 60 Hz.)

The BOKA machine uses auditory clicking externally to the mastoid processes bilaterally. This can induce an internal state of entrainment, increasing resilience and flexibility when the patient is in a crisis. Entrainment means that by exposing one cerebellar hemisphere to a frequency of 30 Hertz and the other cerebellar hemisphere to a rate of 10 Hertz, we entrain both regions to resonate at a frequency equal to the difference, that is, 20 Hertz. This machine incorporates the apparatus for up to six individual medical devices. It is the only prototype in which the bilateral stimulation can be delivered to up to twelve patients simultaneously. It is the only machine currently available in which the frequency can be set ranging from 1–60 Hertz and varied bilaterally. The main advantage of this machine is the ability to treat patients simultaneously. This would benefit a family who had experienced the death of a loved one from an accident involving a motor vehicle or suicide. A sports team can better prepare for competition. Activating their imagination will promote the development of resilience.

This is the first prototype of a bilateral stimulation multi-user machine. It integrates bodily experience with cerebral knowledge. This helps the patient process their traumatic experiences. Having done this, they can move forward, giving them the freedom to push forwards towards optimal or peak performance.

I integrate foot-tapping by the patient into the process of SF-EMDR psychotherapy. This way I can kick-start the integration of bottom-up neurological processing, combined with the top-down neurological processing of information from the cerebral hemispheres.

As the left foot taps, the sensory and motor aspects of the right hemisphere activate. This information passes along the fibres of the corpus callosum. As the right foot starts to tap in synchrony, the signal reaches the left hemisphere. This increases inter-hemisphere connectivity and, hence, coherence.

Further use of this machine can be to help people and their companies with increased levels of behaviour within an organisation. The primary distinction between good and bad bosses within companies is the extent of their behaviour. Rarely does an employee complain that their boss was a bad accountant, engineer, or surveyor. Instead, they will complain about him being a bully, ignorant, and of the existence of a blame culture.

There is an altered frequency of waves produced by the brain with increasing states of wakefulness. Deep sleep generates delta waves (0.5–3 Hz). When in deep meditation or dreaming we produce theta waves (4–7 Hz). When we close our eyes for in-depth visualisation and meditation, we create alpha waves (8–13

Hz). During wakefulness, we make beta waves (14–40 Hz). Finally, during times of heightened awareness we produce gamma waves (<40 Hz), which are associated with heightened states of perception and consciousness. Further research will identify to what extent externally applied frequencies compare with the brain waves recorded during an SF-EMDR psychotherapy session. The goal is to stimulate gamma waves equal to a state of heightened perception. I hypothesise that using the BOKA machine at a frequency of 40–60 Hertz will start this state of increased awareness. As a result, it will improve reprocessing. This can benefit both clients in the business sector and patients in the health sector.

Summary

In this chapter, I have introduced the concept of SF-EMDR psychotherapy. This is based on the processing of information from the enteric nervous system (gut-brain), cardiac nervous system (heart-brain), and central nervous system (head-brain). I explain the interrelationship of the gut-brain and heart nerve pathways along with the role of the heart's magnetic field. Research on the gut-brain is updated with my five-year prediction. I hypothesise it will be possible to have a blood test for the diversity of the gut flora, making it possible to correct any deficiencies with the appropriate supplements. Schumann resonances are proposed to influence the five stages of SF-EMDR psychotherapy. The changing evolution of the brain as well as the reduced size of the cerebral cortices and a corresponding increase in size and functional importance of the cerebellum bilaterally, is also discussed. The European Organisation for Nuclear Research or CERN is developing hadron or proton therapy. SF-EMDR psychotherapy is ideally placed as a neurobiologically based therapy to take advantage of these novel therapeutic technologies. I review recent research on the mechanical influence of sound waves on the brain propagating neural activity. This makes our thoughts go around and provides scientific evidence for the mechanism of action of SF-EMDR psychotherapy. I explain the benefits of coherence of ideas via interhemispheric connectivity. This is influenced by thalamic rhythms acting on the cortex during sleep. I propose that this state is achievable during SF-EMDR sessions of psychotherapy. I discuss the thoughts of the Dalai Lama and meditative practice, as well as the links to neuroscience. We look at the concepts of consciousness from the perspectives of Carl Gustav Jung and Roberto Assagioli. We delve into my bilateral stimulation machine for administering SF-EMDR psychotherapy. I show the different brainwave frequencies with the proposal that gamma wave frequency correlates to a state of heightened perception.

Chapter 2

Activation of the chakras using SF-EMDR for psychotherapy and peak performance

The following description outlines the nature of the main chakras, both external and internal to the body itself. These are illustrated, in ascending order of the most well-known chakras, in my previous book, *The Art of BART* (p. 32).

The pattern starts with the earthstar or subpersonal chakra. It is about 30 cm below the feet. It grounds all the other chakras and is the keeper of the law of karma and past lives stored in the Akashic records. The earth-star chakra connects us to earthly and universal energy. Activation helps to keep us grounded and in touch with mother nature. It releases any negative energy practitioners may have picked up from their clients. It connects the etheric and physical bodies preventing the soul from becoming fragmented. It helps to align you with earth's magnetic core while drawing up the well of pure, divine earth energy. The tree meditation activates the earth-star chakra. This involves the use of the Reiki power symbol Cho Ku Rei, the emotional and mental healing symbol, Sei He Ki, and the distance healing symbol, Hon Sha Ze Sho Nen.

Instructions

Visualise connecting through the earth layers down to its magnetic core. Visualise the powerful energy as pure white light. Bring this energy forward while imagining the Reiki power symbol. Bring this up into your body from your feet. Take it into your ankles, shins, knees, thighs, and hips. From here it enters the root chakra. Ascending through the sacral, solar, heart, throat, third-eye, and throat chakras until the energy runs in a brilliant current, electrifying cells throughout your whole being. Finally, it will exit through your shoulders, elbows, wrists, hands, and fingertips.

Imagine leaning against or sitting under your favourite tree. The energy enters the earth through its roots, drawing water to nourish the trunk and bark. This is bottom-up SF-EMDR processing. It combines with sunlight and the chlorophyll in leaves via photosynthesis. This provides top-down nourishment (EMDR) with an outcome of coloured blossoms, reflected by your emotional, physical, as well as your spiritual health and well-being.

Figure 2.1 gives a picture of the combination of top-down and bottom-up reprocessing in SF-EMDR psychotherapy. Patients usually register emotional disturbance at the level of the enteric nervous system or gut microbiome. This is transferred to the cardiac nervous system via the thyroid to the head-brain at the level of the cerebrum. Eventually, it hits the prefrontal cortex. Before that, I will often ask the patient to tap with their feet to encourage reprocessing downwards of any distressing emotional phenomena associated with their traumatic memories. The notation psyche and iatros at the top of the image draw the attention of patients with prior meditation and mindfulness experience, especially the ultimate symbol of healing, the Caduceus. The mythology of the wings is a link to Hermes or Mercury as messengers to the Gods.

Only in the last 100 years has it become associated with medicine. It is in its original meaning that patients may describe a level of transcendence and even contact with relatives who are no longer alive.

First (spinal cord/root) chakra (lotus Muladhara)

The grounding energy centre, it anchors spiritual reality and converts it into physical reality. The Tau symbol sits on the heart symbol, containing both within the four-petal lotus.

The Muladhara chakra has four petals, bearing the Sanskrit letters *va, scha, sha*, and *sa*. The seed sound in the centre is *lam*. A yellow square represents the earth.

There is minimal perception at this level. SF-EMDR psychotherapy activates the patient's inbuilt survival instinct in a containing way. This helps establish belief in a reality more significant than the root chakras' sense of separateness. The imbalance here translates as insecurity. There may be a history of insecure attachments in early childhood (from six months to three and a half years). For diagnosis of these, see the initial section of comprehensive mental health assessment in Chapter 13.

Healing this chakra helps to restore security, well-being, and self-esteem. The physical body masters increased stability courage and patience. The second (II) or sacral chakra can now activate during the continuation of psychotherapy (Table 2.1).

Second (sacral) chakra (Lotus Svadhisthana).

This is believed to be the centre for both relationships and social interactions, as well as being responsible for dealing with issues related to the inner child aspects of our personality (Table 2.2).

Third (solar) chakra (Lotus Manipura).

This is assumed to be the centre of personal power. It is believed to be a centre for both chi energy and intuition. In addition, it is thought to give rise to functions of the auras, etheric, and astral sensitivity. Here ten petals each with their own individual symbol contain the yellow sun. Each triangle reveals the

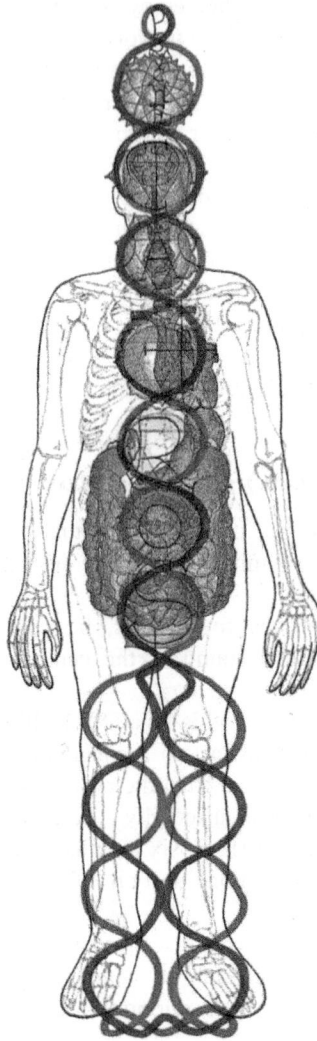

Figure 2.1 The stages of SF-EMDR for psychotherapy and peak performance:

a. Core feelings at the level of the bony skeleton;

b. Energetic systems at level of chakras meridians, endocrine and immune and primo vascular systems;

c. Top-down and bottom-up reprocessing at level of circulatory system and DNA;

d. Information reprocessing at level of gut-brain, heart-brain and head-brain;

e. Integration of Psyche iatros and caduceus. Link to soul healing and consciousness of higher vibrational resonance.

Table 2.1 Spinal cord or root chakra functions

Mantra	Lam
No. of petals	4
Physical functions	Gives vitality to the physical body. Associated with being "grounded" and survival instincts.
Metaphysical functions	
Endocrine glands/organs	Adrenals, kidneys, spinal canal, colon (for digestive action), legs, feet, and bones.
Symptoms if chakra is "out of balance"	Violence, greed, anger, concern over physical survival,
Lessons learnt once chakra is activated using SF-EMDR psychotherapy	Mastery of one's physical body, "grounding" your individuality, stability, security, stillness, health, courage, and patience. Helps to develop emotional well-being and self-esteem,
Gemstones that crystallise this energy	Ruby, Garnet, Obsidian, Red Jasper, Smokey Quartz.
Element	Earth.

Table 2.2 Second or sacral chakra functions

Mantra	Vam
No. of petals	6
Physical functions	Oversees personal belongings, partnerships, and relations. Seat of creativity and procreation. Involves making money and achieving financial support or investment.
Metaphysical functions	Vitality, sexuality, procreation. Linked to conscious creativity and inner child.
Endocrine glands/organs	Genital, spleen, bladder, kidneys, and uterus.
Symptoms if chakra is "out of balance"	Insecurity, violence, greed, anger, sciatica, arthritis, anorexia nervosa.
Lessons learnt once chakra is activated using SF-EMDR psychotherapy	Emotional balance, love, intake of new ideas, working harmoniously and creatively with others.
Gemstones that crystallise this energy	Amber and Carnelian.
Element	Water.

symbol of power in chi, aura, etheric, and astral realms. These are based on gut instinct; the starting point for SF-EMDR psychotherapy (Table 2.3).

Feelings, sensations, and emotions of the patient vibrate at higher frequencies. The third chakra or Solar Plexus (as outlined above) actively links these to

Table 2.3 Third or Solar Chakra functions

Mantra	Ram
No. of petals	10
Physical functions	Sympathetic nervous system, digestion, metabolism.
Metaphysical functions	Seat of emotions and clairsentience and spirituality
Endocrine glands/organs	Stomach, pancreas, gall bladder, liver, and central nervous system
Symptoms if chakra is "out of balance"	Abusive power, anger, ulcers, hypoglycaemia, and diabetes mellitus.
Lessons learnt once chakra is activated using SF-EMDR psychotherapy	Authority, mastery of desire, awakening of consciousness, transformation of self, laughter, and morality.
Gemstones that crystallise this energy	Amber, Yellow Tourmaline, Citrine, and Topaz.
Element	Fire.

the gut feelings of the enteric plexus or gut-brain. Its colour is yellow, and it generates warmth; like the ambient radiation from the sun.

Opportunities and willpower emerge from the location of the third chakra. Intellect from the head-brain registers through the reprocessing of the patient's gut feelings. Self-control and discerning behaviour are experienced. If this chakra is out of control, the patient remains in an angry, aggressive state. The ability to appraise genuine threat occurs at the level of the solar plexus. Patients can choose the necessary battles to tackle with SF-EMDR psychotherapy. This allows them to refrain from being in a continued state of anger ("battle mind.")

The goal of aligning willpower with intellect occurs by activating the necessary neural networks. By breathing into the solar plexus and holding the breath, you can pull the heart-brain and head-brain into synchrony. This aligns with the gut-brain; allowing focus and decision to emerge for the patient.

Blood flow changes in our patients and clients in the context of the perceived threat. Blood is withdrawn from the prefrontal cortex at the instant of traumatic stress. This is the reason patients experience the sensation of not being able to think. The brainstem receives increased blood flow, orientating the person towards survival strategies. The problem arises when these are often still engaged once the threat has passed. SF-EMDR psychotherapy can reverse this blood flow. This allows a realistic appraisal of danger. In turn, it gives the patient time to develop thinking space and rational response.

Blood diverts to the amygdala at the precise moment of trauma or stress. In response, it reacts automatically to the threat. Only information perceived as relevant to survival is processed, leaving the individual vulnerable to instinctive reactions.

SF-EMDR psychotherapy encourages the patient to be conscious and mind-ful. They are required to keep one foot in the present and the other in the memory of the past event being processed. Once the energetic levels of the first three chakras are balanced, the patient's senses awaken. This sensation unlocks creativity with an appreciation of beauty. In my dissociation model, I encourage patients to imagine being soothed by the calm WATER level (Window of Affect Tolerance and Emotional Reprocessing). Together with the patient, we reprocess a range of emotions. We aim for the sensations, feelings, and emotions associated with either the hyperarousal state (RAPIDS) or the hypoarousal state (FROZEN). I often explain these different states to the patient before therapy. Doing so allows the patient to prepare for any distressing emotions experienced. I consider this a prerequisite to efficiently reprocessing their trauma. It helps them overcome their stress and enables them to move on in their lives. This is conducted along with a seven-element relaxation exercise.

The heart chakra is believed to be the centre of emotional empowerment (Table 2.4). It can be seen to deal with the expression of feelings through the heart such as grief, loss, and love. By resonating with this chakra through SF-EMDR psychotherapy our patients become more receptive to love and emotional healing. The green heart in the centre of this chakra has twelve

Table 2.4 Fourth or heart chakra functions

Mantra	Yam
No. of petals	12
Physical functions	Centre of personal self-esteem, power, and ethics. How a person makes decisions, handles crises, and takes risks. Conquers fear and creates happiness and satisfaction. Responds to appreciation with empowerment.
Metaphysical functions	Anchors a higher self. Direct link to the intuitive or sensing right hemisphere. Opens awareness to universal energy (to love one's neighbour as oneself).
Endocrine glands/organs	Thymus, lungs, arms, hands, and circulation.
Symptoms if chakra is "out of balance"	Disturbed emotions, repression of love. Asthma, high blood pressure, lung and heart disease.
Lessons learnt once chakra is activated using SF-EMDR psychotherapy	Oneness with life, forgiveness, compassion, understanding, balance, conscious awareness, acceptance, peace, openness, harmony, and contentment.
Gemstones that crystallise this energy	Emerald, Tourmaline, Jade, and Rose Quartz. Primary colour is green. Secondary colour is pink.
Element	Air.

petals surrounding a six-pointed star. The central symbol represents emotional healing. The symbol strikes me as resembling a person holding and soothing a baby.

Further SF-EMDR psychotherapy brings the patient towards the "path of the heart." They can let go of their psychological defences. One patient explained to me that he felt that an arrow tipped with a rose was released from an angelic "eros" before gently entering his heart. This left him with a feeling of warmth and love. This is just one example of how activating the fourth chakra using SF-EMDR psychotherapy connects the individual energy of the first three chakras with their universal life energy. The patient's personal and spiritual life energies become integrated, both bilaterally and vertically. This allows mindfulness to emanate from the heart centre towards higher chakra levels.

Fifth (throat) chakra (Lotus Vishuddha).

This is considered the centre for the encouragement of communication, as well as being the centre of truth, personal expression, responsibility, faith, and creativity (Table 2.5). The blue throat-chakra contains sixteen petals. The symbol within the equilateral triangle represents truthful expression, responsibility, faith, and creativity.

During SF-EMDR psychotherapy the patient often experiences a lump in their throat. The patient must clear this before reprocessing can take place.

Table 2.5 Fifth or throat chakra functions

Mantra	Ham
No. of petals	16
Metaphysical functions	Seat of communication. Centre of speech, sound, and clairaudience. To show increased abundance.
Endocrine glands/organs	Mouth, thyroid, parathyroid, and hypothalamus.
Symptoms if chakra is "out of balance"	Problems with speech, communication, and hearing. Ignorance, depression, lack of discernment. Unwise use of knowledge. Sore throat and thyroid dysfunction
Lessons learnt once chakra is activated using SF-EMDR psychotherapy	True communication of the spoken word. Creativity in speech, writing, and the arts. Peace, truth, knowledge, wisdom, honesty, reliability, gentleness, and kindness. Throat chakra mediates between the head thoughts and the heart feelings. It is the seat of willpower, courage, and guidance.
Gemstones that crystallise this energy	Lapis Lazuli, Azurite, Turquoise, Aquamarine, Celestite, and Blue Topaz.
Element	Akasha (Ether).

It is often a reflection of the traumatic event that the patient has been unable to speak due to the associated dysregulated affect. At the time of the traumatic event, the inflow of sensory information was extreme. It was so great the neural fibres leading to the switching station of the thalamus became overwhelmed, causing the amygdala to detect an unsafe or life-threatening situation. The priority was survival. This caused the fight, flight, or freeze neural pathways to activate. The speech pathways involve the left frontal cortex of Broca's area and the inferior frontal gyrus of Wernicke's area for expression and comprehension. No information was allowed through from the thalamus to these cerebral cortices, meaning the patient did not have enough time to comprehend, review, or talk about their experience. Indeed being rendered speechless would have dramatically increased their chances of survival. However, many carry the speechlessness for months or years after the event.

SF-EMDR psychotherapy reversal

Simon Weston was severely wounded following a bomb explosion. He was caught off-guard on the *Sir Galahad* in the Falklands in 1982 in the conflict between the UK and Argentina. For six months he was not expected to live. Between the accident and now he has lived through eighty-seven operations. Over that time he received 500 units of blood or blood products. That is not a patch on the psychological problems that occurred as a result. He relived the explosion every night in nightmares for twenty-four years after the event. He woke up in a sweat each night unable to process the experience. He was still in survival mode and speechless. Then one night the metaphorical elastic band around his chest snapped. He could dream about the experience and talk to his dead colleagues in the trenches. I would hypothesise that the tightness around his chest was a constricted heart chakra.

Once active, the blockages at the level of the throat chakra could be addressed. This, in turn, allowed the thalamic circuits to switch off from survival mode. Nightmares or non-REM sleep phases were negotiated without waking up in a sweat. The REM dreaming circuits were switched on. This transferred healthy imagery and emotional experiences to the left cerebral hemisphere. This activated Simon's comprehension and expression. He has since been able to ascribe meaning to his ordeal eloquently. I believe that had Simon been able to avail himself of the staged approach of SF-EMDR psychotherapy, he would have overcome these hurdles years ago. He would not have had to wait twenty-four years for his own spontaneous healing reprocessing to occur.

In my experience using SF-EMDR psychotherapy, patients tend to "get stuck" at the level of the throat chakra. This is felt to be "like a lump in their throat" and represents an emotional or mental block in their traumatic memory. Their fifth chakra is their source of expression of emotions, feelings, and creativity. By direct bilateral stimulation of the throat, patients can shift this "blockage." They are then able to "find their voice" and speak truthfully and calmly about the traumatic memory. The throat chakra has a sky-blue colour and resonates with the clarity of speech and sound when activated.

It is essential to manage the patient's reprocessing during SF-EMDR psychotherapy within their window of affect tolerance, and emotional regulation (WATER), otherwise hypo or hyperarousal can occur. The resultant anxiety can trigger panic attacks and nervousness. Safely negotiating this stage allows the emergence of inspiration and intuition for the patient. By now, a quantum leap in consciousness has occurred, and the patient is ready to ascend to the vibrational levels present in the quintessential mind. Individual and collective unconsciousness start to merge, and innovative thinking consolidates with knowledge acquisition. The patient begins to view their life with a new perspective.

The middle picture (Figure 2.2(b)) is of Narrow Water Castle in Warrenpoint, Co. Down, Northern Ireland. This was the location for the greatest loss of life of the security forces in the troubles in Northern Ireland and occurred in 1979. It is designed to illustrate how the state of calm represented by "WATERS" can change in seconds. It quickly switches to the destructive states of chaotic "RAPIDS" and numbing "FROZEN." This can lead clinically to the dissociative states described above. The consensus view of trauma therapists is that the state of hyperarousal is also a form of dissociation. Patients in either the RAPIDS or FROZEN state require a different therapeutic approach to restore their state of equilibrium to calmer "WATERS."

Plans were at an advanced stage to erect a bridge over this span of water near Warrenpoint. Metaphorically this represents new neural networks spanning the twin states of being either frozen or in the rapids. This could be symbolised by an arc or a rainbow of light reaching over the cavernous depths of water below.

As the neural synapses fire, they rewire. By doing so, the window of tolerance widens. It is as if the banks of the river in the photograph have been strengthened, protecting itself against flooding and freezing over. This allows the patient to tolerate greater degrees of effect and regulate their emotions better. By using the seven-element exercise to strengthen this reservoir, they can safely contain any dysfunctional emotions. The information is then fed up to the sensory gateway known as the thalamus. Here there is a low-grade level of analysis computing any signs of danger. This could be high winds and turbulent waters or the hidden danger of an iceberg. Once the threat has passed, the cortex can convert any significant or traumatic life experiences so that meaning can be made from the event. Unfortunately, the EU funding of 14.5 million euros for the bridge construction has been withdrawn. This came down to a lack of matching funding. It was not forthcoming from the Irish and Stormont governments.

	R.A.P.I.D.S	
	Racing thoughts	
	Affective dysregulation	
	Partitioned personality	
	Impulsivity	
	Distress	
	Suicidality	

(a) Hyperarousal and dissociation

	C.A.L.M.	W.A.T.E.R.S
	Consciously	Window of
	Aware	Affect Tolerance:
	Level headed	Emotions
	Mindful	Regulated &
		Stabilized

(b) Integration of affective states

	F.R.O.Z.E.N	F.E.A.R
	Freeze Reaction	Feigned death
	Oblivious to outside world	Entrapped
	Zonked out	Anguish
	Emotionally	Rigidity
	Numb	

(c) Hypoarousal and dissociation

Figure 2.2 Model of altered levels of arousal dissociation and stability linked to the window of affect tolerance and emotional regulation. The middle picture is of Narrow Water Castle, a fifteenth-century Elizabethan Castle in Warrenpoint, Co. Down, Northern Ireland. This was the location for the greatest loss of life of security forces in the Troubles in Northern Ireland. It is designed to illustrate how the state, represented by "Calm Waters," can change in seconds to the destructive states of chaotic "Rapids" and numbing "Frozen in Fear." This can lead clinically to the dissociative states described above with corresponding features of hyperarousal and hypoarousal, which can occur interchangeably during SF-EMDR.

Source: Top and middle images from Shutterstock.com, bottom photograph courtesy of Fran S Waters USA.

Integrating the intuitive art of psychotherapy with the rational perspective of neuroscience regarding the shutdown dissociation continuum associated with complex PTSD. Introducing a new therapeutic paradigm in thetreatment of traumatic dissociation or dissociation identity disorder (DID)

The Shutdown Dissociation Scale (Shut-D) was designed to test for vulnerability to the types of complex PTSD associated with dissociative symptoms. It was developed by Elbert and Schauer, to allow for the expression of derealisation and depersonalisation. It is assumed that the survival advantage of the shutdown continuum is to inhibit actions that may threaten survival and stimulate actions that promote survival when in a life-threatening situation.

These symptoms arise from the shutting down of emotional, cognitive, sensory, and other behavioural responses that would otherwise lessen the survival prospect in the face of overwhelming threat. The following are the six stages of the dissociative shutdown:

1. Avoidance

The first response to threat is avoidance in the first place. However, in situations of sexual abuse, war, torture, or terrorist attacks this is rarely possible.

2. Freeze

Second, freeze occurs due to sympathetic stimulation and attentive immobility. The person is immobile but alert (initial orienting response to danger). The client/patient is silent, paralysed with frozen defensive reactions. Their heart-rate, pulse, and blood pressure are increased so that they are in a state of readiness to act.

Analogy: Dr Chris Gantor, an Australian psychiatrist describes an evolutionary perspective on trauma. His view is that humans deploy mammalian defences when faced with life-threatening situations. An example of this might be on a safari, and you see a lion 200 metres away. Your reaction is to back up to your vehicle carefully. Alternatively, you attempt to blend in with the surroundings and remain motionless. This shifts the lion's attention to other moving or noisy stimuli. This is often the beginning of speechless terror; a feature of unresolved trauma.

A patient described how his heart raced whenever he recalled past events with his dog. A car had hit the dog, and he was powerless to help. This was a natural first part of the survival response. This memory became reactivated during the therapeutic session and needed to be reprocessed. His speechless terror was responsive as the traumatic memory was reprocessed using SF-EMDR psychotherapy.

Another patient described an encounter with a frog, cat, and dog on the stairs of her family home. At the time, she experienced overwhelming anxiety. Her heart quickened when she was confronted by the conflicting demands of holding onto her dog at the bottom of the stairs. She was frozen to the spot with the thought of the cat attacking the frog. She was repulsed by the sight of the frog, which appeared to be watching her. Unknown at the time, this was directly linked to unconscious memories. One was of a time she ran into an army of frogs crossing the road. Another was of her former cat, who had died after a collision with a car. She described how, previously, "kamikaze sheep" jumped onto the bonnet of her car. These previous memories emerged by floating back to a first or worst time when she felt in a similar life-threatening experience. This was dealt with using the three stages of trauma recovery:

- Safety and stabilisation: overcoming dysregulation;
- Coming to terms with traumatic memories; and
- An integrated understanding of self, which can move on around a healthy present and healed self.

3. Withdraw by flight, or 4. Aggressive defence by fight

The person initiates their active defensive response by activation of the sympathetic branch of the autonomic nervous system. In turn, this causes a range of flight and fight responses:

- Increases in heart rate, blood pressure, deeper inhalation and exhalation;
- Sweating, which cools the body and leads to moist palms. This improves the grip if the person decides to flee through the undergrowth and lessens the chance of injury from twigs and branches, etc;
- The thalamus acts as a sensory gateway after a traumatic event. It decides on the information that is transferred to the cerebral cortex. As it becomes activated in this role, resources are diverted away from the cerebral cortex. The hypothalamus can then act on the pituitary, stimulating the adrenal glands. Adrenaline is later released into the bloodstream. This explains why cognitive behaviour therapy is unable to access thalamically stored information. It provides evidence for the effect of buzzers placed on the abdomen, renal, and other affected body areas during SF-EMDR psychotherapy (O'Malley, 2016, 2017);
- The heart and musculoskeletal system become energised via increased blood flow for a snap decision either to take flight or to fight the oncoming danger;
- The peripheral vascular system (i.e. peripheral blood vessels) constrict to reduce potential blood loss in the event of an injury from the marauding lion;
- If the person is injured by the lion the peripheral pain receptors (nociception) shut down. This prevents the person from engaging in the premature recuperative behaviour, which could impede healing and recovery. Any effort to resist could lead to death from the lion's instinctive attack; and

- Thinking is limited during this stage of the dissociative process. Any delay in the person's instinctive reaction could be fatal. It takes 40ms for the muscles to be activated by brainstem control of synaptic reflexes. It takes 500ms for a thought to be generated in the cerebral cortex. Thus, to delay ½ sec or 500ms to decide consciously could be fatal. This physiological response explains why at the point of overwhelming trauma, information is stored in the body and brainstem. Dr Bessel van der Kolk discusses this in his seminal work: "The body keeps the score." I have described a novel way to titrate this information into the ventromedial prefrontal cortex and onto the prefrontal cortex. This is where the patient can think about and learn from the event. In my clinical experience, it is only at this stage of trauma recovery that a trauma-focused CBT approach can be most effective.

RAPIDS: reactive racing thoughts, angry at affective dysregulation, panicky, intrusive imagery, impulsive or high-risk behaviour, dissociative, self-harm, and suicidal ideation. My symbolism of the RAPIDS acronym represents hyperarousal with dissociation.

Analogy: in this half-second, the person may have become the lion's lunch. This happened in a recent safari in South Africa. The victim was photographed seconds before death. They were attempting to take a picture of the lion from the open window of their vehicle. Unannounced, the lion pounced on what it perceived to be prey. Its predatory instincts kicked in and killed the tourist.

5. Immobility

Fifth, the person enters a state of tonic immobility, where they are unable to move or respond. This increases the survival chances even when the lion has attacked. Any movements made now may act as a stimulus for the lion to continue its attack with increased ferocity. It would respond in this manner, as its instincts perceive a threat to survival. Thus, it is very dangerous if the prey or victim fights back. This stage of the autonomic response involves the activation of the parasympathetic system, especially the dorsal vagal nerve, which causes a range of instinctive reactions.

The immobility of the victim helps to avoid tissue damage when threatened with sharp objects or when penetrated. This has relevance for a victim raped at knife- or gunpoint.

Surrender signals to the attacker may prevent counter aggression by the assailant.

Anger is suppressed, and the victim experiences emotional numbness. This is a parasympathetic response mediated by the dorsal branch of the vagus nerve.
In my three-dimensional model below, I describe the FROZEN acronym (Freeze Reaction Oblivious, Zonked-out, Emotions Numbed).

There is an increase in the production of endorphins and enkephalins by the victim to diminish the physical pain. Aggressive and defensive reactions are also inhibited.

Blood flow is directed away from Broca's and Wernicke's areas in the left cerebral cortex. Thus, the patient often can't speak about the experience either at the time or subsequently. This is an adaptive survival strategy, as any noise could threaten survival chances. Following the trauma, the patient may be unable to speak about the event. In my clinical experience, patients describe feeling a lump in their throat. This has been described as speechless terror. It is maladaptive and counterproductive in achieving recovery from the trauma. SF-EMDR psychotherapy therapy sessions reverse this effect. To counter this reaction, buzzers are placed either side of the throat. There they remain until the blood flow is encouraged to flow back along the neck veins and arteries. The buzzers relax the muscles of the vocal cords, allowing them to function as they should. The patient's speech then returns. Hundreds of patients report that the lump in their throat disappears after therapy.

Assessing the level of dissociation in your patient and deciding on a therapeutic approach

The Dissociative Experiences Scale (DES) was developed as a tool to assess dissociative symptoms in the general population. It doesn't allow for interaction with the client by the therapist, as it is a self-rating scale. The Shut-D scale illustrated below is much more interactive. It helps to pick up dissociative disorders. These include non-epileptic attack disorder (NEAD) and other types of conversion disorders. The patient can experience either predominantly hyperarousal or hypoarousal symptoms associated with their dissociative experiences.

There is now widespread acknowledgement that dissociation with a predominance of hyperarousal or hypoarousal symptoms requires different therapeutic approaches. In my opinion, the approach to treatment should be discussed in clinical supervision with a psychotherapist. They should be experienced in the clinical management of primary secondary and tertiary dissociation, as is outlined by Van der Hart Nijenhuis and Steele.

The Shut-D scale below has proved to be a satisfactory way to quantify dissociative symptoms in patients. There were four different samples recruited for this study:

1. The subjects recruited for the study were female refugees with multiple traumatic experiences from the university refugee clinic;
2. This included German psychiatric patients and healthy controls;
3. Another 130 patients were recruited from inpatients at a psychiatric hospital in Germany; and
4. Additionally, fifteen female patients with dissociative identity disorder were recruited from psychiatric outpatient departments and private practitioners.

Results of reliability and validity studies on Shut-D questionnaire

All items on the Shut-D scale were found to be significantly correlated with dissociative symptoms.

Shut-D dissociation scale

This scale applies to multicultural populations of differing education and income. Those included suffer with various psychiatric disorders. Among the dysfunctions are acute and complex PTSD, developmental trauma disorder, depression, psychosis, personality disorders, and dissociative identity disorder.

The authors of the article on the development of the Shut-D questionnaire state that:

> First, disruption of the ongoing perceptual and behavioural processes provides the basis for shutdown dissociation and interferes with an integrative representation of the environment and the self. It is likely that this ongoing disruption of integrative processes plays a vital role in the development and maintenance of PTSD.

Read each question thoroughly and mark yourself on a scale of 0–3. Zero is not at all, 1 is once a week, 2 is two to four times per week, and 3 is five or more times a week.

1   Have you fainted or been passing out?
2   Have you felt dizzy? Has your vision gone black? Have you felt dizzy and couldn't see anymore, as if you had gone blind?
3   Have you felt as though you couldn't hear for a while, as though you were deaf? When people were talking to you, did they sound far away?
4   Have you had an experience of blurred vision and not being able to see things around you properly?
5   Have you felt as though your body or a part of your body has gone numb?
6   Have you felt as though you couldn't move for a while, as though you were paralysed?
7   Have you felt as though your body or a part of it was insensitive to pain?
8   Have you ever been in a state in which your body suddenly felt heavy and tired?
9   Have you ever experienced your body becoming tense or rigid for a while?
10 Have you felt sick or nauseous? Have you felt as though you were about to throw up or vomit? Have you felt yourself break out in a cold sweat?
11 Have you ever had an out-of-body sensation?
12 Have you had moments when you have found yourself unable to speak? Have there been occasions when you could only speak with great effort?

Have there been occasions when you could only speak in a whisper for a period?

13 Have you ever suddenly felt weak and warm?

39 is the maximum score achievable. Any results scoring 20 and above are noted as highly significant.

6. Final stage of dissociative collapse

The sixth and final part of the shutdown continuum involves feigned death, fall, faint, vasovagal collapse, non-epileptic attack disorder (NEAD or pseudosei-zures), and excessive desire to please.

- Repeated activation of the parasympathetic system activates the dorsal vagus of the reptilian brain. This comes from the Latin *"reptilio,"* which means to crawl. Blood pressure is lowered in case the victim's skin and muscle tissue are damaged. This is a good survival strategy, as potential blood loss is minimised. There is recent evidence that reptiles like the bearded dragon are capable of imitative behaviour. This offers new potential for helping patients reprocess brainstem-based behaviour during SF-EMDR psychotherapy. You can link somatic experiences by focusing on brainstem responses;
- When the victim is crawling, or prostrate, oxygen and essential nutrients are carried by the circulatory system to the essential organs: the gut-brain, heart-brain, and head-brain. SF-EMDR psychotherapy is uniquely placed as an integrative approach to allow reprocessing at all these levels;
- The vagal stimulation of the heart reduces heart rate. Circulation and metabolism is maintained. This is again an instinctive survival strategy. When I was nine, I was standing at an open kitchen door leading to a hallway. In an instant, I was prostrate with hands outstretched to break my fall in a reptilian or crawling posture. A split second later there was a massive explosion from a rocket attack launched by the Irish Republican Army (IRA) at the joint British Army Royal Ulster Constabulary (RUC) military base. This was 100m away from our family home. Reflecting on this event over the years since I studied medicine and neuroanatomy I came to the following conclusion. The sound wave of the explosion was initially processed by my autonomic nervous system. All my sensory receptors conveyed information to the brainstem and thalamus and interpreted this as a danger. Within milliseconds the thalamus sent effector responses to my musculature, activating the reptilian posture response. Between 100 and 500ms later my auditory nerve processed the sound of the explosion, breaking glass, and falling masonry. Only then did I become consciously aware of my environment. My brainstem had instinctively protected my key organs of the heart lungs and the gastrointestinal system. As I was only nine, my

default mode network was in the early stages of development. It is following life-threatening traumatic experiences like this that your destiny and fate can be decided. Thankfully neither I nor any members of my family were physically injured by the 1971 explosion. Our town in "bandit country" went on to experience over forty more terrorist conflicts I came to know as "the troubles." It is for this reason I left to study medicine at Trinity College, Dublin, and my interest in the neurobiology of trauma was kindled;

- If the assailant tortures the victim, cortisol is released as adrenocortical and mineralocorticoid. This can help to protect the heart and any subsequent stress reaction. This occurs after extreme punishments such as waterboarding or radiation poisoning;
- The victim releases their analgesia in the form of endogenous opioids to aid survival until hopefully help arrives;
- All emotions are numbed (FROZEN in FEAR). Flat affect, Frozen reaction, Oblivious, Zonked-out, Emotions numb, Feigned death, Entrapped, Anguish, Rigidity. This helps to inhibit an emotional reaction, which may threaten survival;
- An excessive frozen reaction can lead to dissociative subtype PTSD, if not adequately addressed; and
- To aid survival, all physiological arousal mechanism and memories of the incident can be repressed. In therapy, the goal is to bring these unconscious memories back into conscious awareness. This can be achieved using SF-EMDR psychotherapy.

My model of the spectrum of autonomic arousal in the wake of trauma embodies these dissociative emotional states. I aimed to contain them through the prism of the NARROW WATER CASTLE. The next step is converting them from gut-brain to heart-brain reprocessing. Activation at a gamma wave frequency of 40 Hertz can help to reverse thalamic activation. This allows thalamocortical binding to occur. Further activation into the head-brain allows computing in the cerebral cortex and prefrontal cortex. This stabilises the patient's level of arousal. Once in their optimal arousal zone, they can tolerate feelings and associated reactions. They start to reflect and learn from previous experiences. They begin to think and feel integratively. Their reactions adaptively fit the imagined or recalled situation.

Dissociative responses help the victim to survive their life-threatening event. If left to continue for prolonged periods of time, it will lead to an inability to reintegrate memories. It can also cause fragmentation of future experiences that are not adequately stored in long-term memory. It is as if the thalamus, as our sensory gateway, is on high alert. It keeps triggering a survival response, and no information enters the cerebrum. This would take 500ms: time the thalamus believes it doesn't have. The patient is unable to think due to dissociation. They have disabled defensive responses and collapse into a helpless and hopeless state (both physically and mentally). It is difficult to tolerate this effect, and the patient may engage in self-harm to attempt to feel normal again. Instead of reaching a sense of CALM WATERS (Consciously aware, Level-headed, Mindful Window of Affect Tolerance and Emotional Regulation and Stability), they are likely to overshoot their window of tolerance or optimal arousal zone. This brings them into the RAPIDS as described above.

I have the solution for patients who have difficulty with this two-dimensional concept of dissociation. I have developed a three-dimensional model inspired by the Narrow Water Castle found at the Burren outside Warrenpoint, Co. Down, Northern Ireland (Figure 2.4). This model is especially helpful with child patients.

Playing with the letters in Narrow Water Castle we make a fantastic acronym. This describes how, with experience, the nerves and synapses make new connections. This can also be used to explain the goals and processes involved in SF-EMDR for psychotherapy and peak performance.

Nerves
Are activated
Repeatedly
Rewiring &
Opening the
Width of the
Window of

Affect
Tolerance &
Emotional
Regulation

Containing
Any
Significant or
Traumatic
Life
Events

Figure 2.4 is an overview of the model of the NARROW WATER CASTLE showing the RAPIDS on one side (Figure 2.6) and the FROZEN lake (Figure 2.5) on the other. It is set on the background of garden paving slabs to give a perspective with the actual model size. The model has a customised wooden cover, which locks into place with clips, allowing for portability. The model has reinforcing metal brackets for durability and protection. It is easy to replicate the model to use with dissociative clients. It would be especially helpful for working with patients on the ASD scale. In my clinical experience, these patients respond well to information they can quickly visually process. The presence of the castle acts both as a safe place and as an area in which to resolve conflicts. It is possible to use this structure to reintegrate compartmentalised aspects of the patient's dissociated personality. In my clinical practice, the emphasis is on reintegration of parts to the state that existed in the pre-traumatic personality. One must do this in the context of a secure therapist–patient relationship.

The diagram (Figure 2.3) shows the effects on the client's apparently normal personality after exposure to increasing levels of trauma. This pattern of dissociation was described by Van der Hart, Nijenhuis, and Steele, 1999.

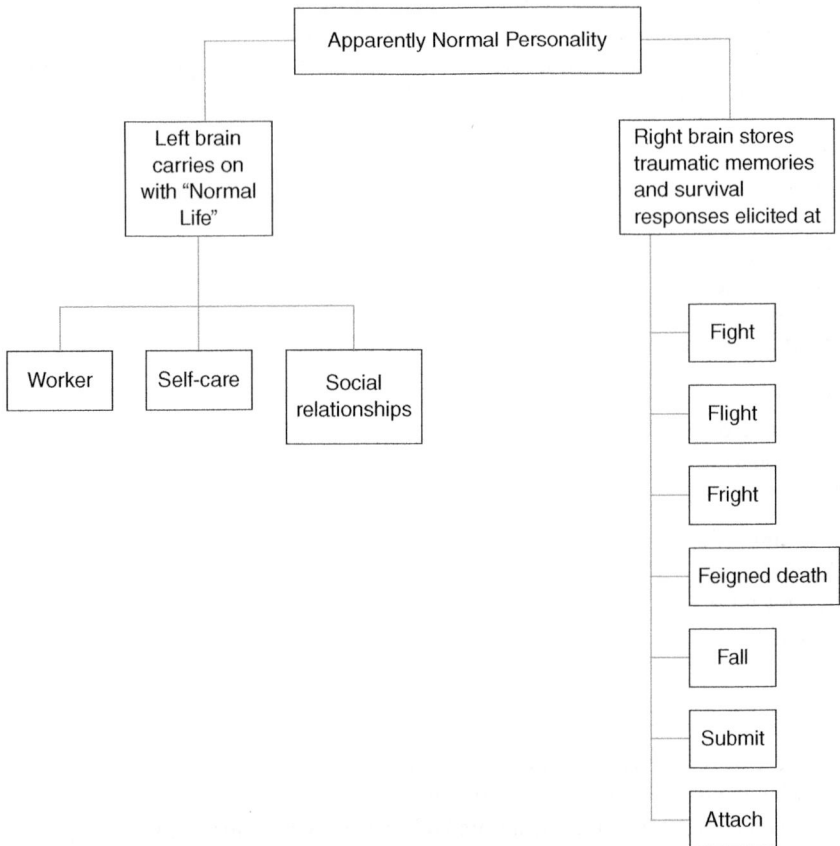

Figure 2.3 Diagram showing the effects on the apparently normal personality after exposure to increasing levels of trauma. The symptoms of this dissociation are best treated by a process of reintegration. This can be achieved using sensorimotor-focused EMDR. When traumatic events happen, the personality fragments in a characteristic way according to Van der Hart, Nijenhuis, and Steele, 1999. These fragmented aspects of the patient's personality can be reassembled using SF-EMDR to bring the patient back under the influence of their original pre-traumatic personality.

Figure 2.4 Aerial view of the castle. The castle can be used to help the patient visualise resources associated with safety and out of a traumatic unsafe or life-threatening situation. With children this can be acted out in play-therapy scenarios. In my clinical experience, patients can easily relate this metaphor to their own somatic and cognitive experience of trauma. This model works well with patients with complex trauma such as dissociative identity disorders. Many patients have drawings or soft toys, which they use to represent different aspects of their partitioned personality. According to Van der Hart, Nijenhuis, and Steele, traumatic events cause the patient's personality to fragment.

Source: Dr Art O'Malley.

Figure 2.5 This shows how if the patient feels shutdown or frozen then there is a window, which can be opened. This can be imagined relating to opening the window of affect tolerance, emotional regulation, and stabilisation. It is a demonstration of the ease of opening the window of tolerance if the patient feels shutdown or "frozen." The window can be opened as illustrated. This can be imagined as relating to opening up the patient to "Calm Waters." I encourage patients to use imaginal resources to lift themselves out of the frozen lake into the safety of the Narrow Water Castle.

Source: Dr Art O'Malley.

Figure 2.6 This shows a way out from the hyperaroused state of dissociation associated with the "Rapids." Various types of imaginational resourcing for adults or creative play for children can assist clients to escape from the white-water rapids to reach the safety of the Narrow Water Castle. The image of the triple spiral on the door can be used to activate magical kingdoms described by authors such as Roald Dahl, Walt Disney, J. K. Rowling and the mythology of the wizard Merlin and King Arthur and the Knights of the Round Table.

Source: Dr Art O'Malley.

Discussion

There has been an explosion of research into the effects of early trauma and deprivation on human development. Editors Charles Zeanah and Edmund Sonuga-Barke characterise this as a move towards understanding developmental mechanisms. Teicher and Samson suggest that different forms of abuse can affect specific regions of the brain. This has been reported in Kennedy et al. 2016 in a twenty-five-year follow-up to the English and Romanian Adoptees Study. Impairing ADHD symptoms persist in this group. Functional magnetic resonance imaging (fMRI) studies are demonstrating under-activation of brain circuits, such as the default mode network (DMN). A study of young children exposed to war trauma found high levels of PTSD, anxiety, and disruptive behaviour disorders and ADHD. To date, this research has not yet translated to a change in clinical practice in Child and Mental Health Services (CAMHS), especially in the UK. Here the emphasis is on treating symptoms with medications. Typically, antidepressants and stimulants are used as the primary intervention. A focused exploration of the management of dissociated traumatic stress would dramatically decrease the need for medication.

McGorry reported on the latest fMRI literature concerning threat and reward processing, emotional regulation, and executive control. The conclusions and implications for clinical practice of this research are profound. They found that maltreatment in childhood led to future mental health problems. It does so by altering neurocognitive functioning. These neurocognitive alterations appear to be adaptive at the time of the adversity. They contribute to the pathogenesis of mental health disorders in adolescence and adulthood. The mechanism seems to be that latent vulnerability is the neurocognitive phenotype. The child experiences indirect cumulative effects and immediate direct effects. This impacts on socio-emotional functioning. Exposure to later stressors then leads to a heightened risk of developing chronic and enduring psychiatric disorders. In my opinion, what is needed in CAMHS is a paradigm shift from prioritising medication to preventive psychiatry.

Conclusion

Trauma survivors with autonomic shutdown and dissociation symptoms or dissociative identity disorder require different treatment to classical exposure-based approaches. The Shut-D scale will enable therapists to systematically document the impact of traumatic experiences on victims where they have been exposed to a high level of danger such as sexual assault. This is especially relevant to the dissociative subtype of PTSD in DSM V. This will also be relevant when ICD 11 is published in 2018. This is expected to incorporate diagnostic criteria for complex PTSD. This research paves the way for innovative treatment strategies for dissociative symptoms in trauma victims.

Case example one

One patient described to me his vision of a fish with bulbous eyes as if linked to the earliest reptilian evolution of visual perception. This became linked to the image of a dolphin riding the crest of a wave and diving into the deep ocean. Since their development, dolphins are believed to have retained the consciousness emerging from the planetary grid of earth. In Prof Brian Cox's documentary, "Wonders of Life," the evolution of human senses is discussed. When jawless fish existed, they breathed via sets of gills. As evolution proceeded, these gills formed arches and gave rise to fish with jaws. These bones then further receded to form the internal ear ossicles, the stapes, incus, and anvil. Similarly, our eyes have evolved from these primitive ancestors. The most primitive aspect of our visual pathway has been incorporated into the brainstem. It is known as the superior and inferior colliculi or corpora quadrigemina. Peripheral bilateral stimulation during SF-EMDR psychotherapy can trigger visual imagery for our patients. Furthermore, many lizards have a third eye, which reacts to light and dark. This is symbolic of the brow or third-eye chakra, which is associated with inner sight or intuition. In many meditative practices, practitioners visualise breathing in through the pineal gland or third eye. This is believed to have the effect of activating both the lower and higher chakras.

This schematic drawing of the dorsal view of the goldfish brain (Figure 2.7) shows the main brain divisions. It is made up of:

- The forebrain: the olfactory bulbs and telencephalon;
- The midbrain: the mesencephalon with the optic lobes, cerebellum, and vagal lobes; and
- The telencephalon: the floor of the telencephalon is the primitive evolutionary structure for the basal ganglia in higher vertebrates.

The roof of the telencephalon is the precursor to the hippocampus. The optic lobes and the cerebellum have their usual higher vertebrate equivalents. The vagal lobes are the locus of cell bodies for the glossopharyngeal nerve, which is important for taste. The mesencephalon is not visible from a dorsal view. It is located at a rostral and caudal position underneath the midbrain optic lobes. The schematic drawing of the lateral view of the goldfish brain shows the level of the sections in the lower part of the diagram. These can be compared with the embryological divisions of the human brain shown in Chapter 8.

It is interesting to observe how the vagal lobe of the goldfish has evolved into the human brainstem. This provides further neuroanatomical support for the theoretical validity of SF-EMDR psychotherapy. A key consequence of bilateral cerebellar stimulation is activation of the brainstem of the patient. Further SF-EMDR psychotherapy activates neural synapses. A tingling sensation is experienced, as new synaptic connections are made, and axon rewiring occurs. As emotional blocks

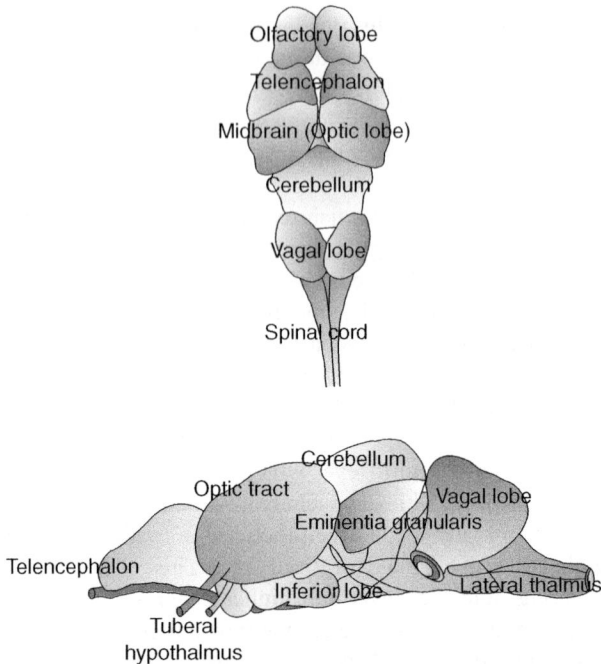

Figure 2.7 Dorsal view of the goldfish brain above and lateral view below.

are overcome in an independent mind, hosts find verbal expression easier. Creativity can flow freely. Broca's area (expressive language) and Wernicke's area (receptive language) become activated. Blood flow increases in the prefrontal cortex, making a better transmission of information possible.

The sixth (brow) chakra

This is also known as the third-eye chakra (lotus Ajna). It is believed to be the centre of psychic energy. This centre is the origin of insight and a doorway into the unconscious mind. Opening the third eye can assist our patients and clients in their exploration of higher realms. Of note, there are only two petals in the third-eye chakra. Anatomically, this is the site of the pineal gland. There is a sculpture representative of the pineal gland in the Vatican, attesting to the significance of this endocrine gland in Catholic belief. This is the largest sculpture representative of the pineal gland in the world.

Many patients experiencing SF-EMDR psychotherapy end their journey of self-realisation here. Here is where they find sufficient meaning from their experiences. Further insight is possible with activation of the seventh or crown chakra. This can provide a link for the patient with what Jung termed "collective unconsciousness."

The pinecone sculpture is believed to symbolise the opening of the brow chakra equivalent to the third eye and the pineal gland, which is located in the centre of the brain.

It is believed to link us to the frequency of our soul energy and greater self-awareness and knowledge. Opening the brow chakra and pineal gland offers the potential of moving from a state of duality to oneness.

This can be achieved by those who meditate for prolonged periods. They are said to become intuitive by opening up their third eye, sixth chakra, or pineal gland. Their pineal gland has enlarged to the size of a real pinecone. The average size of someone who does not meditate is the size of a pea, apparently.

This area in the forehead is marked by many eastern cultures with a bindi. This comes from the Sanskrit *Bindu*, meaning "a drop, small particle, or dot." It is believed to be the seat of concealed wisdom and the exit point for kundalini energy. The bindi is said to retain energy and strengthen concentration. Bindis come in different shapes and colours according to their meaning. Red represents honour, love, and prosperity, whereas yellow symbolises the power to influence the intellect.

In many eastern traditions the energy, prana, or chi is inhaled through the third eye. Some animals have a vestigial third eye which is sensitive to light and dark. The inhaled energy is directed upward to the crown chakra and then downward infusing all the remaining chakras until it exits the earthstar chakra.

As we ascend further to the level of the sixth (brow) chakra (Table 2.6), we link to Maslow, the highest hierarchy of need. This is the search for transcendence or self-actualisation. The indigo or dark-blue colour becomes resonant. Patients often report experiencing an indigo-coloured beam of light around their brow. This may represent the release of Kundalini energy. As we continue SF-EMDR psychotherapy, the patient's imagination synthesises images. These pictures enable target memories to be reprocessed. Intuition is developed at this stage in the treatment. An awareness of "all there is" may seep into consciousness. By developing mindfulness, the patient can become an outside observer or witness of events, allowing them to enter a state of calm where they experience a world of recovery and triumph (stage five of SF-EMDR psychotherapy).

Advocates of Taoist philosophy claim a connection to the electromagnetic heart field. The "third eye" of the sixth chakra reaches above the level of the personal ego where transcendence can occur. Activation of the sixth-chakra energy lays the foundation for discarding duality. It also enables attunement with oneness. Further SF-EMDR psychotherapy activates the collective unconsciousness represented by the seventh chakra.

Table 2.6 Brow chakra image and functions

Mantra	Om
No. of petals	2
Physical functions	Visualisation of the brain stem and cerebellum. Vision and balancing of the two cerebral hemispheres.
Metaphysical functions	Clairvoyance and insight.
Endocrine glands/organs	Pituitary, nose, left eye, and ears.
Symptoms if chakra is "out of balance"	Lack of concentration, cynicism, tension headaches, nightmares, and disturbed vision.
Lessons learnt once chakra is activated using SF-EMDR Psychotherapy and Peak Performance	Realisation of the soul, insight, imagination, peace of mind, concentration, wisdom, and perception beyond duality.
Gemstones that crystallise this energy	Fluorite, Tourmaline, Azurite, Quartz, and Ophrys.
Element	Light.

Seventh (crown) chakra (lotus Sahasrara)

This is known as the spiritual gateway centre and is the seat of the soul (Table 2.7). This centre is believed to filter soul energy otherwise known as Prana. There are sixty outward petals, which lead to one thousand towards the middle. By activating this chakra, we can access the realms of the soul and cosmic consciousness. It is necessary for the patient to reach a higher vibrational plane to achieve this level of conscious awareness.

The seventh chakra is one of knowledge acquisition at all the energy levels of the body. It involves getting in touch with your own unique purpose and path and direction. Patients start to experience a state of oneness instead of duality. This realisation of oneness can lead to a greater understanding of the role of humanity on earth.

During SF-EMDR psychotherapy, one patient experienced purple healing light entering the third eye of the pineal gland (sixth chakra). This was then followed by a band of white light penetrating through the crown chakra, before washing over the rest of their body. This appeared to be a way in which they connected to the universal cosmic energy.

The dance of body, mind, and spirit may equate to the processing of gut-brain, heart-brain, and head-brain, as I have discussed earlier. Development of the patient's individual chakra energies mirrors these processes. This can be achieved by gentle activation of the chakras by SF-EMDR psychotherapy. Explanation of the functions of the chakras can help patients and clients understand how their body is processing information on these different levels.

Table 2.7 Crown chakra image and functions

Mantra	None
No. of petals	1,000
Physical functions	Vitalises cerebral hemispheres and integrates the spiritual and physical self.
Metaphysical functions	None.
Endocrine glands/organs	Pineal gland, central nervous system cortex, and the right eye.
Symptoms if chakra is "out of balance"	Confusion, depression, alienation, and reduction in inspiration.
Lessons learnt once chakra is activated using SF-EMDR Psychotherapy and Peak Performance	Higher self becomes linked to one's personality. Spiritual will, inspiration, unity, divine wisdom, understanding, continuity of consciousness, and perception in higher dimensions.
Gemstones that crystallise this energy	Amethyst, Diamond, Quartz, Crystal, and Celenite.
Element	None.

A manual summarising the critical aspects of "the Art of SF-EMDR" will be made available for therapists and business coaches.

Case example two

A client had been through two years of complicated abdominal surgery. This had included removal of the gallbladder for acute cholecystitis. The surgery was done the old-fashioned way and had left the client feeling bloated and wanting to retch. Now several years later the client was still complaining of abdominal discomfort.

During the SF-EMDR psychotherapy session, the zappers were placed against the abdomen. Initially, the left side felt bloated, and the right side felt full of adhesions.

The headphones were placed behind the mastoid process, the frequencies set to create entrainment between the cerebral hemispheres with the stimulation frequency greater in one region than the other. I encouraged the client to perform imaginary psychic surgery cutting the adhesions away and removing the bloated feeling. This led to a reprocessing of the last memories of going under the anaesthetic and the first memories of waking up. These were successfully reprocessed. The client started to feel a headache and was able to use one of the zappers to lessen its effect. She began to rock back and forth, reliving the posture associated with recovery from the anaesthetic. She then spontaneously placed both zappers at the pingala and ida positions at the base of the spine. This is the point of activation of the kundalini energies, and a fundamental tenet of kundalini medicine and yoga is to activate these points. As these points were activating, my client became aware of a warm sensation of heat over the sacrum (Lotus Svadhisthana). The session concluded with my client standing upright. Her abdominal contents felt more relaxed, and the sensation of bloating was gone. I also used the zappers to activate the brainstem and shoulder; loosening the gallbladder meridian. My client felt the whole process had been healing and integrative.

The soul star (transcendental) chakra

This is believed to filter divine light. It is the chalice of soul energy and facilitates access to the Akashic records, which are found to hold the soul memories of our ancestors.

The soul chakra is also known as the avatar of synthesis. Its purpose is to integrate the patient with planet earth and raise their energy levels.

This is believed to be 20 cm above the crown chakra. It is a keystone for the other chakras and is supposed to connect the patient to the source of all energy.

According to string theory, universal information comes from the eleven dimensions of a multiverse world. The origin of the word universe is from the Latin "*unus*," for one and "*verses*," to turn. One could hypothesise that when the space-time of the eleven dimensions becomes one, that we have the singularity of the Big Bang. This again shows the links between ancient mythology and modern theoretical physics. As our knowledge expands, the worlds of myth and science appear to coalesce. My goal is to seek the common ground between the east and west and between ancient myth and modern scientific thought.

The divine-star gateway chakra

This chakra governs your link to higher powers and god. It handles the flow and regulation of universal rays into your conscious awareness.

It is located 20 cm above the head and is coloured gold. When I visited the site of Tynwald in the Isle of Man, accompanied by a CAMHS colleague of mine, something interesting happened. She was acutely aware of the spiritual energies around this stone circle, which is only several metres in diameter. The circle is off the beaten track and well away from the official locations that tourists are funnelled to. It is in an isolated area close to a small stone church. I held a pair of divining rods 20 cm above my head. As I traversed the outside of the circle, the divining rods started to move spontaneously in circles. As I stopped at that point, they continued to rotate as if driven by an invisible energetic ley line or meridian. In total, at this precise spot, the ancient civilisations had marked out the triskelia. This is the intersection of three meridians: one travels east, south, and south-west through Glastonbury, Avebury, Cornwall, and Penzance. Another travels to Iona and north through Scotland, intersecting with the Atlantic Ocean at Findhorn on the north coast of Scotland. The third heads north-north-west, intersecting with the middle of Ireland and the sacred sites of Knowth Dowth and Newgrange before exiting by the Carrowmore hills in Sligo and the lake isle of Innisfree. This is conclusive evidence to me of the power and influence of the chakras outside the body that interact with the multiverse galaxies and source of all that is.

The stellar gateway (or transcendental) chakra

Some believe this to be the centre of the divine essence, seeing as the Light Portal that connects the soul to the divine source; as if it is the doorway into other worlds, the Stellar Gateway chakra above the divine star where it links the patient to the sun and solar system. At the centre of this chakra is a black wormhole. According to string theory, this gives us access to the multiverse, as well as another eleven dimensions of possible existence. We have not yet evolved a capacity for interplanetary and intergalactic travel. There may be evidence from Sumerian cuneiform writing that advanced human civilisation existed 3,600 years ago. Dr Michael Heiser refutes the assumptions concerning the Nephilim and other cultures made by Prof Zecharia Sitchin, in his book *The Twelfth Planet*. As Dr Heiser has a PhD in Hebrew Bible and ancient Semitic languages he seems eminently qualified to dispel these myths.

Links to ancient civilisations on earth

On 19 October 2013, Melissa Hogenboom, BBC News' science reporter, reviewed an article by Prof David Lordkipanidze. This describes a complete skull from Dmanisi, Georgia and the evolutionary biology of early Homo. Dmanisi is the archaeological site in the Kvemo Karti region of Georgia, 93 km southwest of the nation's capital, Tbilisi, in the river valley of Mashavera. The article concludes that the site has yielded remains consistent with the presence of the single human species Homo outside Africa around 1.8 million years ago. It describes the world's first completely preserved adult hominid skull from the early Pleistocene. This could range from 0.8 to 2.6 million years ago. The brain volume was 546cc, compared to almost 1600cc today. The article concludes that this implies the existence of a single evolving lineage of early Homo with phylogenetic continuity across continents.

Also, the earliest example of dyed flax was found in a cave in Georgia, dating back 34,000 years. This again provides evidence of human habitation dating to modern times.

Chris Stringer (2011), from the Natural History Museum in London stated that the large jawbone makes an excellent case for the single evolving-lineage theory, but he was doubtful of a direct link to Homo erectus.

The Tbilisi team maintain:

- Their hominids represent an early expansion of human ancestors outside Africa;
- They are the most complete collection of Homo species from 1.8 million years ago to 3000,000 BC;
- They had human-like spines and limbs suited for long-distance upright travel;
- The male was larger than the female; and
- They had brains thirty times the size of Homo sapiens. Their primitive limbs resembled Australopithecus. Known as "the southern ape," they existed two to four million years ago.

The Happisburgh prints (Kennedy, 2014) in Norfolk are approximately 850,000 years old and the oldest outside Africa. Findings show them to be from a group of children and adults. At the time of imprinting it was possible to walk from Africa to Britain. These prints are the first direct evidence of people at the most northerly edge of habitation in Europe. Professor Stringer (a world authority on early humans) believes the Norfolk hominids are relatives of Homo antecessor or pioneer man. They became extinct in Europe after Homo Heidelbergensis took over, followed by Neanderthals around 400,000 years ago. The Neanderthals interbred with modern humans. Many of our inherited genetic diseases may have emerged from this interrelationship.

This is important in the context of SF-EMDR psychotherapy. If confirmed, this places our ancestors on earth alongside the great apes for more than one million years. The process of brain evolution was more gradual than previously thought, lending further support to the Darwinian theory of natural selection.

The impact of SF-EMDR psychotherapy will be most substantial on the hardwired parts of the human brain. This includes the brainstem, cerebellum, and the limbic system, all parts of the early human's brain.

As the PFC was the latest part of our brain to evolve, it is the most susceptible to traumatic stress. It also explains why unmodified CBT is unlikely to reach the primitive reptilian parts of our central nervous system. This has significant implications for the initiative "Improving access to psychological therapies," or IAPT, in the NHS. This tends to involve practitioners with limited training in CBT. It does not include training in trauma-focused therapy such as SF-EMDR psychotherapy.

The Stellar Gateway chakra exists far from the physical body. By activating this chakra, we gain energy and knowledge, and any excess energy cascades down into all the other chakras before revitalising the earth, the patients, and important others in their lives.

The ascending chakras are equal to earth, water, fire, air, ether, ajna, and the third eye. This is a different perspective from that of Western medicine but can be accommodated within the framework of SF-EMDR psychotherapy. The petals and colours represent the chakras, matching the spectrum of colours in a rainbow. The repeated figure of eight contains the first five chakras on their ascent to the brow and crown. This analogy is used to reflect the flow of information during SF-EMDR psychotherapy reprocessing. This allows for the possibility of activating the high heart chakra. This is represented by the colour turquoise and the thymus gland. This chakra is most active in children and as the thymus becomes vestigial in adulthood is said to merge with the heart chakra.

The theosophical society

Charles Webster Leadbeater (1847–1934) was a clairvoyant. He wrote over thirty books on the spiritual life and man's psychic nature. In 1884 he went to India with Madame Blavatsky. He also joined her in Alexandria. In 1895 he began to examine the atomic structure of over sixty elements. He took the five vows of a Buddhist, although a loyal Christian. He moved to Australia where he died in 1934.

His work is essential, as he brought the eastern ideas of the chakras as vortices of energy to a western audience for the first time, in 1927, in his book *The Chakras*. He illustrated what he termed, "The streams of vitality," which originate from the sun. And the "serpent-fire," which has its roots deep in the earth.

He refers to the kundalini energy with the activation of the lateral Ida and Pingala channels. He expressed how the central Sushumna rises in tandem. This is compared to the linga outside Hindu Temples and the peripheral nervous system.

The individual schools of yoga activate the chakras differently. Charles Leadbeater has stressed the activation of the second or splenic centre. Stimulation of the third, fourth, and fifth chakras can enable the patient to awaken some of their astral planes.

The third-eye chakra when awakened brings forth the image of the serpent projecting from the centre of the forehead. You see this on the headdress of the Egyptian Pharaohs, as their country's chief priests were thought to have occult powers. When the crown chakra is active, the patient can leave their body in full consciousness. Few except the most adept yogis have reported this level of conscious awareness. The arousing of the kundalini coincides with activation of the HPA axis. It is recognisable in mythology by the caduceus symbol. Of interest, the rod of Asclepius has only one serpent coiled around the staff.

Leadbetter could divine the number of petals and colour of each chakra. These had different locations, shown in Figure 2.8, especially the sacral chakra, which he termed the splenic chakra. Of note, the chakras break down into these

THE CHAKRAS

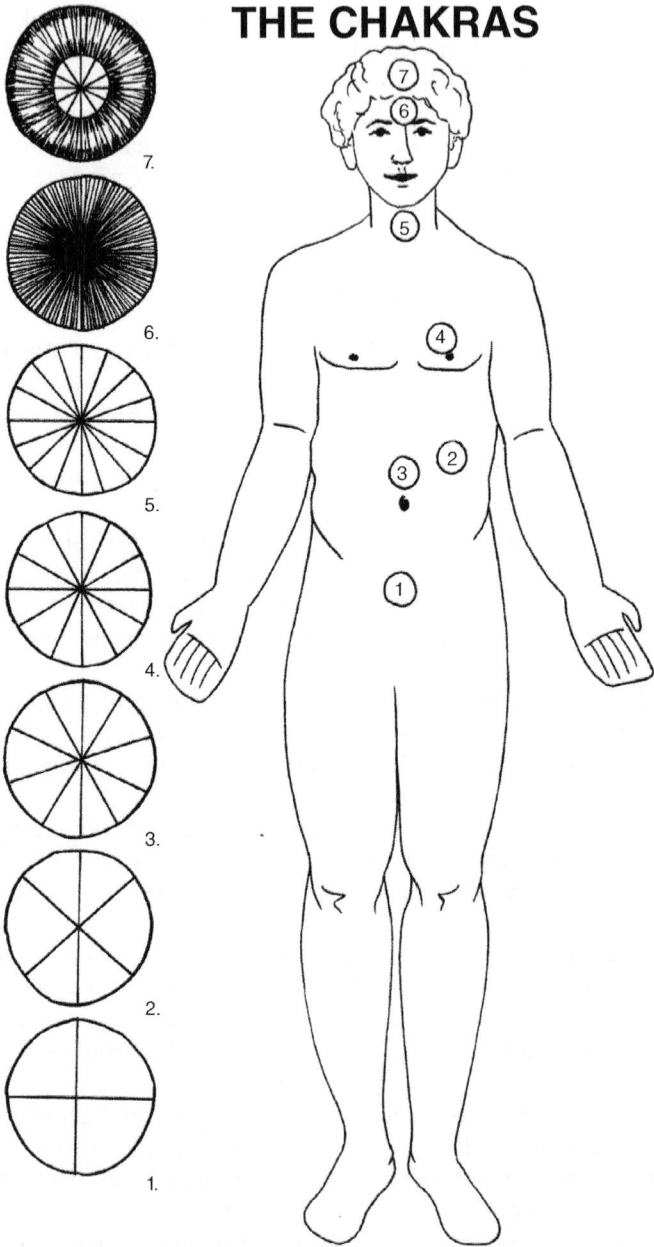

Figure 2.8 The chakras according to Charles Leadbetter. Note the different location for the sacral plexus or chakra.

divisions: four, six, eight, twelve, sixteen, one hundred, and one thousand. The third eye and forehead chakra appear to merge as a combined sixth chakra.

Edwin Babbitt wrote a treatise on principles of light and colour. In it he drew a vision of the atom: seen below (Figure 2.9). He founded a school of chromopathy,

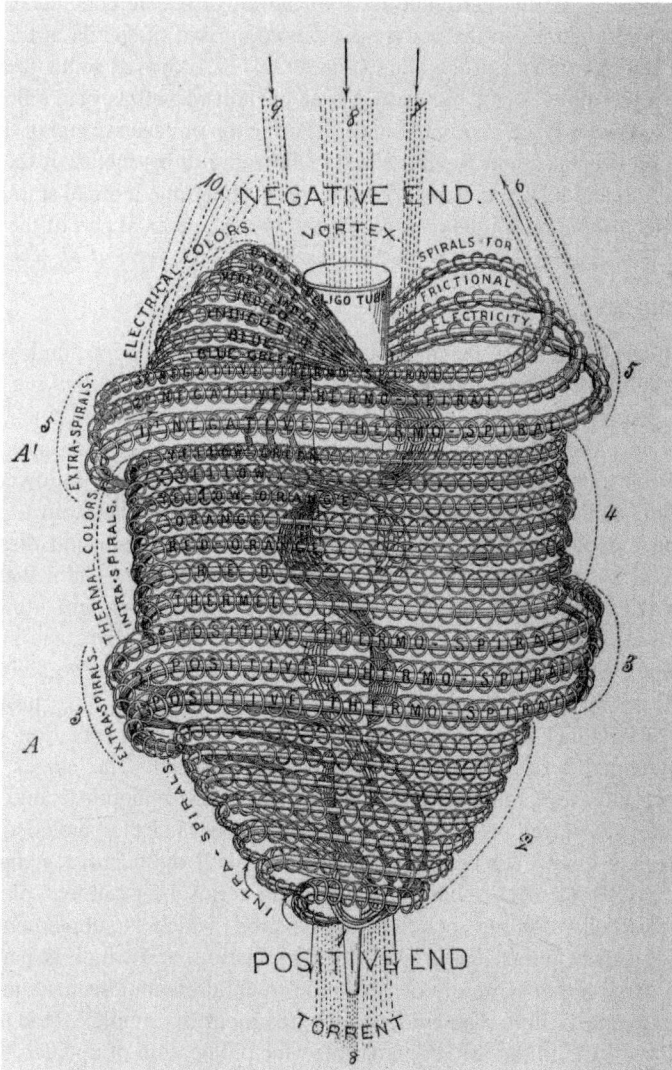

Figure 2.9 Spiral image of the atom by Edwin Babbitt. Principles of light and colour
Source: 1878 edition Literary Licensing, LLC p102. Creative commons license.

known as the new science of healing by light and colour. His lamp-shade is a translucent paper covering of a graded blue tint, producing a soft blue light, to "sooth and strength the eye and nerves." He also produced a chromo lens which when filled with water concentrated and focused rays of light that had a penetrating healing power over areas of the body after exposure. We can incorporate features of this chromo lamp into the buzzers to provide bilateral stimulation in SF-EMDR psychotherapy.

He also discussed the harmonic laws of the universe. He concluded that like other tubular structures in the body, the atom comprised of spirals in the form of tubes. In Babbit's model of the atom (Figure 2.9) he proposed in his treatise that colours of light flow around the atom. Using his notation efflux ethers flow out of the model of the atom at locations 6 and 10. At the top or negative end of the model or vortex he proposed that the influx ethers flowed into his model of the atom at locations 7, 8, and 9. He maintained there were seven thermo luminol spirals, which become electroluminal spirals on reaching the vortex and axial part of the atom.

Conclusion

This chapter focuses on the nature of the chakra energies as understood by eastern traditions with a superimposition of western scientific thinking in terms of the endocrine organs they represent. There is also a proposed link to sacred geometry and intentional prayers. The chakras, in ascending order, are the Earth Star, root or spinal cord chakra, and sacral chakras. These are followed by the solar, heart, and throat chakras. I illustrate the reaction of the brain to fear and stress and I explain the concepts of altered levels of arousal and dissociation experienced by the patient. This model introduces the Rapids, Calm Waters, and Frozen in Fear concept into the literature. A new paradigm for treating dissociative identity disorder is explained. This article explains the six stages of the shutdown dissociation continuum that involves progressive activation of the sympathetic and parasympathetic system. To explain this process the analogy of an attack by a safari lion is used. The Shut-D dissociation scale has been developed based on the defence cascade model. The stages include: avoidance, attentive immobility, flight, fight, tonic immobility, and feigned death from vasovagal collapse. The Shut-D questionnaire is included for use by practitioners who are dealing with patients with dissociative symptoms of complex PTSD or DID. This is important in terms of treatment planning. I reintroduce readers to my model of dissociation, which is supplemented with the use of a three-dimensional model of dissociation, and which is particularly useful to explain this symptom constellation to children adolescents and patients on the autism spectrum. The evidence for treatment of complex PTSD is being assessed by NICE in the UK in preparation for publication of updated treatment guidelines on PTSD.

A case example shows how images of early brainstem and visual origins in fish can appear in the reprocessing of a patient. The remaining chakras are brow, crown, soul star, stellar gateway, and universal gateway. These are the energy centres that, when activated, allow the patient to access transcendent or elevated levels of consciousness. The use of the bindi symbol by many Eastern cultures is explained. A case example showing how SF-EMDR psychotherapy can lead to the release of kundalini energy following abdominal surgery is presented. The chakras according to Charles Leadbetter are illustrated. These show slight modification from the more traditional ones associated with the individual schools of yoga. A description is given of how the kundalini energy can be awakened. An early model of the structure of the atom as conceived by Edwin Babbitt is shown, as well as reference to his treatise *The Principles of Light and Colour* and the development of a school of chromopathy.

Chapter 3

Neurodevelopment of the head-brain, heart-brain, and gut-brain

Development of the embryo and clinical implications

The blastocyst forms soon after fertilisation and retains a memory of the circumstances of conception. There is debate about the moment that this group of cells show signs of life. There is some evidence that following two cell divisions, i.e. the eight-cell blastocyst stage, there is pluripotential for life. The question of when the soul enters the body remains open and is hotly debated between those who say there is no scientific evidence and others who have attempted to show that the body is lighter post mortem compared to ante mortem. The heart is often mentioned as the seat of the soul. It is of note that the first heartbeat occurs at eight weeks' gestation.

The ancient Egyptians believed that the soul had five parts, i.e. the:

1. Ren;
2. Ba;
3. Ka;
4. Sheut; and
5. Ib.

The heart was seen as the seat of emotion, thought, will, and intention and was the key to the afterlife. Archaeological remains confirm that in death all the body organs were removed except for the ancient Egyptian's heart. It was believed to be the key to a successful transition to the afterlife. If the heart was lighter than a feather, the person went to heaven. If it weighed more than Maat's feather, the monster Ammit consumed it. This may give rise to today's expression, "with a heavy heart."

Maat personified truth and justice. Her blue ostrich feather represented truth. In Egyptian mythology Maat bound the universe, world, state, and individual together.

The impact of violence during conception

When conception has been because of violence, such as rape, this has a profound impact on the mother's ability to accept the pregnancy. Often her feelings of loathing can be translated into dislike of self or be projected onto the developing embryo. When the infant becomes an adult this intrauterine stressful experience is remembered by any events that mimic from a sensory point of view the early months of pregnancy. Imagine a millimetre-sized embryo being transported down the fallopian tube before crash landing during implantation as a foetus against the uterine wall. This journey is normally eventful. With the added influence of cortisol from the mother's umbilical cord on foetal development, you can imagine a terrifying ordeal for the developing embryo. If we fast-forward to when that baby becomes an adult it is essential to explore their knowledge of their own conception, their attachment relationship with their parents, and how this history might impact on their current symptomatology. For example, they may be reluctant to travel in circumstances where they are unsafe and not in control. Classically, this involves flights over water with the unconscious fear of a crash landing. In addition, journeys in a coach may cause re-experiencing of that terrifying journey along the fallopian tube. In my experience, this gives completely new avenues to explore with patients and clients where the genesis of their phobias is from traumatic circumstances of conception.

Physiological evidence for the gut-brain and head-brain connection

According to Cryan and Dinan, there is a pathway of communication via the gut, heart, and brain axes that impinges on cortical functioning of brain regions such as the anterior cingulate cortex. These are affected by both chronic pain and chronic stress. Thus, disorders such as irritable bowel syndrome may be a brain-mediated disorder with associated deficits in cognitive functioning. The techniques I will describe in Chapter 13 outlining how to conduct SF-EMDR psychotherapy sessions could benefit this cohort of patients. More work is needed in this developing field of research.

Synaptic potential of foetal brain during pregnancy and some clinical implications for infant development

The central nervous system starts to differentiate at ten weeks' gestation. Sufficient organisation has occurred at twenty-four weeks to sustain independent life. However, most myelination and sensory development occurs in the final trimester, which is why nature has optimised forty weeks for human gestation. At birth the foetal brain is 50 per cent adult size. This rises to 90 per cent by age five, provided the infant experiences normal developmental environment.

The environment the expectant mother is exposed to can directly influence the stress levels of the baby. This is being extensively investigated by the "Predo" preeclampsia project in Finland. Stress hormones produced by the mother end up in the foetus via the placenta. This project is attempting to identify the times in pregnancy when the foetus is most vulnerable to stress according to Raikkonen-Talvitie. The pregnancy experiences of 5,000 mothers are being collated to predict and prevent preeclampsia and intrauterine growth retardation. Evidence points to how exposure to prenatal stress can lead to both temperamental difficulties in children and paradoxically increased resilience. From studies of the Dutch hunger experienced by mothers in the winter of 1944–1945 and the attack on the Twin Towers on 11 September 2001, it is known that these traumatic events may have lifelong consequences for childhood development. Low birth-weight may also give rise to diabetes, cardiovascular disease, ADHD, depression, and even schizophrenia.

The development and expression of the six core emotional states in patients and clients

For face processing, we must be able to match the labelled emotion to the facial expression. We start processing faces moments after birth, as illustrated by the breast crawl reflex. We become more sophisticated, recognising fear and disgust with age. However, our ability to sense sadness and anger disimprove in comparison. This appears to be related to both hormonal development and maturation of the prefrontal cortex. There is recognised to be a drop in performance in emotional recognition of ten around puberty.

- This angry person (Figure 3.1) is shaking their fist and metaphorically has steam coming out of her ears. The explicit message is "keep away." Anyone approaching this person is likely to place themself in danger. Knowing when to approach someone and assess their readiness for therapy is essential if a therapeutic rapport is to be established;
- In disgust the subject's revulsion is palpable. The downturned mouth coupled with frowning forehead conveys the subject's emotional state (from Latin *dys* and *gustatory*, to taste) This emotion links to potentially harmful foods or tastes. The reflex would be to spit out the food and act as a warning to others to be careful. This is a good example of gut, heart, and brain neurological connections;
- This person is pouting their lower lip and appears close to tears. The sense is of him welling up with the emotion of sadness. You might say he is burdened by a weight on his shoulders or has a heavy heart. He also appears to have regressed to how infants are when they feel upset. The key goal of this emotion is to induce compassion in the other person and a sense of empathy for their suffering. It is this quality of compassion and caring for others in distress that is our essential human characteristic; and
- The brilliant smile of radiant white teeth helps to illuminate this expression. Not only are they radiating the warmth and happiness of a contented internal state but also they are implicitly saying "approach me." This may also act as

Figure 3.1 The six core emotional states and corresponding facial expression.

a preamble to attachment by sending out a bonding signal to a prospective partner.

- This person shows a wide-eyed expression and the whites of her eyes, expressing fear. This is likely to move from the mobilised response to the point of frozen watchfulness associated with activation of the dorsal motor nucleus of the tenth cranial nerve or vagus nerve. This has been most clearly elucidated by Dr Stephen Porges. This person may be close to collapse via the vasovagal response and must be dealt with sensitively to avoid a dissociative response. The fear response can also be associated with a state of high arousal. The person's heart is racing but they are rooted to the spot.
- This person has experienced something unusual, which has led to a sharp intake of breath and an expression of surprise. This emotion is felt to be pivotal as a means towards resolving the emotions of disgust, anger, sadness, and fear. Thus, inducing curiosity or surprise during the therapeutic session is a key goal of SF-EMDR psychotherapy.

Brain regions that are important for emotion state include brainstem – amygdala and prefrontal cortex, feeling of emotion – insular and prefrontal cortex, and level of consciousness – frontal and parietal lobes. Other components of an emotion state, and the content of consciousness, are presumed to rely on more variable and distributed structures that would depend on the particular kind of emotion or conscious experience and, therefore, are not depicted here. The hypothalamus, amygdala, brainstem nuclei, including Periaqueductal gray and Parabrachial nuclei, orbitofrontal cortex, anterior and posterior cingulate cortex are important for the expression of emotion. Intralaminar thalamus and the ascending reticular formation are necessary for the maintenance of arousal and wakefulness – that is, the level (state) of consciousness. The insular cortex is an important structure for the experience of emotion. Bilateral, prefrontal, and parietal cortices are broadly important for the level of consciousness. Other important central nervous system components of emotion include the rostral ventrolateral medulla (important for control of autonomic function) and components of the spinal cord itself, all of which contribute to substantial processing that is related to interoceptive and homeostatic information and also parts of the nucleus accumbens and ventral pallidum that participate in reward and positive affect.

Development of head-brain, heart-brain, and gut-brain from birth onwards

Babies have 100 billion neurons in their brain at birth, but few are connected into networks to form the connectome. Input and subsequent experience determine how these neural networks and ultimately form into intelligences (Howard Gardner). There is an initial overcapacity, and additional synaptic pruning occurs.

There are 100 million neurones in the enteric plexus, which is greater than the number of neurons in the spinal cord. These neurons and receptors develop at the same time as those of the cerebral cortex. This is because the neural crest divides in the embryo at ten weeks' gestation to form both the head-brain and gut-brain.

Professor David Paterson from the University of Oxford has been studying how the brain and heart work together. Nerves from the brain directly affect the heart. The sympathetic nerves cause the heart to pump faster while the parasympathetic ones slow the heart. However, he has discovered that there are 10,000 specialised neurons in the heart itself. These are integrated into the cardiac muscle of the right atrium. These neurons are known as the "heart's little brain." In the same way as the cerebellum is the brain's little brain this could be termed the cardiac bellum. By electrically exciting these neurons, Professor Paterson has been able to show how much neural control is in the heart itself. His experiment was as follows: a rat's right atrium was suspended in a glass container containing nutrients and infused with oxygen. Although isolated from any other tissue it was observed to be beating independently. The heart rate was at 200 beats per minute but by electrically stimulating these neurones externally, messengers were released to slow the heart down to 100 beats per minute within a second. When the electrical activation was switched off the contractions of the right atrium returned to their previous rate of 200 beats per minute. This experiment shows that there is a detailed neural network in the heart, which is independent of the brain's descending sympathetic and parasympathetic control. Hence, we can conclude that the heart can function independent of the brain or central nervous system. This provides scientific evidence for the Egyptian belief that the heart deals with truth. This means that the heart is important both scientifically and philosophically. This can be illustrated by some common sayings that are related to the role assumed by our hearts in society down the ages, some of which are mentioned in the following section.

The relationship between the heart and the head and how it can be expressed in language

The heart and the head are part of the mind–body continuum and live in a synergistic partnership, with one dependent on, rather than subservient to, the other. Over the centuries poets and philosophers have referred to affairs of the heart in their literature. The following are some examples with translations where necessary.

A generous heart, kind speech, and a life of service and compassion are the things that renew humanity. *Buddha.*

A good head and a good heart are always a formidable combination. *Nelson Mandela.*

There are a number of expressions that we use today that include the heart:

- "To wear your heart on your sleeve" is to be open with your emotions and express feelings openly
- "The heart of the matter" relates to the crucial or essential points.
- "Heartfelt feelings" is to be truthful.
- "Straight from the heart" is to say something directly without duplicity or deceit.
- "To do with all your heart" is to put complete effort into something.
- "In your heart of hearts" refers to your innermost or soul feelings.
- "From the bottom of my heart" is with the greatest sincerity I can muster.
- "To have a change of heart" is to do things differently based on new feelings and a changed perspective on your life and values.
- "To pour one's heart out" is to be emotionally overwhelmed.
- "To set your heart on something" conveys a sense of passion, drive, and commitment.
- "Take heart" means to have courage (from the French "*cœur*").
- "To trust with all your heart" relates to our earliest attachments and feelings of security.
- "Heartthrob" is a sign of attraction as the heart speeds up or even "skips a beat," as in the recent song in the pop charts by Olly Murs.
- "My heart goes out to his family" is a sign of empathy towards a bereaved or otherwise distressed family. This could be interpreted as allowing your heart's magnetic field to resonate with that of those around you.

- "Eat your heart out" has various meanings but is generally used to draw attention to one's achievements in bettering someone else's.
- "Not for the faint hearted" means that you need strength or courage to complete this task.
- "The way to a man's heart is through his stomach" means that by satisfying man's hunger he will be able to feel love and affection. From a literal perspective this was exploited by the Russians in their battle against German forces in the Second World War. By prolonging the conflict into winter, the Russians knew that the German supply lines would be nullified. Without provisions the German soldiers would become demoralised and easier to defeat.
- "Cross one's heart and hope to die" – children usually say this when they wish very strongly for something to come true. There is a belief that this originated as a religious oath based on the signs of the cross in the early twentieth century (Poem, 2014).

The heart can vary position in these idiomatic sayings, so conveying different meanings:

- In the right place; activating the central chakra;
- In your boots; conveying a sense of depression; and
- In your mouth; meaning an extreme state of excitement.

The process of SF-EMDR psychotherapy pays attention to all the patient's idiomatic use of language to better assess which part of their body is registering sensations, emotions, feelings, and thoughts. To quote Blaise Pascal:

> The heart has its reasons, of which reason [(i.e. the head-brain or cerebral cortex] knows nothing; one knows it in a thousand things. I say that the heart loves universal being naturally and also itself naturally, insofar as it gives itself to them and it hardens itself against one or the other at its own choice. You have rejected the one and kept the other; it is by reason that you love yourself?

Thus Pascal postulated that the heart was capable of reflective thought. This has not been fully accepted by western scientific thinking. It is often said that better decisions are made when the head rules the heart. However, in eastern philosophical traditions such as Confucianism and Buddhism the True Path to follow is that of the heart and mind. Indeed, the heart is seen as the governing organ of the brain.

During therapeutic sessions of SF-EMDR psychotherapy the patient is often unable to speak, as the trauma leaves them in a state of speechless terror. They can be encouraged to imagine speaking from the heart, liver, gut, spleen, lungs, pancreas, or any other relevant organ. Often the tone and pitch will change and they are able to access a kinder more tolerant voice within. This relates to the Chinese philosophy where one organ governs another. The heart governs blood, controls the blood vessels, manifests in the complexion, houses the mind, opens into the tongue, and controls sweat. The liver stores blood, ensures the smooth flow of Qi, controls the sinews, manifests in the nails, opens into the eyes, and houses the ethereal Soul. The lungs govern Qi and respiration, control channels, and blood vessels. They both disperse Qi all over the body and as the uppermost organ in the body their Qi travels downward to the kidneys, bladder, and large intestine. The lungs regulate the passage of water, controls skin and hair, opens into the nose, and houses the corporeal soul.

The spleen is referred to as the central organ in the digestive process. It governs transformation and transportation. It controls blood, muscles, the four limbs, and rising Qi. It opens into the mouth and manifests in the lips and houses thought. The kidneys are said to store the essence, which comes from parents and is established at conception. The kidneys govern birth, growth reproduction, and development. They are the origin of skill and intelligence and are physiologically related to the brain. This is uncannily like the hypothalamic–pituitary–adrenal axis familiar to western medicine. The kidneys work with the lungs to control the flow of Qi. They open into the ears and manifest in hair. Kidney Qi controls the anal canal, urethra, and vas deferens. Finally, in Chinese medicine it is said that the kidneys are the residence of willpower or chi.

There are six yang organs: small and large intestine, gall bladder, stomach bladder, and triple burner. The latter opens, discharges, and lets out Qi. Overall the lungs and heart are the upper burner. The stomach and spleen are the middle burner and the kidneys, bladder, and intestines are the lower burner. Knowledge of these theories of Chinese medicine alongside that of western medicine allows the principles of SF-EMDR psychotherapy to be applied with the best of both worlds for the benefit of the patient.

The role of the heart in interpretation of facial expressions conveying emotion

The independent filmmaker David Malone sought to undergo an experiment where he received a brain MRI while rating the intensity of faces with a range of emotional expressions. Sarah Garfinkel and Prof Hugo Critchley (2013) from Brighton and Sussex Medical School designed this experiment. The key variable was whether the faces were shown in time with the heartbeat. When shown in synchrony with his heartbeat, David rated them as more intense. Particular faces, which displayed explicit fear, were registered in the amygdalae (the brain's threat-appraisal centres). The conclusion from this experiment is that the heart helps you to connect with your emotional state. The heart is believed to be the main conduit or channel for emotional information such as compassion and concern for others and the capacity to share feelings such as joy, which help us to bond socially as a human species. In this book, I explain how the heart's intrinsic nervous system interacts with both the enteric plexus or gut-brain and cerebral cortex or head-brain. These interpretations of our feelings and sensations are the emotional heart's gift to the rational mind. A few final quotes place things in perspective:

I am certain of nothing but the holiness of the heart's affections and the truth of the imagination. *John Keats*

A loving heart is the beginning of all knowledge. *Thomas Carlyle*

Lessons from mythology, language, and film in relation to neurodevelopment and symbolism of the brain, heart, and gut

In Egyptian mythology, one's life's deeds were measured by weighing the heart against a single feather. The more burdened or heavy the heart, the less likely one was to pass on to the next kingdom. Thus, the concept of "a true heart" anchors much of Egyptian philosophy. We know that the heart, which automatically tells the truth over the rational mind, mediates facial blushing due to embarrassment. It cannot help but give you away:

False face must hide what the false heart doth know. *William Shakespeare.*

The depiction by the ancient Egyptians of the Mythological Eye of Horus bears an uncanny resemblance to a sagittal section of cingulate cortex, thalamus, brainstem, and cerebellum. This suggests that the ancient Egyptians were skilled in human dissection and understood functional neuroanatomy.

From this we can surmise how knowledgeable the Egyptians were in their accurate representations of the brain. Might we assume that they too understood the impact of affective neuroscience on the developing brain?

Role played by body's autonomic nervous system in informing this historical legacy

Our organisational drives and behaviours are fuelled by instinct and emotion, with intellect providing direction. As described above, the amygdalae can easily hijack information-processing in the prefrontal cortex. This can lead to a maladaptive reaction to complex trauma or "toxic" stress. The sports psychiatrist Dr Steve Peters (2012) explores this concept further. He describes how all information comes first to the chimp brain, which is governed by its instinctual, drives, desires, and processes. It needs to be nurtured by the human brain's prefrontal cortex before it can exert control over it. This idea is explored further in the section on peak performance. The computer brain is a reference point for both the chimp and human brains. It processes information four times faster than the chimp brain and twenty times faster than the human prefrontal cortex. Dr Peters introduces readers to the metaphorical concepts of the computer brain functions as:

- Autopilots, which are constructive, helpful, automatic behaviours and beliefs;
- Gremlins, which are destructive, unhelpful, automatic, programmed behaviours and beliefs, which can be deleted;
- Goblins, which are destructive, unhelpful behaviours and beliefs, which are hard-wired or fixed;
- The Stone of Life, which contains the patient's life truths, values, and life force or vitality; and
- Mindset, which is the patient's perceptions, and influences their overall approach to life.

Improving heart, brain, and gut communication is an essential component of SF-EMDR psychotherapy. The aim is overcome the instinctive gut reactions to incidents so that patients can be reconnected to their higher-order functioning in the prefrontal cortex. This can be achieved by having their gut, heart, and brain activate their respective chakras to vibrate at an increased frequency.

In the Chinese pictogram for listening, the symbols represent:

- Watching with your eyes;
- Listening with your ears;
- Thinking with your mind;
- Feeling with your heart; and
- Focusing with undivided attention.

In this oriental philosophy, the brain is linked to the heart and our relation to authority within society. For thousands of years, the yellow heart symbol was seen as the centre of consciousness and represented both soul and spirit. Thus, the heart was the source of thoughts, feelings, and emotions. Integrating the functions of eyes, ears, heart, and the selfless act of undivided attention using the mind, captures the essence of listening. This implies activation of executive functions within the prefrontal cortex. It also symbolises the holistic approach to communication taken by the most populous nation on earth. I think this pictogram form of communication has some links to the hieroglyphics of the ancient Egyptians and the wavelengths associated with the twenty-two letters of the Hebrew alphabet. The symbolism was an intrinsic part of the communicated message. All these pictogram and glyph scripts appear to have originated from African languages composed of click sounds. Thus, this shows that as a species we started with 100 phonemes of sound. This reduced with migration. English has forty and Hawaiian only thirteen. This offers the possibility of changing the audible clicks in the bilateral headphone stimulation of SF-EMDR psychotherapy to mimic the language of our ancient ancestors.

In Chinese mythology, Ma Gu is the goddess of longevity, and is represented in a late nineteenth-century mural in the long corridor of the summer palace. She is depicted with cannabis plants and peaches.

Chinese alchemy comprises outer (waidan) and inner (Neidan). In traditional Chinese medicine, there are three treasures:

1) Jing, known as the essence of life. This is said to be in the adrenal glands;
2) Chi, which is the vital energy of life and is found in the lower dantian just below the umbilicus. This would correspond to the sacral chakra, the site of Kundalini awakening; and
3) Shen, which translates as spirit or mind. This spiritual energy is located at the upper dantian. This is between the eyebrows, and corresponds to the site of the pineal gland and third eye. It may give rise to our western expression of advanced intellect being "highbrow."

Neurological representation of bottom-up and top-down processing (Figure 3.2)

Bottom-up processing

Subcortical route eventually feeds back to the orbitofrontal cortex for eventual processing at end stage of SF-EMDR psychotherapy onset from 120ms.

Detailed perception and core processing through the amygdala produces an emotional reaction in the body and mind; onset from 170ms.

Interaction occurs between the visual and somatosensory areas.

Top-down processing

This involves recognition of faces and emotional processing (ventral vagus). Conscious awareness starts; onset from 500ms (cerebral hemispheres).

It is only now that CBT-based approaches are active.

Bottom-up processing

Subcortical route eventually feeds back to the orbitofrontal cortex for eventual processing at end stage of SF-EMDR psychotherapy onset from 120ms.

Detailed perception and core processing through the amygdala produces an emotional reaction in the body and mind; onset from 170ms.

Interaction occurs between the visual and somatosensory areas.

Top-down processing

This involves recognition of faces and emotional processing (ventral vagus). Conscious awareness starts; onset from 500ms (cerebral hemispheres). It is only now that CBT-based approaches are active.

The Wizard of Oz can be interpreted to support the basic tenets of psychotherapy in relation to how different body organs relate to intrinsic human characteristics.

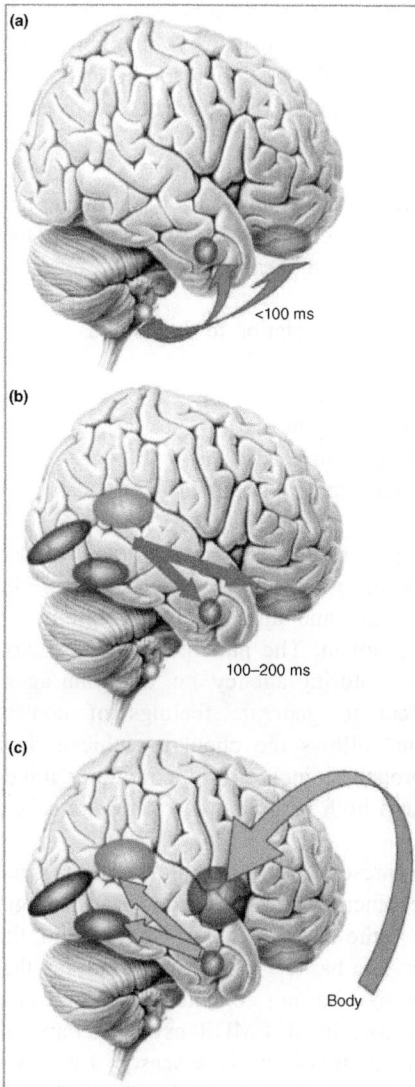

(a)

Responses to emotional visual stimuli can be registered in the amygdala and prefrontal cortex due to subcortical input from the peripheral nervous system. This BOTTOM-UP processing lasts from 40-100ms.

<100 ms

(b)

At 100-200ms the different areas of the sensory cortex provide input to the amygdala. The superior temporal cortex (green) encodes facial expression, while the fusiform gyrus (blue) encodes static information e.g. identity. MIDDLE-LEVEL processing.

100–200 ms

(c)

At around 500ms conscious processing occurs. The brain evaluates the meaning of the emotional stimulus. This involves the medial prefrontal cortex projecting to brainstem nuclei, hypothalamus and the insular cortex. This is an example of TOP-DOWN processing. Thus an emotional state involves a complex interaction of these different stages of reprocessing.

Body

Figure 3.2 This diagram illustrates the timeline for neuronal processing from unconscious processing neuroception to conscious awareness. It takes half a second or 500ms for the patient to register events consciously.

Source: reprinted with permission from Prof Ralph Adolphs.

Symbolism of the movie, *The Wizard of Oz*

The Wizard of Oz was a collective effort of multiple directors and was an adaptation of the 1990 book. It has been interpreted in ways that reflect the cornerstones of my approach to patients in SF-EMDR psychotherapy.

Movies are often inspired by dream states giving rise to archetypal images. Often, after SF-EMDR psychotherapy sessions, patients will report profound dreams, which I see as continued reprocessing after the session.

The Wicked Witch of the West represents that which seeks to dominate and control the patient's life, much like Adolf Hitler did in the 1930s and 1940s. Dorothy is on a spiritual journey towards self-actualisation, which is highest in Maslow's hierarchy of needs.

The different stages of the pyramid bear some relation to the chakras:

1.   Root and sacral equate to physiological needs;
2.   Solar and heart represent love and belonging needs;
3.   Throat represents confidence and self-esteem needs; and
4.   Third eye, forehead, and crown can represent self-actualisation needs.

The development of an individualised optimum healing environment for each patient will allow Maslow's hierarchy of needs to be met. This will be comfortable and supportive, free from pain and anxiety. There will be an atmosphere of acceptance, hope, and optimism. The patient is able to relax, be honest and feel free to be themself. Restoring agency, i.e. being an agent in one's own life, enables the patient to generate feelings of control necessary for recovery from trauma and allows the client to achieve their peak performance goals. Spiritual approaches, including encouraging mindfulness and meditation, can similarly help both patients and clients transcend their individual experiences.

In *The Wizard of Oz*, the dog, Toto, represents the inner intuitive instinctual animalistic part of us. SF-EMDR psychotherapy allows venting of these gut instinctive reactions related to incidents at the onset of therapy. In the film, the witch tries to capture Toto by putting him in a basket. He escapes, implying that our intuitive voice can sometimes be ignored but not contained. Due to Toto's actions, Dorothy undergoes a transformation. In SF-EMDR psychotherapy the purpose is to notice our intuitive gut feelings. It is from these sensory fragments that reintegration occurs and our imagination can be unleashed.

The Tin Man needs a heart, but his love is already present, waiting to be connected. There is a need to draw in the intellect represented by the Scarecrow's missing brain. This can occur when the Lion has received courage, *cœur*, or a heart. We find that he already has inner strength. The oiling of the Tin Man could represent a blood transplant. The blood metaphorically flows down to Dorothy's ruby-red slippers. By clicking her heels, she realises there is no place like home and she realises where her heart is. It was there all along.

The electromagnetic field around the heart helps to transit mechanical pressure-waves along the blood vessels. The nerve plexus around the gut, heart, and brain are nourished with oxygen and become fully activated and integrated. Thus, in Dorothy's journey, the Tin Man, Lion, Scarecrow, and Toto represent aspects of herself that she needs to become aware of internally. This can only happen as she follows the Yellow Brick Road, which, I believe, represents centring on the solar, or third, plexus. There are also parallels to the Chinese pictogram of the heart described above.

Knowledge of arterial and venous blood flow through capillaries can inform therapists as they help patients resolve their traumatic experiences during SF-EMDR psychotherapy. The therapist can help the patient to tune into areas of heat or tension associated with the RAPIDS phase of dissociation, or areas where they feel numb, associated with the FROZEN in FEAR phase of dissociation. The heart and lungs are central to the person's survival. The oil sought by the Tin Man might represent lubrication of his circulatory system so that he may perceive emotions. The heart of the Lion will also give him courage, while the Scarecrow, when he has a brain, will be able to rationally appraise the environment rather than instinctively reacting with fear. This symbolism shows that SF-EMDR psychotherapy, by emphasising the reactions of gut, heart, and brain, will optimise the potential of the patient.

Embryonic development

In the human embryo, the heart starts beating at around eight weeks' gestation. Initially a cardiogenic area with primitive blood vessels forms at the head of the embryo at eighteen days. Then two endocardial tubes form to distribute embryonic blood flow. These fuse into a primitive heart tube at twenty-one days. A day later the truncus arteriosus, bulbus cordis forms along with a primitive ventricle and atrium. By thirty-five days the heart folds into the characteristic four-chamber structure, which is fully functional at eight weeks' gestation. Knowledge of these developmental processes can inform history-taking, in relation to relevant details of the patient's pregnancy. At around twelve weeks, the embryonic neural crest divides into tissue destined to form both the foetal brain and alimentary canal. This explains why so many serotonin or 5HT receptors are in the gastrointestinal tract, which is then responsible for the gastric side effects of psychotropic medication. It could also explain why drugs that are slowly metabolised by the liver's metabolic enzymes are associated with further adverse effects.

Role of anterior, medial, and posterior cingulate cortex in processing emotions

The anterior cingulate cortex (ACC) is the frontal part of the cingulate cortex. It acts as a clutch between the frontal cortex and the limbic system. The sagittal ACC is involved in the integration of sensations from the body's viscera.

The anterior cingulate cortex or ACC deals with emotions, while the sagittal cingulate cortex or SCC is responsible for integration of visceral sensations. The

MCC deals with response selection, while the anterior and posterior parts deal with avoidance of fear and orientation of the skeletomotor musculature. The PCC deals with personal orientation. Its dorsal and ventral aspects code for visuospatial orientation and assessment of the self. Finally, the retrosplenial (RSC) cortex is involved in memory access and formation.

The corpus callosum

The corpus callosum (from the Latin for "tough body") is a collection of 300 to 800 million nerve fibres connecting similar areas in each cerebral hemisphere. This leaves 98 per cent of cortical neurons unconnected. Most of the remaining two cortical neurons are inhibitory via the GABA receptors, with the minority using the excitatory transmitter, glutamate. The ratio of the corpus callosum to the volume of the hemispheres has reduced over time. The main function of the corpus callosum is to inhibit the other hemisphere.

The corpus callosum fibres continue to develop at least up to the age of thirty and perhaps throughout life. In a study of subjects with high-functioning autism, they had smaller parts of the relevant corpus callosum compared to controls. This suggests a deficit in their integration of information at both neural and cognitive levels. This might also relate to aberrant default network connectivity. It could also explain why they have difficulties with information processing.

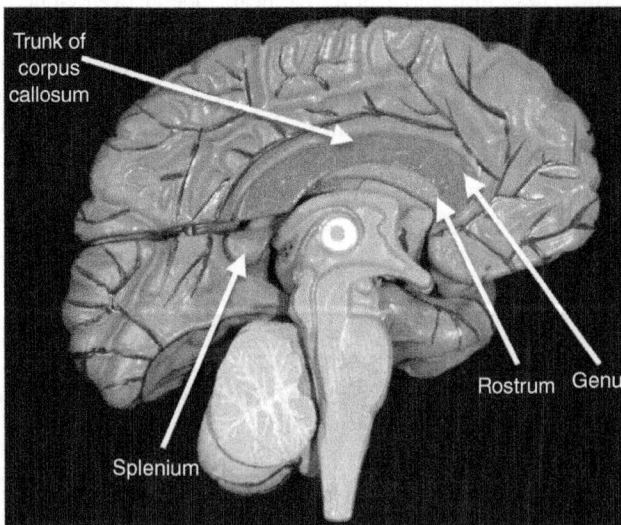

Figure 3.3 Cross-section of the corpus callosum showing different sections.
Source: Shutterstock.

This shows the small volume of fibres involved in interhemispheric communication. The corpus callosum contains 200–250 million white-matter contralateral axonal projections. It only exists in placental mammals or eutherians. Myelination of callosal axons occurs rostrocaudally, that is, from back to frontal regions. It doubles in size from birth to age two, just like the cerebellum. It continues myelination throughout life. Axonal connections undergo pruning or synaptic refinement while the CC increases in area. These developmental processes may further functional specialisation of the cerebral hemispheres. Several studies show that the CC connecting the left cerebral and right cerebral cortex is larger in musicians. This is because the CC is activated by a motor task using both hands. The bilateral auditory and tactile stimulation of SF-EMDR psychotherapy may replicate this stimulus. The band of fibres within the CC act to separate functions of the left and right hemispheres. The goal of SF-EMDR psychotherapy is to help reunite these hemispheres so that they function as a coherent whole sphere.

The CC is divided up into the rostrum (named after its resemblance to a bird's beak), genu, or anterior part (or knee), trunk, and splenium (posterior part). It is the largest fibre-tract pathway in the brain. These tracts are essential to the transfer of interhemispheric information. The pathway supports memory, learning, and sensory functions of the head-brain (Figure 2.2).

SF-EMDR Psychotherapy and peak performance are underpinned by Dr Iain McGilchrist's thesis, articulated in his book, *The Master and His Emissary*. This is essential to understanding higher cortical functioning and to achieving stages four and five of SF-EMDR psychotherapy and peak performance.

Do humans have a sixth sense?

In 1992 Kirschvink et al. from the California Institute of Technology in Pasadena discussed biomineralisation of magnetite in the human brain. Paramagnets act like magnets in the presence of a magnetic field applied externally and thus have a small positive susceptibility to magnetic fields, e.g. magnesium, molybdenum, lithium, and tantalum. Diamagnets act like magnets in opposition to an externally applied magnetic field and therefore have a weak susceptibility to magnetic fields. This includes most periodic-table elements such as copper, silver, and gold. The common elemental property is that they repulse magnets.

However, ferromagnets have a large positive susceptibility to an external magnetic field. They retain their magnetic properties after the magnetic field has been removed, e.g. iron, nickel, and cobalt. Ferromagnetism is one million times stronger than either diamagnetism or paramagnetism. The human brain and meninges were found to contain ferromagnetic material. This allows for the intriguing possibility that human magnetoreception can interact with both T lymphocytes and CNS neurons.

In July 2016, Joe Kirschvink progressed from dissecting human brain tissue to in vivo human experiments. He believes that he has demonstrated, in a sample of twenty-four human volunteers, unconscious magneto reception. In other words, this could be a sixth sense. It is believed that it may be the primal sense evolved from members of the animal kingdom. This magneto reception acts like a GPS system for all migratory animals such as birds and fish. It is also found in lobsters, worms, snails, frogs, newts, cattle, deer, rats, mice, and dogs. They all orientate according to the weak magnetic field surrounding earth.

Two theories have been proposed for the neurobiology of magnetoreception:

1) Electromagnetic field triggers quantum reactions in cryptochromes, which are found in the retina;
2) Miniature compass needles sit within receptor cells, either near the trigeminal nerve or in the inner ear. These needles are presumed to be made up of magnetite, which somehow interacts with neural pathways.

The magnetic field generated by an MRI is one thousand times stronger than the Earth's magnetic field, which ranges from 25T (microtesla) at the Equator to 60T at the poles. In the experiment, it was found that while sitting in a Faraday cage and being exposed to a magnetic field rotating anticlockwise, volunteers suppressed their alpha-wave production. This implies brain processing and that humans have functioning magneto receptors. The heart generates a powerful magnetic field and sends out waves of information to all cells including all foetal cells affecting its development from the moment of conception. I believe that listening and thinking from the heart is possible and can be facilitated by SF-EMDR psychotherapy incorporating this latest research on magneto reception.

Summary

This chapter examines the interrelationship between the gut-brain, heart-brain, and head-brain by examining research on the brains' neurodevelopment. The clinical implications of embryonic development are discussed. A new link has been proposed between chronic pain and stress and their negative impact on cognitive functioning. The synaptic potential of the baby's brain in pregnancy is illustrated along with some clinical implications for infant development. The patient's six core emotional states are described from a neurological perspective along with their corresponding facial expressions. The inter-relationship of heart and head is described in terms of language and recent scientific experiments. This can be used therapeutically to encourage the patient to listen to the internal voice of their bodily organs. The principles of the yin and yang organs of traditional Chinese medicine are described. This can be used to increase the effectiveness of SF-EMDR psychotherapy. The role of the heart in the interpretation of facial expressions conveying emotion is explained by the experimental observations of Professors Hugo Critchley and Sarah Garfinkel from Brighton and Sussex Medical School. Lessons can be learnt from the mythology of the ancient Egyptians, the Chinese language, and *The Wizard of Oz* film from 1939. The autonomic nervous system of the body underpins this legacy and the concept of top-down and bottom-up processing is explained. The crucial roles of the cingulate cortex in integration, orientation, and memory formation and the corpus callosum in interhemispheric transfer of information are illustrated. Finally, reference is made to Dr Iain McGilchrist's book, *The Master and his Emissary*. Recent discoveries in magneto reception are presented. This can be conceived of as a sixth sense and has implications for heart processing during SF-EMDR psychotherapy.

Chapter 4

Vibrational frequencies related to accelerated information processing in patients

Development of vision from initial sensory input to the superior colliculus to movement of eyes scanning the natural environment

Ephrin ligands are a family of proteins that bind onto the Ephrin receptors. They are involved in axon guidance, visual mapping from the retina to the superior Colliculus. This is analogous to a computer keyboard and mapping in terms of the American Standard Code for Information Interchange or ASCII on screen characters. These Ephrin molecules ensure sets of neurons project and connect to other appropriate sets of neurons.

In mammals, seeing is mediated by projections to the thalamus and onto the cortex. The retina senses and transmits light to retinal ganglion cells (RGCs). There are more than twenty types of RGCs projecting from the retina to parts of the brain. The expression of these ephrin ligands on the axons of the RGCs is linked to development of the retinotectal projection.

The most important area for eye movements is the superior colliculus. It mediates reflexive eye movements, head turns, and shifts in focus of attention. When RGCs mutate and fail to make the appropriate connections, the patients may go on to develop autism, schizophrenia, Tourette's syndrome, and other neurodevelopmental disorders.

In the peripheral stimulation with zappers that is a central component of SF-EMDR psychotherapy, the sensory stimulation reaches the superior colliculi on either side of the brainstem. This, in turn, sets up the cascade of protein binding that leads to visual mapping and scanning of the environment by the eyes. I first noticed this in 2007 when I was treating a teenager who was bedwetting at age seventeen. He was very motivated to change this behaviour, as he had signed up for the army cadets and was going on field trips. I used resource installation with visual imagery and drew a diagram showing neural control of the bladder. I got him to imagine responding to the bladder signalling him to wake up in the night to void urine. He visualised the image with his eyes closed while holding on to both zappers held against the contractile muscles of the bladder. I observed his eyes moving in saccades in time with the rhythmic pulses of the zappers. This was analogous to rapid eye movement and he was in a relaxed but fully conscious state. Since then, I never ask the patient to follow either a light bar or my fingers. I believe this is unnecessary to reprocessing trauma and might interfere with the natural pontine geniculate occipital waves, which are generated by stimulation of the brainstem, and activate the mechanisms associated with REM sleep.

Key reason for effectiveness of SF-EMDR psychotherapy and peak performance

The heart has an intrinsic beat of sixty to eighty beats per minute. Its magnetic field is forty to sixty times stronger than that of the brain. SF-EMDR psychotherapy taps into the internal commonality of sensory experience within each patient and client. The bilateral stimulation is optimised in intensity and amplitude. The resonance is experienced bilaterally at the level of the skull mastoid processes. This enables the cerebellae to be activated bilaterally. Over a ninety-minute therapeutic session, the patient experiences relaxation at the level of the cerebral cortex. The key to the success of SF-EMDR psychotherapy is placing the auditory signal bilaterally over the area of maximal bone density. The evolutionary process of natural selection has strengthened this area of the skull to afford maximal protection to the cerebellum (little brain) and brainstem. Dr Seth Pollak from the University of Illinois is one research scientist to have discovered the multiple functions of the cerebellum in terms of processing sensations, emotions, and feelings apart from solely movement impulses. The cerebellum has more neurons than the rest of the cerebral cortex put together. There are forty-five billion axons sent out from each cerebellum to the prefrontal cortex on the contralateral side. Thus, the combination of auditory and aural bilateral resonating frequencies helps to quell brainstem instinctive reflexes. Also, the intuitive reflective capacities of the prefrontal cortices are enhanced. Patients frequently report to me that the cerebellar resonance often fades into the background as the session progresses. The regular background rhythm appears to maintain their attention, cognition, and memory while allowing them to reprocess their adverse life experience and the accompanying unwelcome body sensations. Thus, the mechanical input to the cerebellum is to help the patient pay attention to the bodily information that is being reprocessed during the session.

Functional anatomy of the cerebellum

The cerebellum has three divisions: spinocerebellum, cerebrocerebellum, and vestibulocerebellum, in relation to the brainstem. The spinocerebellum regulates muscle tone and contributes to voluntary movement. The cerebrocerebellum plans and modulates voluntary movement and is involved in storage of procedural memories. Finally, the vestibulocerebellum maintains balance and is involved in the control of eye movements. Together, the cerebellum plays a crucial role in the processing of thoughts, feelings, and emotions. Bilateral activation of the cerebellum is an essential prerequisite for effective SF-EMDR psychotherapy.

Pollak and his colleagues have shown that there is a loss of cerebellar volume in children following institutionalisation. I believe the effects of this trauma can be effectively treated with early intervention using SF-EMDR psychotherapy. This would need to be tested with longitudinal studies.

These CT scans (Figure 4.1) contrast the volume of a normal three-year-old's brain with that of a child from an Eastern European orphanage who was exposed to extreme neglect (right-hand side of the CT scan). The types of neglect included being allowed to cry and being left to feed from a bottle propped up with a towel. The brain shown has failed to grow from birth. The anterior foramen ovale has closed and this skull will now prevent future outward brain growth, worsening the outlook for this child in the future.

The gyri and sulci are now growing inwards and this will further compromise brain function and specialisation. This child is likely to grow into adulthood with severe disorganised attachments, to have an inability to sustain meaningful relationships, and become a heavy user of adult mental health services. Children like this often become revolving-door patients, resistant to effective treatment. This makes the case for investment in parental and infant mental health services, which are currently not delivered by a substantial majority of the UK's current National Health Service trusts.

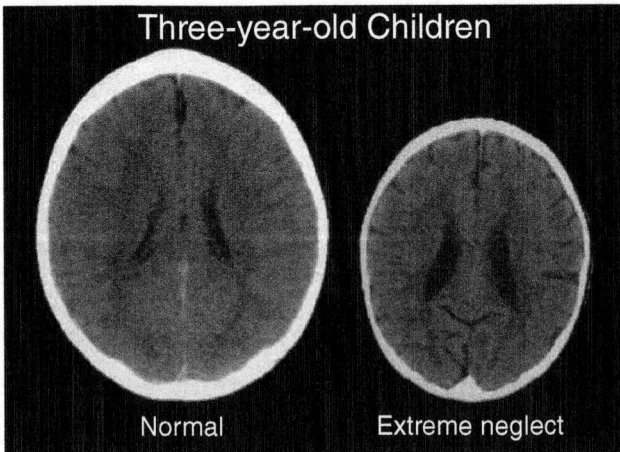

Figure 4.1 CT scans of a normal three-year-old and one exposed to extreme neglect.
Source: reprinted with permission from the Child Trauma Academy.

The image of the brain of the child exposed to a deprived environment contrasts to the healthy neural network of the normal three-year-old exposed to an enriched environment. Such deprived neurons experiencing fear are unable to reach out and synapse with their neighbours. This causes major physical and emotional ill health in future adult life.

According to Dr Bruce Lipton, cells exposed to fear are fed this information via their cell membrane. Its receptors are like human senses, but in microscopic form. Essentially, they are sentient beings and their growth mechanisms shut down when exposed to a fearful atmosphere. Dr Rupert Sheldrake read of the work by Alex Gervage on the growth of mushrooms in 1920. He then proposed morphogenetic fields as a mechanism to explain how the environment could control the cell's genetic code or DNA. Thus, the normal child who has been exposed to a loving environment stimulates the neurons to grow and synapse, enhancing their ultimate potential. Early child abuse has been shown to damage normal development of the corpus callosum, and the development of the brain. Thus, neglect, abuse, and trauma can be "toxic to the developing brain."

Interaction of the autonomic nervous system with the social engagement system and historical perspectives on the ANS

In 1872, Darwin recognised the dynamic rural relationship between the heart and the brain:

> ... When the heart is affected, it reacts on the brain... and the brain reacts through the vagus nerve on the heart so there will be mutual action and reaction between these two most important bodily organs.

(Darwin, 1872)

In 1921, John Newport Langley wrote a book titled *The Autonomic Nervous System*. In it, he described a purely motor system, not linked to the brain. Then, in 1949, Walter Hess won the Nobel Prize for medicine/physiology. He described how the autonomic nervous system was a paired antagonism system of the internal visceral organs, involving sympathetic and parasympathetic innervations. This idea is based on the evolution of our nervous system over time.

Social behaviour was noted to be a uniquely mammalian feature and was linked to the distribution of nerves to the heart and muscles of facial expression. The heart also became recognised as an endocrine organ, producing both oxytocin and vasopressin. Reptiles, on the other hand, produce vasotocin (a combination of the previous two hormones). We have, therefore, evolved a complex integrated nervous system. This has a hierarchical response to challenges from the environment, involving four stages.

1. Changes have occurred through evolution, which have involved endothelial heart regulation shifting from older unmyelinated nerve circuits to newer myelinated ones;
2. The quest for safety via regulation of metabolic output of the heart;
3. The social engagement system for safety became integrated over time; and
4. A process of neuroception in the cerebral cortex that exhibited downward inhibitory control of the vagus nerve.

Introduction to the polyvagal theory developed by Dr Stephen Porges

This theory evolved during the 1990s, when Dr Stephen Porges was in discussion with neonatologists involved in caring for very premature infants. They were very susceptible to infection and often succumbed. Porges set out over the next few years to understand the multiple functions of the infant's vagal nerve. Porges proposed the vagal paradox in 1992. This emphasised that respiratory sinus arrhythmia (RSA) represents the outflow from the vagus to the heart, otherwise known as cardiac vagal tone (CVT). Vagal mechanisms were found to mediate both the protective RSA and the potentially harmful bradycardia associated with the activation of the dorsal motor nucleus of the vagal nerve. The paradox existed only if a single central vagal source was assumed to be operating.

The concept of the social engagement system (SES) is part of Porges' polyvagal theory and involves myelinated vagal nerves, which inhibit sympathetic influences on the heart and dampen the hypothalamic–pituitary–adrenal (HPA) axis. This branch of the vagus nerve is involved in regulating heart rate and breathing and is involved in self-soothing and calming behaviours. Only mammals have a myelinated vagus nerve. It originates in the nucleus ambiguus with preganglionic nicotinic and postganglionic muscarinic receptors. Under challenge, these are switched off by the sympathetic nervous system.

The polyvagal theory developed by Porges is based on the long, wandering pathway and innervation of the tenth cranial, or vagus, nerve. The old, unmyelinated vagus nerve is designed to preserve metabolic resources. Although initially protective, it can also kill you by causing panic and immobilisation. When Porges was working in a neonatal intensive care unit, he found that, in newborns, vagal tone was protective when associated with heart rate rhythmicity. A paediatrician wrote to him, stating that too much of a good thing can be bad. This led Porges to pursue his vagal paradox theory. He discovered that the phylogeny of the autonomic nervous system (ANS) was not well described. He proposed that, in the embryo, the vagus had two primary divisions:

1. The dorsal motor nucleus of the vagus nerve, which has its origin in the nucleus tractus solitarius; and
2. The ventral motor nucleus of the vagus nerve, which has its origin in the nucleus ambiguus in the brain stem.

The ventral motor nucleus of the vagus nerve controls the striated muscles of the face and head, the larynx, the pharynx, and the common nuclei of the facial and trigeminal cranial nerves. Thus, the innervation of the heart goes with that of the head, as they are wired together from early embryonic development. This provides further scientific evidence for the theoretical underpinning of SF-EMDR psychotherapy.

How does the body respond to environmental challenge?

The body's hierarchical response to an environmental challenge is initially regulated by the ventral nucleus of the vagus nerve in its control of the face and heart. Preterm babies are vulnerable to this challenge, as their facial muscles do not fully work at birth. They exist in an unsafe state. The main mode of change is to involve neuro-regulation of the periphery by the brain. SF-EMDR psychotherapy starts with stimulation of the peripheral nervous system at the level of the gut-brain and heart-brain, before reprocessing at a head-brain level. This helps to rewire faulty neuronal networks associated with traumatic events at conception during pregnancy, infancy, and throughout the lifespan.

Relationship between the Jacksonian theory of dissolution of the ANS and Dr Porges polyvagal theory

When humans are in a safe environment, visceral homeostasis promotes growth and restoration. The myelinated vagus acts on the cardiac heart rate, slowing the heart and inhibiting the fight-or-flight mechanism of the sympathetic nervous system (SNS). It also reduces cortisol secretion from the hypothalamic-pituitary-adrenal axis and decreases immune mediated inflammation by decreasing circulating cytokines. Throughout the process of evolution and natural selection, the brain stem nuclei of the nucleus ambiguus merged with those the face and head. An integrated social engagement system (SES) then emerged. To ensure survival in dangerous or life-threatening situations, further evolution of the nervous system was necessary. This involved progressive recruitment of the SNS and freeze or feigning-death behaviour associated with activation of the dorsal motor nucleus of the vagus nerve (DMX). Normally the vagus nerve acts as a brake on the heart rate. The resting heart rate is 70–85 beats per minute. If this vagal brake is released, e.g. by being cut, the heart rate goes up to 100–110 beats per minute. This occurs every time we suddenly stand up and scan the environment.

Our heart rate is therefore regulated by these distinct phylogenetic systems. For social engagement to occur, we must first assess risk in the environment and inhibit limbic control of our fight, flight, or freeze responses (Table 4.1).

The nervous system is continuously evaluating risk via an unconscious process (Table 4.1), which Dr Stephen Porges has called neuroception. Safe is illustrated as the first reaction, dangerous is the second reaction, and life-threatening is the third reaction. This helps us to distinguish safe, dangerous, or life-threatening situations

Table 4.1 Illustration of the three stages of reaction predicted by the polyvagal theory of Dr Stephen Porges.

Dissolution following trauma	Evolved in brainstem (Time in years)	Behavioural functions	Autonomic nervous system	Environmental stimulus
1st reaction	10,000	Social communication, self soothing, calming, inhibition of arousal (social engagement system)	Ventral vagal complex	Safe
2nd reaction	1 million	Mobilisation, (fight, flight, fright, active avoidance)	Sympathetic nervous system	Dangerous
3rd reaction	100 million	Immobilisation (freeze, fall, feigning death, passive avoidance)	Dorsal vagal complex	Life-threatening

from environmental cues. The key brain areas thought to be involved in this process are the temporal cortex, amygdala, and periaqueductal grey. Together with activation of the SES we can interpret voices, facial expression, and hand movements or gestures.

The above diagram (Figure 4.2) shows how Cranial Nerves V, VIII, IX, X, and XI provide input to bronchi, heart, turning the head, pharynx, larynx, facial muscles, and muscles of the middle ear and mastication. There is an exchange of information between brainstem, cortex, and environment.

The dorsal vagal cortex (DVC) includes sensory nucllei in the nucleus of the solitary tract (NTS), the area postrema, and motor nuclei in the dorsal motor nucleus on the tenth cranial or vagus nerve (DMX). As shown in Figure 4.3, when the environment is perceived as safe by the patient or client, they release oxytocin from the hypothalamus. From here oxytocin goes to the sensorimotor DVC and systemically to the viscera as shown by the dashed arrows.

Figure 4.4 illustrates the activation of the amygdala and dorsal motor nucleus of the vagus nerve (DMX) when the patients' cerebral cortex is exposed to an unsafe environment. When the patient perceives danger, they begin active mobilisation and arginine vasopressin (AVP) is released from the hypothalamus to both the NTS and the area postrema of the dorsal vagal complex (DVC). This changes the set point of several vagal reflexes, such as the baroreceptor reflex. This reflex inhibits the sympathetic system and activates the parasympathetic nervous system. This drops peripheral resistance to blood flow and decreases heart rate and contractility. The combined effect is a reduction in blood pressure. This activates the patient's SNS for fight or flight.

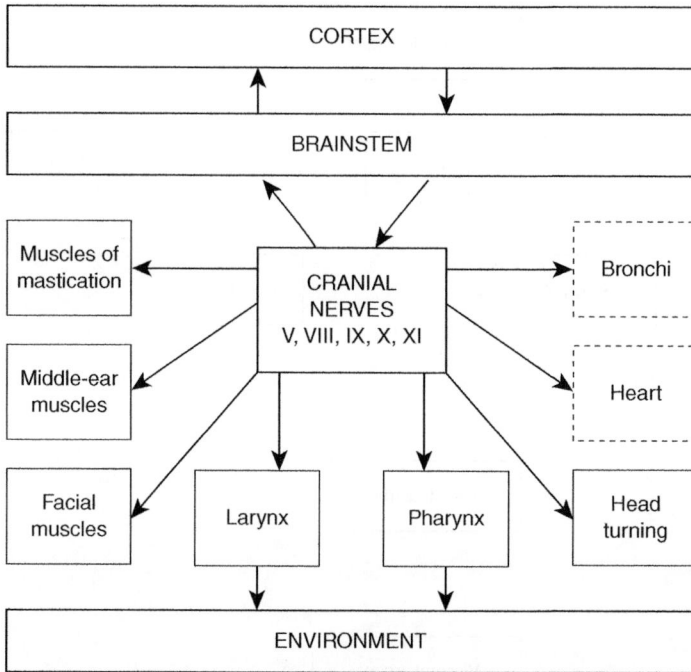

Figure 4.2 Relationship between the cortex, brainstem, cranial nerves, and the environment.
Source: reprinted with permission from NYAS Porges, S., 24 January 2006, "Social engagement and attachment: a phylogenetic perspective." Doi10.1196/ annals 1301.004 Figure 1, Social Engagement System.

Figure 4.5 shows what happens when the dorsal vagus nerve is further activated by exposure to a life-threatening environment. In life-threatening experiences both fight and flight responses are disabled. Rather the patient or client responds with a frozen-in-fear response. FROZEN in FEAR stands for: freeze reaction, oblivious, zonked, emotionally numb, feigned death, entrapped, anguish, and rigid. The DMX provides vagal input to the viscera which also receives input with AVP systemically from the hypothalamus. AVP stimulates both the NTS and the area postrema. The dorsal vagus or primitive unmyelinated fibres of the vagus nerve are fired.

The connections of the sympathetic nervous system are shown in Figure 4.6. The pupils are dilated improving visual acuity. Lung and heart function are improved. The gut's motility is reduced freeing up energy resources. Glucose, adrenaline, and noradrenaline are released for immediate decision-making. Urination is inhibited. This is in preparation for a fight-or-flight response by the patient in response to the threat of imminent danger. For this to be effective the sympathetic system must be able to override the parasympathetic system.

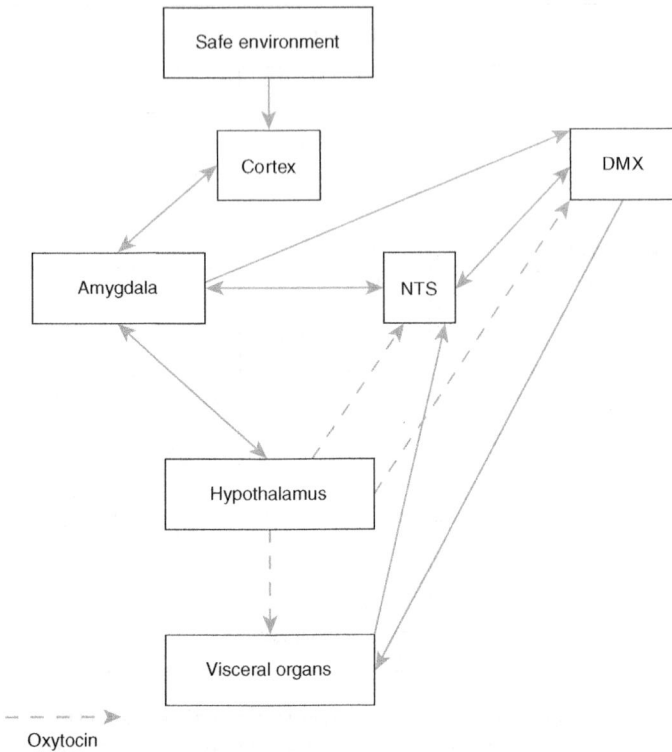

Figure 4.3 Regulation of the dorsal vagal complex in a safe environment (DVC).

The extent of the path of the vagal nerve in the body is illustrated in Figure 4.7. The word vagus means wanderer and reflects the tenth cranial nerve's journey from head to lung, heart, liver, stomach, spleen, kidney, small and large intestine, and bladder. The bilateral cerebellar auditory and tactile stimulation during SF-EMDR psychotherapy activates the nerves and, hence, the feelings associated with each of these organs where relevant in either trauma resolution or peak performance.

According to Porges' polyvagal theory, the dorsal vagal unmyelinated fibres become activated when the patient is exposed to a life-threatening environment. This means that their reptilian brainstem processes all the incoming sensory information. Traumatic experiences can become locked in at this level of the brain. During SF-EMDR psychotherapy, I often ask patients to hold the tactile units on either side of their brainstem. This has the dual advantage of stimulating bilaterally the origins of several of the cranial nerves processing this traumatic sensory information. Also, this allows for activation of the reticular activating system and consequent production of pontine-occipital-geniculate

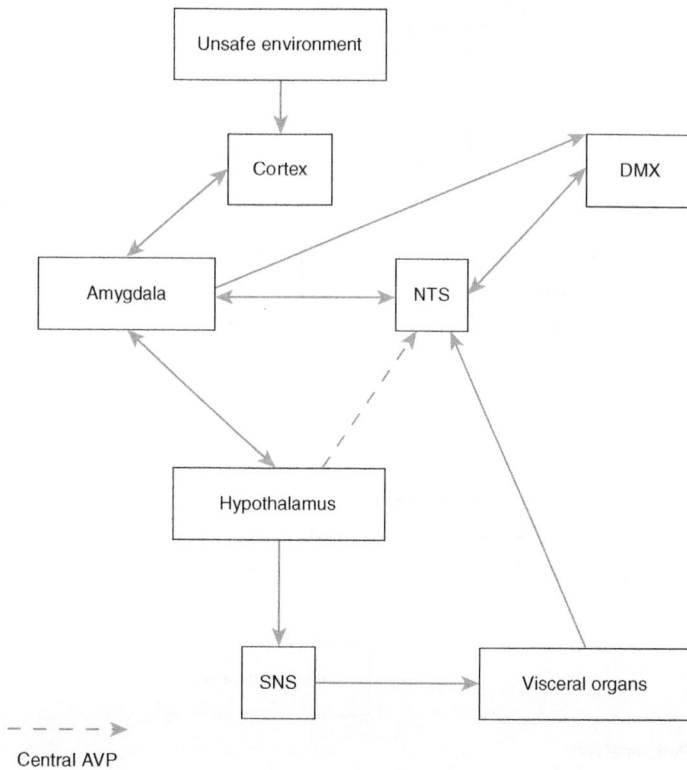

Figure 4.4 Regulation of the dorsal vagal complex in an unsafe environment.

waves. These are a precursor to REM, and towards the end of SF-EMDR psychotherapy sessions, I have observed most patients yawning as if about to enter a REM-like state. Processing continues after the SF-EMDR session and I ask patients to provide written feedback of any new meanings or insights gained. This can provide a useful starting point for the next session.

Characteristics of the reptilian brain

Reptiles have no cortex but well-developed cerebellum and predominant olfactory lobe. They also have a predominant medulla oblongata. Thus, their behaviour is mediated at a brainstem level. This is the same response humans have in any life-threatening situation.

Our reptilian ancestors are natural predators with a strong survival instinct driven by their medulla oblongata, cerebellum, midbrain, forebrain, and olfactory lobe.

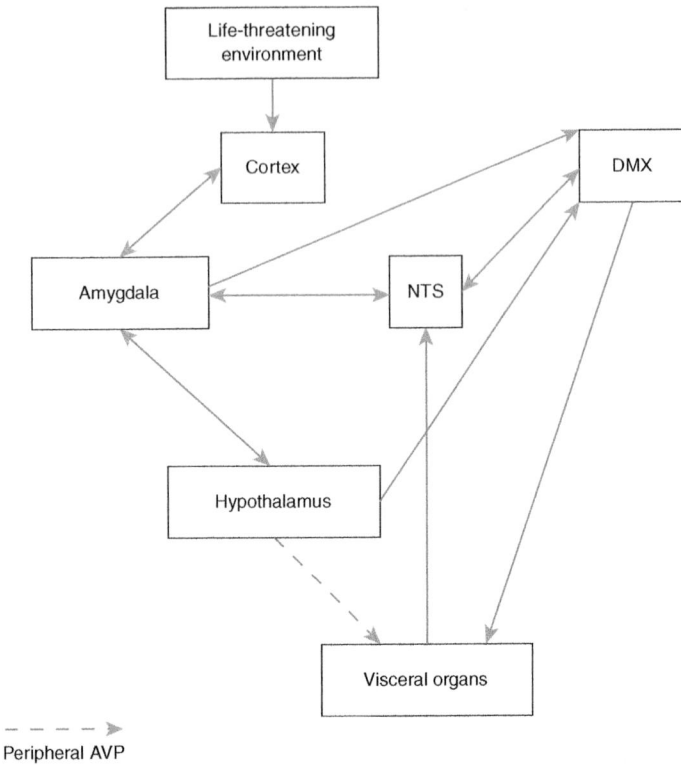

Figure 4.5 Regulation of the dorsal vagal complex in a life-threatening environment.

Dampening human brainstem reactions are a key goal of SF-EMDR psychotherapy. The reticulating activating system in the centre of the brainstem plays a key role in this process. The inferior and superior colliculi process the inputs from the cranial nerves oculomotor, trochlear, and abducens. These act on the eye to perform all known eye movements. This explains why during SF-EMDR psychotherapy bilateral stimulation induces eye movements naturally. In my clinical opinion they don't then have to be artificially activated as in EMDR or brainspotting.

Role of the periaqueductal grey matter in mediating the patient's response to trauma and the client's optimisation of performance

The Periaqueductal Grey is an area of grey matter surrounding the third and fourth ventricles. It plays a key role in mediating the brain's response to trauma.

Sympathetic system

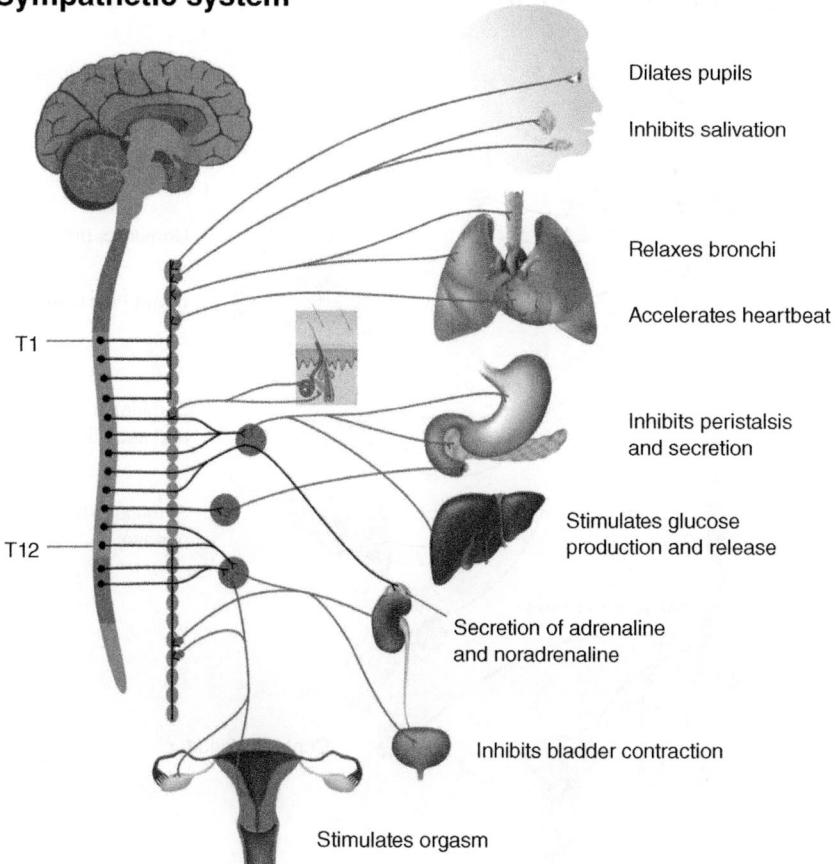

Figure 4.6 The connections of the sympathetic nervous system.
       Source: Shutterstock.

Neuroception has evolved below the level of consciousness. If the nervous system appraises the environment as dangerous when it is safe, an inappropriate response can occur. Table 4.1 illustrates the various responses to safe and dangerous situations.

For the SES to work, these instinctive responses and gestures must be switched off. This involves a level of top-down control from the prefrontal cortex to the bilateral almond-shaped amygdalae. When the risk is rated as high in the environment by a patient's nociceptive processes, both amygdala and the PAG are activated. The PAG's dorsolateral, ventrolateral, lateral, rostral, and caudal nuclei trigger instinctive defensive responses (passive or active) or escape behaviours. I

Parasympathetic system

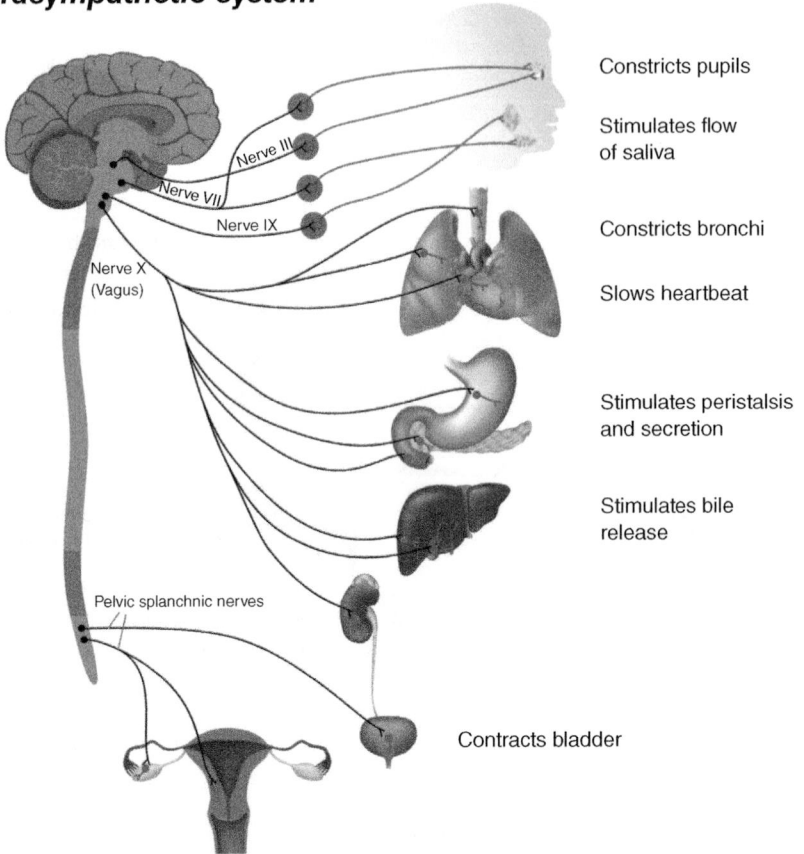

Figure 4.7 The connections of the parasympathetic system.
Source: Shutterstock.

believe this has major implications for the evaluation of risk in the setting of patients attending our mental health services.

Risk assessment (RA) is an evolved threat-detection system that can go wrong. Threats may be ambiguous or complex and require an orienting response. The medial defence zone (MDZ) of the hypothalamus becomes activated. Input to the MDZ comes from the amygdalae (our threat detector), the hippocampus, and lateral septum (which provide contextual information on possible threats). Output is from the dorsal midbrain PAG. These structures are also involved in panic attacks.

Mirror neurones are involved in the perception of risk and in identifying the aggressor's emotions from body posture and facial expressions. The shutdown

Table 4.2 Outline of different stages of reactions of the autonomic nervous system dependent on sympathetic or parasympathetic activation.

RESPONSE	LEVEL OF AROUSAL	NERVOUS SYSTEM ACTIVATED	NEURO-ANATOMY/ENDOCRINE SYSTEM
Fight	Increased (hyper)	Sympathetic	H.P.A Axis – Adrenaline
Flight	Increased (hyper)	Sympathetic	H.P.A Axis – Adrenaline
Fright	Increased (hyper)	Sympathetic	H.P.A Axis Adrenaline
Freeze	Decreased (hypo)	Unmyelinated branch of vagus	ParasympatheticAcetylcholine
Faint (vaso-vagal syncope)	Decreased (hypo)	Unmyelinated branch of vagus	ParasympatheticAcetylcholine
Feigned death	Decreased (hypo)	Unmyelinated branch of vagus	ParasympatheticAcetylcholine

continuum ends with tonic immobility (TI). TI presents with intense fear and a perception of entrapment. It occurs in complex PTSD and DID patients who describe being scared stiff or frozen with fear. A loss of sense of self and dissociation can occur. Knowledge of our patients' threat appraisal system and the shutdown continuum can inform risk management and guide therapist in their successful application of SF-EMDR psychotherapy.

Assessment of risk for a patient in a clinical setting, such as with hospital inpatients or in an outpatient department, involves an evaluation of these six different states. Thus, each patient can enter a state of fight, flight, fright, freeze, faint, and feigned death. This is part of what I term a progressive shutdown dissociation continuum.

Neuroception in the patient is always evaluating threat or risk and triggering a cascade of viscera-motor and somatomotor reactions as an unconscious process in our patients and clients. If the nurse or therapist assumes these are conscious behaviours, then the level of intervention is likely to be unsuited to the patient's internal state. For the therapist to gauge the neurological level of risk, it is important that a detailed history of development both in utero and infancy is taken. The more traumatic the history, the more likely that the patient will have relied upon the primitive, or unmyelinated, vagal nerve responses as a defence against perceived threat.

Rate of myelination of nerve fibres

The level of myelination of nerve fibres occurs in a linear fashion from twenty-six to forty weeks of gestation. During the first three months of infancy, further rapid myelination occurs in preparation for bonding between the primary caregiver and the infant. From six months to three and a half years of age, attachment patterns are laid down. If the adult patient has had a sufficiently traumatic childhood (or was born with a pervasive developmental disorder), then opportunities for optimal SES development are minimal. The risk of self-harm and harm to others is increased because of this altered neuroception, leading to the misinterpretation of a safe environment as unsafe. The use of seclusion in such a patient might trigger aspects of their PAG. This could stimulate phylogenetically older responses of the dorsal vagal complex.

Aspects of early infant brain development

The first three years of brain development primarily involve the right cerebral hemisphere. It processes sensory information, positive affective information, and the adaptive expression of negative affect.

The right hemisphere also appears to have a primary role in regulating cardiac function, represented by cardiac vagal tone (CVT). This is the sum of the inhibiting influences on the heart of the myelinated vagal pathways, namely, the ventral vagal complex (VVC), originating in the nucleus ambiguus (NA) and the immobilising effects of the dorsal motor complex (DMC) of the vagal nerve, originating in the nucleus tractus solitarius (NTS). The NTS is located at the origin of the vagal nerve and has evolved to mediate sensory information from the periphery. This relationship can be represented by CVT = VVC (NA) + DMC (NTS).

I believe that SF-EMDR psychotherapy represents a unique opportunity to combine the high frequency of the ventral vagal complex with the low-frequency bands associated with the dorsal motor complex. These become integrated with the gut- and head-brains, enabling the patient to resolve their traumatic experiences.

During the process of SF-EMDR psychotherapy, attention is paid to heart-rate variability, ensuring that neither the VVC nor DMC are over activated and that the patient remains within his or her window of tolerance (Figure 2.2, a,b,c).

Afferent feedback from the viscera is emphasised in the early stages of SF-EMDR psychotherapy by accessing and reprocessing gut reactions. The insular cortex is also thought to be involved by bringing integration of the diffuse visceral feedback and allowing cognitive awareness to emerge. This is the goal of the latter stages of SF-EMDR psychotherapy.

Links between our unmyelinated vagus nerves and ancient reptilian ancestors

The unmyelinated branch of the vagus nerve is common to all those animals with a vertebral column, or spine. The integrated social engagement system links both the heart and head. If someone is then confined in a small space and is unable to escape – for example, through torture or ongoing trauma – the dorsal motor nucleus of the vagus nerve is triggered in this potentially life-threatening situation.

The heart then slows and metabolic needs for oxygen and food supply are reduced. The gastrointestinal tract is stimulated to eliminate its contents so that scarce metabolic resources are not expended in digestion. We have evolved this survival technique from our reptilian ancestors, such as the Komodo dragon from Indonesia. They could survive anoxic conditions for hours because their brains were small and oxygen needs were limited.

Turtles are the oldest form of our reptilian ancestors and lived 210 million years ago in the age of the dinosaurs. The first probable mammal-like animal was known as lystrosaurus (the Therapsid missing link). It paved the way for the evolution of the Mesozoic mammals millions of years later.

The distinguishing features of these Mesozoic mammals are:

- Milk-producing mammary glands to suckle young;
- Hair or fur;
- Warm blooded (endothermic metabolism); and
- External ears with the presence of small bones in the inner ear.

In reptiles these inner-ear bones are part of the jawbone and therefore reptiles are unable to easily distinguish between low- and high-frequency sounds. Hence, we have a hierarchy to our response to environmental challenge. The neural feedback starts at the level of the visceral organs – which are subdiaphragmatic – before moving to the level of the heart. The sequences applied in SF-EMDR psychotherapy enable this information to be activated towards the fifth (or throat) chakra before entering the brain at the level of the sixth chakra (or pineal gland). Ultimately, the goal is to raise consciousness by activating the seventh (or crown) chakra.

Evolution of the human brain from reptilian ancestors

As I have explained, the human brain has evolved from the primitive reptilian brain. While reptiles have no biological imperative towards socialisation, humans require interaction with other humans to survive. Humans reciprocally regulate each other's emotional and mental states through love, attachment, and intimacy. This can also occur maladaptively via bullying and oppositional behaviour. The human's neural pathways for social support and adaptive behaviour are the same as those stimulating health, growth, repair, and restoration. The governing principle in this neurological hierarchy is our quest for safety. Ideally, we achieve this in our interactions with others. This makes sense from a physiological perspective. By providing a safe haven to a sick or otherwise compromised individual, they then do not have to defend themselves from attack (conscious or unconscious). Hence, scarce metabolic resources are not used up. If this individual is frightened, they will not physically improve and their body might, indeed, shut down. Information coming from our nervous system helps us to feel calm through this human interaction. All humans are constantly monitoring the immediate environment to check whether it is safe or dangerous.

Figure 4.8 shows how the adrenal glands sit on top of the kidneys and produce adrenaline aldosterone and cortisol. The outer cortex produces steroid hormones and is divided into three zones: zona glomerulosa, zona fasciculata, and zona reticularis. The steroid hormones from the adrenal cortex are mineralocorticoids, glucocorticoids, and androgens. Mineralocorticoids such as aldosterone regulate blood pressure and electrolytes. The glucocorticoids such as cortisol and cortisone regulate metabolism and suppress the immune system. They are known as the stress hormones. The inner layer adrenal medulla produces the catecholamines adrenaline and noradrenaline, which cause the fight, fright, and flight response in an emergency, anxiety, or a panic attack.

Thus, understanding the role of the adrenal gland is fundamental to how we can treat the patient's reaction to acute and chronic stress and acute and complex PTSD.

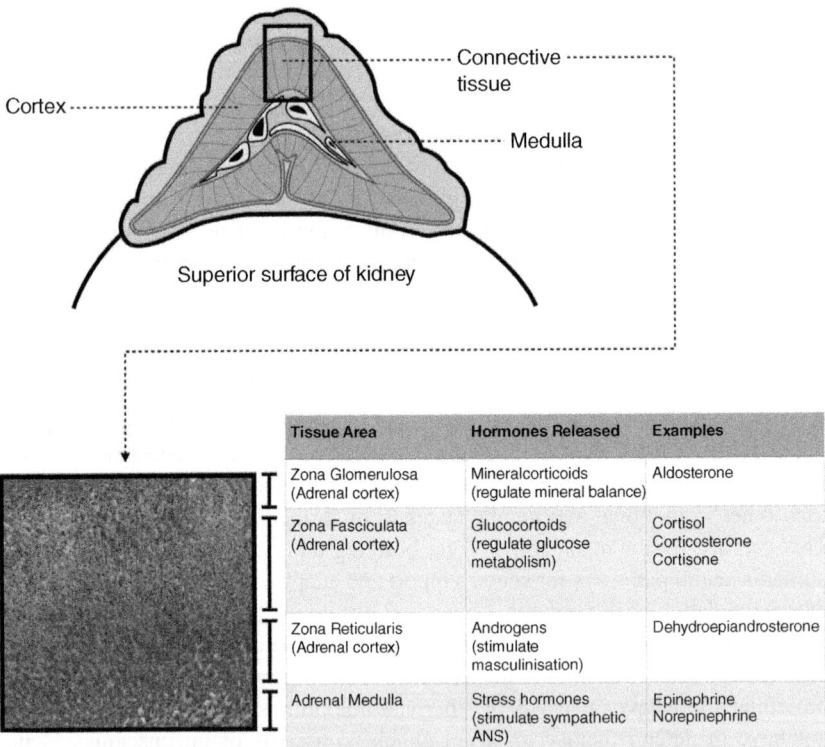

Tissue Area	Hormones Released	Examples
Zona Glomerulosa (Adrenal cortex)	Mineralcorticoids (regulate mineral balance)	Aldosterone
Zona Fasciculata (Adrenal cortex)	Glucocortoids (regulate glucose metabolism)	Cortisol Corticosterone Cortisone
Zona Reticularis (Adrenal cortex)	Androgens (stimulate masculinisation)	Dehydroepiandrosterone
Adrenal Medulla	Stress hormones (stimulate sympathetic ANS)	Epinephrine Norepinephrine

Figure 4.8 Schematic diagram of the adrenal gland showing the different tissue areas and the different hormones released. It is now accepted that depression is linked to inflammation of the mind. The adrenal gland doubles in size with severe depression and cortisol secretion causes regulation of mineralocorticoid and Glucocorticoids receptors. This has an impact on the immune system and triggers an inflammatory response. The SF-EMDR psychotherapy approach is designed to reduce the inflammatory response associated stress and traumatic life events.

Inflammation and hypertrophy of the adrenal gland can initiate depressive symptoms such as low mood, anhedonia, fatigue, psychomotor retardation, social withdrawal, and sleep disturbance. This may also worsen coexisting conditions such as rheumatoid arthritis, chronic pain, obesity diabetes, and cardiovascular disease.

Focusing on reprocessing the stressful events at an abdominal, heart, and endocrine level using SF-EMDR psychotherapy can help to alleviate the inflammation and the severity of the psychiatric and psychological symptoms in these disorders.

Stress and inflammation

Experiencing stress in our patients' and clients' lives triggers a mind–body inflammatory response. In infancy, early childhood, and adult life proteins are secreted at a cellular level. These include cytokines, transcription factors affecting DNA replication, and even faulty genomics. Major stressors to look out for are: conflict, rejection, isolation, exclusion, and poverty. Interpersonal loss and unresolved grief or bereavement can act as triggers. The neural mechanisms involved in processing the physical pain from intense heat or cold appear to be involved in processing emotional pain from social rejection or bereavement. As I have already explained this gives rise to language such as "I was heartbroken" and "My feelings were hurt."

We now know that neural networks in the brain communicate directly with the body's immune system. Inflammatory cytokines may trigger the cognitive mood and behavioural symptoms of depression. Thus, a picture is emerging of genetic factors, personality traits, and social-environmental conditions predisposing the individual to psychopathology.

This leads to a cycle of mild inflammation causing anxiety linked to a perception of social threat. This causes further inflammation at a neurological and immune system level. Full-blown anxiety and depressive disorders are then likely in adulthood. A combination of medication such as SSRIs, SF-EMDR psychotherapy, mindfulness, and meditation approaches such as T'ai Chi can treat these disorders before they become chronic and intractable.

A lot is known about both the adverse socio-environmental conditions that precipitate and the cognitive and emotional processes that mediate depression. Stress and inflammation play key roles in the aetiology of depression by altering social, cognitive, and affective processes. Identifying and modifying negative cognitive appraisal and the sensitivity of neural networks to social threat and intimidating behaviour and dysfunctional parenting can be targeted. This will help to reduce the prevalence of depression and its burden on society.

One of our earliest ancestors was the tortoise. When threatened, it would shut down neurologically by retracting its head into its shell. Its tenth cranial nerve (vagus nerve) was unmyelinated and it could stay in this state for long periods until the environment was safe again.

Humans have a myelinated vagus nerve, which originates in the brainstem. Its nuclei send branches to the middle-ear muscles, the larynx, and pharynx, along with branches to the muscles governing facial expression. As therapists, when listening to the voices of our clients (intonation and prosody) and monitoring their gaze, facial expression, and gestures, we are, in fact, tuning in to their physiological state. This includes motor impulses, bodily sensations, emotions, feelings, and instinctive reactions. Paying attention to, and processing, these aspects of our patient's experience is integral to SF-EMDR psychotherapy. If the patient's tone is flat, lacks prosody, is hard to understand, and their posture is slouched with minimal gestures, they may be experiencing stimulation via the dorsal motor nucleus of the vagus nerve.

For too long, clinicians have been told an event must be life-threatening in order to diagnose PTSD. However, we are each wired up according to our own experiences from infancy and childhood to adulthood. The response of our nervous system to the event is of more critical importance to the eventual diagnosis than the event itself.

In setting up therapy, the client should be able to have a say in negotiating their proximity to the therapist. This will promote a shift in their physiological state towards safety. It is best to avoid loud environments with low-frequency sounds, which might evoke a "threat" state, associated with a perceived predator nearby. Ideally, we should talk in a modulated way to our patients to trigger an appropriate nociceptive response, filtering out low-frequency, and preferentially tuning into higher-frequency, sounds.

Direct vascular channels connect skull bone marrow and the brain surface enabling myeloid cell migration

Inflammation is essential for defence and repair after injury. The sympathetic nervous system recruits neutrophils and other immune cells from the bone marrow. Animal studies revealed that most neutrophils came from bone marrow in the skull. Myeloid cells travel to the inflamed brain via microscopic channels. These cross the inner-skull cortex connecting the dura with the bone marrow cavities in the skull and occupy 2.5 per cent of the brain volume.

Herrison et al. 2018, when studying the intersection of the skull and the brain noticed there were channels connecting the bone marrow in the skull with the brain's dura mater to the inner cerebral cortex. The research team were able to track different cell types from bone marrow to organs affected by inflammation in the human. Stress causing depression and inflammation in the brain therefore has the potential to recruit neutrophils from the adjacent bone marrow in the skull. Myeloid cells were found to traverse the small vascular channels to reach the site of inflammation in the brain. The current dogma taught in medical school is that the bone marrow releases anti-inflammatory cells into the systemic circulation. Here they were thought to pool in the blood before delivery to the site of inflammation. The meninges contain cerebral and external carotid arteries and the diploic veins. Diploic veins connect the pericranial and endocranial venous system through the skull. Meningeal vessels have access to the cerebrospinal fluid through the arachnoid granulation. These newly discovered vascular channels provide a direct route for immune competent cells to reach the site of acute or chronic inflammation in the brain. Trauma to the skull has the potential to disrupt these channels and make the consequences of concussion or mild traumatic brain injury worse.

Skull-bone-marrow–derived neutrophils appear to migrate directly to the brain. Thus, pathogenic cell types may also travel along these micro channels. The role of these channels in acute and chronic brain inflammation remains to be fully elucidated.

Prof Ed Bullmore, in his book *The Inflamed Mind*, discusses the role of brain inflammation in the aetiology of depression. He asserts that auto-immune disease, arthritis, obesity, physical and traumatic stress can all cause bodily inflammation (p. 125). Now the existence of these micro channels could explain how this reaches the brain and triggers a depressive episode. These channels may transfer information in the form of soluble inflammatory factors, alerting the skull-bone-marrow to brain pathology such as a bleed, ischaemia, or traumatic encephalopathy due to a head injury.

This is an exciting new area for research and SF-EMDR psychotherapy is ideally placed to take advantage of these advances in medical knowledge in treating medical, physical, and psychological health problems to arrive at a state of improved resilience and peak performance.

Newly discovered structural and functional features of the immune system and the head-brain (cerebral meninges)

Louveau discovered the presence of lymphatic endothelial cells in the CNS. They demonstrated that these endothelial cells transported fluid and immune cells from the CSF to deep cervical lymph nodes. This enables a connection to the rest of the lymphatic system, namely lymph nodes, thymus, spleen, and bone marrow. Lymphatic vessels were found lining the dural sinuses. The dural sinuses drain blood from both the internal and external veins of the brain into the internal jugular veins. Blood from the meningeal lymphatic network appears to start from both eyes and track above the olfactory bulb before aligning next to the sinuses. The glymphatic system is the waste clearance pathway for the CNS. The glymphatic system was so named by Maiken Nedergaard, a Danish neuroscientist, as it is dependent on glial cells.

Louveau et al. (2018) discovered that lymphatic vessels exist in the meninges of the CNS. This provides evidence for a link between the CNS and the peripheral immune system. The meningeal lymphatic system helps to drain components of the cerebrospinal fluid. These meningeal lymphatics regulate processes of inflammation and provide surveillance at an immunological level of the CNS.

The discovery of this CNS lymphatic system calls for reassessment of neuroimmunology fundamentals. Also disorders with an immune system dysfunction may have malfunction of the meningeal lymphatic vessels as a significant aetiological factor. SF-EMDR psychotherapy has the flexibility to work with other medical and surgical treatments to stimulate the nervous system to improve immune-system function improving the outcome in these conditions.

Role of the immune system in the gut or enteric nervous system

The word glia is derived from the Greek word for "glue." These cells act as the glue of the enteric nervous system. Enteric Glial cells (EGCs) form a neural network in the intestinal mucosa. They interconnect with somatosensory, circulatory, nervous, and immune systems. Evidence suggests EGCs modulate gut functions by regulating mucosa permeability and neural activity of Meissner's and Auerbach's plexus. They also interconnect with the body's immune and endocrine systems. They are involved in electrolyte secretion, absorption, and vascular tone of the gut. These can all be related to processing of gut feelings or gut instinct in stage one of SF-EMDR psychotherapy.

Disease states such as infection, inflammatory bowel disease, irritable bowel syndrome, ischaemic bowel, slow transit constipation e.g. in depression, diverticular disease, neurodegenerative diseases such as Parkinson's disease that decrease gut motility, are all worsened by a reactive EGC phenotype.

Knowing this, the therapist can initiate signalling of mirror neurons in the gut-brain of the patient using bilateral stimulation as described in SF-EMDR psychotherapy (Chapter 8). This can restore proper EGC function and lessen the onset and progression of intestinal inflammation, which is a key component in many of the above intestinal diseases.

Neural aspects of immunomodulation with a focus on the vagus nerve

The thymus and lymph nodes regulate cellular immunity. Bone marrow and spleen regulate humoral immunity while skin and mucosa are the first line of defence of innate immunity. T lymphocytes result from cellular immunity and B lymphocytes from humoral immunity.

The vagus or "wandering" nerve modulates the immune system and has links to the immune system of the heart and the CNS. The nucleus tractus solitarius (NTS) is a major relay station for neural-immune communication. Use of tactile BLS on either side of the brainstem during SF-EMDR psychotherapy can enhance communication between the neural networks and the immune systems. The hypothesis is that cerebellar activation at a frequency of 40–60 Hz (gamma waves) will dampen brainstem responses, both minimising inflammation and boosting immune-neural communication and thalamocortical binding.

The NTS connects to the dorsal motor nucleus of the vagus nerve and the nucleus ambiguous. The vagally mediated Heart Rate Variability (HRV) is positively associated with activity in the anterior cingulate cortex, insular cortex, and amygdala. This pathway from the brainstem to the prefrontal cortex is activated in the final stages of SF-EMDR psychotherapy. This neural network involves the autonomic nervous system, the endocrine system, and immune systems as well as reprocessing of pain, emotion, and changes in behaviour. SF-EMDR psychotherapy is one of the few therapeutic approaches to take account of these multi-organ systems.

Unexpected role of interferon gamma in regulating neuronal connectivity and social behaviour

Human meningeal immunity was previously known to influence spatial learning and memory and has now been shown to affect social behaviour. Mice, whose adaptive immunity has been compromised, show enhanced connectivity of the frontal cortex and this is associated with marked deficits in their social behaviour.

Interferon gamma (IF) appears to mediate an adaptive immune response and promote social behaviour at the same time. Gaba aminobutyric acid (GABA) is produced by inhibitory neurons that react with IF. The subsequent neural circuits that are recruited promote social behaviour. This confirms the link between the brain's meningeal immune system and social behaviour at a molecular level.

This also suggests a possible evolutionary link going back to the origin of life. A conflict existed between social aggregation of the social behaviour of species and an anti-pathogen response that is protective in situations where new species are encountered. Thus natural selection appears to have worked out that the risks of encounters with a new species (acquisition of potentially fatal diseases) is outweighed by the potential benefits in terms of survival and reproduction. For Homo sapiens this involves the promotion of mental health, consequent to adaptive social behaviour resulting from closer contact between species.

Many neurological and psychiatric disorders show disturbance in social behaviour e.g. ASD, ADHD, OCD, dementia, and schizophrenia. These are also linked to immune-system dysfunction, for example, altered levels of cytokines, T lymphocytes, and natural killer cells. This discovery many help to elucidate how immune-system dysfunctions disrupt neural circuitry responsible for social behaviour in these disorders.

SF-EMDR psychotherapy has now been modified to stimulate improved immune neural communication. It is now clear that the brains of the head, heart, and gut interact to achieve integrated information processing at all levels of hormonal, circulatory, central, cardiac, and enteric nervous systems. Recent discoveries show a network of connections between the lymphatic meningeal pathway of the brain and the normal immune system. As far as I am aware SF-EMDR psychotherapy is the first to incorporate this knowledge.

Patients with ASD show hyper-connectivity in the prefrontal cortex and insular regions of the frontal lobe. CNS neurons respond to IF, which comes from T lymphocytes, which produce this inhibitory neurotransmitter GABA. The activated inhibitory interneurons act to prevent hyper-excitability and connectivity in the prefrontal cortex. Thus, abnormal immune responses may be the root cause of many neurological and psychiatric disorders presenting with deficits in social behaviour. These pathways between the nervous and immune systems have evolved slowly over millions of years. Consequently, they may be especially vulnerable to fast-evolving pathogens such as meningitis and the Zika virus. It was previously thought that the brain was immune privileged; this research shows it to be immune competent. The activation of imagination during SF-EMDR psychotherapy may not only stimulate mirror-neuron activity but also enhance immune-neural communication at the level of multiple body systems.

Summary

The relationship between the three parts of the cerebellum and its connections to the brainstem and frontal cortex are described and give rise to the unique technique of bilateral cerebellar stimulation, which is the foundation for SF-EMDR psychotherapy. The historical descriptions of the autonomic nervous system have changed from John Langley to Walter Hess to Dr Stephen Porges. The latter's polyvagal theory is discussed with respect to safe, unsafe, and life-threatening environments. The wandering path of the vagal nerve is discussed, along with its ventral branch associated with the SES and the dorsal branch associated with the freeze response. The role of the periaqueductal grey matter in mediating the patient's response to trauma and the client's optimisation of performance is discussed. A new model for the assessment of risk for a patient in a clinical setting such as an inpatient or outpatient clinic is proposed. This is based on an understanding of their nociceptive responses to threat. This differs dramatically from the checklist approach adopted by most NHS hospital trusts at present. It is my conviction that risk assessment based on an individual's neuroception and activation of their polyvagal complex will enable more appropriate targeted therapeutic interventions. There are links between our vagus nerve and that of our reptilian-brained ancestors. The evolution of the human brain from our reptilian ancestors is discussed. The shutdown dissociation continuum is described in detail along with explanations of how SF-EMDR psychotherapy can be used to alleviate symptoms of traumatic stress associated with specific stages along this continuum. Structural and functional features of the meningeal lymphatic vessels in the CNS are discussed. The influence of enteric glial cells as part of an enteric immune system is explained, with the implications of this for SF-EMDR psychotherapy. The neural aspects of neuromodulation focussing on the vagus nerve allow for SF-EMDR psychotherapy to enhance all levels of neural-immune communication. The latest research on the role of interferon gamma in regulating neuronal connectivity and social behaviour are discussed, with implications for modification of SF-EMDR psychotherapy. This becomes one of the first textbooks to integrate this information about the therapeutic effects of the connections between the brain's immune and nervous systems.

Chapter 5

Proposals for SF-EMDR psychotherapy with special populations and effects of abuse and neglect on the developing brains of the patient

Introduction to the information-processing difficulties of children and adults with autism spectrum disorder

Play by children with autism stimulates their mobilisation responses. The fight-or-flight defensive reaction can be activated. Normally, by looking at one's playmate, these defensive behaviours are down-regulated. If someone accidentally hits the other during play, then saying "I'm sorry" normally diffuses the situation. Neurotypical children use their tone of voice and facial expression to communicate emotions. This prevents their playful behaviour from being interpreted in an aggressive manner by the nervous system of their playmate.

This moment-to-moment facial interaction is difficult for both children with autism and those who have grown up in an unsafe environment through trauma, neglect, or abuse. My clinical experience using SF-EMDR psychotherapy with traumatised patients leads me to believe it will help patients with autism spectrum disorder (ASD). The goal here is: bringing affective regulation of tone.

In a safe play environment, children with autism would be mobilised and encouraged to develop behavioural reciprocity. This initial stage of interaction can progress to a "play-fighting" stage. The reciprocal behaviours are accompanied by face-to-face encounters so that each participant can maintain their playful engagement without straying into aggressiveness. To create this safe play environment, teachers must learn to understand the neurological impact of autism on the child. This will enable them to modify the child's environment and alter the intonation and prosody of their own voices when communicating with these children. A safe state of socialising, learning, and feeling good is then realised for these autistic children.

Dr Stephen Porges set up a listening project for children with autism. He could determine which sounds pass into the middle ear via the eardrum and which simply bounce off it. The ideal situation is that the middle-ear muscles contract. This allows the higher frequency sounds of the human voice through to the brain, once they have been processed by the auditory nerve. Porges found that as aural sensitivity is reduced, children's language development improves. In the listening project, music was amplified to emphasise the tone and prosody of a human voice.

The vocal music was modified by computer algorithm so that it would wax and wane. Patients' auditory systems would strive to hear the sound as it faded, and, as it started to come back, they would feel better. The project aimed to present high-frequency sounds promoting safety while excluding low-frequency sounds, which can be interpreted to mean danger. When the child's nervous system is no longer hypervigilant, then the middle-ear muscles can adaptively modulate the ambient sounds. These muscle reactions are not dependent on voluntary control.

Auditory hypersensitivity is present in sixty per cent of patients with autism. They find it difficult to extract the human voice from other environmental sounds. Their social engagement system (SES) is compromised. They can pick out low-frequency sounds, and they are often aware if someone is walking behind them. Usually, in potentially dangerous environments, for example, walking home late at night, people shift unconsciously from the SES to a system associated with hypervigilance. Patients with autism remain in the hypervigilant state. They employ neural tone of the middle ear to hear low-frequency sounds, for example, footsteps, at the expense of hearing and understanding the human voice. Children with autism grow up in a sensory and auditory world where it is difficult to filter out low-frequency sounds. It is as if they are always aware of the possibility of danger with their heightened sensory awareness.

Treatment of autism spectrum disorder and traumatic stress disorders

Once the patient with autism is made to feel safe in the therapeutic context subtle neural connections are activated. These neural connections occur by stimulating the ventral vagus or tenth cranial nerve. Other muscles are activated via the muscles of facial expression. This helps to regulate emotions in the face, heart, and gut and the patient can enter a relaxed physiological state. Use of SF-EMDR psychotherapy can help these patients achieve a positive outcome. The neural connections of the heart, face, and head are accessed through regulation of the muscles of facial expression. This will inhibit the responses associated with hyper and hypoarousal. Ideally, the child with autism is then able to learn through play. They experience the environment as safe and their senses become less sensitive.

Porges found that the children with autism who were enrolled in the listening project were better able to hear their own voices. They did not have to talk as loudly or shout out and they were better able to engage in conversions with their families and at school. The treatment is simply passive listening to sounds, specially programmed to stimulate the child's nervous system. They tune in to voice intonation and prosody. The treatment comprises five one-hour sessions repeated daily, and Porges found that beneficial effects would occur by day three of the treatment. More research is necessary to test the repeatability of these results in the UK population of children with autism spectrum disorders and in those with quasi-autistic behaviours because of extreme neglect and abuse. The cohort of children brought to the UK from Romanian orphanages would be a good sample to study.

The response of the patient to stress

On exposure to extreme stress, many human bodily systems become "stuck" as stress hormones are secreted by the hypothalamic–pituitary–adrenal (HPA) axis. The human being continues to live in the world as if the trauma is still present. Often, a chronic pattern of hyperarousal exists. In childhood trauma, the response is one of alternating hyperarousal and hypoarousal. The immune and perceptual systems are also affected by this exposure.

Memory is stored in both a verbal (or narrative) form and as somatic maps. The brain often becomes overwhelmed and the thalamus shuts down under the influence of traumatic stress. Hence, sensory fragments appear as flashbacks. The incident is not remembered as a story. Instead, it is stored at an organic level, for example, as a sense of fear with a lack of context. The patient might experience repeated nightmares due to unprocessed, non-REM sleep.

Implications for clinical practice and psychotherapists

Following trauma, information is encoded without its social context. The person's body organises itself as if the trauma is still present. Through SF-EMDR psychotherapy, I enable the patient to tolerate traumatic emotions as they are experienced. The shock has often changed the patient. The initial process involves shifting to experiencing the trauma at an internal bodily level. Talking can be a defence against feeling and may be a distraction from noticing the body's reactions. We know that different parts of the brain are activated when feelings are experienced, compared to when the patient is talking. Thus, in SF-EMDR psychotherapy, the goal is to enable patients to feel their feelings, notice bodily sensations, and allow a flow of information to occur within themselves. Initially, their bodies feel under threat. However, as clinician and patient notice together how these fearful sensations dissipate over time, the process continues; their feelings and emotions become more tolerable.

Giving patients a degree of control over any procedure helps them to stay calm by engaging the observing or ego state of their mind. This ensures that there is less chance of them re-experiencing the traumatic event during the therapeutic session. SF-EMDR psychotherapy provides verbal scaffolding, enabling the patient to undergo the process of therapeutic change.

Effects of abuse and neglect on the developing brains of the patient:

1. The functions of the prefrontal cortex are changed with impaired ability to pay attention and focus;
2. Neglect and abuse can reduce the ability of the person to experience emotions appropriately;

3. IQ can be reduced by up to thirty per cent;
4. It interferes with the person's ability to engage with others;
5. Patients become less productive members of society; and
6. Self-reflection, understanding, and caring for others do not develop adequately, following neglect and abuse.

Another symptom is that the patient dissociates from the reality of neglect and abuse. In general, people want to believe that the world is a safe place. When trauma occurs, the dissociative defence emerges. For example, one dissociative identity may be able to learn and have friends, while the other can be the aspect of the personality that stores the traumatic event.

The level of brainstem arousal is related to heart-rate variability. Mindfulness and posture are also interrelated. I believe activation of gut responses stimulates processing in the insular cortex. This is crucial in linking the gut and heart-brains by tapping into the senses of both proprioception and body awareness. The aim of treatment with SF-EMDR psychotherapy is the reintegration of the whole body at the level of the gut, heart, and brain, to keep the patient within their conscious awareness, level-headed, mindful window of affective tolerance and emotional regulation (see Figure 2.2(b), CALM WATERS). They remain fully alive in the present, having reprocessed their traumas. The patient should feel safe and powerful following treatment.

Implications of Dr Stephen Porges' polyvagal theory for the treatment of trauma and autism

Stephen Porges discovered, from his work on newborn babies, the importance of the social engagement system (SES). Initially, babies are indiscriminate in their affections. Only at around six months of age do they become attuned to the sound of their primary carer's (usually the mother's) voice. This voice has a high frequency of approximately 900 Hz. The middle-ear muscles in the infant allow the spectrum and intonation of these sounds to register acoustically when the infant is in a safe environment. However, children who have been abused, traumatised, or have autism are often afraid of their environment. This may include sudden noises or the low tone of their father's or male carer's voice. This is because it resonates with a low frequency and might be associated with their being held down or attacked by a predator. These events can activate the most primitive part of our reptilian brain: the dorsal (unmyelinated) branch of the tenth cranial, or vagus, nerve.

In 1902, it was noted by Wundt that "[r]espiratory movements are regularly accompanied by fluctuations of the pulse, whose rapidity increases in inspiration and decreases in expiration."

In 1910, Hering reported that "[i]t is known with breathing that a ... lowering of heart rate ... is a function of the vagal nerves."

Back then we can see that there was a connection between breathing and heart rate. With the polyvagal theory, there is a common cardiopulmonary oscillator, autonomic function governs primary emotions, and there is a link between vagal control of the heart and neural control of the face and head muscles (Table 5.1).

In a safe environment, the patient is in a state of visceral homeostasis, allowing growth and restoration. The heart rate slows, and the production of cortisol and cytokine is decreased, resulting in a decrease in immune-mediated inflammation and an inhibited flight/flight response. Brainstem nuclei integrate these responses with muscles regulating eye gaze, facial expression, listening, and prosody.

However, humans have evolved to avoid dangerous and life-threatening situations. The modulating response of the integrated brainstem nuclei promotes social engagement and reciprocal communication. The faster-reacting bottom-up and phylogenetically older circuits kick in when our survival is endangered. These occur in sequence via the dorsal vagal complex and the endocrine system. Conversely, the newer myelinated vagus inhibits both the sympathetic nervous system and dampens HPA-axis activity.

Importance of myelination in utero and early neurodevelopment

Developmentally, myelination occurs rapidly in the last trimester of pregnancy. There is a linear increase in the rate of myelination, equivalent to that present in adolescence. During the first three months after birth, further myelination prepares the infant for bonding. The ventral vagal complex, from six months until approximately three and a half years, lays down attachment patterns. An adult who experienced abuse, neglect, or trauma in childhood, or who developed a pervasive language or developmental disorder, will have suboptimal SES development. They will be at an increased risk to self, others, and property in any environment appraised as unsafe by their unconscious neuroception.

Table 5.1 Anatomical divisions of the autonomic nervous system

	COMPONENT	BEHAVIOURAL FUNCTION	LOWER MOTOR NEURONS
III	The myelinated vagus (ventral vagal complex)	Social communication, self-soothing, calming	Nucleus ambiguus
II	Sympathetic-adrenal system	Active avoidance (mobilisation)	Spinal cord
I	Unmyelinated vagus (dorsal vagal complex)	Immobilisation (feigning death or passive avoidance), vaso-vagal syncope (fainting), bodily shutdown (potential death)	Dorsal motor nucleus of the vagus

Social engagement in newborns to the infant stage of development depends on the regulation of their visceral state (or gut feelings) by the myelinated fibres of the tenth cranial nerve, which act as a "vagal brake." If the environment of the infant is one of stress and threat, then defensive behaviours are activated. These are preferentially initiated by the infant's endocrine system via the spinal cord and by the unmyelinated fibres via the dorsal vagal complex. Myelination and, hence, social engagement are not prioritised and this might have crucial implications for the genesis of attachment disorders, autism, schizophrenia, and personality disorders in later life.

These myelinated pathways connect to the heart's sinoatrial node, or pacemaker. This ensures that the resting heart rate is lower than the intrinsic pacemaker rate. The heart rate occurs at the frequency of spontaneous breathing. This respiratory sinus arrhythmia (RSA) provides a connection to the brain, heart, and gut via diaphragmatic breathing. However, the rapid breathing of a panic attack is initiated by brainstem nuclei activation.

The mechanisms that enable humans to engage facially (i.e. through facial expression and eye gaze) are shared with those needed to listen to the human voice. Problems in these areas are a feature in many psychiatric conditions, such as autism and pervasive developmental disorders. An integrated activation of these pathways will reduce heart rate and blood pressure and levels of autonomic arousal. This will promote social engagement and enable patients to reprocess feelings, sensations, and thoughts in their window of affect tolerance and emotional regulation (Figure 2.2).

The frontal cortex influences the inhibition of heart rate, blood pressure, and autonomic arousal via descending corticobulbar pathways. The SES links the HPA-axis and social-neuropeptides (oxytocin) to the patient's immune system. It is believed that exposure to chronic stress interferes with immune-system function, thereby weakening patients' resistance to infection. It is likely that a compromised antigenic response to viral inflammation is a component of chronic fatigue, fibromyalgia, and other immune-system–related disorders. These conditions often appear many years after the initial traumatic events: for example, soldiers from the first Gulf War in 1990 exhibited such symptoms by the year 2000. There are clear neuro-physiological links to the somatic-motor system in patients with ASD. Deficits in eye gaze, minimal facial expression of emotions, monotonous intonation, lack of prosody, and difficulty eating are all linked to immature somato-motor development. Lung, heart, and digestive problems are secondary to impaired viscera-motor regulation. Both somatic-motor and visceral-motor dysfunction lead to a deterioration of the myelinated fibres' ability to activate the SES. Consequentially, spontaneity, social skills, detection, and expression of emotions, language prosody, and intonation are weakened.

Treatment aimed at neurological regulation of the SES would enhance appropriate spontaneous behaviour, expression of affect, prosody in expressive speech, and the ability to extract the human voice from ambient background noise. This would improve the triad of impairments associated with autism: that is, communication, reciprocal social interaction, and stereotypical behaviours. The hearing and understanding of language is dependent on filtering out low-frequency sounds (associated with shouting and aggression) in favour of high-frequency sounds (900 Hz) consistent with a soothing human voice. This explains the calming effect of a lilting lullaby on a newborn's state of affective regulation. Preferential filtration of high-frequency sounds depends on appropriate innervation of the middle-ear muscles. These are the stapedius muscle, innervated by a branch of the facial nerve, and the tensor tympani muscle, innervated by a branch of the trigeminal nerve. These nerves are impaired in children with language delay, learning disabilities, and autism. Repeated middle-ear infection related to otitis media may also delay language development. Early detection and restoration of function of both these nerves will improve the patient's SES.

The role of experience-dependent plasticity on the development of the cerebellum or little brain

In 2006, Schutter and van Honk reported an electrophysiological link between the cerebellum, cognition, and emotion. Frontal theta EEG activity was recorded in response to single-pulse cerebellar transcranial magnetic stimulation (TMS). Dr Pollak estimates that forty per cent of cerebellar connections are with the prefrontal cortex. These occur via the dentate nucleus of the cerebellum and correlate with complex cognitive processes. The neocortex and cerebellar hemispheres develop experientially. Cerebellar neurogenesis continues until the age of two. Children abused through neglect or trauma have smaller cerebellar volumes. This has major implications for their future emotional, physical, psychosocial, and intellectual development. Dr Pollak reported on children adopted into an enriched family from institutionalised care. In the group comparison of cerebellar regional volumes, there were smaller volumes, bilaterally, in the right and left superior–posterior lobes in institutionalised children compared to controls. The left superior–posterior lobe of the cerebellum was associated with visuospatial memory and the right superior–posterior lobe was correlated with planning and executive function. From these results we can conclude that cerebellar function is dependent on neuroplasticity.

Dr Pollak further concluded that physiological and social deprivation impacts negatively on cerebellar development. Environmental distress can lead to limited neural activity between the cerebellum and the cortex, especially during the first two years of life. It might only be in adolescence, with renewed brain development, that this "faulty wiring" manifests in behaviours linked to psychiatric disorders.

When I read an article by Hanson, Suh, Nacewicz, and colleagues I became interested in the role of the cerebellum in emotional development. I attended a neural developmental seminar given by Dr Pollak at the University of Manchester, where he discussed his research on this topic (Pollak, 2012). Until then,

I had been using bilateral auditory stimulation, using the standard BOKA-9 machine, built by Dr Gerhard Karl (of Karlware). As my SF-EMDR psychotherapy involved a lot of therapeutic feedback with reframing of somatosensory and visceral-motor experiences, I found that placing the headphones directly over the ears interfered with the therapeutic alliance. I hypothesised that if the auditory tones were applied bilaterally, directly over the mastoid processes, there would be maximal resonance via bone conduction within the patient's posterior fossa.

The posterior fossa contain both cerebellae and brainstem. I have since used this technique during sessions lasting 90 to 120 minutes. It appears that exposure to bilateral auditory tones, placed at the level of the level of the mastoid processes, inhibits brainstem responses and strengthens connections to the prefrontal cortex.

Inhibition of instinctive brainstem responses helps to modulate primitive gut reactions, including abdominally registered feelings of anger and anxiety. Levels of arousal in the aftermath of traumatic experiences are contained within the patient's conscious awareness, level-headed, mindful window of affect tolerance, emotional regulation, and safety (CALM WATERS). Information then flows at a higher level of organisation within the body, that is, from the cardiac plexus to the insular cortex and from the cerebellum to the prefrontal cortex, bilaterally. The patient is left with both time and space to reflect on their traumatic experiences in a calm and safe state. Through this reflection, they can learn from their experiences to help them in the future.

The making of who we are: down to the cerebellum

The cerebellum has been estimated to have 101 billion neurons (Anderson et al., 1992) compared to 26 billion neurons in the cerebral cortex (Pelvig et al., 2006). It may be the most evolved region of the brain. Those with damage to their cerebellum, like the Romanian orphans, had emotional and cognitive problems like depression and ADHD. A small percentage of connections of the cerebellum are with the motor cortex while the majority is with the parts of the cortex involved in cognition, perception, language, and emotional processing. These connections are bidirectional. The cerebellum talks to the cortex which sends signals back. This information is reprocessed and sent back to specific cortical regions. The cerebellum is now at the heart of the links between the sensorimotor aspects of the body and the mental information processing of the mind. This new information confirms the reasoning behind bilateral continuous cerebellar resonance accompanied by tactile stimulation at multiple locations on the body surface employed in SF-EMDR for psychotherapy.

Throughout evolution the cerebellum increased in size at the same rate as the rest of the brain. The apes, forerunners to Homo sapiens, branched off from the other primates. The ape cerebellum had a phenomenal growth spurt, becoming disproportionately larger as it evolved first in the lesser apes then in the great apes and finally in humans.

As the connections with the frontal lobe were evolving simultaneously it may be that the increased size of the prefrontal cortex was secondary to the rise in volume and increased density of neuronal connection and function in the cerebellum. As far as we can tell, the cerebellum was present in a wide range of living species. It is large and complex in fish. The circuits are similar in fish, reptiles, birds, and mammals. It has evolved from our earliest ancestors, the bilaterians and Devonians, from 600 million years ago. Thus, it is hardwired to respond to all incoming stimuli from the sensory and motor nervous system. At the moment of trauma the least well myelinated prefrontal cortex goes off line. This may be an instinctive reflex to preserve cerebellar function, which fires off signals to the brainstem to take evasive and protective action.

Little brain, big impact

In the human brain the cerebellum is thirty-one per cent larger than that expected from a scaled-up model of the non-ape primate. This equates to about twenty billion extra neurons. The brain devotes a lot of oxygen and nutrients to sustain these neurons. This shows the evolutionary imperative given to the cerebellum compared to the cerebral cortex.

King of the swingers

This is the title of a song from the film of *The Jungle Book*, produced by Disney. The lyrics are widely available and suggest that evolution from monkey to human form would come with revelation of the secret of "man's red fire." It highlights that we evolved from a species that was initially able to move quickly through the trees.

Robert Barton, an evolutionary neuroscientist at Durham University in the UK, suggests that growth of the cerebellum was related to the movements of our primate ancestors. When small, these primates would swing from the branches of trees without their feet touching the ground as they moved about in search of food and mates. As the apes increased in size to that of gibbons the branches could no longer sustain their weight. It is likely that this necessitated apes manoeverability bipedally on the ground. This led the human cerebellum to have four times as many neurons as the neocortex. Given the role of the cerebellum in sensorimotor control and sequence learning, cerebellar neuronal organisation may have helped humans evolve both technological capacity and languageThis process, known as braciation, involves fine sensorimotor control and good organisation to visualise and plan your route to get to the desired destination without incident.

Planning a route involves predicting the future. This involves constant readjustments to your direction of travel and movements in terms of speed and strength while scanning the environment for potential pitfalls. I believe this explains the success of SF-EMDR for psychotherapy and optimising performance as mind and body are integrated around the fulcrum of bilateral cerebellar resonance. The hand-held tactile units provide continuous bilateral stimulation analogous to our primate ancestors swinging through the trees. The continuous stimulation of the cerebellum bilaterally enables focus of the mind on the bodily reactions during the therapy session.

The cerebellum is believed to use forward models to compute the likely outcome. This is a rapid-fire process as the mind and body integrate to move in the optimum manner without neurofeedback, which would add an unnecessary delay in response time. It is likely that the primo vascular system, which transmits biophotons as light energy, is also mobilised to signal the brain to respond as quickly as humanly possible.

The cerebellum contains rows of neurons called Purkinje cells linked by parallel sensory fibres and vertical climbing fibres, which are believed to convey error messages which continually correct the forward model used to predict the future. These units are laid out in modular form and connect to different parts of the cortex. This suggests that the cerebellum interacts with the cortex to modulate motor, cognitive, emotional, social, and perceptual function in a similar manner.

It is likely that the ability to learn, plan, predict, and update information was central to the development of the complex behaviours that make us human. Perhaps the driving force behind this was the "eyes in the back of our head, i.e. both cerebellae rather that the prefrontal cortex, as is conventionally believed. The growth of the cerebellum may also have set the scene for language to develop. Some neuroscientists are suggesting that the cerebellum ("should we rename it big brain?") is behind achievements in art, science, and culture.

According to Andy Clark, a philosopher at the University of Edinburgh, UK, the cerebellum may seamlessly synthesise movement, language, and thought as we go about our activities of daily living. These processes occur unconsciously, melding with conscious experience. The conscious learning that is initiated at the cortical level establishes social emotional and perceptional rules. These are transferred to unconscious learning at the cerebellar level. Scarce resources in the cortex are freed for anything urgently needing our attention.

The advantage of this learning model is that subtle social cues are processed with minimum energy expenditure. Rules we already know are applied and revised only when something happens unexpectedly. We can conceive of the cerebellum as our automatic source of cognitions or thought. Having the cerebellum at the back of the brain enhances our capacity for multitasking. Women may be better at this due to cross wiring between the left and right cerebellum at the level of the cerebellar vermis. Thought can now be considered as a kind of movement trapped in the cerebellum. Planning for action is both part of cognition and movement. When you say "Thank your lucky stars" you can thank both cerebellae. It is my belief that SF-EMDR mobilises recovery and peak performance by stimulation of the cerebellum using bone resonance headphones placed over the mastoid processes.

Adolescent brain development

Adolescents have a greater capacity for self-reflection than younger children. Experiments in the 1970s and 1980s have confirmed that adolescence is a time of structural change in the prefrontal cortex.

Glial cells produce myelin, which then envelop brain axons, thereby increasing their rate of transmission 100 times. This process continues throughout childhood and adolescence. In the prefrontal cortex, the brain axons are the last to be fully myelinated, and this may not be completed until the patient is between the ages of twenty-five and thirty.

The sensory pathways (i.e. vision, hearing, taste, touch, and smell), as represented by synapse formation, are entirely dependent on the child's early experiences. Typically, they start to develop at twenty-four weeks' gestation, peak at four months, and complete their development by age seven. Thus, the vision and hearing of a premature baby will be significantly delayed. Language development starts at thirty-two weeks' gestation, peaks at nine months, and reaches maturity at seven. Finally, higher cognitive functions start to develop before birth, peak between one and two years of age, and complete their development around thirty.

There are approximately 100 billion neurons, both at birth and in the adult brain. In the months after birth, new synapses form, that is, synaptogenesis, thus increasing the density of synapses in the infant brain compared to the adult brain. The frequently stimulated synaptic connections are strengthened while infrequently stimulated ones atrophy (i.e. synaptic pruning). The initial period of rapid brain growth is dependent on the infant's environmental experiences and lasts for approximately three to four years, before synaptic density is reduced to adult levels.

In the prefrontal cortex, synaptogenesis occurs in the sub-granular layers during both childhood and adolescence. Following puberty, new synaptic growth plateaus, leading to elimination and reorganisation of the synapses. This synaptic pruning in adolescence decreases synaptic density in the frontal lobes. This has implications for learning and teaching. The superior anterior cingulate cortex is involved in the integration of sensations from the body's viscera.

Why is synaptic pruning an essential component of development of the prefrontal cortex in adolescents?

In adolescence, neural networks become more efficient, and sounder categorisation occurs. There are increased connections between Wernicke's receptive and Broca's expressive areas of the left cerebral hemisphere. In 1993, Pujol, Vendrell, Junqué, and colleagues observed that the fibres of the corpus callosum continue to grow until the patient is in his late twenties. This facilitates inter-hemispheric communication.

The volume of grey matter in the frontal lobe peaks at twelve in males and eleven in females, before declining in adolescence. The peak volume may equate to the wave of synaptogenesis, which occurs before the onset of pruning.

This excess of grey matter at the beginning of puberty allows for the processing of information.

The volume of white matter in the temporal lobe peaks at seventeen for both males and females. As grey matter reduces in the frontal cortex, during adolescence, the myelinated white matter increases in volume. As children develop, their sensory and motor regions mature first, followed by the cerebral cortex in a back-to-front manner. The phylogenetically older parts of the brain develop before the newer areas, such as the prefrontal cortex. The prefrontal cortex is a recent evolutionary development and has been present for about 10,000 years. In comparison, the reptilian parts of the brain have evolved over the past 200 million years. This means the reptilian brain is more hardwired than the neuroplastic prefrontal cortex.

The peak of grey matter development, at the onset of puberty, is due to a new wave of synaptic proliferation. Refinement then occurs, pruning out or eliminating the least-used synapses. This prepares the adolescent brain for more controlled sensorimotor, emotional, and cognitive processing. Testosterone levels in boys may slow down synaptic pruning, making boys clumsier at this stage. Gender differences remain to be fully explained. Some studies suggest grey matter in the frontal cortex continues to be lost until the age of thirty. Others suggest until the age of sixty or longer. There is now felt to be a linear increase in myelinated white matter throughout life, increasing the potential for lifelong learning.

Development of executive functions in the brains of patients and clients

The term "executive function" means coordination of thoughts, feelings, and behaviour. It includes selective attention, working memory, and problem solving, which all improve during adolescence.

Multi-tasking is believed to be a test of perception. This is the ability to hold in mind an intention to carry out an action at a future time. This was tested in children between the ages of six and fourteen, and in adults. An improvement was found between the ages of six and ten, which tailed off between the ages of ten and fourteen. It is possible that the lack of improvement in performance for children aged between ten and fourteen was related to their pubertal status. In the matching-face-and-word task the results revealed that between the ages of eleven and twelve performance declined, compared to the younger children.

Reaction time increased by up to twenty on the match-to-sample task in girls aged ten to eleven and boys aged eleven to twelve, compared to the nine to ten and ten to eleven age groups, respectively. Performance gradually improved from age thirteen to fourteen, reaching pre-pubescent levels by age sixteen to seventeen.

This may explain why adolescents are clumsy during this period of new synaptic development. These new synapses are not fully pruned or connected, making the pubertal frontal cortex less efficient. Only at the end of puberty are these synapses pruned in specialised, efficient networks, allowing performances in general to improve.

Social-cognition development

The development of social cognition is influenced by the person's social experiences consequent to entering a new school. On entering secondary school, both social cognition and self-consciousness are affected. The child's theory of mind, the understanding of others' desires, intentions, and beliefs, is challenged.

Social communication skills are dependent on the perspective of the individual and their understanding of another's perspective. When an action is observed and then performed by an individual, mirror neurons fire. With regard to face-processing of the six Ekman emotions (2003), it was noticed that recognition of fear and disgust improve most with age. There was no improvement in the recognition of sad and angry expressions between the ages of six and sixteen. These findings suggest that puberty interrupts the developmental course of facial recognition (Carey, Diamond, & Woods, 1980). Recovery in recognition of these basic emotions occurs from ages fourteen to sixteen. Future research could involve working with endocrinologists to take saliva swabs of pubertal hormonal levels. This would give a more accurate measure of pubertal status when testing other cognitive and emotional functions.

Risk-taking in adolescents

Adolescents find it difficult to recruit circuits in the brain associated with motivation. This means that more extreme incentives are sought by adolescents in order to compensate. This might include behaviours such as deliberate self-harm, joy-riding, alcohol and drug misuse. By attempting to activate the dorsolateral prefrontal cortex (motivational circuit), more effort is required, as these circuits have not yet matured in the adolescent brain.

When confronted with risk, adults link their gut response to the associated visual image. This is the somatic motor hypothesis (Damasio, 1996). Adolescents try to directly engage their prefrontal cortex, which requires more effort. By helping adolescents to understand this propensity, we might help to minimise their risk-taking behaviour. Based on my clinical experience of dealing with adolescents affected by traumatic events, SF-EMDR psychotherapy can limit their risk-taking behaviours. Girls may have an increased ability to both regulate and contextualise their emotions due to an earlier maturation of their prefrontal cortex. In 2005, Nelson, Leibenluft, McClure, and Pine developed the social information processing network model (SIPNM). A group of young people aged seven to seventeen and a group of adults aged twenty-five to thirty-six viewed faces showing different emotional expressions. The young people showed greater activation of the amygdala, orbitofrontal cortex, and anterior cingulate than their adult counterparts. However, when asked to switch their attention from the emotional expression to a non-emotional property, only the adults were able solely to engage and disengage the orbitofrontal cortex. This suggests that the adults had further development of their emotional processing and cognitive appraisal system compared to the group of young people.

Implications for learning by and teaching of adolescents

Executive function and social cognition are fundamental prerequisites for optimal learning by, and teaching of, adolescents in our secondary schools. Can the curriculum be modified to adapt to key changes in the pubertal brain that reflect this crucial period of neuroplasticity?

How do the processes of axonal myelination, synaptogenesis, and pruning influence learning of subjects such as languages, maths, science, and creativity?

How does the school's physical environment and teacher's knowledge of central nervous system development in their pupils influence the learning process?

The development of social and communication skills from age eight to twelve (known as the skill-hungry years) is a key life stage but is currently mapped against Key Stages Two and Three in settings of two different schools (primary and secondary). Integrating the learning of these years is a challenge in our current educational system but offers the prospect of tackling both antisocial behaviour and lack of engagement in the learning process (Figure 5.1).

This will not only address the intellectual, physical, and participatory aspects of the curriculum, but also foster emotional development and resilience. Teachers having knowledge of the art and science underlying SF-EMDR psychotherapy will be in a strong position to foster the integration and optimisation of these attributes.

During the past ten years, Dr Neil Mercer, Professor of Education and Educational Psychologist at the University of Cambridge, has explored collaborative learning in the classroom.

When children think together, they solve problems with better reasoning. By airing ideas openly and allowing criticism to be non-judgemental, teachers found that the best results were achieved when the classroom sought agreement.

Learner profile

Conversely, an emphasis on individual acquisition of knowledge and on purely analytical reasoning, as is most commonly practised in schools, tended to confirm children's pre-existing biases and prejudices.

Exploratory talk was used to stress sharing relevant knowledge with reasoning and a commitment to collaboration. Teachers agreed the ground rules for talking with the class in advance. Children were divided into groups of three to work on the scheduled task. In evaluating this approach, Professor Mercer (Littleton & Mercer, 2013) noticed the following:

LEARNER PROFILE

Academically capable, qualified, and multi-skilled; self-reliant and rounded; morally responsible and happy

EMOTIONAL

Responsible and mature
Confident, positive, and ambitious
Self-reflective and empathetic
Cooperative and collaborative
Disciplined and resilient
Culturally and globally aware

PHYSICAL

Fit and active
Health-conscious
Presentable
Practical

PARTICIPATORY

Performing arts
Sport
Outdoor activities
Public service and charity

INTELLECTUAL

Versatile
Skilled
Knowledgeable
Inquisitive
Committed

Figure 5.1 An ideal learner profile for children in secondary school. The Student Learner Profile concept is courtesy of Steve Pagan, formerly of Cheadle Hulme School Cheshire, England. This means pupils are academically capable, qualified and multi-skilled, self-reliant and grounded, morally responsible and happy.

1. Improved quality of work of the whole class;
2. More improved reasoning when solving problems;
3. Improved individual attainment surprisingly; and
4. Children showed synergistic social and psychological development.

A future goal for SF-EMDR psychotherapy is to apply the multi-user BOKA machine to a group of ten to twelve teachers to induce them to adopt this approach by overcoming their natural fear of change and the conception that a previous didactic approach was the only route towards achieving high grades for their pupils.

The process builds on the concept that integration of information at the level of the cerebral hemispheres is aided by the concept of three brains in one, explained below.

We can conceive of three brains in one within the human brain. This is a refined hypothesis of the gut- and heart- and head-brain plexi being reflected within the insular cortex and limbic system. The initial information processing occurs at the level of the splanchnic nerves of the gut nervous system. This gut instinct is referred up to the heart, where the cardiac nervous system processes heartfelt emotions and sensations (e.g. tugging at your heartstrings). From here, information is filtered via the sensory thalamus. Depending on the patient's level of arousal, further processing occurs at a conscious or thinking level. This gives further impetus to the theory of cerebellar reprocessing with the patient during SF-EMDR psychotherapy.

Conclusion

An introduction is given to the information-processing difficulties of children and adults with autism spectrum disorders and traumatic stress disorders. The response of the patient to stress in general is discussed, along with the implications for clinical practice and psychotherapists. The developing brain is affected by neglect and abuse. This is related to the polyvagal theory first postulated by Dr Stephen Porges. The relationship between myelination of nerve fibres and the social engagement system is highlighted. This is also related to the development of the cerebellum in the first few years of life. The stages of adolescent brain development are further described, with attention to the role of pruning in the formation of executive functions. The development of social communication skills is a consequence of this pruning and it is related to risk-taking in adolescents. The implications for learning by, and teaching of, adolescents are discussed with an outline learner profile for a child in high school. The role of collaborative learning in the classroom is outlined. This is tied in with the concepts of the gut-brain, heart-brain, and head-brain, as represented within the cerebral cortex.

Chapter 6

The mystery of consciousness and the definition of mind

In his book *Creating the Conscious brain*, Antonio Damasio discusses this mystery. According to Damasio, when the self meets the mind we experience consciousness. He describes the mind as a flow of images and a conscious mind as one containing a self. The self introduces a mental subjective perspective. We become fully conscious when the self comes to mind.

The unison of mind and self creates auditory, skin and neural "maps." The mental experience is closely related to the firing of retinal neurons. Islands of image-making perception provide signals to the association cortex or memory-holding regions of the brain, before sending images back for perception. The self is more elusive. Our brains generate "maps" of the body internally that are used as the reference for all other neural "maps." The "I" in our processing must be stable so that the reference point is one body. The internal milieu must be maintained in a state of homeostasis, otherwise sickness or death occur. The brain and body are tightly coupled, and the brainstem governs breathing, heart rate, and blood pressure. The brainstem nuclei provide neural "maps" allowing the grounding of self to occur, regarding primordial feelings. There is a wealth of cognitive and emotional content stored in the cortex.

The self is built in three stages. The first stage, or proto-self, is a neural description of relatively stable aspects of the organism. The main product of the proto-self is the living body's spontaneous feelings (primordial feelings). In the second stage, a pulse of the core self is generated when the proto-self is modified. This modification is due to an interaction between the person and the object, which results in alteration of the object also. The modified images of both person and object become momentarily linked. The resultant coherent pattern between the person and the object becomes a sequence of images, some of which are also feelings. In the third stage, or autobiographical self, objects in the person's life-story activate the second stage. The second and third stages are subsequently linked logically.

John R. Searle, in his review of Antonio Damasio's book, quotes the following:

...The distinctive feature of brains...is their ability to create maps. Minds emerge when the activity of small neuronal circuits is organised across large networks...to compose momentary patterns (which represent events located outside the brain).

(Damasio, 2010)

The decisive step in the making of consciousness is not the image-making that is at the basis of our mind, but the fact that the images we make are unique to us.

The proto self is an integrated collection of separate neural patterns, mapping moment by moment the most stable aspects of our body. It produces primordial feelings, which are acknowledged and reprocessed in stage one of SF-EMDR psychotherapy.

The core self involves a process whereby images modify the proto self. These images are made conscious by the person's actions.Finally, the autobiographical self contains our sense of person and social identity. It contains a tapestry of life's memories. This analysis adds to the ongoing debate defining and distinguishing the concepts of the mind, self, and consciousness.

The ratio of the corpus callosum to the volume of the hemispheres has become smaller from Homo erectus to Neanderthals to Homo sapiens. It has been surmised that this is due to the specification of language in the left hemisphere (LH).

People who lose the function of their right hemisphere (RH) have a pathological narrowing of the window of attention. In extreme cases, they fail to acknowledge the existence of the left half of their body.

Both hemispheres work together and communicate via the band of fibres known as the corpus callosum.

As humans have evolved, the ratio of corpus callosum to volume of hemispheres has decreased. This has led to different functions between the right and left hemispheres. In conditions such as autism, there is less potential for hemispheric integration.

This shows the consequences for mankind of individual functional tendencies concerning the LH and RH. The static, fixed, and isolated functions of the LH are contrasted with the changing, evolving, and interconnected world of the RH.

The right hemisphere yields a world of the individual. This is changing, evolving, interconnected, implicit, and incarnate. Living beings are represented in the context of their lived world yet are never perfectly known.

The world of the left hemisphere involves a network of small, complicated rules. It is vocal of its own accord. I hypothesise that SF-EMDR psychotherapy, by accelerating interhemispheric neural networks and proliferation of synaptic connections in the patient's connectome, can help reverse the trend of separate hemispheric function.

Thus, two versions of the world, which are combined in different ways, exist inside our heads. In the early part of the sixth century, the hemispheres were more balanced. However, in the fifteenth and sixteenth centuries, the left hemisphere came to dominate, and the more we tended to pursue happiness, the more we were left feeling resentful. This led to an explosion of mental illness. As civilisation pursued freedom, De Tocqueville stated how this was "strangled" by a network of small complicated rules that covered the surface of life. There were limits to rationality, as rationality itself was grounded in a leap of intuition and, according to McGilchrist, the left hemisphere is:

> The Berlusconi of the brain because it controls the media, it's the one with which we … it's very vocal on its own behalf. The right hemisphere doesn't have a voice and it can't construct these same arguments.
>
> (McGilchrist, 2009)

Einstein (Calaprice, 2011) declared that the intuitive mind (RH) is a sacred gift and the rational mind (LH) is a faithful servant. In his world (1888–1955), he felt that society honours the servant but has forgotten the gift. McGilchrist suggests that a fundamental bicameral difference is that the left hemisphere rationalises (the "what" from its narrow perspective) while the right hemisphere "intuits" (the "how" from its much broader perspective). I believe that SF-EMDR psychotherapy can help to redress the tendency of a dominant left hemisphere and restore the primary function of the RH in its intuitive role, as mentioned at the beginning of this book.

The role of asymmetry in the human brain

The divided brain gives us two different, but ultimately complementary, views of the world. The hemispheres are in a power struggle to bring us their own unique experience of the world. As I will explain later, this is influenced by Eastern and Western cultures.

The structure of the brain reflects its history. Each part evolves from, and in response to, an adjacent part. The outer cortex evolved from the subcortical structures, responsible for unconscious biological regulation. The frontal cortex further evolved from the neocortex. The prefrontal cortex has evolved over the last 10,000 years and now comprises forty per cent of the frontal cortex. Our planning abilities, perspective-taking, decision-making, and consequential think-ing arise from here. This may give rise to our quintessential human personality characteristics.

The key components of the peripheral and central nervous systems are:

1. Spinal cord with connections to the periphery;
2. Brainstem with origin of the cranial nerves;
3. Cerebellum with links to prefrontal cortex and brainstem;
4. Limbic system with amygdala, basal ganglia and hippocampus;
5. Neocortex with occipital, parietal, temporal, and frontal lobes,

The neocortex is further divided into the allocortex, which comprises paleocortex and archicortex. These are the cortical parts of the limbic system and have four or five and three layers of neuronal cell bodies respectively. The number of cell body layers relates to the information processing capacity. Thus, the neocortex does the greatest amount of information processing. I have described this as the "quintessential model of the brain."

Sherrington (1906) described "opponent processors" in the brain, which control the sensorimotor system. Kinsbourne (1988), from New York, described three pairings within the head-brain:

1) "Up/down": The cortex exerts downward inhibition of the automatic sub-cortical responses;
2) "Front/back": The frontal cortex inhibits the posterior cortex; and
3) "Right/left": The interrelationship between RH and LH via the corpus callosum, which is discussed in detail in Chapter 7.

The embryological development of the foetal brain

The forebrain is the forward, or rostral, part of the brain. The prosencephalon, or forebrain, divides into the telencephalon and diencephalon. The telencephalon, or cerebrum, contains the cerebral cortex. The diencephalon consists of thalamus, hypothalamus, subthalamus, and epithalamus. The mesencephalon forms the midbrain. Finally, the rhombencephalon, or hindbrain, forms the metencephalon and myelencephalon. The descending neural tracts aggregate as the spinal cord.

At eight weeks' gestation, the heart starts to beat. At ten weeks' gestation, the neural crest divides into tissue that will form both the brain and the gastro-intestinal tract (GIT). Therefore, the GIT has similar neurotransmitter receptors in the brain. This explains why drugs acting on the CNS also exhibit side effects on the GIT. Good examples are the antidepressant drugs known as selective serotonin reuptake inhibitors (SSRI). While it takes up to three weeks for these drugs to show a therapeutic effect, the adverse impact on the GIT (nausea and vomiting) are more immediate.

Frontal lobes of the brain

The frontal lobes have expanded rapidly since they first evolved. Although the latest region of the brain to "come online," they are also the first to shut down at the onset of traumatic stress. Currently, they represent forty per cent of total brain volume. They contain more myelinated white matter for faster neuronal transmission. Under the effect of toxic or traumatic stress, the brain is, therefore, forty per cent less efficient in processing information. The frontal cortex comprises forty per cent of the neocortex and is engaged in the following functions: planning, organising, problem-solving, memory, impulse control, decision-making, selective attention, and controlling our behaviour and emotions.

Frontal lobe injury may affect emotions, impulse control, language memory, and social and sexual behaviour. The left frontal lobe contains Wernicke's and Broca's areas and is responsible for receptive and expressive language.

The frontal lobes help to inhibit the limbic system, or emotional brain and help us to read other people's minds and intentions. By seeing the other person's perspective, we can allow empathy to occur. This is known as "theory of mind" and is crucial for communication and reciprocal social interaction to develop.

At the onset of trauma, blood flow is diverted away from the frontal lobes towards the brainstem. This ensures that breathing, heart rate, and other functions essential to our survival are maintained. Thinking processes are temporarily shut down as they could hamper our instinctive survival reflexes. This blood flow is gradually reversed, as confirmed by feedback from patients during SF-EMDR psychotherapy. They describe a tingling sensation moving from the back of their head to their forehead, which is accompanied by a gradual return to homeostasis. This is often accompanied by a release of light energy from the area of the forehead associated with the sixth chakra and pineal gland. The significance of the pineal gland in processing emotion has been known to cultures as diverse as the Egyptians, Romans, Hindus, and to the philosophers of Ancient Greece.

Yakovlevian torque (Toga & Thompson, 2003) means there is bilateral asymmetry regarding the midsagittal plane of the brain. This might relate to the evolution of language dominance in the left cerebral hemisphere. I would suggest that this bilateral asymmetry provides theoretical support for the use of continuous bilateral cerebellar auditory stimulation during SF-EMDR psychotherapy sessions. The right hemisphere directs its attention to whatever is going on in the outside world. The left hemisphere focuses narrow attention directed to our immediate needs. The left hemisphere prefers what it knows and is led by its expectations. The right hemisphere sees things, and in their context, while the left hemisphere sees things broken up, from which it reconstructs a whole perspective. The brain, therefore, attends to the world in two distinct ways. In one reality (RH), we directly experience the "live" version. In the other (LH), we experience our presented version of reality. Working together, the two hemispheres allow us to know, learn, and make things. We become powerful and authoritative.

What are the functions of the individual hemispheres?

The hemispheres can distinguish five types of attention:

1. Vigilance;
2. Sustained;
3. Alertness;
4. Focused; and
5. Divided.

The intensity axis of attention is a function of the right hemisphere and the selectivity axis of attention is a function of the left hemisphere. Thus, globally, attention is served by both cerebral hemispheres.

Development of ideas on the theory of mind

The right hemisphere explores the environment for attentional intensity. When the right hemisphere prioritises something, this orientates the left hemisphere to focus on it. It grasps the salient features with input from the right half of the body to which it is connected.

The right hemisphere is involved in the person's theory of mind. This is the capacity to "put oneself in another's shoes" and imagine what their feelings, ideas, beliefs, and motivations are. The right hemisphere understands emotions and mediates social behaviour.

The pars opercularis of Broca's area contains mirror neurons for imitating finger movements. The right frontal pole regulates the HPA Axis. The right frontotemporal cortex helps to dampen emotional hyperarousal. The right superior temporal sulcus recognises emotion in faces. Focal intonation (prosody) and gesture are both interpreted by the right hemisphere. The left hemisphere reads blunt emotions by examining the mouth, for example, whether friend or foe. The right hemisphere, on the other hand, can interpret tertiary theory of mind from the eyes alone. All emotions, apart from anger, are connected to the right frontal lobe. The second order theory of mind can be assessed using the Sally–Anne Test.

This false belief task was developed by Wimmer and Perner. Anne has a box and Sally has a basket. Sally puts a marble into her basket and goes outside for a walk. Then Anne mischievously takes the marble from Sally's basket and puts it in her own box. When Sally comes back, she wants to play with her marble. Where does Sally think the marble is? Most four-year-old children say that Sally will look inside her basket, as that is where she thinks the marble is. Younger children, and those with autism, often point to the box, showing that they believe Sally will look where the marble is located. They have not yet developed a second-order theory of mind. This ability is independent of intellect. Thus, children with Down's syndrome have a normally developed theory of mind, whereas many patients with high-functioning autism will have an abnormally developed theory of mind. It appears that this ability is genetically hard-wired in the brain. It remains to be seen whether SF-EMDR psychotherapy could reverse this process in some patients with high-functioning autism.

Baron-Cohen and Wheelwright devised the "revised mind's-eye tests" as a pure test of theory of mind (TOM). There are thirty-six pictures of eyes in total. Each set of eyes is accompanied by four words describing feeling states. Only one is correct. Examples include playful, upset, and desire. Patients with autism are unable to read these facial expressions, as they tend to avoid eye contact, which is a traumatic experience for them. SF-EMDR psychotherapy has the potential to help them overcome this trauma and learn how to process and make sense of this visual information.

In autism, the functions of the right frontal cortex are impaired. These patients have problems with social language, irony, metaphor, empathy, prosody, and the ability to convey meaning and feeling through vocal intonation and inflection. Initial results with SF-EMDR psychotherapy suggest that it helps to integrate cerebellar function and improve impaired frontal cortex function.

Professor Colwyn Trevarthen at the University of Edinburgh first studied the interaction between mothers and infants. His pioneering work shed light on the incredible interactive abilities of the newborn and infant in terms of their functional ability to engage all their senses to enhance the mother–infant interaction (Figure 6.1).

There is a dynamic evolving interaction between mother and infant, which dramatically grows the infant brain from fifty to ninety per cent of adult size in the first four years.

Infants are normally cradled to the left and, therefore, come to attune to their primary caregiver's right hemisphere. This controls the emotionally expressive left side of the adults' face. Close exposure to the left hemiface of the mother puts the baby in touch with emotions and aware of the impact of touch. The first three years of the child's life allow the mother's expressed emotions to be actively perceived. During this time, it is primarily the right hemisphere of the baby that experiences connectome development from the process of synaptogenesis.

In primary intersubjectivity, emotions between mother and baby are both expressed and actively perceived. This lays the foundation for the speech type of communication known as "motherese."

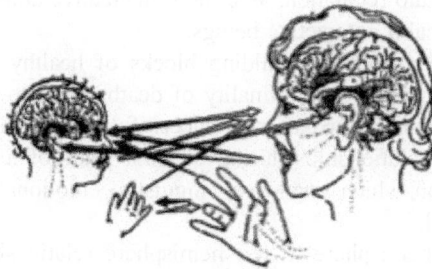

Figure 6.1 This is an illustration of mother–infant protoconversation and rhythmic turn-taking of expressive acts. Mother watches and listens, intuitively anticipating the baby's expressions. She replies playfully with touches, motherese speech, and face and hand expressions. The baby, attracted to the sound of mother's voice, facial expressions, and hand gestures, replies playfully, with affection, imitation, and provoking imitations.
Source: reprinted with the permission of Prof Colwyn Trevarthen.

The baby is attracted to the mother's voice in tone and rhythm. Facial expressions of warmth and positive emotion and hand gestures from the mother elicit playfulness, affection, and reciprocal imitation from the infant. As the mother watches and listens, she intuitively anticipates the baby's expressions. The mother mirrors the infant's vocalisations with "motherese" speech, touch, facial expressions, and hand gestures. A proto-conversation is initiated with this rhythmic turn-taking of expressive acts. As positive emotions are processed, the baby expresses joy freely. A happy, responsive mother matches her infant's arousal. The mutual delight evoked via turn-taking promotes resilience and attunement. However, in these early years, the infant must be allowed to express negative emotions such as moodiness. A mother who can tolerate anger, sadness, and fear in herself and her infant will encourage interactive repair and mutual attunement. If the baby–mother interaction becomes stressed, there may be minimal mother–infant play. The interactive levels of arousal become mistuned, and the mother and infant can become overwhelmed.

Another type of stressful interaction involves the baby withdrawing or becoming non-responsive. This induces negative feelings in the mother, which she is unable to tolerate. The result is mutual frustration and, if prolonged, can lead to developmental delay. The earlier CT scans of a healthy three-year-old and a neglected one demonstrate the profound deleterious effects on growth of the infant's brain that deprivation can have. This was recently brought to media attention in the UK. A child aged four was discovered under a pile of blankets in his cot, having been dead for over two years. His emaciated, shrunken frame was estimated to be the size of a six-month-old baby. The mother was sent to prison, having been convicted of starving him to death.

When the mother and infant are in a state of interactive regulation, the infant seeks out the mother for cooperative regulation and learns self-soothing behaviours. The mother then seeks to regulate her infant's inner state of being. This assists the infant's auto regulation. With both interactive attunement and frequent play, both become calm, interactive beings.

Human relationships are the building blocks of healthy development. From the moment of conception to the finality of death, intimate and caring relationships are the fundamental mediators of successful human adaptation.

These important relationships during the first years of life form the foundation and scaffold on which cognitive, linguistic, emotional, social, and moral development unfold.

When the right hemisphere to left hemisphere relationship is dysregulated, the infant averts their eye gaze, disconnects from the mother, is easily startled, and feels unsafe. The mother is angry and hostile and averts her gaze from the baby. If she suffers with postnatal depression, her still or unresponsive face fails to react to the inner distress of the infant. The infant starts to auto-dysregulate by crying, arching, and then displaying a blank stare and becoming motionless. The baby is exposed to a chronic state of threat with no sense of safety. The mother can be threatening to her baby if the depression becomes delusional. She might be intrusive, unresponsive, or even dissociative to her infant's stimuli. The result is that the mother's confidence as a "good enough mother" is shattered and both she and her infant can become agitated or withdrawn, with little capacity for affect regulation.

The corollaries are an impaired window of tolerance in later life, and this shows the necessity to develop capacity within national health systems for perinatal and infant mental services. This would lay a firm foundation for identifying those at risk of mental health problems in later life. Along with several colleagues, I was trained in the "watch, wait, and wonder" (Muir, Lojkasek, & Cohen, 1999) parent–infant dyadic psychotherapy technique. This involves the mother and infant being together on a mat on the floor surrounded by age-appropriate toys. For the first twenty or thirty minutes, the mother is encouraged to watch her infant and stay near. She then waits for the infant to take the lead in initiating contact. This might prove very difficult for the mother, and the therapist's role is to be supportive at this stage. For the last half an hour of the weekly session, the mother is asked to reflect or wonder what the experience was like, both for herself and for her infant. There is the opportunity to put in place repair of any damage to mother–infant bonding both by the practice of the techniques at home and addressing any unresolved trauma issues for the mother. In our use of this technique in an adult inpatient setting, we found that all the mothers had experienced traumatic stress. This was because of abuse in their own childhoods, trauma at the infant's birth, or from postnatal depression or psychosis. This meant that significant direct trauma-focused therapy was needed by the mothers before they could benefit from the "watch, wait, and wonder" therapy.

Further neuronal development in the infant brain

In later years, the right anterior superior temporal gyrus is activated when the child starts to speak and count. The precuneus exists bilaterally in the parietal lobes. They are activated when we can relate to a first-person perspective, and episodic memory has been established. The right ventromedial prefrontal cortex links emotion and feeling with cognitions and meaning. This is activated by bilateral auditory stimulation during both EMDR and SF-EMDR psychotherapy, due to the use of continuous bilateral cerebellar activation. The RH, which is embodied with the self, produces body language and tone of voice. Body dysphoria and anorexia combine body image disturbance with significant affective distress. SF-EMDR psychotherapy can help to relieve emotional dysregulation associated with these disorders.

The RH regulates the sympathetic nervous system; the parasympathetic nervous system is more under LH control. The former regulates heart rate and blood pressure; the latter boosts body relaxation. The RH pays attention to whatever exists apart from us while the LH attends to its created virtual world. Both hemispheres are involved in all brain functions, despite their lateral specificity. This explains why integration of cerebral hemispheric function would be enhanced during SF-EMDR psychotherapy.

Development of language in the left cerebral hemisphere

The RH is engaged in processing new experiences. Once this is familiar or routine, this information is embedded in the LH. We then know someone, in the sense of a feel for what is distinctive about him or her. This is the kind of knowledge we first think of when talking about the living. The second type of knowledge is facts. Factual knowledge is general, impersonal, fixed, certain, disengaged, put together from individual bits and mostly associated with the LH.

Languages other than English refer to these types of knowledge with different words. In Latin, *cognoscere* is used, in French, *connaître*, and in German, *kennen*. Another Latin example is *sapere*, in French, *savoir*, and in German, *wissen*. Jung said, "all cognition is akin to recognition." This means we come to know (or *cognise/wissen*) something only by recognising (*erkennen*) something we already know (*kennen*). The RH apprehends things when new. The LH takes over when things become more familiar. Thus, initial holistic knowledge becomes fragmented. Knowledge perception and experience exist in the differences between things. Our senses quickly acclimate to constant input (e.g. bilateral auditory cerebellar stimulation). From the age of three, language in the form of sentences tends to emerge.

The neuroplasticity of the brain is such that, in the first eighteen months, infants have a synaptic development of Wernicke's area to such an extent that they can fully comprehend any languages they hear consistently. By the age of two, Broca's area for spoken language has lagged in its development. This explains the frustration of the toddler–parent dyad known as the "terrible twos." It takes about one year for the expressive and receptive parts of the cortex to make sufficient connections for the infant to express their wants and desires. Vulnerable mothers need to be supported during this critical stage of language development.

The BOKA machine used for SF-EMDR psychotherapy can be conceptualised as a "body of knowledge activator." For half a million years, our nearest ancestors had the capacity for some form of communication. The Homo erectus species appeared around 200,000 years ago. Spoken language appears to have evolved around 60,000 years ago. Children use intonation, phrasing, and rhythm as a precursor to syntax and vocabulary. Newborn babies enjoy motherese, which is the music of speech. They have a sense of prosody and rhythm from birth, even if born completely deaf. They do this via right hemispheric holistic processing.

Music was built upon the prosodic mechanisms of the right hemisphere that allow us affective emotional communications through vocal intonations.

Music helps to communicate emotion, which came before language, both phyllo and ontogenetically. Human language may have developed from the gestures of the Ogham language, for example. The metaphor of "grasping" has roots in the description of thinking in different languages. In Latin, *comprehendere*, in German, *be-greifen* or *handeln* describe meaningful, goal-directed human activity. Derivations of the Latin word *tendere* mean to reach out with the hand. This shows the link between gestures and the development of language.

Metaphor links language to life experience and is a function of the RH. Its Greek roots are "*meta*," across, and "*pherein*," to carry. This enables purposeful thought via embodiment and placing it within a living context. In practising SF-EMDR psychotherapy, I am constantly drawing the attention of the patient to their statements using a metaphor.

McGilchrist argues that thought, structure and content have an earlier bodily existence before being processed in Broca's area of the LH as speech. Language is an extension of life. As Wittgenstein stated:

> Our language is an ancient city: a maze of little streets and squares and of houses with additions from various periods and this surrounded by a multitude of new boroughs with straight regular streets and uniform houses... And to imagine a language means to imagine a form of life.
>
> (Wittgenstein, 1973)

Language is an embodiment of emotion. It has origins in music and rhythm (e.g. drumbeat) and is registered via the anterior cingulate cortex before cerebral reprocessing. Music is beneficial to the group rather than the individual, and both dolphins and whales have comparatively enlarged anterior cingulate cortices, which facilitate their ability to communicate across large distances. Indeed, the brains of dolphins and humans are of equal size, despite their diverse evolutionary habitat.

Evolution of the infant's brain into functioning adult right and left hemispheres

During infancy, the RH matures first, followed by the LH from the third year onwards as speech and language areas become myelinated and activated. By years five and six, the RH starts to evolve the capacity for emotionality and prosody of language. The right frontal lobe serves functions such as empathy, humour, irony, imagination, creativity, capacity for awe, music, dance, poetry, art, love of nature, moral sense, ability to conceptualise, to think consequently, and how to change your mind. My experience of using SF-EMDR psychotherapy is that patients experience new sensations in their frontal lobes at the final stage of reprocessing. At this point, it can be postulated that both frontal lobes are benefiting from activation by continuous bilateral cerebellar stimulation.

Consequentially, these functions may be enhanced. According to McGilchrist, the RH reaches out while the LH has an end in mind, as if directed by conscious will. The RH tends to seek out hemispherical coherence while the LH is its master's valued emissary. The LH is purposeful while the RH attends to what is out there. Thus, the brain evolves a dual perspective according to the perspectives of both hemispheres. The LH might initially be unaware of the primary awareness of the RH. Which version of the "truth" are we to believe?

On the one hand, there is broad vigilant attention and wholeness of the RH worldview, whereas, on the other hand, trans-formation and re-presentation by the LH occurs using its functions of separation, division, and analysis. The LH makes the implicit explicit and is directed by conscious will. In its turn, the RH delivers an experience to the LH, which is bound by context and incorporates affective awareness. According to Panksepp (1988), this affective awareness is the prerequisite for perception and cognition.

SF-EMDR psychotherapy focuses on the primacy of our affective experience. Descartes opined, "*cogito ergo sum*" (I think; therefore, I am) and led the movement for mind–body dualism. In the twenty-first century, we are entering an era of reintegration of mind and body. I believe a more prescient axiom is "*affectio ergo sum*" becoming "*sum ergo sum.*" Feeling (from Latin *affectio*) is at the heart of our being and from emotion humankind has developed logic and reasoning. This is a significant shift from Cartesian dualism. Damasio states, in *Descartes Error*:

> Nature appears to have built the apparatus of rationality not just on top of the apparatus of biological regulation but also from it and with it.
>
> (Damasio, 2006)

Achieving affective regulation for the patient is a key function of SF-EMDR psychotherapy along with the parallel integration of the influences of nature and nurture.

The Mindful Therapist by Dan Siegel is a clinician's guide to mindsight and neural integration. Over a period of thirty years Dan has been working with a group of scientists from a variety of disciplines to come to a consensus about a definition of the mind. They concluded:

> *After much discussion, they decided that a key component of the mind is: the emergent self-organising process, both embodied and relational, that regulates energy and information flow within and among us.*" It's not catchy. But it is interesting, and with meaningful implications.
>
> (Siegel, 2010)

As the mind has a regulatory function, this involves both monitoring and modifying our immediate environment. A good example is what happens when driving a car. The learner driver displays conscious competence. With increasing practice this becomes unconscious competence. However, we may have other things on our mind than the traffic and the road ahead. This causes highway hypnosis, which is one of the earliest signs of a dissociative process. As the mind's working memory becomes overloaded with conversation, information from the radio, telephone, or other devices, the mind becomes less well able to regulate the flow of energy and information, conscious or unconscious incompetence can result in an accident.

To help develop these functions of the mind Dan has outlined a series of exercises in his book. Many are based on mindfulness practices such as the seven-element exercise described in this book.

The thirteen chapters are hypothesised in the letters PAR & 12 Ts:

1. **Presence.** This is the ability to create an integrated sense of being that develops from a temporary state into a permanent trait. We are then flexible, adaptable, coherent, energised, and stabilised. This links to my description of RAPIDS, CALM WATERS, and FROZEN in FEAR states described in Figure 2.2.

2. **Attunement.** This occurs during SF-EMDR for psychotherapy and peak performance as the client becomes aware of all incoming sensations related to the target memory. It involves focused attention and clear perception. Both practitioner and client use different sets of cortical mirror neurons to establish postural and therapeutic rapport and even internally simulate the other's mental state. In a recent case the patient was about to describe a traumatic childhood memory on the way to school. This was a twenty-minute journey and dad nagged me incessantly. . . . . .

I interrupted to say, "He got you to say your times tables and you were frightened in case you made a mistake."

He was astonished to discover that this was exactly what had been on the tip of his tongue to say. I also noticed that as he was talking, his mouth and cheek muscles became contorted. When I drew his attention to this sensorimotor memory he remembered events as an infant. He was born with torticollis. This meant that his neck muscles were weak on the right side and his head was permanently tilted to the left. For the first six months, his mother had to do daily exercises to push his head to the opposite side to allow him to hold his head up straight. This was extremely painful. A consequence of this was that for years in early childhood he could only speak using the cheek muscles on the left side of his mouth. He was extremely conscious of this, especially as his dad would embarrass and tease him at home and in public for 'looking stupid." My client said that he consciously tried to use the muscles on the right side of his cheek to talk properly. It was this somatic perception that led to his contorted facial expressions and meant that applying the buzzers to each cheek had an instant remedial effect.

3. **Resonance.** This helps to make the psychotherapist and patient or executive coach and client part of one system. We become immersed in the unknown and face-to-face with uncertainty. This idea resonates with the four-stage creative cycle discussed by Prof Ernest Rossi. Bringing the repressed feelings up to the skin surface from the inside for reprocessing along new neural pathways has been my clinical experience during the ten years I have practiced SF-EMDR for psychotherapy, optimal functioning, and peak performance.

1. **Trust.** This involves the experience of love without fear. It develops in the first year of life with good-enough parenting. If the infant experiences fear through neglect, abuse and trauma the resultant absence of love causes mistrust. In later life trust emerges with acts of compassion and loving kindness. We move from states of possibility to actuality to a series of probabilities. This brings us to a quantum state of consciousness. Different transformation of energy occurs including sound, kinetic, meridian, light, electrical, chemical, magnetic, gravitational, and involves photons and subatomic particles.

2. **Truth.** This involves an integrated coherent world-view. The mind can be conceived to be like an ocean. Becoming mindful of the inhalation and exhalation of the breath can help to bring you to the calm depths and the bottom of the ocean. You are then able to cope with the storms and choppy waters at the surface, trusting that you will be safe until the storm abates and the calm waters return.

3. **Tripod.** We shape our inner world through observation, openness, and objectivity. John O'Donoghue, the Irish poet and author of *Anam Cara* and *Eternal Echoes* said to Dan Siegel;

    > I'd love to live like a river and be carried by the surprise of my own unfolding.
    >
    > (Siegel, 2010)

    This is a perspective that recognises the integration of time and how, like sand, it slips easily through our fingers.

4. **Triangle of well-being.** This involves the mind, body, and relationships. The brain is integrated, you have empathic relationships and a coherent resilient mind. Information and sensation are forms of energy flowing through the body mind and can now be added to the biopsychosocial and spiritual model of completely integrated health.

5. **Tracking.** This involves paying attention to sight, smell, sound, touch, taste, and bodily information of our mental activity and outside relationships. The gamma-frequency range of stimulation used in SF-EMDR helps tracking of these different sensations bringing about thalamocortical binding neuroception and conscious knowing.

6. **Traits.** Dan Siegel and others explored personality pathways as patterns of developmental pathways involving core motivations, emotional reactivity, primary orientation bias, and adaptive strategies. They showed that traits can change over time.

7. **Trauma.** This has been thoroughly discussed throughout this book. As described, traumatic experiences impair integration of the calm waters, and patients oscillate from rapids to frozen in fear states. Implicit memory is ninety to ninety-five per cent SF-EMDR, while explicit memory is five to ten per cent cognitively stored. Implicit awareness usually emerges at the

level of the umbilicus and travels to the head via the heart and the throat. Once these body memories have integrated, healing of the traumatic wounds is activated.

8. **Transition.** This involves staying with degrees of probability and diversity. Also, as time passes peaks of activation are noticed. This leads to plateaus of probability and the planes of possibility leading to actuality. In the quantum state, we can allow all these ways of being to exist and associate. In my opinion, for the treatment of dissociative identity disorder (DID), more time should be spent on integrating or associating parts than encouraging them to be perceived separately.

9. **Training.** I will be commencing training for suitably qualified psychotherapists interested in the top-down and bottom-up model of reintegration using SF-EMDR for psychotherapy, optimal functioning, and peak performance. Details of presentations are posted on the website www.artomalley.com

10. **Transformation.** At the end of therapy, consciousness should be integrated in the following domains; horizontally, vertically, temporally, narratively, via states of self, interpersonally, and with calmed and contained memories.

11. **Tranquillity.** The optimally functioning patient will experience a sense of wholeness, with intuition, creativity realising their full potential. The word "no" is reframed as "know," increasing receptivity and potential for change. The world is engaged with a tranquil heart and body-mind.

12. **Transpirational integration.** This is a breathing across interconnected states of awareness. It is a recognition of connection of communities and between selves and is essential for our survival as a species. I hope you can understand the need to widen our circle of compassion, as in helping others we help ourselves.

Conclusion

The work of Antonio Damasio in his book *Self Comes to Mind: Constructing the Conscious Brain* is discussed, where he illustrated the mental maps in the brain. He described three stages of development: the proto self, core self, and autobiographical self. The relationship of these self-stages to SF-EMDR psychotherapy is compared.

Dr Iain McGilchrist has written a classic text, *The Master and His Emissary*, outlining the respective roles of the right and left hemispheres. A YouTube video presentation highlights the significant differences in function between the hemispheres. As the volume of the corpus callosum has decreased over time, so specialisation between hemispheres has increased. The role of asymmetry in the human brain is discussed, along with its embryological development.

The concepts of theory of mind are explained alongside its facilitation by appropriate attunement of mother and infant. The early development of the infant brain is explained, including the development of language. A potential way forward for perinatal and infant mental health services is described, using the "watch, wait, and wonder" psychotherapeutic approach. This links to the ancient origins of language, music, and communication between animal species such as birds, whales, and dolphins. The evolution of the infant brain into adult right and left hemispheres is dependent on experience. SF-EMDR psychotherapy can play a role in optimising this process and focuses on the primacy of affective, compared to cognitive, experience. Hence, I make the case for it being an effective, if not essential, precursor to cognitive-behavioural therapy. Until the affective component of trauma has been activated and reprocessed, it has not registered in the prefrontal cortex for cognitive reappraisal. Hence, CBT initiated before this stage is more likely to prove ineffective. This has implications for the effectiveness of trauma-focused therapy within mental health services. This chapter concludes with a summary of the 15 aspects of mindful consciousness referred to by Dr Dan Siegal in his book, *The Mindful Therapist*.

Chapter 7

Development of thought and the role of SF-EMDR for psychotherapy and peak performance in reprocessing thoughts

Conscious thought accounts for about five per cent of brain activity. The first manifestation of thought is its global synthetic form generated by the right hemisphere (RH). Hand and other gestures become integrated with speech production once the left hemisphere (LH) becomes activated. The words generated from thought patterns are segmented linearly and hierarchically as both hemispheres and gestures combine. These influences reverberate reciprocally in the forebrain. The thought processes that begin in the RH are sent to the LH for processing and re-presentation. This is recycled to the RH, becoming a new synthesis of the original recalled experience. This helps to explain why bilateral cerebellar activation in SF-EMDR psychotherapy facilitates patient's reprocessing. I would argue that all forms of psychotherapy would benefit from this augmented form of inter-hemispheric communication. It promotes unification between the left hemispheric division of information and the right hemispheric tendency towards wholeness. In other words, thesis and antithesis are combined as a synthesis. The role of individuation from the LH is integrated with that of coherence from the RH. The rationality of the LH is subject to the intuitive wisdom of the RH. Knowledge of the five stages of SF-EMDR psychotherapy and of peak performance helps to bring these perspectives together. Also, as the therapist seeks to identify and locate anatomically points of maximum distress, this can highlight areas resistant to information reprocessing. They can use this knowledge to hypothesise which hemispheric functions are most compromised and need to be accentuated.

Theories on the origin of consciousness

Panksepp (1988) believes it starts at the periaqueductal grey matter in the midbrain before migrating through the cingulate, temporal, and frontal regions of the cortex. An analogy is made of a forest canopy being akin to a cerebral canopy. This is like a tree growing upwards from roots deep within us. The primacy of affect in generating consciousness is the approach of this neuroscientist. As our cerebral canopy has evolved, we are aware of greater empathy with the world at large and develop the capacity for abstraction.

Dr Stuart Hameroff and professor Sir Roger Penrose have collaborated over the last twenty years in this field. Their hypothesis is known as orchestrated objective reduction or ORCH OR and was first proposed in the 1990s. The orchestrated "OR" relates to the quantum state and is assumed to result in moments of conscious awareness. In 2013 Penrose and Hameroff introduced the concept of beat frequencies of speeded-up vibrations of microtubules. The activity of microtubules was below the level of neurons at 10^{16} operations per second. Three theories of the origin of consciousness have been proposed:

1. Consciousness is not an independent quality but arose, in terms of conventional processes, as a natural evolutionary consequence of the biological adaptation of brains and nervous system;
2. Consciousness is a separate quality, distinct from physical actions, not controlled by physical laws, that has always been in the universe. In the view of Descartes, panpsychism, and religious viewpoints, consciousness lies outside science. Many critics of the first edition of this book spoke of it as being "pseudoscience," as they were unaware of the scientific evidence linking consciousness and spirituality; or
3. Consciousness is considered to result from discrete events, that have existed as non-cognitive or proto-conscious moments. Their interaction with universal physical laws is yet to be fully elucidated. In this view consciousness is an intrinsic feature of universal action.

Unexplained features of consciousness

These include the following:

- How and why do we have the phenomenon of consciousness as an inner life of subjective experience? This is known as the "hard problem";
- How does the brain bind its different sensory inputs into unified conscious content? I have discussed the theory of thalamocortical binding earlier in the book and SF-EMDR psychotherapy is believed to help significantly with this "binding" problem;
- Brain activity may be synchronised over large zones. It may be that the synchrony problem reflects discrete unified conscious moments. It is my belief that SF-EMDR psychotherapy's continuous bilateral stimulation at gamma-frequency range can optimise this synchronisation;
- Penrose has shown in Gödel's theorem that "understanding" comes from a non-computable effect. This effect has yet to be fully explained; and
- Single cells without a nervous system engage in intelligent behaviour. How do they swim, find food, mate, learn, and remember without a single synapse? This brings us to the microtubules, which may encapsulate quantum consciousness. In dendrites and the cell body of neurons microtubules are interrupted and interconnected by microtubule-associated

proteins. Microtubules in axons are continuous. Gap junctions exist and may enable entanglement and integration of information at the level of microtubules from nearby neurons. Dendrites, cell body, and microtubules combine to trigger synaptic firing along the axon. It is these axonal firings that control behaviour and are an essential component of quantum computations postulated in ORCH OR.

Quantum physics and consciousness

Penrose published *The Emperor's New Mind* in 1989 to examine the inter-relationship between consciousness and quantum mechanics. He further refined the measurement problem in quantum theory by introducing an objective form of quantum state reduction (OR). The energy (E) of a particle is related to the fundamental frequency (v) of its oscillation. If h = Planck's constant, then E=hv.

This emphasises the fact that quantum phenomena have both wave and particle qualities. In classical mechanics objects have specific locations and states. In quantum mechanics particles can exist in two or more states at the same time, i.e. superposition. Non-local entanglement is another property of the quantum state, which can combine with classical signalling to result in quantum teleportation. Objective reduction occurs when there is conflict between unitary evolution (U) and collapse of the wave function due to observation denoted by R.

Schrödinger's cat thought experiment

The cat is in a box exposed to a quantum event involving radioactivity that would, according to superposition, result in the cat being dead and alive at the same time. Both Einstein and Schrödinger considered quantum mechanics an incomplete theory needing improvement to deal with the problems of this thought experiment.

Diósi-Penrose proposed a bridge between quantum and classical physics as a "quantum-gravitational" phenomenon. The ORCH OR model proposes a quantum-state reduction leading to a moment of proto-consciousness.

Quantum conductance through photosynthesis

During photosynthesis photons are absorbed into a protein complex and this is converted to chemical energy to make food. This appears to have similarities to the collapse of the wave function proposed in tubulin and microtubules. The exciting finding is that mechanical vibrations administered through the skull to the brain modify electrophysiology, behaviour, affects, and mood. This may be by direct excitation of brain microtubules. My hypothesis is that this can be achieved during the continuous stimulation that occurs in SF-EMDR psychotherapy.

Beat frequencies

Beat frequencies arise when orchestrated objective reduction (ORCH OR) is applied to super-positions of energetically different quantum states. The periods identified are 25ms for 40 Hz gamma synchrony and within a range of 30–90 Hertz of gamma synchrony. My current BOKA machine for delivering this beat frequency has a range of 1 to 60 Hertz. The next iteration will have a range compatible with the wider gamma range to facilitate greater thalamocortical binding during SF-EMDR psychotherapy sessions. Penrose and Hameroff propose heightened enhanced conscious moments occurring every 12.5ms at a frequency of 80 Hz gamma synchrony combined with low-intensity conscious moments occurring every 250ms and interspersed with 4 Hz delta frequency. These gamma waves represent conscious moments nested in delta waves and may represent beat frequencies exhibited by faster vibrations of microtubules. This relates to the buzz of thought discussed earlier in the book. During quantum superposition, reprocessing of information and regulation of neurons occurs. Microtubules are central to this process in the theory of ORCH OR. In the human brain, up to 100,000 neurons are believed to be involved in conscious moments. Microtubules evolved from symbiosis among prokaryotes, mitochondria, and spirochetes in eukaryotic cells 1.3 billion years ago. This led to pursuit of pleasurable conscious experiences, e.g. food and sex. As ORCH OR evolved, quantum cognitive systems become more powerful.

Components of orchestrated objective reduction as it applies to consciousness

This theory proposes that consciousness consists of a series of distinct events or moments of "objective reduction" (OR) of a quantum state. These quantum states are assumed to exist because of quantum computations occurring in neuronal microtubules. There needs to be orchestration of the OR events for consciousness to occur. OR is designated as the bridge between the worlds of classical and quantum physics. In brain science Alzheimer's disease, body and brain trauma, and other psychiatric disorders are related to microtubule disturbances. ORCH OR conscious moments at 40 Hz gamma synchrony are now seen as beat frequencies coupled to neuronal membrane physiology and account for some correlates of consciousness. The ORCH OR proposal suggests that there is an intrinsic link between conscious experience and the structure of four-dimensional space-time geometry. In summary, SF-EMDR psychotherapy for all the reasons underlined is ideally placed to apply the ORCH OR theory for the clinical benefit of a wide range of patients.

Quantum field theory (QFT) of neuroscience underpinning SF-EMDR for psychotherapy, optimal functioning, and peak performance

Psychosocial and genomic influences interact with the body-mind during EMDR. A crisis develops at the peak level of arousal. The therapist–client relationship stimulates mirror neurons, activating intuition. There is an opportunity for gene expression via DNA translation and transcription. The gut mesentery (mesentery) acts to regulate immune nervous endocrine and circulatory systems. The messenger proteins, neurotransmitters hormones, and immune cytokines are linked to the mind–body response and its mental, physical, emotional, and spiritual energy fields (cf. Chapter 2). QFT, when formulated as underlying EMDR, leads to reduced stress and psychosomatic illness and a meditation-like REM state that is ideal for reprocessing. Finally, after 90–120 min continuous BLS the client reaches their peak performance in terms of problem-solving and creativity.

Quantum Bayesianism (QBism)

This theory predicts that the wave function used by the observer (patient) has no objective reality as quantum and probability theory are combined. Instead Quantum information exists only in the imagination. Prof Rossi can now outline a QB theory (Figure 7.1).

Complex cycle of information exchange occurs in psychotherapy

This includes consciousness, unconscious factors, emotion, sensations, feelings, and sensory-motor aspects of physical and mental health all in a network of the Quantum Field. This can be perceived at the level of psychoneuroimmunology. There is an integration of the cells of mind with the central and peripheral nervous systems and the soma. This facilitates development and reprocessing of memory, learning of new behaviour, and verification, reintegration thinking, and meaning at the end of the 120 min therapeutic encounter. There is extracellular RNA flow between mind and body in all body fluids, i.e. saliva, tears, blood, sweat, urine, and lymph.

The diagram below (Figure 7.2) starts with stage 1 of the four-stage creative cycle. This is the initial process of assessment to document the presenting problems and their associated SUDS level (0-10), which the patient or client wants resolved in their day-to-day life. As the consultation progresses we enter stage 2. The patient looks inside for a solution and confronts any cognitive dissonance and uncertainty. This stage has been referred to metaphorically as the "storm before the light" or the "dark night of the soul." I refer to stage 3 as the "lightbulb" or "aha" or "eureka" moment. This is the point at which intuition breaks through into insight and a

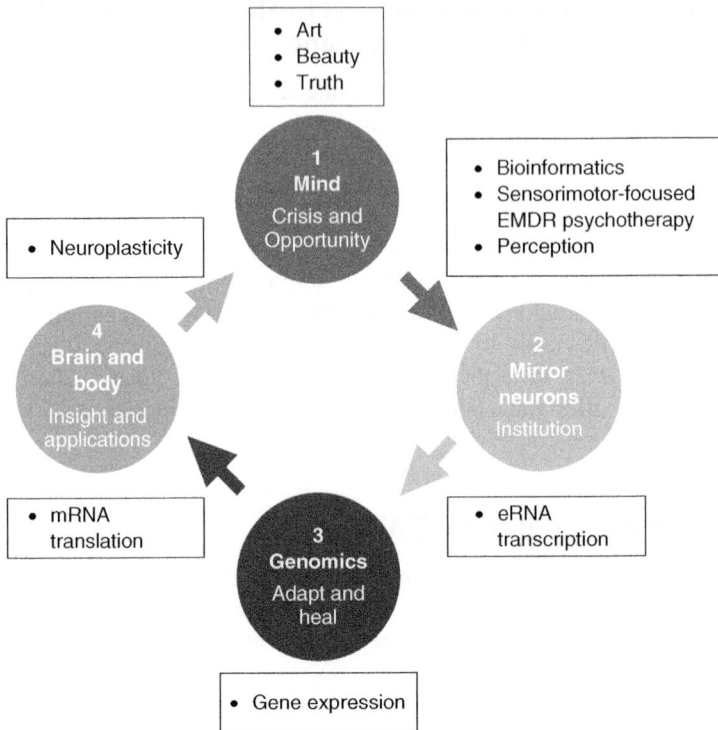

Figure 7.1 There is a classical cycle of body-mind and gene interacting with molecular biology, consciousness, and cognition. Circle 1 reflects just-noticeable differences (JND) from research in 1890s. This is combined with art, beauty, and truth as quantum biology merges with psychology. Prof Rossi now proposes that subjective novelty evokes Numinosum. This incorporates fascination, mystery, and tremendousness. These are translated at a genomic level causing growth of the brain and evolving consciousness and cognition. Circle 2 represents how two million enhancer RNAs in the environment convey signals to genes with over three million docking sites or receptors. This modifies genes and their cellular messengers to Circle 3. Healing and adaptive regions on the DNase sites promote transcription and translation of healthy DNA with preserved length of telomere. Circle 4 shows the links between brain and body-mind. The behaviours associated with the dopamine DRD4 receptor gene appears to be an example of the novelty-numinosum-neurogenesis-effect (NNNE). This is hypothesised to act via the observer/operator interaction at a quantum level.

Source: reproduced with permission from Prof Ernest Rossi.

solution to the problem being worked on emerges. The 120-minute time frame is essential to allow new neural patterns to develop on the background of new gene expression producing amino acid combinations that interact with DNA and RNA translation and transcription as new proteins. Finally, stage 4 consolidates the

CRISIS/OPPORTUNITY

$$\Delta x \Delta p \geq \hbar/2$$

$pq - qp = -i\hbar$

$pq - qp = I\,\hbar/2$

2 Ob/Op Period of private inner work and creative replay

3 Illumination:
Breakout and insight
Positive experience
Intuition

Incubation:
Review and conflict
Negative experience
Feeling

AROUSAL

RELAXATION

Proteomics

$|\psi>$ **1**

$<\Phi|$ **4**

Data collection:
Initiation
Sensations

Genomics

Verification:
Reintegration
Thinking

Time in Minutes

0   30   60   90   120

Ultradian performance peaks

Ultradian healing responses

AWAKE

Breaking point

Maximum Cortisol Peak

Maximum testosterone peak

Maximum growth Hormone release

Nightly dreams

ASLEEP

Midnight   Noon   Midnight

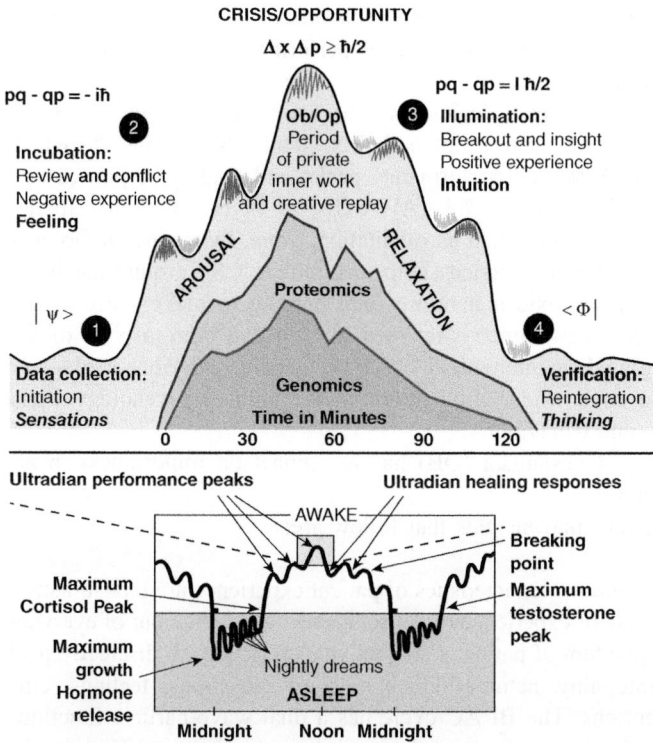

Figure 7.2 This illustrates a fundamental scientific principle of body–mind psychotherapy such as the sensorimotor-focused EMDR Human Givens approach and brief effective psychotherapy. The therapeutic encounter is mapped onto the 90 to 120 min basic rest–activity cycle or BRAC. The creative cycle is composed of: (a) initiation sensations and data collection; (b) incubation with review of any conflict negative emotions and feelings. These are activated with buzzers, bone resonant headphones and a "magic" remote. This facilitates some private inner work and creativity to rework and rewind the trauma (Human Givens); (c) a Eureka moment of illumination. The patient's body language becomes animated. The use of the light-stream guided visualisation helps illuminate the problems. The negative emotions and feelings are dissolved. Once the subjective units of distress scale (SUDS) levels at 0 or 1 there can be installation of positive thoughts, feelings, and experience once the traumatic event can be viewed ecologically (SF-EMDR and Human Givens); and (d) with all bilateral stimulation finally switched off there is the prospect of rewired neural networks in the prefrontal cortex allowing for thinking space and internal verification. Later reappraisal, over the next few days, with final reintegration of traumatic memories, allows the patient to move on in their life with increased self-confidence and self-esteem. The lower part of the diagram shows how consciousness, cognition, emotions, and feelings are experienced within the circadian and ultradian cycles. Note, with increasing stress there is a point where healing responses are overwhelmed and the person snaps (breaking point or nervous breakdown).

Source: reproduced with permission from Prof Ernest Rossi.

growth cycle with these neural networks synapsing in the frontal cortex as positive cognitions and an adaptive information process. This can lead to improved self-esteem, emotional resilience, and peak performance in the chosen goals decided by the patient or client.

The small rainbows depicted in the lower half of Figure 7.3 illustrate the multiple phases of activity of both RNA and DNA during the REM dreaming cycle (ASLEEP). The performance peaks and healing responses are shown in the top half of Figure 7.3 (AWAKE). It is believed that therapeutic and relaxation techniques such as meditation, yoga, hypnosis, Qi Gong, Buddhism, and other prayerful practices help to circulate CSF around the brain, cleaning any build-up of toxic metabolites and helping to make sense of daily experiences. There is asymmetry between the top and bottom parts of the diagram. This integrated quantum field has been generalised from maths, physics, and biology to cover wider applications in the field of psychology, consciousness, cognition, and behaviour.

Quantum Bayesianism (QB) has an impact on mindfulness in all forms of psychotherapy

The fundamental insights that follow are:

1.   The quantum characteristics of patient experience are probabilistic, not definitive, in their experience of consciousness and behaviour of everyday life;
2.   The quantum of patient's subjective experience are discreetly packaged into separate, tiny, natural Planck units of sensations, feelings, emotions and perceptions. The BRAC cycle has a dual wave-particle function like light, and what we see depends on how we observe. This is the ultimate demonstration of Heisenberg's uncertainty principle;
3.   QB dynamics can be observed at all levels from body-mind to genes in all living systems on planet earth. This was the great insight of Bohr, Dirac, Heisenberg, and Schrodinger. Thus, from microscopic to the entire universe quantum field theory applies; and
4.   There is a central role for QB expectancy in a world full of uncertainty. A new consciousness is being recognised, with emergent cognitive emotions, feelings, sensations, free will, and even reality itself. The merging of this mathematical view of psychotherapy allows for a coherent scientific rationale of the healing therapeutic relationship to emerge. This will hopefully lessen the need for different schools of psychotherapy to seek self-justification and lessen the influence of politics as has happened with the predominance of CBT as the preferred model of psychotherapy in improving access to psychological therapies (IAPT) in the NHS of the UK.

Development of the basic rest–activity cycle or (BRAC)

Dreaming is an expression of the incubation stage two of the BRAC cycle. The theory of probability in QB relates to the transition and translation of adaptive

The Domain of Hypnotherapeutic Work

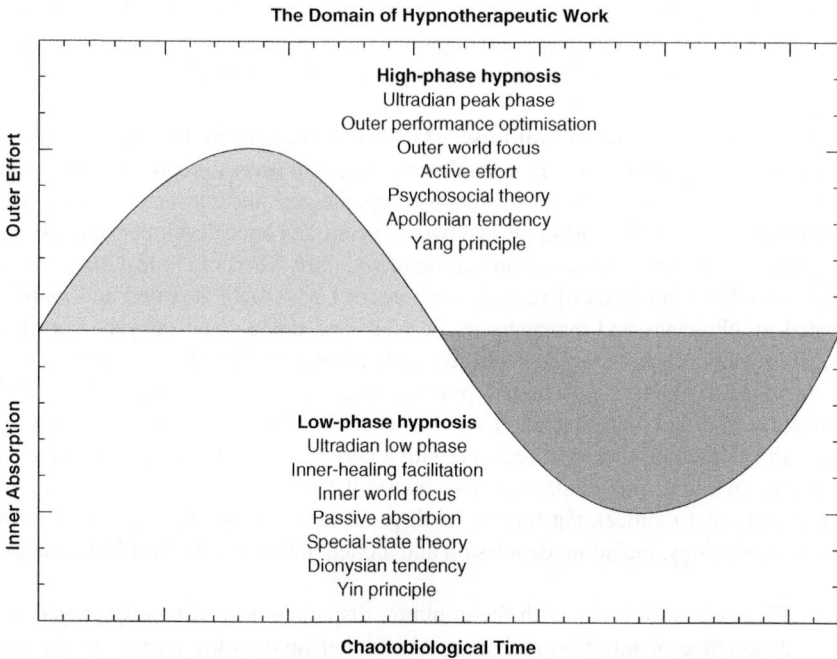

Figure 7.3 Some research illustrates how the overarching domain of psychotherapy is a wave function of chatobiological time from the maths of chaos theory. This has led to a call to reorient the education, theory, and practice of psychotherapy, especially the sensorimotor-focused EMDR Human Givens approach, and brief effective psychotherapy. This represents a two-dimensional pyramid profile of the four-stage creative process. The performance peaks are illustrated in red and alternate with low phases of healing and recovery shown in green. These occur during the 90–120 min BRAC cycle. This must become the default time period for effective psychotherapy and has been my practice for the last ten years. In my clinical experience four two-hour sessions are much more cost-effective in promoting recovery than eight one-hour sessions. The one-hour session is a throwback to the fifty-minute hour common to psychoanalysis and has no neuroscientific rationale as Prof Ernest Rossi's definitive research proves. The bottom half of the figure shows the clearing of the daily build-up of toxic metabolic-waste products associated with the activities of daily living (ADL) during sleep (green) and dreaming (rainbow colours).

Source: reproduced with permission from Prof Ernest Rossi.

replication of both RNA and DNA. This changes the experience dependent dynamics of gene expression during the consultation. The patient develops brain neuroplasticity which allows for enhanced therapeutic possibilities.

Following a good night's sleep the client's brain is cleared of toxic metabolites, which allows gene and protein expression. Brain neuroplasticity is activated allowing a new consciousness and thinking space to emerge for verification and reintegration in BRAC stage four. This cycle occurs twelve times each day. This allows optimal evolution of life consciousness and cognition and reprocessing of sensations, emotions, and feelings interlinked with endocrine, immune, nervous, lymphatic and other second-messenger systems.

Practical implications of Prof Rossi's QFT of physics, maths, biology, chemistry, and psychology are to tune in at an observer/operator level to reprocess acute and chronic stress, which generates most psychopathology and substance-misuse disorders and addictions. During the last twenty years, as I have developed and refined my therapeutic approach based on neurobiology, thirty years of clinical experience, feedback from hundreds of related conferences I have both attended and participated in, clinicians and managers in the NHS and doctors and lawyers from the GMC have persistently targeted, bullied, and harassed me for what they perceive as a focus on trauma. They claim I practise in a way not promulgated by NICE guidance and that I am not fit to practice as a CAMHS consultant. This is even though I am on the specialist register, with a certificate of completion of specialist training in child and adolescent psychiatry (CCST) since 2004. They fail to appreciate that reprocessing trauma in all patients will lessen the impact of most psychopathology, including depression and anxiety disorders. As Prof Rossi states:

> We need to do away with the common disparagement of merely subjective experience of intuition and imagination that favours the pursuit of the so-called virtues of objective and rational thinking ... We need to transcend the stale, reductive ideologies and manipulative models of psychotherapy as stimulus/response conditioning, gaming, programming, suggestion, and dry cognitive behavioural transactions.
>
> (Rossi, 2004)

This considered statement has major implications for NICE and the NHS which employ a CBT model, as political influence is greatest for this treatment modality.

Prof Rossi has elucidated the novelty-numinosum-neurogenesis-effect (NNNE). I propose that SF-EMDR and brief effective psychotherapy alongside the Mirroring Hands Protocol are consistent with QFT cognition and consciousness. The unconscious processes referred to by Freud and Jung can now be updated using QFT and the ZX calculus. The subjective experience of the patient can achieve unconscious communication with the psychotherapist. According to Milton Erickson this is of paramount importance during the four-stage creative cycle.

The role of sleep is crucial in homeostasis when well but impaired in PTSD, and disturbed sleep is a key early-warning sign of psychopathology

The body-mind during sleep is cleared by sixty per cent more cerebrospinal fluid, which is washed through the spinal cord and brain to remove any toxic by-products of metabolism that may have accumulated during that day. Sleep is a chance to optimise self-care and health via epigenetics and RNA/DNA transcription and translation.

The rise of drama in Ancient Greece initially objectifies the thoughts and feelings of others and us. Through ownership of these thoughts and feelings, we gain insight. Crucially, we achieve the capacity for empathy and objectivity. These concepts have been recognised in different ways through both culture and language. Initially, words for thinking and seeing are similar. Then the word "*theorein*" is added to the lexicon and relates to theory and "*noein*" or "*noos*" related to reflection, generation of ideas, and images. In the sixth century BC, "*apeiron*" means indefinite or ill defined, but later becomes the essence of "*sophia*," or wisdom. "Thymos" becomes instinct and couples motion and emotion. This gives us our current nosology for mood disorders and the word euthymic. The latter can be translated as having normal instinctual drives and impulses.

The connectome

This refers to the title of Seung's recent book (2012). In it, he discusses how the wiring of the brain is the main factor driving our individual personalities. It took twelve years to map the connectome of the worm "C. Elegans," which has 300 neurons. We have eighty-six billion neurons, as estimated by Azevedo, Carvalho, Grinberg, and colleagues, each with millions of connections, emphasising the mammoth task involved in mapping the human connectome.

Neurons are influenced by four main factors:

1. They adjust or reweight strengthening or weakening connections according to experience;
2. They reconnect by new growth or pruning of synapses during periods of neuroplasticity;
3. They rewire when firing action potentials, which stimulates branches to both grow and retract; and
4. They regenerate depending on epigenetic influences and where in the forest of the neuronal brain's synaptogenesis occurs. Alongside regeneration apoptosis occurs where existing neurons shrivel, degenerate, and die off like leaves falling from the tree.

According to Seung, "You are more than your genes. You are your connectome."

Also as the maxim goes, "If you do not use it [neural synapse and corresponding muscle reflex], you lose it."

This has major implications for the rehabilitation of stroke patients and those with major limb or spinal injury. The body and brain can reshape and remould, gaining lost function, especially when the injury occurs in childhood. However, the Holy Grail of those working in rehabilitation technologies is to apply the research from biomechanical engineering to the neural maps of Hebbian learning to effectively regain lost muscle and nerve function.

Brain size is not related to the functions of the conscious mind. Both Anatole France, the celebrated writer and anatomist, and Albert Einstein had brain sizes smaller than average (Seung.) What appears to be important is the way neurons intricately cooperate to perform mental tasks. The cerebral cortex can remap following injury, showing that the Brodmann areas are not rigidly defined. Each functional brain area may contain over one hundred million neurons.

Seung hypothesised that the different brain functions are heavily dependent on how these neurons are connected

These famous words were written by John Donne in 1624.

> XVII. *Nunc Lento Sonitu Dicunt, Morieris*
> Now, this bell tolling softly for another, says to me: Thou must die.
> XVII. Meditation
> No man is an island, entire of itself; every man is a piece of the continent, a part of the main; if a clod be washed away by the sea, Europe is the less, as well as if a promontory were, as well as if a manor of thy friend's or of thine own were; any man's death diminishes me, because I am involved in mankind, and therefore never send to know for whom the bell tolls; it tolls for thee . . .

For man, we can substitute the word neuron. By means of mechanisms yet uncertain, these neurons form a body-wide web of interconnectivity. This results in our ability to sense, feel, perceive, think, and generate the remarkable capabilities of our mind.

In the same way that we expectorate, sweat, and urinate, so it is the function of the gut-brain, heart-brain, and head-brain to secrete thoughts and feelings.

There are more than one million synapses per cubic millimetre in the head-brain. Each connection may have many synapses. The influence may be chemical, electrical, or mechanical. It is unidirectional and passed on when neurotransmitter (key) meets receptor (lock). These neurotransmitters may be excitatory or inhibitory and the resulting synapse may strengthen or weaken the neuronal connection. All these interactions take place in a timeframe of 40–500 milliseconds.

In 2005, the Royal Society in England voted Isaac Newton an even greater genius than Albert Einstein (Seung, 2012, p. 64). Newton (1675), stated in his reply by letter to Robert Hooke,

> What Descartes did was a good step. You have added much several ways and especially in considering the colours of thin plates. If I have seen further

it is only by standing on the shoulders of giants ... your humble servant, "IS. NEWTON."

If we say there is nothing new under the sun, then all ideas pre-exist in some form or another. Many discoveries are spontaneous, seemingly unconnected, and simultaneous. Examples include Newton and Leibnitz's discovery of calculus and the work on AC and DC electricity generation by Nicola Tesla and Thomas Edison. Similarly, if one neuron can make stronger connections, it is because a longer, taller, and thicker trunk in the interconnected neural network, or connectome, has supported it.

Each neuron lower down the neural hierarchy sends excitatory synapses to higher-up neurons that can detect the whole sum of its individually detected parts. According to Seung: "The function of a neuron is defined chiefly by its connections with other neurons."

This is defined as connectionism and a complete picture of neural function can only be determined by studying both its inputs and outputs.

I am reminded of the acronym, GIGO, from the computer industry. This stands for gold inputs = gold outputs. However, it could also imply garbage inputs = garbage outputs.

The nature of memory

To secrete coherent thoughts, we need to have access to a database, or memory bank, in brain terms. Neural connections have been compared to both wax, in that they can remain the same for long time periods, and plastic, in that they can be shaped and moulded quickly. In the same way that a strengthened synapse gets bigger, so perhaps can a revisited memory coalesce and become stronger, feeding into different synaptic neural networks. In the case of traumatic memories, these are stored piecemeal and dysfunctionally. Here, the normal hierarchical structure of memory storage and retrieval has broken down. Lower excitatory sensory inputs have overwhelmed the normal upper-inhibitory mechanisms. It seems likely that memories are stored as patterns generated from interconnecting neurons. Connectionist neuroscientists have proposed that "if two neurons are repeatedly activated simultaneously then the connections between them are strengthened in both directions."

They also proposed that "if two neurons are repeatedly activated sequentially, the connection from the first to the second is strengthened."

These rules have become known as Hebbian rules of synaptic plasticity, from Hebb's 1949 book *The Organisation of Behaviour*. The connectome is where nature meets nurture and experience plays a key role in the development of memory. The links between memories and connectomes is a key task for the future as technologies advance to become equal to the task. In summary, Seung stresses that we can change who we are for the better by means of the four Rs:

- Reweighting;
- Reconnection;

- Rewiring; and
- Regeneration.

I would add a fifth R: Reprocessing. This can be achieved with SF-EMDR psychotherapy, as described in the text.

In the same way that the water in a stream and the earth underneath are involved in a constant two-way exchange of information, so the neural network in our brains works the same way. I have explained how our moods can fluctuate from the FROZEN in FEAR state of numbness to the hyperaroused state of the RAPIDS. When our neural activity is becalmed, we operate within an effective window of tolerance. As the waveform patterns of neural activity are produced, our connectomes drive our present experiences, leaving an impression behind that becomes accessible memories of the past. If the waveform of neural activity enters the frozen state, we can become dissociated with hypoarousal. If, on the other hand, the pattern of neural activity enters the rapids, then the dissociation will be because of hyperarousal. Through attuned use of SF-EMDR psychotherapy, we can guide our patients and clients towards the safety of the calmer Narrow Water Castle. Recent research published in *Science* (6 April 2017), challenges the traditional view of memory. Short-term memories were believed to be stored in the hippocampus and the process underlying long-term storage of memory was not fully understood. Tonegawa and a group of colleagues at the RIKEN-MIT Centre for Neural Circuit Genetics, highlight the critical role of the PFC in forming long-term memories (LTMs). In experiments on mice, LTMs were found to have a similar mechanism to how sounds and smells trigger expansive recall of an experience.

Engrams are theorised to be a means by which memories are stored as biological brain changes in response to external stimuli. Tonegawa found that engrams form immediately in the cortex but are in a "silent state," meaning they are unresponsive to natural cues. They mature fourteen days later into an "active" state, which is responsive to these cues. Hippocampal engrams, however, are active immediately memories are laid down but gradually fade into a "silent" state. Thus, complementary memory systems exist. One has limited capacity but allows memories to form rapidly. The other is longer lasting but takes longer to become fully activated. As Tonegawa explains;

> There is a division of labour. The hippocampus can form active memories very quickly, while the prefrontal cortex takes care of long-term stability. If you don't need prolonged memory, the hippocampus is enough; if you don't have to form active memory quickly, the cortex is enough; but we want both. The key question this work resolves is whether engrams move from the hippocampus to cortical sites over time or are established in the cortex during learning and unmasked as time passes. This is strong evidence for the latter.
>
> (Makin, 2017)

In the experiments,

[t]he cells that allow a mouse to remember the fear (aspect) of a memory are maintained from day 1 to three weeks later. But there is a switch in the use of connections: at three weeks when the hippocampus engram is not active anymore, the connectivity between the PFC engram and the amygdala engram allows the animal to recall the fear memory.

(Makin, 2017)

In my opinion this provides further evidence for the clinical effectiveness of SF-EMDR psychotherapy. Towards the end of a two- or three-hour processing session patients will typically place the buzzers on the right and left PFC. They report a tingling sensation in this region which is likely to be indicative of fading engrams in the limbic system (amygdala and hippocampus) and activation of the specific LTM related engrams in the PFC. As Eichenbaum speculates, the role of the PFC may be in organising and choosing between alternative outcomes as new meanings and learning are attributed to the previously traumatic memory.

Thus, this new concept of memory formation shows that the PFC contains the specific memory information at the same time as the hippocampus. This is contrary to the standard theory of memory consolidation, which maintains that Hippocampal memories are gradually transferred to the PFC. We now know that both are formed simultaneously. Those in the PFC become stronger while the Hippocampal ones become weaker.

Further studies are needed to discover whether memories fade completely from the hippocampus or remain in trace form. It is possible that the hippocampus retains memory traces, which are retrieved only occasionally. To differentiate two similar episodic memories, the silent engram in the hippocampus may become reactivate so that the patient can then retrieve the detailed episodic memory even many decades later.

Clinical example illustrating this form of memory consolidation

This was evident in my use of SF-EMDR psychotherapy in a sixty-one-year-old man with Asperger's Syndrome. During the reprocessing sessions, his body was writhing and contorting as he was remembering the physical abuse he suffered on many occasions at the hands of his father. In retrospect, he could realise that his father probably also had features of Asperger's and was unable to empathise, lacking an adequate theory of mind.

As reprocessing continued, the nature of my patient's shaking changed and resembled that of an infant trying to escape a painful grip. My patient could relate how age eighteen months he was travelling on a bus and sitting on his dad's knee. He felt uncomfortable and attempted to escape. However, his dad merely tightened his grip and my patient was unable to wriggle free.

As this memory was somatically experienced, another body memory surfaced. My patient shook violently from side to side with such force that I asked him to lie on the sofa with his head supported at one end and his legs supported at the other. He started to arch his back and move all four limbs in rapid jerking movements. He also experienced seeing a yellow aura in his visual field. After a period of approximately ten minutes he entered a calmer restful state, which to my mind seemed postictal. When he had fully regained consciousness and was able to meaningfully talk about this experience he recalled witnessing his mother have a series of severe epileptic seizures. At the age of five he remembered her being brought to hospital from home in an ambulance. In another he described how his mother fell in the yard outside the house. As her seizures progressed his dad put a knife forcefully between her locked jaw and clenched teeth. This was to keep her airway patent and prevent her biting her tongue.

I asked my patient to enquire about the onset and nature of his mother's epilepsy. At his next appointment, he explained that his mother first developed epilepsy after seeing her own father collapse, vomiting blood from a burst peptic ulcer. Her epilepsy remained untreated and continued throughout her pregnancy with my patient. During the reprocessing with SF-EMDR psychotherapy my patient somatically experienced seizures, which gradually came under his control. My hypothesis is that the physical sensations he had experienced of his mother's epilepsy in utero were like a silent engram in the hippocampus which then become activated in the PFC. As if on cue at the end of the session my patient placed both buzzers on his right and left PFC. During the session, he also experienced bilateral bone resonance via headphones placed next to the mastoid processes. My hypothesis is that this continual resonance activated the "buzz of thought" linking the Hippocampal stored memories with those of the cerebellum. The cerebellum on each side was then able to activate the silent engrams in the PFC, leading to consolidation of this memory stored initially at the in-utero stage of development.

The origin of philosophy

According to Bertrand Russell (1945), philosophy as a discipline emerged with the work of Thales in the sixth century BC. The famous words "*Gnothi Seauton*" ("know thyself") were inscribed over the entrance to the Temple of the Oracle in the Greek city of Delphi. This was said to be the site where the flight paths of the male and female golden eagles intersected. Thus, x marked the spot where these two birds landed. A camp was set up and civilisation began. The gods, such as Zeus, were all-powerful and had dominion over land and sea and all creatures on earth. This can be another creation myth to help explain in aural tradition some of life's mystery.

As Greek culture developed, the LH, as represented by the god Apollo, gradually took precedence over the RH, as represented by the god Dionysus. Gradually, over the centuries, the dominance of the LH worldview prevailed. The influence of the Greek and Roman cultures, which sought to integrate the hemispheric perspectives, waned.

SF-EMDR psychotherapy is designed to reattune the LH (emissary) to its master, the RH. This can help to rebalance the global approach and unconscious attention from the RH with the representation and analysis from the LH. I also see this as a realignment of Eastern and Western medical viewpoints, which can be collaborative and not mutually exclusive, as explained in the following illustrations. The myth behind the Oracle at Delphi was that two golden eagles were sent out in opposite directions from the same point. They were to drop a stone at the point where their paths crossed. These stones landed at the Delphic Oracle, symbolising the meeting of east and west. I would also suggest that the intuition of the right hemisphere and the rationality of the left hemisphere intersect at this famous landmark. The Oracle can be likened to the corpus callosum.

An amazing analogy occurred in July 1969 with the Apollo 11 moon-landing. Neil Armstrong, the commander of the spacecraft, announced as the lunar module commenced its descent: "Mission Control in Houston. The eagle has wings." Later, he was to famously declare "Houston! Tranquillity Base here, the eagle has landed." This was the site on the moon chosen for landing. Eagle was the name of the lunar module that separated from the spacecraft, taking Neil Armstrong and his crew both to the moon and back to the mother craft. An eagle was also the astronaut's symbol and was worn as an emblem on their space suits. In Native-American culture, the eagle is revered as representing their essential spirit: it is one of the three components of the scorpion astrological sign. The eagle is believed to be closest to the spirit, as it can climb higher and see further than any other bird. This again shows the confluence of scientific achievement and mystical symbolism. In the same way that the astronauts blasted off from earth in a Saturn V rocket, perhaps the stones dropped by Zeus's eagles were rockettes, or small rocks.

I believe a new philosophy is possible through the application of SF-EMDR psychotherapy. Patients can be helped to achieve new insights and awareness towards the Delphic goal of *Gnothi Seauton*. They will have greater knowledge of the feelings deep inside themselves. They will be supported to allow an intense dialogue to be initiated with these feelings at a cellular, visceral, and linguistic level.

The Renaissance saw a resurgence in the RH perspective on the world. This meant opening the eyes to the world of experience. The body and soul were considered inseparable. Primacy was afforded to implicit understanding, intuition, myth, and metaphor. This was not to last, and soon individual ambition and competition thrived alongside the influence of the LH. The Era of Enlightenment and the Age of Reason dawned on civilisation. Thus, over time, we have seen the foundations laid for the concepts behind the evolution of thought across cultures and time.

- From the Greek we get nous or wisdom which is allied to the RH worldview;
- From the Latin we derive *intellectus*, which is allied to the primacy of the analytic LH; and

- From the English language comes *sensus communis* or common sense. This, I believe, integrates both hemispheres and links their perspectives to the meaning derived from sensation and feeling. It may also be related to the primacy of the word commons. In the rural village of Newtownhamilton where I grew up, the site of the agricultural mart where pigs and cattle were bought and sold was known as the Commons. It was where all farmers would meet to conduct trade and exchange local news and information. Today the most important part of the legislature is the Commons. If we take the neural network analogy, the trunk neuron would be the Houses of Parliament at Westminster leading to millions of branches of smaller common areas across the country. Taking the analogy further it could be said that lines of communication from one to the other have become severed and that MPs are disconnected from the grassroots. The parallel to nature is striking and may suggest a root-and-branch review to restore interconnectivity from the epicentre of political power to the peripheral regions. This would be like the connections already outlined between our central and peripheral nervous systems.

Nous grasps first principles by induction. Thus, the primacy of the RH is that it is the basis for the LH's rationality. The body and soul are integrated, and reason is subservient to unconscious awareness, metaphor, and imagination. Descartes' world was one where the mind and body were separate, and primacy was given to the role of the LH. The integration of the world of art and science involves the embodied ambiguity of the RH with its implicit investigation. Creations of the RH come to us via the senses and are a forerunner of the English common-sense approach. I conceive this book as an integration of the art and science of both psychotherapy and peak performance.

Implications in the field of psychiatry

Patients with the diagnosis of anorexia nervosa, multiple personality disorder, and deliberate self-harm share the symptom of dissociation. The patient feels cut off from their feelings. The self is fragmented and emotions lack depth. The patient's capacity to empathise is reduced. There is an underactive RH and overactive LH. In autism-spectrum disorders, the LH is especially relied upon, with consequent hypofunction of the RH. One of the goals of SF-EMDR psychotherapy is to reverse the imbalance in these disorders via continuous bilateral cerebellar activation followed by affective reprocessing and conscious directed thoughts.

In autism, there are deficits in social intelligence and difficulties in understanding implicit meaning. Patients with autism have difficulty interpreting tone of voice, prosody, humour, irony, and deceit. The functions of empathy and imagination are more dependent on the RH than the LH. The over-analytical LH of the child with autism may interpret parts of the person rather than the holistic whole. There could be an obsession with mechanical parts, such as the spinning drum of a washing machine, which occurred in a three-year-old child with autism referred to me. Children with autism often refer to themselves as "he" or "she" as they become alienated from self and develop a distorted self-perception. As the eyes convey a pure form of theory of mind, children with autism find meaningful eye contact difficult. One of the pathognomonic features of autism is poor eye contact. This scores highly in the autism diagnostic observation scale, or ADOS. The function of face recognition is dependent on global cerebral function and is, therefore, impaired in autism.

My hypothesis is that SF-EMDR psychotherapy assists with the rebalancing of hemispheric functioning with improved oxygenation and blood flow to the compromised areas of the hypoperfused RH. In autism, there appears to a compensatory hyperfunctioning of the LH. From a SF-EMDR perspective, immobility would be expected on the left side of the body, consequent to RH hypofunction. Careful attention to, and scaffolding of, fine body movements would be the goal of stage four SF-EMDR psychotherapy to rewire right-cerebral-hemisphere brain axons ready for transmission.

It seems essential for our full consciousness and imagination that the RH is put in a position whereby the LH cannot overrun it. The RH "believes" but does not know; the LH "knows" but is unable to believe. The master "trusts" his emissary, yet this very trust may be misplaced. With cooperation between both hemispheres, they become invincible whereas, if there is domination by the LH over the RH, then both hemispheres suffer. Chaos ensues when the RH (or left hand) does not know what the LH (or right hand) is doing.

Our brains reflect the substance of the universe around us both structurally and functionally. We come to understand our world through the metaphorical use of language. I believe this is helped by bilateral activations of the cerebral hemispheres being enabled to reprocess thoughts, as in SF-EMDR psychotherapy.

Theories on the origin of the universe

Ideas about origins of the universe are related to the development of conscious awareness in man. There are new ideas emerging from the Perimeter Institute in Toronto about these origins. Its director, Professor Neil Turok (Leonard, 2010), hypothesises that as one big bang ends another bounces into existence to explain conservation of space–time and the laws of physics. Lerner, in his book *The Big Bang Never Happened* provides a counter-argument to the pre-eminent theory on the origins of the universe. The corollary for psychotherapy is that the Jungian concept of collective unconsciousness is timeless. By increasing the vibratory frequency of our own individual consciousness, we may be able to tap into this universal awareness, or cosmic mind. I believe that doing this during sessions of SF-EMDR psychotherapy has the potential to further resolve traumatic memories.

Analysis of dreams that have had a significant impact on religion and science

It is during dreams that we suspend the physical three-dimensional world of daily life on planet earth. In dreamtime, it is believed that we have access to eleven dimensions of space–time. This is analogous to the eleven multiverse dimensions predicted by superstring theory and quantum mechanics. Many cultures speak of the predictive nature of dreams, from the stories in the Bible to the Aborigines in Australia.

In Western science, Frederick August von Kekule was having difficulty conceptualising the structure of the benzene ring – the organic chemical compound made up of a ring of carbon atoms. He had a dream of whirling snakes. He reported the dream in a speech made in 1890 at a dinner commemorating his discovery many years after it took place:

> I turned my chair to the fire [after having worked on the problem for some time] and dozed. Again, the atoms were gambolling before my eyes. This time the smaller groups kept modestly to the background. My mental eye, rendered more acute by repeated vision of this kind, could not distinguish larger structures, of manifold conformation; long rows, sometimes more closely fitted together; all twinning and twisting in snake-like motion. However, look! What was that? One of the snakes had seized hold of its own tail, and the form whirled mockingly before my eyes. As if by a flash of lighting, I awoke ... Let us learn to dream, gentlemen and then perhaps we shall find the truth ... but let us beware of publishing our dreams before they have been put to the proof by the waking understanding.
>
> (Roberts, 1989, p. 80)

There is a Gnostic gem from Roman-era Egypt (first century AD), with an ouroboros surrounding a scarab and *voces magicae*, characters representing magic words. This shows that the ouroboros symbol is ancient and can resonate effectively with the patient undergoing SF-EMDR psychotherapy (Figure 7.4).

During SF-EMDR psychotherapy, I get the patient into a state of information flow. When they are in the zone, the information travels up from the initial gut reaction to the heartfelt sensations associated with grief and loss before registering in the quintessential elements of the brain. Crucially, for resolution of the traumatic stress, I get the patient foot-tapping. This aids the circulation of sensations throughout the body from top to toe and vice versa. There is a parallel in ancient history for this form of processing as illustrated by the ouroboros symbol above, which shows the snake or serpent completing the circle by biting its tail. Clockwise represents the flow of information across the body from left to right and vice versa. This is also the image in von Kekule's dream that led him to discover the chemical structure of the benzene ring.

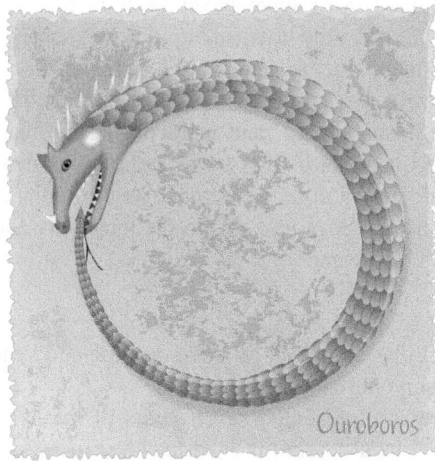

Figure 7.4 The ouroboros in von Kekule's dream depicts his snake grasping its own tail.
Source: Shutterstock.

Often, the ouroboros symbol involves the image of two serpents each biting its own tail. I use this metaphor to conjure up a figure-of-eight image positioned either vertically or horizontally in space. Patients are encouraged to track the movement of sensations and feeling from their root, or sacral, chakra up to the crown and third-eye chakras.

At this point, the reprocessing can often become stuck and I suggest to patients and clients that they tap each foot in turn to kick-start the reprocessing. Sometimes I notice that this can happen spontaneously.

Dan Siegel reported, in a lecture of his that I attended, how one elderly patient was unable to speak about the traumatic grief he had experienced. Thus, his Broca's area needed stimulation. Once his right foot started to tap, due to the crossing of the corticospinal tract in the brainstem (pyramidal decussation), his Broca's area was activated and he started to speak. Siegel's definition of mind is as an emergent self-organising embodied regulator of the flow of both energy and information. This linking of body and mind is fundamental to the raison d'etre of this book.

In his book *The Act of Creation*, Koestler called this the second most important dream in history after that of Joseph predicting seven years of plenty followed by seven years of famine. In this story, none of the Pharaoh's magi could interpret his dream. Then Joseph was called for and then Pharaoh said to Joseph,

Behold, in my dream I stood on the bank of the river. Suddenly seven cows came up out of the river, fine looking and fat; and they fed in the meadow.

Then behold, seven other cows came up after them, poor and very ugly and gaunt, such ugliness, as I have never seen in all the land of Egypt. In addition, the gaunt and ugly cows ate up the first seven, the fat cows. When they had eaten them up, no one would have known that they had eaten them, for they were just as ugly as at the beginning. Therefore, I awoke. In addition, I saw in my dream, and suddenly seven heads came up on one stalk, full and good. Then behold seven heads, withered; thin, and blighted by the east wind, sprang up after them. In addition, the thin heads devoured the seven good heads. So, I told this to the magicians, but there was no one who could explain it to me.

(Koestler, 1964)

Joseph could explain that the seven fat cows represented years when the harvest was plentiful and everyone had enough to eat.

The seven lean cows represented seven years of hardship and famine when disease and pestilence would befall the world. The crucial part of the dream was the sting in the tail in that the thin heads devoured the fattened heads.

Joseph, through his interpretation of the dream, could predict the future. Most countries would feast during the good years but not put any provisions aside for the lean years, when millions would starve to death. Therefore, he suggested to Pharaoh that a good percentage of the harvest should be set aside and preserved so that his people could be fed enough to survive the seven years of famine.

The Pharaoh was so pleased with Joseph that he put him in charge of all of Egypt. In due course, the seven years of plenty arrived and there was much merriment, laughter, and wastage. When the lean years arrived, people in every land fought one another for food. Only in Egypt did everyone have enough to eat and God saw that Joseph had listened to him.

An experienced manager of an NHS trust stated that during the years 2001–2007, money was poured into the NHS. Then, when the financial collapse happened in 2008, he predicted that there would be seven years of hardship for the cash-strapped NHS. No money would have been put aside during the good years to help with the economic crisis and many trusts would struggle to survive. Many more would perform so poorly that they would be subjected to a rescue plan equivalent to emergency resuscitation. The parallels with the biblical dream of Joseph are apparent.

Summary

Conscious thought is believed to represent only five per cent of human brain activity. Research is ongoing into ways we can usefully access the brain activity of the remaining ninety-five per cent of non- or unconscious activity. Most of the techniques so far have examined military applications. The role of the connectome and how the brain's wiring makes us who we are is discussed. This includes a recent definition of the field of connectomics and how this features in our understanding of memory. SF-EMDR psychotherapy will prove useful in treating the effects of dysfunctional memory storage via the fifth R, which is Reprocessing. Various ideas of the neuroanatomical origin of consciousness are proposed, such as the periaqueductal grey matter in the midbrain. New theories on the origin of consciousness are presented including, ORCH OR, quantum physics, and the underlying role of quantum field theory (QFT). The complex cycle of information exchange occurring in psychotherapy is explained. This links the mind, mirror neurons, genomics, brain and body with the 4 stages of the basic rest activity cycle or BRAC. This is further developed in terms of different phases of hypnosis and chatobiological time. The implications of QFT in psychotherapy are poorly understood by the medical profession and the commissioners of health services in the NHS.

Philosophical origins are also mentioned. New insights, such as those once achieved by the Ancient Greeks at the Delphic Oracle are proposed. As we moved from the Age of Enlightenment to the Age of Reason in society, so did our world perspective shift from the right to the left hemisphere. This has had major implications in the field of psychiatry, with many more patients experiencing mental ill-health because of being cut off from their feelings. The role of SF-EMDR psychotherapy in redressing this balance is proposed. Comparisons with the American moon landings are made. This leads on to scientific and mythological ideas on origins of the universe, which are proposed to be compatible. There is a final section on dream analysis, with an account of the scientific breakthrough made by von Kekule in his discovery of benzene's structure and Joseph's interpretation of the Pharaoh's dream, which saved the people of Egypt from starvation.

Chapter 8

Applying quantum field theory within SF-EMDR to overcome patient resistance and achieve a transformation of consciousness

The Schrodinger wave equation was introduced 100 years ago. According to the Copenhagen interpretation developed by Heisenberg and Bohr, measuring causes the wave function to collapse. The implications of measurement are involved in integrating QFT and mind–body psychotherapy. This has evolved since the work of Jung and Pauli in 1952. They considered: time, space, the unconscious, opposites, connection, and energy. They failed to consider: sets and subsets of motion, opposites regarding motion, yes sets, implied directive, sources of comfort, and the role of position.

All the above are incorporated by subsets of consciousness, focus of attention, and activity-dependent gene expression. The four-stage creative process (Poincaré, 1905; Rossi, 1996) includes:

The Dirac equation has been developed to quantify the interrelationship between quantum field theory and psychotherapy, increasing the potential for therapeutic change during the process of SF-EMDR for psychotherapy and peak performance.

- **Stage 1** Data collection and preparation. This means exploring possibilities and logical reasoning, equivalence correspondence, substitution alongside creative visualisation;
- **Stage 2** Incubation involves trusting the unconscious to creatively problem-solve. In SF-EMDR psychotherapy there is continual bilateral stimulation of the limbic system. This can facilitate Krebs-cycle initiation of activity-dependent gene expression (Kandel & Squire, 1999; Rossi, 2002). This unconscious machinery must first be activated before moving to Stage 3;
- **Stage 3** or inspiration. The light-bulb moment comes after a period of private inner work and creative replay facilitated by my "magic remote." A Eureka moment is possible with the development of insight illumination and intuition; leading to
- **Stage 4** At the end of the session when all stimulation is switched off a period of verification, reintegration, and thinking allows for the development of new neural networks in the cerebral cortex.

In 1980, Erickson emphasised the role of the unconscious mind in therapy:

> ... Just be comfortable while I am talking to your unconscious mind, since I don't care what your conscious mind does.
>
> (Erickson, 1958/1980)

He showed his trust and dependency on the unconscious, the use of opposites, and the possibilities of QFT to hold and contain attention (superposition). He was aware of the role of failure and how to utilise time in the session by pacing interventions. His quote suggests that the psychotherapist's consciousness may be the act of measurement that collapses the wave function. Erickson used quantum principles such as opposites, momentum, and uncertainty to transform resistance and treat trauma by focusing the patient's attention and creatively introducing novelty. These are all features of SF-EMDR psychotherapy. Erickson used time and space in a way that was consistent with both the Dirac equation and concepts of Buddhist meditative practice. Many others contributed to the integration of QFT and psychotherapy. These included Mindell, Goswami, and Rossi. Rossi recognised sensory receptors at levels of the eyes, ears, skin, the lipid membrane of cell wall, and RNA in the cell nucleus. This mirrors some of Bruce Lipton's work in *Biology of Belief*. Attention could now be focused using the novelty numinosum neurogenesis effect. Physiological and meditative practices both showed the following characteristics:

1. Capacity to receive;
2. Value of receiving;
3. Development of trust and safety;
4. Value of openness;
5. Balance and harmony; and
6. Value of connecting to one's "centre."

Erickson's resistance protocol

This was developed in 1964 to act as a template for transformation of patient resistance. As a subset of consciousness its opposite is receptivity. He would focus his attention like a vector in mathematics, redirecting the motion of the patient's resistance. He applied these principles in a similar way to the work of Dirac and Heisenberg whose equations validated the reality of momentum. Redirecting attention is also seen in Tibetan Buddhist meditation exercise. In T'ai Chi, there are three components:

1. Peng or validation;
2. Lu or redirecting attention; and
3. The holding of attention once redirected. This signified that the patient's resistance had been transformed.

As in SF-EMDR psychotherapy, Erickson had sessions of ninety minutes duration, which was consistent with ultradian rhythms and activity-dependent gene expression. Erickson could hold and redirect attention like the quantum effects of T'ai Chi and classical music-composition theory. His guiding principles were trust and appreciation of opposites and uncertainty, which combined group-theory consciousness and quantum physics.

Transformation of consciousness

Validation
Focus of attention
Hold and redirect attention
Utilisation of opposites
Utilisation of time and appreciation
Utilisation and appreciation of creativity
Quantum Electrodynamics

Dirac only accepted this theory forty years after its discovery. The collaboration of Feynman, Gregory, Wilczek, Crease, and Rossi and Rossi implied that the electron had consciousness. This led to the development of yes-sets for the electron. By using axioms (truisms), opposites, pacing, and associative indirect chaining, QED theory was eventually validated. Feynman explored how matter and light or electrons and photons interacted stating:

1.   A photon can go from one place to another;
2.   An electron can go from one place to another; and
3.   An electron can emit or absorb an electron.

Wilczek won the Nobel Prize for explaining how the strong nuclear force influenced quarks at short distances. He considered mass as the embodied energy of fundamental particles. This has parallels to Rossi's connection of the mind and body. It also appreciates the novelty of Erickson's connections between conscious and unconscious minds, as well as the dynamics of quantum entanglement by Goswami, and Gregory. Rossi and Erickson discussed the need to build bridges for patients while in a state of REM or trance so that different levels of connection can occur.

Quantum chromodynamics

This is the theory of the strong nuclear force. Gluons and quarks support protons and neutrons in the atom. There are six flavours of quarks: up, down, strange, charm, top, and bottom. The name comes from a line in "Finnegan's Wake" by James Joyce:

Three quarks for Muster Mark!
Sure, he hasn't got much of a bark
And sure, any he has it's all beside the mark

A gluon is an elementary particle that acts as an exchange particle for the strong force between quarks. They "glue" quarks together to form protons and neutrons. There are eight colours of gluons. These fundamental particles in psychotherapy can be metaphors for: deeper resources, forming a bridge to connect to one's centre, subsets of centring, having a deeper level of being, acting as a bridge to the four forces, facilitating the development of yes-sets for these forces.

Once attention is focused on the core or centre, more connection possibilities emerge. The patient becomes more balanced and can achieve more harmony. The patient is more receptive, less anxious, and less isolated. They will allow themselves to be human beings and feel safer in the context of opening up to the psychotherapist.

Figure 8.1 above outlines a four-dimensional model of consciousness. This is known as a hypersphere and is built by superimposing two three-dimensional spheres into a toroidal structure. This model can explain the binding of distant nuclei within the brain as well as interacting with the wider environment. The essential steps of gravitational fields, dark energy, zero-point energy, and electromagnetism shown in this figure appear to have existed from the very origin of the universe and our biological evolution.

Figure 8.2 represents a global workspace model. It can explain how instantaneous binding of distant nuclei numbered 1 to 4 is related to integral observation and sensing of the outside world. These broadcasting hotspots exist in the neural networks of the brain. Communication can occur by standing waves, phase coupling or spiral vortices. Integrating this binding of distant brain nuclei with broadcasting of information is believed to be central to how consciousness is realized. Knowledge of these mechanisms can be used in SF-EMDR to bring unconscious information into conscious awareness for reprocessing.

How does the evolution of quantum physics relate to the evolution of molecular biology and psychotherapy?

Stage 1: Work of Planck's constant, Einstein's identification of light as particle, Bohr's work on the atom. This relates to protein formation and electron sequence in the ATP cycle. In psychotherapy, this led to psychoanalysis' interpretation of dreams and collaboration by Jung and Pauli.

Stage 2: Quantum Mechanics introduced by Schrodinger and Heisenberg and the concept of wave-particle duality and the double slit experiment. Cross-fertilisation of science and psychotherapy with the concept of consciousness of the electron. In psychotherapy the work of Rossi and Erickson built upon the four-stage creative cycle and the 90–120 minute ideal for maximum therapeutic change.

Stage 3: Dirac's equation integrated quantum mechanics and special relativity. In molecular terms ideas of personal and cosmic consciousness are

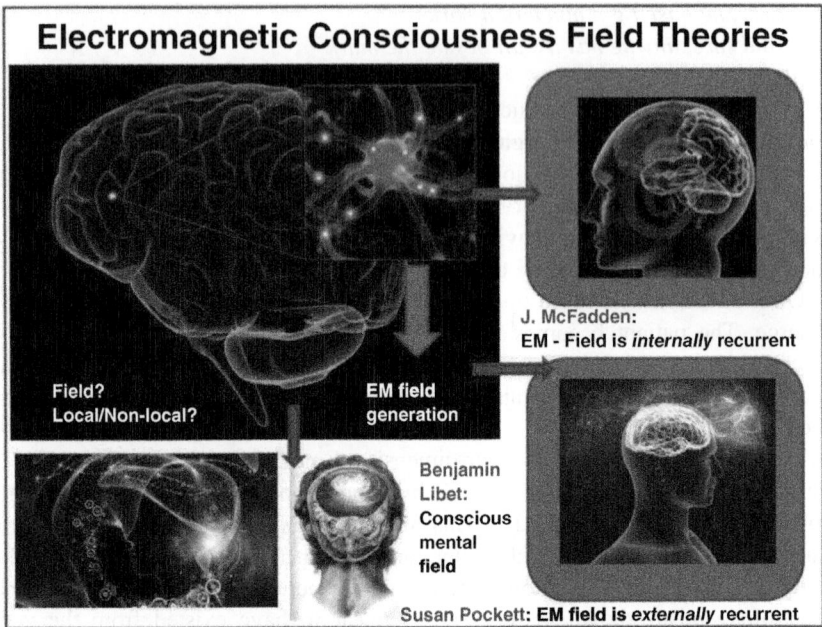

Electromagnetic Consciousness Field Theories

Field?
Local/Non-local?

EM field
generation

J. McFadden:
EM - Field is *internally* recurrent

Benjamin
Libet:
Conscious
mental
field

Susan Pockett: **EM field is *externally* recurrent**

Figure 8.1 Consciousness is based on long-range electromagnetic fields. Current models of consciousness are based on long-range electromagnetic fields that may explain the binding simultaneously of distant brain nuclei involved in integration perception and neuroception during SF-EMDR psychotherapy. This implies that a receptive field resonates at a workplace level of brain memory. It is then superimposed by a mental workspace in a toroidal geometric shape. A comprehensive quantum physics theory should be able to explain the cosmos at a micro and macroscopic level. The links between individual and collective or cosmic consciousness are now being further investigated. The event horizon contains information at a 2D level. This can stimulate 3D representations of the personal function of the brain. The 4D field of resonant workspace is superimposed on these other dimensional levels. The resting brain has patterns of connectivity. This signature of consciousness may reflect a stream of ongoing cognitive processes.

Source: reprinted with permission from Prof Meijer.

explained by quantum entanglement. Ideas of short- and long-term memory formation are simultaneously laid down in the hippocampus and cerebral cortex.

Stage 4: Feynman helped consolidate the quantum electrodynamics of Dirac. He explored connections between matter and light and introduced renormalisation. In psychotherapy, this led to an explanation of how we can more deeply connect to resources and to conscious and unconscious processes.

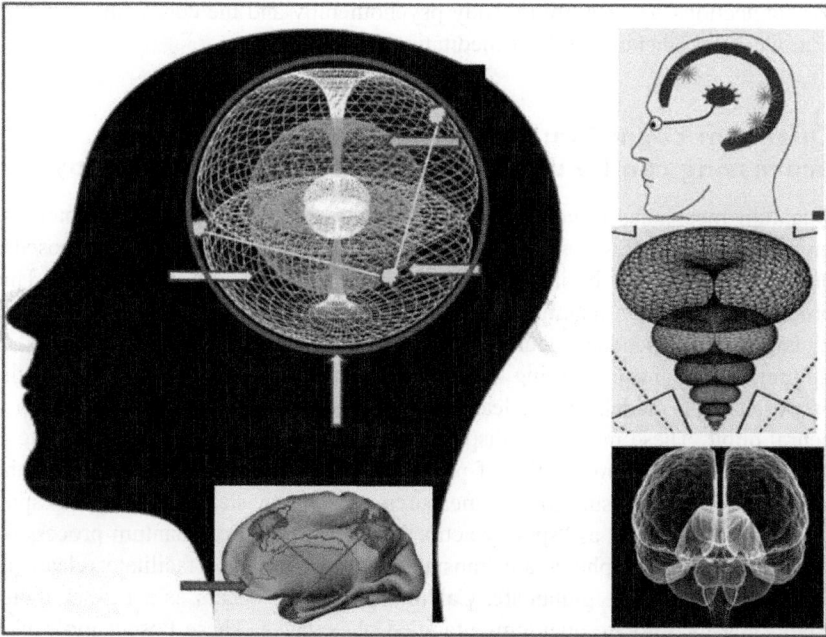

Figure 8.2 Various representations of the event-horizon model of consciousness. The main picture: postulated double-toroidal field integrating the 4D hypersphere workspace with the event-horizon surface, projecting the integral individual information as an internal model of the self. Note that the 4D hypersphere is pictured within the skull, but that it can exhibit an extended location, surrounding the brain or even the whole person. This is due to fractal properties at a microscopic scale, within the brain cells or in extracellular space. Embedding of the 3D toroidal domain of the brain within a 4D hypersphere is both multidimensional and fractal at different levels of organisation. This symmetry is broken from the 4D hypersphere to the 3D internal brain torus. fMRI brain scans can detect antipodal activity domains in the brain tissue itself (middle picture on right).

Insets A: proposed broadcasting centres in the brain which may explain binding, and global synchrony. **B:** organisation of fractal information scales in the extended brain. **C:** Hemispherical anatomy of the brain resembling a toroidal geometry.

Source: reprinted with permission from Prof Meijer.

Stage 5: The development of QCD by Gell-Mann. From the viewpoint of psychotherapy, the application of QFT to the basic-stage activity cycle consolidated Rossi and Rossi's theories at the macro and microscopic levels.

Stage 6: In 1979 the Nobel Prize in Physics was won by Glashow, Salam and Weinberg for helping to unify the weak and electromagnetic interaction between elementary particles. As quarks are the only particle to exhibit all four forces –

weak, strong, gravitational, and electromagnetic – this help lay the groundwork for connections between mind–body psychotherapy and the core components of T'ai Chi and Tibetan Buddhist meditation practice.

Quantum cognition: how a new "spin" on neural processing can be utilised in SF-EMDR psychotherapy

Quantum mechanics is now believed to partly explain the neural mechanisms involved in consciousness and synaptic function. Fisher (2015) has proposed a model for how the brain stores and processes quantum information. This proposes a role for quantum processing in glutamatergic neurotransmission, glutamatergic-dependent neurocognition, and psychiatric treatments such as lithium. Quantum processing is based on quantum bits or qubits. In the proposed brain model, the nuclear spin of phosphorus functions as a qubit or a neural qubit. These molecules display quantum entanglement. Pyrophosphate is hydrolysed into two molecules of phosphate. Measuring the state of one of the spins dictates the result of the measurement on the state of the other spin. Einstein referred to it as "spooky action at a distance." For quantum processing these entangled phosphates are transported into neurons to facilitate release of neurotransmitters like glutamate. Calcium phosphate occurs as a Posner molecule. They incorporate quantum-entangled phosphates. These Posner molecules are involved in quantum memory storage and glutamatergic neurotransmission.

These Posner molecules:

1) Are protected, remain coherent and can therefore function as a qubit memory;
2) Chemical binding of two Posner molecules is dependent on nuclear spin. This quantum entanglement represents a measurement of their spin states;
3) As Posner molecules spin around one another they become further entangled. When at rest, they release calcium into the cytoplasm influencing calcium levels; and
4) They contain six phosphorus atoms and potentially could mediate quantum entanglement and non-local quantum correlations in postsynaptic firing across multiple neural networks. This can occur through the vesicular glutamate transporter (VGLUT). As a phosphate transporter VGLUT moves Posner's molecules from extracellular space to the cytoplasm of presynaptic neurons. This could then lead to post-synaptic neural firing that is correlated across neural networks, by quantum processes.

What are the implications of quantum processes for neuropsychiatry?

Quantum-cognitive processes appear to be diversely distributed throughout the brain. Quantum processing is involved in information processing and neural cognition. This has implications for the bottom-up and top-down processing in SF-EMDR psychotherapy. There also appears to be a quantum-processing role in somatic, affective, cognitive, and behavioural dysfunction.

Electromagnetic fields influence nuclear spins and the therapist–patient relationship. This model requires further testing to be validated. In vitro and quantum computing methods have been proposed. When validated, the fundamental biological basis of brain-information processing will be inextricably linked to quantum field theory and the quantum world.

Consciousness in the universe is without scale but implies existence of an event horizon in the human brain

Consciousness is defined as a system that has developed cooperatively so that it observes itself. This was essential for survival and social communication. Fisher (2017) proposes that individual minds are part of universal consciousness and involved in the entire fabric of reality. Consciousness involved integration of information and feeling of events in the past and future. To explain the rapid response times of the brain, a photon/soliton mediated the information-processing network that connects neural networks to a holographic mental workspace. The hard problem of consciousness is to explain how different sensations acquired their characteristics such as colours and tastes. There is a bottom-up flow of information from atoms, molecules, organs, and neurons to neural networks. There is a second, lateral information flow in which non-local quantum entanglement and holographic projection appear to play a role. The torus is the favoured geometric structure to account for this model of consciousness.

Top-down resonance

There appears to be a standing-wave brain pattern resonating at a top-down level. It encodes spatial information and helps to synchronise neural networks to assist conscious perception. In *A Brief History of Time* Stephen Hawking asserted that the universal force of electromagnetism controlled all biological responses. This form of energy may synchronise spatial and temporal responses at the levels of head-brain, heart-brain, and gut-brain. This provides further evidence for the efficacy of SF-EMDR psychotherapy. This combined form of bottom-up and top-down resonance can impose a three-dimensional imprint in the cerebral cortex and integrate our modality of consciousness.

Universal or cosmic consciousness

This concept is well known from the work of David Bohm who introduced implicate order and Edwin László (2007) who introduced the Akashic-field concept. This bears similarity to the Akashic records of Eastern traditions. This has been linked with the zero-point energy field (ZPE). There appears to be communication between 3D and 4D workspaces associated with consciousness and the brain. There are many recorded episodes of clairvoyance, distance viewing, telepathy, psychokinesis, and near-death experiences (NDE). These phenomena may point to a radiant resonant mind field involving a fourth spatial dimension.

Event horizons in the human brain

Figure 8.3 illustrates how broadcasting centres in the brain might explain the binding of distant brain nuclei. Integration of observation and sensing the outside world assumes multiple broadcasting hot spots in the brain's neural networks. The different conscious experiences are described in numbers 1 to 4. This brain communication is felt to involve resonance of standing waves, phase coupling, and spiral vortices. It has been suggested that integrating and broadcasting this information is the key component in the realisation of consciousness.

Relation with the connectome and default mode networks (DMN)

The DMN operates spontaneously when the brain is at rest. It is involved in day-dreaming, introspection, monitoring of the mental self, and integration of cognitive processes. The human connectome is the proposed candidate for the complex toroidal information flux in the brain. This inner awareness competes with external awareness to effect goal-directed behaviour. This can allow for communication between conscious and unconscious states. The extended brains seen have been derived from universal consciousness. A meta-consciousness model proposed three dimensions: time, awareness, and emotion. Prof Meijer adds a fourth toroidal dimension of self-consciousness, in contact with universal consciousness. This is conceptualised as the source of all that exists. The proposed mental workspace in a 4D context is related to geo-magnetism, zero-point energy field, and dark energy. This also supports the ORCH OR model previously discussed by Hameroff and Penrose.

Summary

Through the development of insights, reflections, meditation, and reasoning, aspects of universal consciousness can be recognised. The human mind is constrained in space, time, and energy and can only partly reflect all of reality. As the population of earth doubles over the next thirty to forty years, the connecting principle of cosmic consciousness offers a potential for humanity to share resources in a way that halts climate change, preserves

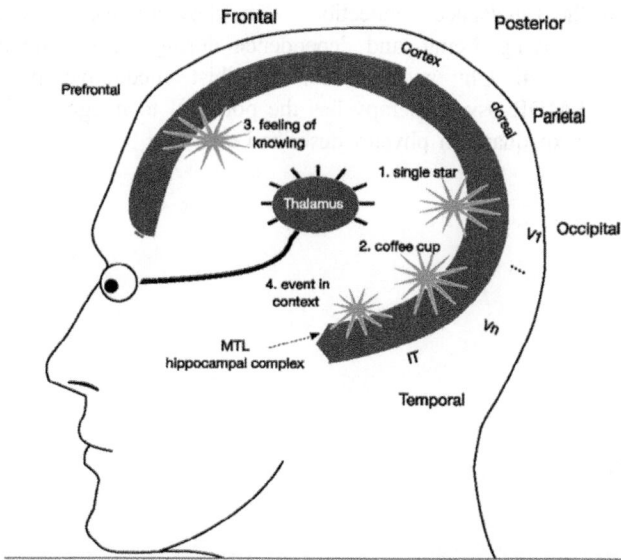

Figure 8.3 Binding and broadcasting from many locations. Four alternative sources of binding and broadcasting in the C-T core. Sites of possible binding and broadcasting are shown as yellow starbursts. Because global broadcasts mutually interfere, only one can occur in any 100–200 ms period. Global interference may explain the limited capacity of momentary conscious contents. Areas V1 and IT: visuotopic maps include area V1, the first cortical map for vision, and area IT, where conscious object representations emerge. Different coalitions of anatomically identical spatiotopic activity maps may lead to different conscious experiences, like the sight of a single star on a dark night (V1) vs. a coffee cup within arm's reach (IT). Prefrontal cortex: non-sensory "feelings of knowing" may bind and broadcast from non-sensory cortex. Area MTL: we predict that the intact medial temporal cortex contributes to subjective event organisation as well as episodic memory coding.

life, and guarantees mankind a real future. By appreciating QFT there can be a greater connection to resources that are beneficial to the patient during psychotherapy. The roles of QED and QCD are explored to show how being at the centre or core of the patient can help to open the unconscious processes that may be responsible for resistance. The psychotherapist has the potential for novelty and creative focusing of attention. This can lead to expansion of conscious awareness and may correspond to opening of the focal setting in Tibetan Buddhist meditation. I have discussed how psychotherapists may expand trust by containment, focusing attention, and activating unconscious healing processes. QCD and QED techniques include relationship between electrons and photons, opposites like electron and positron, validation of the time/space connection. Also, they involve applying yes-sets for opening, receiving, being, and dependence during the therapeutic session. Overlaps with T'ai Chi and Tibetan Buddhist meditative practice were discussed. SF-EMDR psychotherapy has the potential to integrate all six stages in the evolution of quantum physics described.

Chapter 9

Guidelines to practitioners for conducting a SF-EMDR psychotherapy session

Procedure

First, headphones are placed over the patient's head and tilted forwards so that the earpiece rests over the mastoid process bilaterally. The aim is to facilitate bilateral stimulation over the bony protuberances known as the mastoid processes. The frequency is adjusted to the highest level tolerated by the patient. This can range from 0 Hertz to 60 Hertz. It is said that 40 Hertz is the optimum frequency for thalamocortical coherence. This point also achieves maximum cerebellar stimulation, enhancing the reprocessing of thoughts during SF-EMDR psychotherapy.

Then, after taking a detailed trauma history, the client is asked to describe the issue or traumatic event that they wish to work on and to continue the narrative from the point of the significant event up to the present moment. They are helped to maintain contact with the narrative by allowing them to reflect on their experiences. I pay attention to their body language during this process, through constant feedback and interaction with the patient.

When I have asked the patient to retell their story, this will be divided into more and less manageable parts, each with a subjective unit of distress scale (SUDS). I then ask them to hold either a "magic remote" (for children) or video/DVD remote (for adults) in their left hand while they are replaying the narrative in their mind. This will tap into the visuospatial and imaginative capacities of their right cerebral hemisphere. I then ask them to allow the worst part of the memory to emerge, which is usually when they felt most upset. They are asked to describe their gut reaction or instinct associated with the specific traumatic experience. If the patient is finding it difficult to tap into their gut reaction, I will give them a "menu" to help them describe their initial instinctive reaction to their trauma (Table 9.1).

Often, the patient will come up with the worst aspects of the traumatic memory spontaneously; if not, it is helpful to have this "menu" to hand. The precise options offered will depend on the nature of their traumatic story and the unprocessed sensory fragments within it. The client then places thier hands, which are holding the tactile zappers, over the area of the body that experiences the above feelings most intensely.

Table 9.1 Menu of options to give to the patient or client if they are having difficulty tuning into their bodily reactions during sensorimotor-focused EMDR therapy

Menu of possible patient reactions

Gut reaction or instinct
Sensation
Taste
Gut feeling
Image
Sound
Expression or word
Odour, smell, or aroma
Butterfly or heaviness in stomach
Knotted feeling in abdomen
Tension or tightness in chest
Shortness of breath or chest pain
Choking or anxious feeling in throat
Speechless terror
Heart racing or palpitations
Thumping in chest
Sweaty palms
Muscle tension or tightness
Feeling of numbness or altered temperature

As SF-EMDR psychotherapy proceeds, the sensations, feelings, emotions, and movements associated with the trauma are brought to the surface from the relevant abdominal viscera. By contacting these experiences, at a more superficial level, they become less intense, lighter, and change position, in line with the chakra energy points, as formerly discussed.

The patient is observed for any change in temperature, sensations, feelings, or emotions being processed at a higher-energy level. The goal is to register these experiences at a heartfelt level consistent with the energy level of the fourth, or heart, chakra. These are often registered as painful sensations in the chest area, associated with loss and traumatic grief. Anatomically this includes the areas of the heart, lungs, and thymus.

As SF-EMDR psychotherapy continues, a block to the flow of information processing is often found at the level of the throat chakra, or thyroid gland. The information must first be transferred to the master hemisphere and then its emissary, as described earlier.

By either crossing their hands to the lateral aspects of their neck and tapping gently, or placing the zappers there, the patient can achieve this. An awareness of body language by the patient is encouraged during reprocessing. The flow of information is facilitated by getting the patient to tap their feet alternately and to track internal bodily sensations in a figure of eight, from head to toe.

If a cul-de-sac in information reprocessing is reached, the patient is encouraged to mindfully connect with the "stuck" feeling and its bodily location. The patient is then asked to float back to the first, or the worst, time they experienced that traumatic feeling or sensation. The patient then recounts the narrative. This is like the recent traumatic event protocol (RTEP) developed by Elan Shapiro.

Invariably, an unconscious memory or physical sensation comes to consciousness. The patient is then able to verbalise these experiences and make sense of them. The patient is asked to allow the most upsetting aspect of the traumatic memory to emerge into conscious awareness. This moment is captured using a freeze-frame technique, which helps to titrate the associated stress within their window of affect tolerance, emotional regulation, and safety (see Figure 2.2).

The patient's original "target" memory is revisited until the SUDS scale is reduced to the lowest possible level. The initial gut reaction will now have been registered at a heartfelt level. This is a sign that the brain is now ready for reprocessing of the information on an intuitive level. My belief is that the extent of learning, reflection, and intuition possible from SF-EMDR psychotherapy is dependent on the person's age and stage of neurological development. Reprocessing may be blocked by earlier traumas stored at a bodily level. That might be in the enteric nervous plexus, where they become isolated in the abdominal viscera, or at the root chakra level, if the narrative is one of sexual assault or abuse.

Information about the trauma may also be blocked at the level of the cardiac ganglia (or nervous system), especially when associated with childhood traumatic grief. Improving gut-brain, heart-brain, and head-brain connections are an essential component of SF-EMDR psychotherapy. The holistic intelligence of the mind and body can be enhanced through the therapeutic process of vibrating at a higher resonant frequency. This is made possible with the BOKA machine, using the zappers bilaterally, within SF-EMDR psychotherapy. When the patient is asked to review the image following reprocessing, they often report that it has faded. One patient said, "It's as if it has been covered by clouds and it is no longer associated with any distress."

I may incorporate techniques from SF-EMDR psychotherapy. If the traumatic memory involved an assault, it is often helpful to ask the patient to stretch out their hands as if pushing the attacker away and creating a safe boundary around them. A change in posture, for example, getting the patient to stand up from a sitting position, allows them to have greater confidence in imagining confronting their assailant.

The continuous low-frequency bilateral cerebellar stimulation is unique to SF-EMDR psychotherapy. This lasts for the 90–120-minute therapeutic session. This maintains the patient within the CALM WATERS and avoids the dissociation associated with the RAPIDS or FROZEN in FEAR states. I attempt continuous psycho-education during the SF-EMDR psychotherapy session as the patient becomes more receptive to language. I ensure attention is paid to any residual affective dysregulation. Over the ninety minutes there is gradual transfer upwards of information from the lower to the higher chakra energy centres. Patients report sensations moving from the right to the left cerebral hemisphere. I believe this is evidence for integration of information as the master hemisphere connects with its emissary. In my clinical experience, at this stage the patient is likely to commence yawning and report feeling tired. This is a reassuring sign that the brain pathways involving REM sleep have been activated. Stickgold (2002) reported that this is secondary to the production of pontine-geniculate-occipital (PGO) waves from brainstem stimulation.

The two forms of bilateral stimulation used in SF-EMDR psychotherapy directly activate the brainstem centrally. This has the effect of neurological activation of cranial nerves three, four, and six. These oculomotor, trochlear, and abducens nerves move the eyes in all possible directions. In my work as a consultant child-and-adolescent psychiatrist, I find that children with immature optic tracts are unable to track movements across the midline. Thus, other forms of bilateral stimulation are preferable. Francine Shapiro asserts that eye movements are the most effective form of bilateral stimulation. My clinical experiences provide a contrary view. Also, adults processing in-utero, neonatal, preverbal, or childhood memories have also benefited from concurrent bilateral tactile stimulation and mastoid resonance. In SF-EMDR psychotherapy, I combine bilateral cerebellar stimulation at the level of the mastoid process with bilateral tactile stimulation using zappers, as it allows for continuous verbal interaction with the patient. In my clinical experience, young children with attachment disorders often report lack of sensation or feeling in their feet. My hypothesis is that lack of neurobiological regulation from poor maternal–infant bonding has damaged neurological processes in the periphery, such as proprioception. I have found that placing the zappers in the child's socks and asking them to stand up while experiencing bilateral stimulation can reactivate impaired neurological connections. The child reports an improved self-image and goes on to draw a more complete representation of self. This can then help the child to repair damaged attachment relationships. During reprocessing, the therapist notices how their distance from the patient, tone of voice, and posture interact and influence the patient's progress in the session. Further awareness of these factors will be achieved by gaining experience in SF-EMDR psychotherapy.

My EMDR supervisees often report feelings of exhaustion after intense EMDR sessions. I believe this is due to negative emotions, feelings, and sensations released from the patient. Supervision must address the need for therapist repair and restoration before the next therapeutic session.

Images used with the patient who is undergoing SF-EMDR psychotherapy and peak performance

Certain images are useful to help the patient understand the process of therapy and help to map out the individual SF-EMDR stages of reprocessing. They also serve as an introduction to the chakra energy fields, which will be unfamiliar to most patients educated purely in allopathic medicine. However, patients from Eastern cultures will have more extensive knowledge of the application of the increased levels of vibrational energy accessed as they get in touch with higher chakra levels.

The total integration of all stages of SF-EMDR psychotherapy is taken from the cover image of *The Art of BART* (O'Malley, 2015). Taken together, this diagram represents the different stages of SF-EMDR psychotherapy. The patient enables their gut instinct (heartfelt sensation, thyroid sensation, lump in the throat) to be reprocessed, and recognition in the brain can take place as a final step in their reprocessing of thoughts. These are crucial stages in SF-EMDR psychotherapy. Once the body sensations are digested and reprocessed via bilateral affective stimulation, the scene is set for the cerebellum to link up with the orbitofrontal cortex so that learning and meaning can emerge from any significant and traumatic life experiences.

The diagram mentioned above illustrates how SF-EMDR psychotherapy relates to the patient's endocrine, immune, vascular, nervous, and chakra energy systems. I believe these show a genuine interrelationship, physically and functionally, between the theories of Western and Eastern medicine.

The initial focus of reprocessing is to identify a bodily location for a physical sensation or gut reaction associated with the traumatic memory. The process then expands to a wider area; the enteric plexus feeds into heartfelt emotions of traumatic grief, loss, and sadness. The throat chakra is often blocked with unexpressed feelings; once overcome, there is interplay of reprocessing between the bilateral cerebellar, which directly connect to the prefrontal cortex, and the sixth chakra, or third eye of the pineal gland. There is also a parallel interplay of reprocessing between the cerebral hemispheres. Thus, the initial ascending reprocessing lessens the trauma intensity, facilitating descending patterns of stimulation, which complete the patient's reprocessing pathway. Alternate foot-tapping and observation of other movements of the body's periphery manipulate the figure-of-eight pathways illustrated in the diagrams above. This allows identification of any blocks to information processing consequent to the patient's information processing. This could be at the level of the gut heart or head. Alternatively, it could relate to information blocked at the level of one of the energy points or chakras which in turn are related to the endocrine, lymphatic, and immune systems

The first endocrine system is located at the lumbar and coccygeal plexus (L5-S5) (Figure 9.1). It is linked to the adrenal glands and therefore to our fight/flight response and physical survival needs, cf. the first level in Maslow's hierarchy of needs. We form our basic attachments and tribal associations at this level, which relates to formation of our musculoskeletal structures. Deficits, i.e. symptoms at this level, must involve activation and reprocessing of this energy system using SF-EMDR psychotherapy.

The second endocrine system is located at the lumbar plexus (T9-L4). It is also linked to the adrenals and to the male and female genital organs. It is mainly involved with the gastrointestinal, renal, and sex organs. Issues of abnormal sexual, renal, gastrointestinal, or emotional symptoms must involve activation and reprocessing at this bodily level.

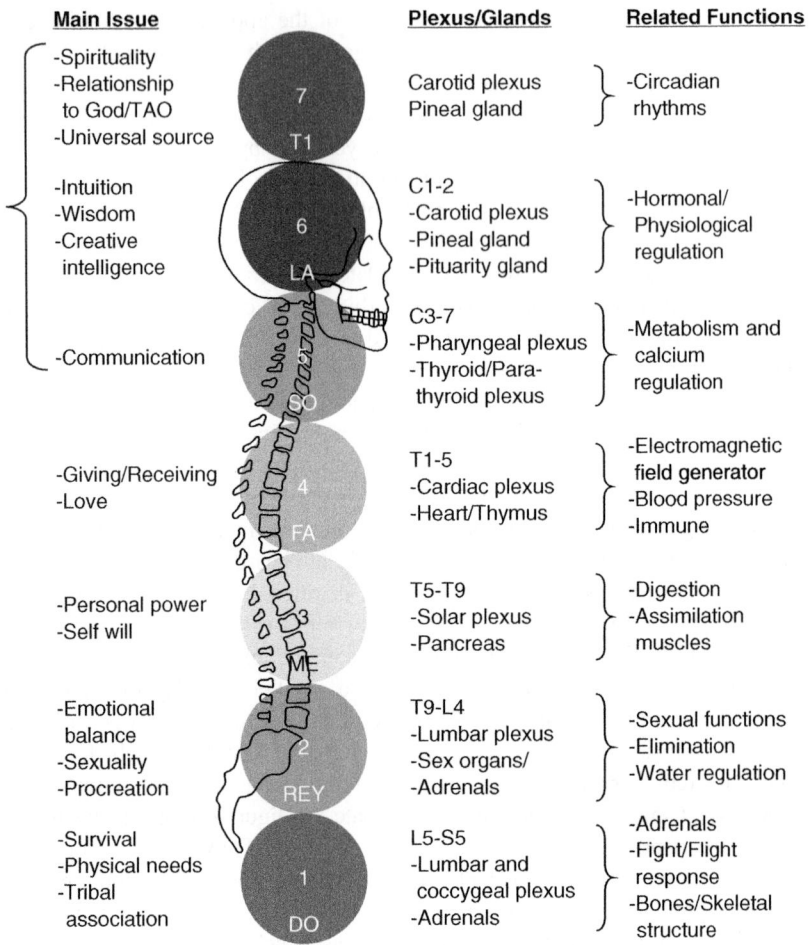

Main Issue	Plexus/Glands	Related Functions

-Spirituality
-Relationship to God/TAO
-Universal source

Carotid plexus
Pineal gland

-Circadian rhythms

-Intuition
-Wisdom
-Creative intelligence

C1-2
-Carotid plexus
-Pineal gland
-Pituarity gland

-Hormonal/ Physiological regulation

-Communication

C3-7
-Pharyngeal plexus
-Thyroid/Para- thyroid plexus

-Metabolism and calcium regulation

-Giving/Receiving
-Love

T1-5
-Cardiac plexus
-Heart/Thymus

-Electromagnetic field generator
-Blood pressure
-Immune

-Personal power
-Self will

T5-T9
-Solar plexus
-Pancreas

-Digestion
-Assimilation muscles

-Emotional balance
-Sexuality
-Procreation

T9-L4
-Lumbar plexus
-Sex organs/
-Adrenals

-Sexual functions
-Elimination
-Water regulation

-Survival
-Physical needs
-Tribal association

L5-S5
-Lumbar and coccygeal plexus
-Adrenals

-Adrenals
-Fight/Flight response
-Bones/Skeletal structure

Figure 9.1 Lateral view of the chakras and bodily organs illustrating the integrated energy systems of the body incorporating Western and Eastern medical beliefs. SF-EMDR psychotherapy is ideally placed to help clients achieve peak performance.

Source: reprinted with permission from Prof Ernest Rossi.

The third endocrine system is located at the thoracic vertebrae (T5-T9) and resonates with the stomach, pancreas, and coeliac plexus. Issues of indigestion, metabolism muscle performance, self-confidence, and will power must be addressed at this bodily location using the buzzers as indicated by the patient.

The fourth endocrine level is located at thoracic vertebrae (T1-T5.) The heart, thymus, and cardiac plexus are involved with generating the body's electromagnetic field. The main issues here are ischaemic heart disease, hypertension, stroke, and immune dysfunction and repair is via giving and receiving love as an energetic field of communication.

The fifth endocrine system is located at the cervical vertebrae (C3-C7.) The pharyngeal and parathyroid plexus and thyroid gland are involved in regulation of thyroxine (T4) and triiodothyronine (T3), and thyroid stimulating hormone (TSH) and calcium and calmodulin. Symptoms here are felt as a lump in the throat and related to the communication of unresolved loss, grief, and traumatic stress.

The sixth endocrine system is located at the first and second cervical vertebrae (C1-C2). This involves the pituitary and pineal glands and the carotid plexus regulating body physiology and hormone production. Reprocessing at this higher level involves understanding and communication of intuition, wisdom, creativity, imagination, and intelligence.

The seventh endocrine system is conceptualised as linked to the body aura, energy field, or Merkaba. It is believed to involve both the crown chakra, pineal gland, and carotid plexus. These regulate ultradian and circadian rhythms. Activation of this endocrine system involves spirituality, relationship to God, the Tao of quantum physics, and the universal source.

Isaac Newton proposed a harmonic synchrony, i.e. do re mi fa so la ti, equating to increasing vibrational frequency of the colours from red, with the lowest resonant frequency, to violet, with the highest vibrational frequency. This also relates to raising the Kundalini energy through meditation. This is practiced in different forms of yoga.

The human endocrine glands correspond to the body chakras illustrated in Figure 9.1, as described below:

Crown | anterior, posterior, and intermediate pituitary gland secrete the hormones regulating homeostasis:

- Growth hormone;
- Thyroid-stimulating hormone;
- Adrenocorticotropic hormone;
- Beta endorphin;
- Prolactin;
- Luteinising hormone;
- Follicle-stimulating hormone;
- Antidiuretic hormone or vasopressin;
- Oxytocin, which regulates mother–infant bonding; and
- Melanocyte-stimulating hormone.

Forehead chakra

This is located one inch above the third-eye chakra and extends outward from the centre of the forehead between left and right frontal lobes. It appears to have been ignored by metaphysical science. However, the hypothalamus is a major endocrine organ. The word hypothalamus is derived from the Greek for "under room." The hypothalamus has many functions, as listed below:

- Medial preoptic nucleus release gonadotropin releasing hormone GnRH;
- Supraoptic nucleus releases vasopressin or ADH;
- Paraventricular nucleus releases thyrotropin-releasing hormone, corticotropin-releasing hormone, and oxytocin. The latter is a fundamental part of maternal–infant bonding;
- The anterior hypothalamic nucleus governs thermoregulation, sweating, and inhibits thyrotropin. Thus, the HPA axis is part of a feedback loop like the rising and ebbing of the chakra energies themselves;
- The suprachiasmatic nucleus regulates circadian rhythms;
- The lateral nucleus governs thirst and hunger;
- Dorsomedial nucleus regulates heart-rate, blood pressure and stimulation of the gastrointestinal tract;
- Ventromedial nucleus governs appetite and neuroendocrine cell secretion in lung and adrenals. Stress can stimulate the hypothalamus to release these carcinogens;
- The arcuate nucleus releases dopamine, growth-hormone releasing hormone, and regulates feeding. Stress can therefore decrease growth hormone and result in stunted growth;
- Mammillary nuclei are part of mammillary bodies and are believed to be important for recollective and spatial memory. It is part of the Papez circuit, which forms a limbus shape around the brainstem; and
- The posterior hypothalamic nucleus is involved in regulation of the autonomic nervous system (Cavdar et al., 2001), with inputs from brainstem and subcortical structures. This study showed that this nucleus connected to the lateral and medial septal nuclei of the forebrain. It also revealed widespread connections to the amygdaloid body, which helps to regulate emotional stimuli. Further studies have shown that the insular cortex receives a visceral input and connects with the autonomic nuclei of the forebrain (Cechetto & Saper, 1987). The midbrain periaqueductal grey matter (PAG) directly connects to this nucleus. The PAG regulates defensive and anti-nociceptive behaviour along with regulation of the cardiovascular system. This nucleus may regulate sympathetic outflow via the raphe nucleus synapses with the adrenal glands. Finally, links to the cerebellum have also been shown.

The hypothalamus receives neural tracts from the nucleus tractus solitarius. This set of sensory nuclei is embedded in the brainstem. It governs input to the viscera, is a centre for cortical integration, and has reciprocal connections with the cerebellum and prefrontal cortex. It appears that the connections are reciprocal, that is, go both ways.

The third-eye pineal gland secretes melatonin, which regulates the sleep–wake cycle and represents intuition and activation of the Merkaba.

Throat | Thyroid and parathyroid balances cerebral rationality with emotional expression of the heart and represents spiritual and physical communication.

Heart | Chest (heart and lungs) and thymus represent harmony and love.

Solar Plexus | Stomach and pancreas represent creativity and personal energy.

Sacral and Umbilicus | Ovaries/testes deal with sexuality and emotional balance.

Root and base of spine | Adrenals relate to fight-or-flight and physical survival and represent grounding and security.

It is interesting that each chakra is anatomically associated with different endocrine glands. When a patient experiences toxic stress, the HPA axis is stimulated. Initially, this causes secretion of adrenaline from both adrenal glands. In severe depression, left untreated, the symptoms will often last nine months. CT scans of the adrenal glands show that they increase markedly in size during the illness (Professor Ted Dinan, personal communication.) Chronic toxic stress further stimulates the adrenal glands. This time, they secrete corticosteroids and mineralocorticoids such as aldosterone. The corticosteroids act on receptors in the central nervous system. This down-regulates the ability of the neuron to function. The chemical neurotransmitters are not released and the lock-and-key mechanism I referred to earlier does not occur.

Each endocrine gland secretes a different hormone. Each hormone has a unique molecular structure, which vibrates with a specific resonant energy. This is akin to the idea of chakras in Eastern medicine (Figure 9.2). Finally, the pituitary gland is associated with ten hormones of different vibrational energy. The crown chakra is said to have 1,000 petals in most Eastern traditions, but only thirty-three in Tibetan culture. Of importance is the recognition that the anatomical location of the crown is associated with the development of pure consciousness. In Judaeo-Christianity, Jesus Christ was mocked and adorned with a crown of thorns. This could be taken to imply that he was able to activate his crown chakra and access higher planetary and cosmic planes of consciousness.

The Primo Vascular system as a new anatomical system

This information comes from the *Journal of Acupuncture and Meridian Studies*, December 2013. Stefanov et al. described the Primo Vascular system or PVS as a system combining the features of the cardiovascular nervous and the neuroanatomical systems.

The article also explains the efficacy of acupuncture points and meridians, the vital energy mentioned in China as Qi and in India as prana. This is an electromagnetic wave that interacts with the DNA of the PVS. The PVS is the earliest embryological tissue and links living organisms with the environment. It exists at animal, plant, and fungi levels.

Long-Hand King, in 1963, first discovered this system and follow-up research has been done by Seoul National University in South Korea. During this

THE CHAKRAS

SAHASRARA
The seventh chakra

Cosmic consciousness,
interior peace.

AJNA
The sixth chakra
aum

Jnana yoga
Recognising and accepting destiny,
confidence in one's own intuition.

WISHUDDHA
The fifth chakra
ham
ether

Mantra yoga
Transformation of energy through
words and images.

ANAHATA
The fourth chakra
yam
air

Bhakti yoga
Love, vitality,
being one with nature.

MANIPURA
The third chakra
ram
fire

Hatha, Karma
and Raja yogas
Firmness and organisational talent.

SWADHISHTHANA
The second chakra
vam
water

Tantra yoga
Ease in relationship, pleasure
in physical contact.

MULADHARA
The first chakra
lam
earth

Hatha and Kundalini yoga
Vitality,
stability, and strength.

name
order
root mantra
element

typical yoga
characteristics

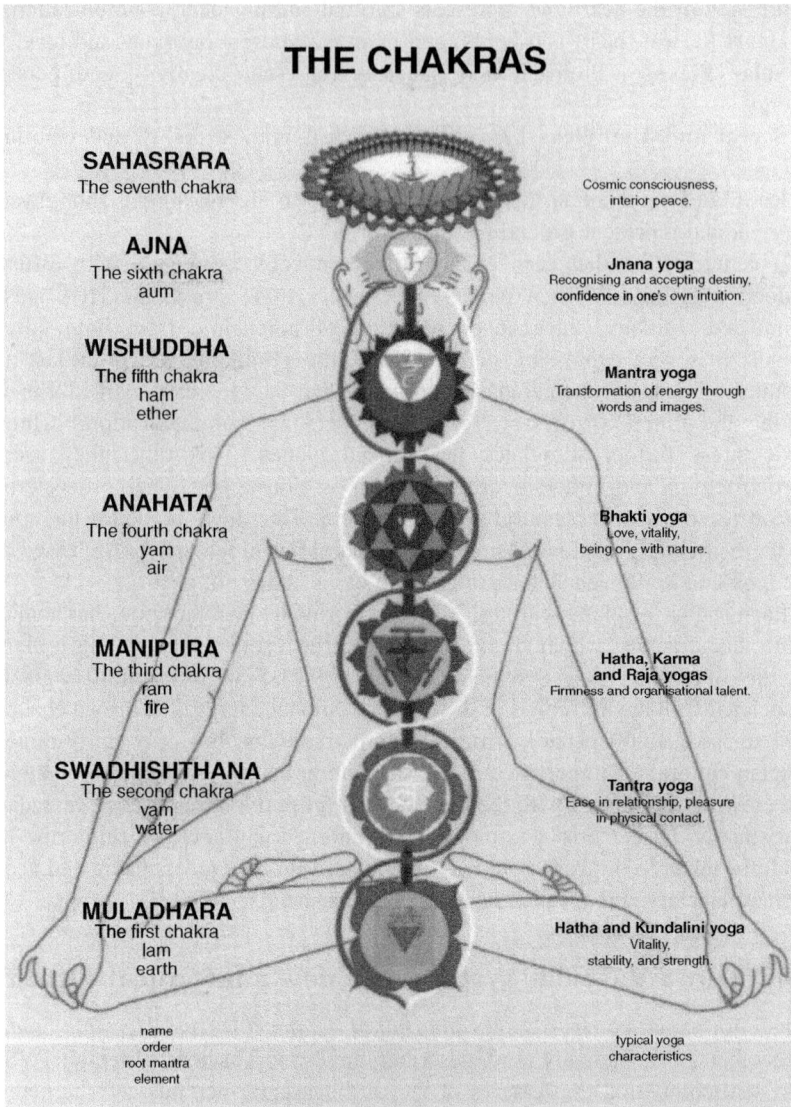

Figure 9.2 Description of the Chakras with name, order, mantra, element, and typical yoga characteristics.

Source: reprinted with permission of Prof Ernest Rossi.

research, channels and nodes known as Primo Vessels (PV) and Primo Nodes (PM) were discovered.

A liquid known as the Primo Fluid circulates in the PVS. It flows at a slower rate than blood and lymph. It contains DNA, RNA, nitrogen, fats, hyaluronic acid, nineteen free amino acids, and sixteen mononucleotides. The sub vessels of PVS contain endothelial cells with smooth muscle cells, large-shaped nuclei, and adventissure. The vessel is surrounded by a membrane. The Primo Nodes are connected to the meridians and the meridians start and end at the PNs for the organs. When the fluid in the PVS changes in its circulation, organ tissues are affected in terms of function. Stimulation of the PVs increases heart rate and intestinal movement and skeletal muscle function. The PV blast cell forms within seven to eight hours of fertilisation. The primordial PV is born within ten hours of fertilisation and the lumen of the PVS has developed by fifteen hours of fertilisation, and the complete vessel is evident by twenty to twenty-eight hours of fertilisation. PVS exists in invertebrates, vertebrates, and plants. Initially, microcells develop in the vasculature of this PVS. The microcells grow into cells, which ultimately develop into channels for transmission of biophotons called sanals. A sanalsome is a type of chromosome that forms when cells divide. The chromosome emerges in the metafields of cell division and organs such as bone marrow, spleen, and lymphatic nodes have a well-developed PVS containing PVs and PMs.

Functional aspects of the PVS

The PVS cells show excitability with calcium channels. They contain collagen, which can react to photon emissions and the PVS may act as an optical channel of biophoton emission with DNA acting as a photon store and coherent radiator. Biophotons may be electromagnetic signals that play a key role in cell development and differentiation. The light propagation function of the PVS can explain the instantaneous effect seen in the brain MRI after shining a torch on the vision point of the foot. This occurs in 0.000007 milliseconds whereas when the light is shone into an eye the respective part of the visual cortex is seen to light up in the MRI scan within 250 milliseconds. The PVS can be categorised as an endocrine organ as the PVS liquid contains adrenaline and noradrenaline and there are chromaffin cells in the acupoints. The PVS appears to be an optical channel to conduct photons. The electromagnetic field travelling through the PVS and DNA is equivalent to the Qi energy that is distributed throughout the body. The DNA in the PVS stores genetic information which is received from these electromagnetic fields. It is possible that these electromagnetic waves of Qi energy are transformed into information stored in the DNA granules in the PVS.

There is increasing interest in converting information to energy. This can also occur in the reverse direction in terms of energy converting into information. The theoretical physicist Steven Hawking once said, "electromagnetism is the basis for life itself."

DNA may produce low-frequency collective motion and the hypothesis of low-frequency phonons in proteins has been proposed. These phonons are able to transfer energy and relate to DNA's role for transforming electromagnetic energy information.

Additional aspects of the Primo Vascular system

The PVS system allows living organisms to communicate with their environment. It is duplicated by the vascular and nervous systems during very early stages of embryological development. The PVS combines the features of vascular, nervous, immune, and hormonal systems. It covers the entire body and regulates and coordinates all biological life processes. For this reason, it is an ideal target for sensorimotor-focused EMDR for psychotherapy and peak performance.

The PVS is the physical substance for the acupuncture points and meridians and is involved in the development and functioning of living organisms. As the PVS occurs in the early hours of foetal development, when other embryonic body systems have developed, this primordial PVS remains connected to all these systems and controls them, as it is the oldest morphological functional system. Until now the PVS has been a missing body-system but, in reality, it can explain the many mysteries of life. This physical substrate for the meridian system is the missing point that can be used to combine ancient Chinese medicine and Ayurvedic beliefs with modern Western science into the successful psychotherapy I have hypothesised in my first book, *The Art of BART*, published in 2015 by Karnac Books.

As the PVS is ubiquitous throughout animal, plant, and fungal kingdoms it may explain why there is a lack of intermediate forms between species, which is a fundamental flaw in Darwinian evolutionary theory. It may be that the PVS as a primordial bodily system, widely disseminated throughout the living organisms on earth, can store and capture information from environmental electromagnetic fields. This stored information will then permit dramatic and sudden changes in an organism's DNA and therefore explain why there is a lack of intermediate forms between species currently in the fossil record.

In March 2018 the interstitium was discovered as the eightieth organ in the body. This is a shock-absorbing tissue underneath the skin, gut, and blood vessels. The dense connective tissue is now known to be interconnected compartments filled with fluid. The interstitium is the largest organ in the body and is supported by a mesh of strong and flexible connective-tissue proteins. It protects organs, muscles, and vessels that keep our bodies alive by absorbing bumps and shocks. The fluid in the interstitium appears to drain into the lymphatic system and is involved in ageing of the skin and inflammatory diseases. It is likely that the PVS is also prevalent in the interstitium and provides a new route for tracking meridian and acupressure-point systems and is another way in which Eastern and Western medicine can be seen to be integrated. This information comes from *Scientific Reports 2018*, "Structure and Distribution of an Unrecognised Interstitium in Human Tissues" by Wells et al.

Summary

The submucosa, dermis, facia, and vascular adventissure are not packed collagen walls as previously believed, rather they are fluid-filled interstitial spaces. These spaces are supported and organised by a collagen lattice and act as shock absorbers, being easily compressed and distended. This impacts on the lungs, aorta, digestive tract, skin, and musculoskeletal system and are a key component of oedema. They also reflect fluid distention and stasis in the interstitial space. These structures may also play an important role in display of malignancy and non-malignant conditions such as biliary atresia, primary sclerosing cholangitis in the biliary tree, scleroderma in the dermis and oesophagus, and inflammatory bowel disease in the digestive tract.

The spaces between tissues demonstrated under the microscope and characterised as the interstitium provide another avenue for communication, for gut feelings, heartfelt sensations, and head thoughts as described in sensorimotor-focused EMDR for psychotherapy and peak performance.

The root of psychiatry is from the Greek words *psyche* and *iatros*. Together they mean soul healing, and I have devised SF-EMDR psychotherapy in the spirit of the Ancient Greek physicians who did not subscribe to the mind–body dualism of Descartes. The discovery of the interstitium as the largest body organ which accounts for 20% of body weight provides further evidence for the clinical effectiveness of SF-EMDR.

Case example one

A heavy-goods-vehicle driver was referred to me in 2011. He had been involved in a fatal road traffic accident in 2008. Since then, he had attended more than ninety individual sessions of CBT. He spoke of how he dreaded these sessions, as he was asked to repeat the history, which became increasingly difficult because of the accompanying dysregulated affect. He was in a state of speechless terror and experienced continuous fear and hopelessness. This had led to severe depression with suicidal intent. During SF-EMDR psychotherapy, I used bilateral cerebellar stimulation to regulate his affect. I asked him to imagine the chair as the driving seat in the heavy goods vehicle. I asked him to hold the zappers in each hand as if holding on to the steering wheel. I used the freeze-frame technique to slow the reprocessing into manageable bytes. His peripheral nervous system became reactivated as if he was reliving the event in vivo. His grip tightened on the tactile zappers and at the point of impact his right leg shot forward. My patient had his eyes closed and was unaware of this motor impulse. When I drew his attention to the instinctive movement, he realised this was when he applied maximum pressure to the brakes. Metaphorically, it was as if his life had been put on hold since the accident, as he, at a somatomotor level, was still applying the brakes. During the SF-EMDR psychotherapy session, he was encouraged to mindfully let go of these brakes to get his life get back on the road. This stoic Yorkshire man could relive the experience and grieve appropriately, realising that the driver who swerved into his path was the guilty party and that his driving was not at fault. The physical injuries he suffered from the accident and the associated traumatic images of the driver he had killed were readily dealt with in several further sessions. His latest feedback was that he had recovered his previous zest for life and was well on the road to recovery.

Troubleshooting with SF-EMDR psychotherapy and peak performance

The patient may show "stuckness" in trauma processing via a movement impulse, as in the above example, a physical sensation, a gut feeling, reaction, or instinct, a core belief, or intense affect or destructive thought process. Individual therapies that focus on one or two of these might miss the vital factor causing the blockage to information reprocessing. In the later stages of SF-EMDR psychotherapy, wider chains of association to the original trauma are made with the patient. This allows any residual pockets of trauma to be located so that they can be actively reprocessed towards resolution and recovery. Patients usually respond by saying they feel lighter and as if a weight has been lifted from their shoulders.

I encourage the patient to notice further reprocessing that may occur after the session. This often comes in the form of a new insight or dream moving on from the original traumatic experience. I encourage patients to write this down and/or email me so that we can discuss its meaning for them at the start of the next session. The patient can then be able to avail themself of peak psychotherapy in moving towards positive psychiatric and psychological change. This is an area often neglected by therapists who are restricted to trauma resolution. Once traumatic stress has been processed, patients are able to ascend Maslow's hierarchy towards an integration of mind, body, and spirit. Specific goals can be worked on to achieve their chosen areas of peak performance.

Summary

This chapter outlines the practical steps a practitioner needs to take to conduct a SF-EMDR psychotherapy and, ideally, peak performance session. A menu of possible patient responses is provided, as this approach will be new to both practitioner and patient. The whole process is made possible by the BOKA machine, which can be explained as the patient's body having the necessary knowledge (in terms of the menu already described). However, this knowledge is not in an accessible form and must be activated by gradually increasing its resonant frequency (i.e. "body of knowledge activator.") To help both therapists and patients, illustrations (Figures 9.1 and 9.2) are included. These shows how the endocrine glands correspond to the chakras, and the surrounding energy fields.

There is a detailed description of the ten hormones secreted by the pituitary gland and comparison is made to the beliefs of the thousand-petalled lotus of the crown chakra. It could be said that when the ten hormones are released, they cascade across the HPA axis and their effect is magnified ten times, giving direct equivalency to the thousand petals of the lotus flower associated with the crown chakra. However, people of Tibetan Buddhist faith ascribe to the view that the crown chakra has thirty-three petals. This can be seen to equate to the number of years Jesus Christ is said to have lived on earth. In the Christian faith, Christ is said to have ascended to heaven on the third day. This equates to a vibrational energy of 0.3 recurring. By ascending, he would have increased his vibrational energy to 1,000. The chapter concludes with a case example illustrating the process and how to troubleshoot with patients.

Assessment of the impact on the cranial nerves by taking a history informed by SF-EMDR for psychotherapy and peak performance

In taking a trauma history, I recommend assessment of the twelve cranial nerves for possible involvement in the relevant significant life events. Any unresolved trauma at a neurological level requires an appropriate intervention to integrate the sensory fragments of the experience into a coherent whole prior to reprocessing.

The cranial nerves originate from the base of the brainstem. The nerves branch out bilaterally in terms of motor and sensory fibres to the rest of the body. These connections are to the senses of smell in the nose, vision in the eye, movements of the eye, muscles, and facial sensation, facial muscles, balance and hearing, the motor and sensory functions of the vagus, motor and sensation of the tongue and pharynx, muscles involved in the startle reflex, and muscles of the tongue. The olfactory nerve synapses with the nerves in the cribriform plate in the nasal epithelium. It is the only cranial nerve not to access the cerebral cortex. In traumatic stress involving smoke, fire, or other acrid smells, these can stay with the patient and be very resistant to resolution. Bilateral olfactory desensitisation can be achieved with SF-EMDR psychotherapy. Using knowledge of the cranial-nerve pathway and function informs the therapist's taking of the patient's trauma history.

SF-EMDR psychotherapy can then be reliably targeted to focus on reprocessing the functions of the affected cranial nerves. The relevant questions in relation to the twelve cranial nerves are as follows.

I Olfactory: The patient should be asked if there are any odours, smells, or aromas relevant to the traumatic episode. This could be the aftershave of a male sexual assailant, or exposure to smoke and fumes from a vehicle accident or house fire. Patients traumatised following a hospital procedure often report the smell of antisepsis, anaesthetics, or the hospital environment itself as traumatic. Patients who have witnessed a decaying body find it difficult to eradicate the smell from their nostrils. I have used bilateral olfactory stimulation to help eliminate these noxious odours. Imagining a favourite childhood smell can do this. For example, using tissue suffused with a favourite natural perfume (placed over the nose and inhaled through each nostril alternately.) I have proposed a device that would allow the appropriate soothing aroma to be delivered to each nostril via a mask separated into two chambers, each connected to a nasal spray.

II Optic nerve: The optic tract travels to the occipital cortex of the opposite side and processes images from the visual fields of the left and right eye. Any distressing image can be processed to resolution during the stages of SF-EMDR psychotherapy.

III Oculomotor nerve, IV trochlear nerve, and VI abducens nerve: These motor nerves act on the eyes to move them in all possible directions. In my clinical experience, peripheral tactile bilateral stimulation and bilateral cerebellar stimulation activates the brainstem where these nerves have their anatomical origin. SF-EMDR psychotherapy allows attention to be paid to the subsequent direction of the patient's eye movements. My hypothesis is that looking upwards is an effort by the patient to extract meaning equivalent to engaging with their prefrontal cortex. Looking with both eyes to the right (or therapist's left) is usually a sign that the patient is accessing a past memory. Looking with both eyes to the patient's left (or therapist's right) tends to occur when working on a future template. Each patient may have a different meaning for their eye movements depending on which cerebral hemisphere is dominant.

The beauty of SF-EMDR psychotherapy is the constant therapist–patient dialogue, which allows each hypothesis to be confirmed or refuted. This is different to neuro linguistic programming (NLP), which has a fixed attribution to the various eye movements. However, when Dr Richard Bandler and Dr John Grinder introduced NLP in the 1970s in California they emphasised reading eye patterns for useful information. These are further described by Molden and Hutchinson.

Visual thinking mode: Looking up and to the left implies recall of a visual memory. Looking up and to the right implies constructing an image. Looking up and to both the right and left alternatively indicates that both recall and construction of images are occurring. The conversation of visual communicators includes phrases such as: Can you see what I mean? It's clear and bright. I'll paint you a picture. Let's zoom in on this point. Patients often speak quickly in a high-pitched voice and use shallow chest breathing.

Auditory thinking mode: A lateral left movement of the eyes implies the patient is remembering sounds associated with the trauma. A lateral right movement implies reconstructing a sound or conversation. An auditory communicator uses phrases such as: I hear what you say. That rings a bell. It sounds OK to me. It's music to my ears.

Internal dialogue thinking mode: When the eyes point down and to the left they suggest that the patient is conversing with themself. The patient may put their hand next to their face or chin in classic "thinker pose." Paying attention to these micro movements is emphasised in SF-EMDR psychotherapy and gives vital information to guide the reprocessing of traumata.

Kinaesthetic or feeling mode: According to NLP, eyes pointing down and to the right imply that the patient is immersed in a feeling experience. They will tend to use phrases such as: That feels right. I can go with that. Let's keep in touch. I hope to be on an even keel from now on. I am getting the hang of this therapy now.

In practice, most patients use a combination of states in learning and social interaction. Several questionnaires are available to assess if there is a dominant style. I use a quick and easy method. The patient is asked to close their eyes and imagine sitting down to taste their favourite dessert. I usually suggest an ice-cream of their own choosing in terms of colour, flavour, and toppings. With their eyes still closed, they move the index finger of either hand to the point in space where they imagined the ice-cream. The commonest point is in the middle of the forehead. This represents the third eye, pineal gland, or sixth chakra and implies that the person is predominantly a visual learner and communicator. If the patient locates the area of the auditory cortex on either side, this implies a preference for auditory learning and communication. Patients who are predominantly kinaesthetic have difficulty pinpointing a location in space and, if pressed, tend to locate either parietal cortex bilaterally.

Three types of eye movement are recognised:

1) Convergence is used for depth perception and ensures that the image of the object lands on the correct spot in each retina;
2) Saccades are short and rapid eye movements, which are unconsciously controlled at a frequency of 4 Hertz. A larger area can be scanned with the high resolution or fovea of the eye; and
3) The eyes make smooth pursuit movements both when tracking an object's movement and when fixed on a single point.

Fixate on a hand 30 cm away, as in EMDR. When the hand moves rapidly from side to side at a greater frequency than 1 Hertz the fingers appear blurred. Now ask the person to hold index and middle finger 30 cm away. Then move your head as fast as possible up and down and from side to side. The person's fingers and hand remain clear. The head-brain can move the eyes in relation to a fixed hand image following a hand movement. When the pursuit system fails, a blurred image results. This tends to explain why the practice of EMDR using simulated eye movements generates a blurred image during its protocol-driven procedure.

V Trigeminal nerve: This nerve is sensory to the mandible, maxilla, and nasal sinuses. It is motor to the muscles of mastication. With the patient, it is important to enquire about any direct damage here during trauma to the face.

VII Facial nerve: This nerve is motor to the muscles of the face, submaxillary, sublingual, and lacrimal glands (tears). It also provides sensation to the anterior two thirds of the tongue and soft palate. I often find that patients reprocessing head trauma will display unconscious movements of the tongue and jaw as they move towards resolution and recovery with SF-EMDR psychotherapy.

VIII Vestibulocochlear nerve: This nerve provides the senses of balance and hearing. Most traumatic experiences are initiated by an orienting response to sound. This then triggers a startle response to look towards the sound source. Hence, we hear the ambulance's alarm before we turn around to see its blue light flashing. The traumatic sound information is stored in the auditory cortex in milliseconds. In taking a trauma history, we must be aware of the disabling impact of sudden unexpected noise before we can initiate reprocessing of the whole event.

Case example two

A twelve-year-old boy described how he was lying asleep on the couch with his parents and sister asleep upstairs around midnight. Suddenly, four gunmen burst in, threatening to shoot. Although the gunmen were disturbed and left suddenly, the sounds of the break-in and the sight of the men in balaclavas haunted him. Using SF-EMDR psychotherapy, we could freeze-frame the initial moment as his auditory cortex via the vestibulocochlear nerve registered the attack. The butt of the gun was used to shatter the wooden door frame and it was the sound of broken wood and glass that activated his startle reflex. By means of a combination of the seven-element exercise (vide infra) and desensitisation to the sounds picked up by the vestibulocochlear nerve, he made a full recovery.

IX Glossopharyngeal nerve: This nerve provides sensation to the posterior one-third of the tongue, tonsils, pharynx, and middle ear. It is motor to the stylopharyngeus and pharyngeal musculature.

Case example three

A thirty-year-old female patient was on holiday in Spain and enjoying an evening meal. She suddenly stood up and drank a glass of water. A lump of meat lodged in her trachea. She started to choke and was having a "café coronary." No one came to her aid until an off-duty fireman realised what was happening. He rushed to her side and performed vigorous abdominal thrusts, causing her to expel the piece of meat stuck in her throat. Several years later, a colleague who worked as a consultant psychiatrist in psychotherapy referred her to me. We ran a weekly clinic in parental and infant mental health. Her obsession with liquidising all her food was affecting her ability to adequately care for her infant. As she progressed through the stages of SF-EMDR psychotherapy, we could adequately reprocess the holiday incident. However, she was left with the fearful sensation of a lump in her throat. By getting her to imagine the fireman reapplying the abdominal thrusts, this sensation dissolved and she could recommence solid food and care for her infant. Any trauma to the throat, tongue, and neck will affect the glossopharyngeal cranial nerve and this trauma had been stored as a somatically accessible memory as opposed to a verbally accessed memory.

X Vagus nerve: The term vagus comes from the Latin word for "wanderer" because of its undulating course throughout the body. It is motor to the pharynx, heart, lungs, bronchi, and GIT. It provides sensation to heart, lungs, bronchi, trachea, larynx, pharynx, GIT, and external ear via the auricular branch. It is now known that gentle massage of the earlobe has a direct calming effect on the heart via these fibres. This might have a role in counteracting a patient's hyperarousal associated with the RAPIDS state.

XI Accessory nerve: This is motor to the sternomastoid and trapezius muscles. It is activated at times of trauma, causing the startle reflex. Cranial accessory fibres of the nerve supply intrinsic muscles of the larynx, pharynx, and palate.

XII Hypoglossal nerve: This supplies the intrinsic and extrinsic muscles of the tongue. These are responsible for automatic/reflex tongue movements and are often implicated in patients' traumatic experiences. The course of the twelve cranial nerves is described in *Gray's Anatomy* (Gray, 1995)

Effects of severe depression on cellular aging

This process is thought to occur at the cellular level of telomeres. Telomeres are specialised nucleic acid proteins that cap the ends of DNA, protecting it from damage during replication. The final part of the telomere fails to be replicated during each cell division in what has become known as the "end-replication problem." This results in progressively shorter telomeres. When telomeres reach a critically short length, cells can die prematurely.

Stress and trauma are believed to contribute to telomere shortening. However, telomerase is a ribonucleoprotein enzyme that elongates telomeres by adding nucleotides to the end of chromosomes. This leaves the possibility of longer telomere length and more accurate DNA replication during cell division. I inform my patients that stress reduction and relaxation is associated with increased levels of the enzyme telomerase. This can result in an anti-aging effect and is mentioned in the following script issued to patients to get them in the right frame of mind for SF-EMDR psychotherapy.

The seven-element relaxation exercise (earth, air, water, heat/warmth, ether, light, and love or universal energy)

For patients who present with affective dysregulation, I have modified Laub and Shapiro's four-element exercise. The description to the patient is as follows:

As you are sitting comfortably in the chair, I want you to mindfully place both feet on the floor. Imagine your feet penetrating through the floor to the earth below. You may want to imagine yourself on a warm, sandy beach with your feet in contact with the sand or standing in a garden next to a tree. Imagine the roots of the tree giving support to you as you lean against the tree trunk.

The second element is the fresh sea or forest air all around you as you let your mind rest on your breathing. As you breathe in and out, notice how more oxygen reaches your brain and your heart rate slows. Breath in for a count of seven seconds and exhale for a count of eleven seconds to stimulate diaphragmatic breathing. This will improve your concentration as SF-EMDR psychotherapy proceeds.

The third element is water. Seventy per cent of the composition of our body is water and, as you drink from the glass, imagine swallowing water mixed with saliva. This contains the enzyme amylase, which will relax your stomach and gastrointestinal tract. Any knots or butterflies in your tummy are eased as the tension relaxes.

The fourth element is heat or warmth, which percolates throughout your body as regional blood flow increases during the session. We will pay attention to any areas of blood flow that are associated with the hot or cold sensations of the RAPIDS and FROZEN states we have discussed. At all times, we will seek to return to the CALM WATERS.

The fifth element is the ether, or atmosphere of calm, generated by you as your trauma is reprocessed during SF-EMDR psychotherapy. I will now draw your attention to your favourite colour of light. This will be imagined coming from the cosmos of universal light energy. It will be drawn down through the gateway, or stellar chakra, to your soul-star chakra and then into your body through the third-eye, or pineal-gland, chakra. As it gains increasing focus and strength, the light connects the third eye to the throat chakra. From here, your favourite colour of light energy moves to the chest, heart, lungs, and thymus, increasing your awareness of harmony and love at your heart chakra. From here, the light energy reaches the solar plexus, giving creativity and concentration. The light reaches your sacral chakra, connecting to your innate sexuality before moving to infuse the root chakra, ensuring that you are secure and grounded to commence therapy. Finally, the light reaches the earth-star chakra under your feet and connects to the roots in the earth below. The relaxation spreads to each organ and cell in your body and you experience an anti-aging effect.

Finally, I invite you to create a mental image of those people whose presence creates a loving atmosphere. You are aware of this room as a safe or peaceful place. You can think of people, real or imagined, or a favourite pet. When you get a strong sense of the nurturing quality of the person or animal tap your feet alternately, tapping into this resource. I ask you to visualise this loving and nurturing energy surrounding, strengthening, and enabling you to deal with whatever trials and tribulations are currently being faced. See yourself hugging these people or pets for at least fifteen seconds, your head resting on their shoulder so that heart-to-heart communication can occur.

This last resource can be augmented with nurturing protector figures and wise inner advisers, as described by Parnell.

The patient will then pause before continuing to resonate at the level of the earth-star chakra. This exercise will return the universal energy to its stellar origins. One of the fundamental laws of physics is that energy can be transformed but can neither be created out of nothing nor be destroyed without a trace.

I encourage patients to be mindful of this state, usually at the end of our 90–120-minute sessions, so that they can imagine that they leave the room enclosed in an insulating bubble of this atmosphere. We rehearse how they can use this to de-escalate any rising tension in the atmosphere when they leave the office to return to home or work.

Each time the patient has reprocessed an aspect of the trauma, they scan the event mentally, aided by the real or "magic" remote. The goal is to isolate or freeze-frame any remaining disturbing images from the replayed traumatic event. To augment processing, I give the patient bilateral tactile units, or, with young children, castanets can be useful. As the patient's somatic map of the territory changes, any negatively charged words used by the patient to describe their experiences are reframed positively. To allow reprocessing to continue at an effective pace, attention is paid to the patient's body language, eye contact, tone of voice, and unconscious movements for any signs of autonomic hyper or hypoarousal. The pace of reprocessing is either slowed down or sped up, to ensure that the patient remains within their window of affective tolerance and emotional regulation.

Typically, the patient will notice that the sensations associated with the trauma move from the solar plexus to the chest to the throat, in line with the chakra-energy system. Any blocks to reprocessing are identified and resolved using SF-EMDR psychotherapy before, ultimately, a transfer of information occurs at the interhemispheric level to the prefrontal cortex at the level of the third eye, or sixth chakra (pineal gland).

Once the trauma narrative appears reprocessed with minimal affective disturbance, the patient assesses imaginally for any remaining disturbance in the past (trace back), present (go above), and future (move forward). Where areas of trouble are identified, patients are asked to cross their arms, with or without holding tactile zappers, to facilitate sequential bilateral transmission of information along neurological channels. Patients who have been grabbed by the throat by an assailant often experience distressing sensations around their throat and neck. I encourage the patient to massage these areas gently with their fingers until relief is felt. Patients who have suffered injury to an arm, chest, shoulder, leg, or another body part will experience a shift in painful sensations in these areas. In my experience, asking the patient to place the tactile zappers gently over the area until the distress is relieved can relieve the emotional component of the residual pain.

As the "stuck" traumatic information is reprocessed, the tension within the patient's neuromuscular system is released. As the physical symptoms diminish, the cerebral hemispheres reinterpret the flow of information. Meaning is made of their experience as linked neural networks are activated. Patients are shown illustrations to facilitate their understanding of the transformation they have experienced. Patients often report tingling sensations, especially in the periphery, at this stage. My interpretation of this is that thinking space in the cerebrum has been created, allowing new synaptic connections to be made. The patient is in a calm state and is able both to learn from the experience and to gain insight into their behaviour. I like to address resilience by asking the patient to imagine coping with the incident if similar circumstances were to occur in the future. Stage Four suggests that brain axons are rewired for transmission, and the patient is set up to be resilient.

The final thirty minutes of a 120-minute session of SF-EMDR psychotherapy allows the patient time for reflection on the reprocessing achieved during the session. By then, the patient will have experienced ninety minutes of continuous bilateral cerebellar stimulation, as well as intermittent peripheral tactile stimulation accompanied by self-tapping if necessary. This may have precipitated a rapid eye movement (REM) state, where patients often report feeling tired and might commence yawning. This promotes an optimum level of integration of information between the cerebral hemispheres before reaching the analytic, executive functionality of the prefrontal cortex. The patient is then asked to review the reprocessed traumatic incidents completed during the session to become aware of any new:

- Thoughts;
- Beliefs;
- Feelings;
- Sensations;
- Impulses;
- Meanings (i.e. things they have learnt about themselves and how they have survived their traumatic experiences.)

Any new positive thoughts, beliefs, feelings, sensations, and lessons learned are reinforced using a future template.

In my clinical experience, I have found that the patient goes through the stages of arousal, followed by the deepening of the experience, and then by relaxation, before having time to think and reflect on the session.

The end of the session allows for reflection on what lessons have been learnt, and for sense to be made of their experience. The patient's thinking space is freed in the prefrontal cortex, and my hypothesis is that new neuronal pathways are laid down in vivo towards the end of the two-hour session. Reprocessing continues after the session in the subsequent days, giving the opportunity for further synaptic potential. This maps onto the four-stage creative process and basic rest–activity cycle outlined by Rossi. I ask patients to notice any continued reprocessing and to note any significant dreams related to the session. Most patients send this information by email so that I can have my formulation hypothesis ready for the next session. These are shown in Figure 9.3. This model has been replaced by the 90- to 120-minute basic rest–activity cycle.

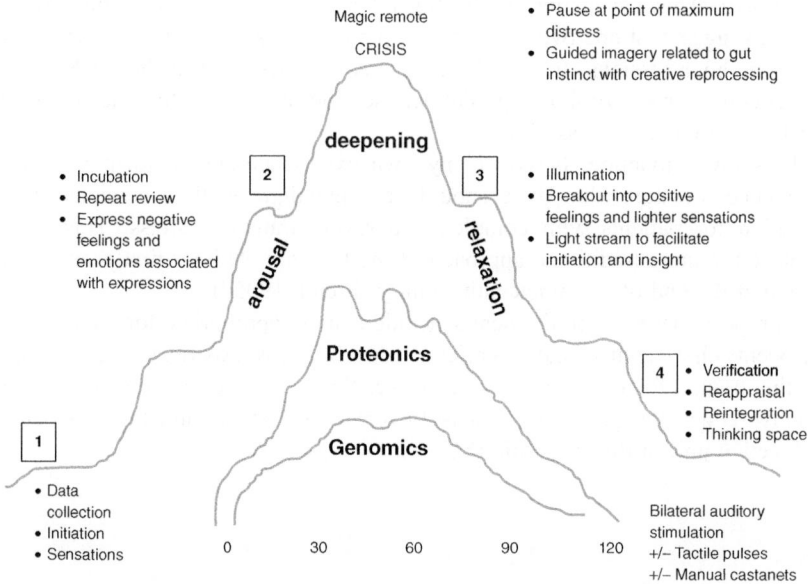

Figure 9.3 Model of sensorimotor-focused EMDR for psychotherapy and peak performance session compared to neuroscience model of Rossi (2004).

Source: drawing created by Sorcha O'Malley and adapted from original by Ernest Rossi.

Summary

In taking a developmental and trauma history of the patient, I discuss how particular attention should be paid to assessing sensory and/or motor involvement of the twelve cranial nerves. All the cranial nerves are included in this, except the olfactory synapse with the brainstem.

As explained earlier, this will trigger a brainstem, instinctive, or reptilian response. Many therapists have discussed with me their difficulties in helping their patients get rid of odours, smells, or aromas associated with the traumatic or abusive experience.

No amount of traditional or trauma-focused CBT or EMDR can relieve this olfactory sensation. I have proposed bilateral olfactory stimulation using SF-EMDR psychotherapy to relieve the patient's distress. A key component of successful therapy is having the patient in a calm, relaxed state. The use of the seven-element relaxation exercise is described, and this can be interwoven into the session. Rossi has proposed a neuroscientific model of psychotherapy. I apply this to SF-EMDR psychotherapy, showing the initial elevating of arousal, then deepening the therapeutic experience, followed by relaxation. The real-time changes of genomics and proteomics are hypothesised to occur in parallel, as illustrated. This has major implications for the effectiveness of therapy and would suggest that one two-hour session per patient is much more effective than two one-hour sessions. In my clinical experience working in the NHS, I have never come across two-hour appointment sessions apart from the ones I have set up in the traumatic stress clinic.

It is my conviction, based on my own experience and reviewing the neuroscience literature, that there should be a paradigm shift to sessions of this duration for patients with complex and severe traumatic stress. This should replace the more traditional approach of the fifty-minute hour first promoted by Freud at the end of the nineteenth century (Freud, 1905d).

I propose that this appointment schedule is more appropriate for the provision of twenty-first-century health services. It has been my experience that six hours of this trauma-focused therapy spread over three two-hour sessions can dramatically reduce the patient's impact-of-events-scale scores and their associated subjective unit of distress scale (SUDS).

Chapter 10

The influence of some research in trauma therapy by neurobiologists, and how this has influenced my development of an integrative approach to SF-EMDR psychotherapy and peak performance

There are several scientists whose work has had a profound effect on my approach to therapeutic work with patients and clients.

Biology of Belief by Dr Bruce Lipton

Bruce Lipton is a cellular developmental biologist who has proposed that multi-cellular organisms use the same proteins for multiple functions. The Caenorhabditis worm has 1,000 cells, compared to fifty trillion cells in humans. It has 24,000 genes compared to 25,500 in the human genome, however. Thus, genes are only part of the story of perception. Thus, he suggests new biology to describe perception and has co-written a book entitled *Spontaneous Evolution*. Dr Lipton's latest work, *The Honeymoon Effect* (2013), develops this idea one step further in an attempt to understand the molecular basis of consciousness. The book introduces the term honeymoon, which refers to the state of married bliss of newly-weds who often go on a romantic holiday. The term was used in 1546 as "hony moone." There are reports that the father of the groom provided mead for a month to the newly-weds. The state was said to wane like the moon in that time. Indeed, today, the twenty-eight-day lunar cycle is close to one month. An extract reveals the honeymoon effect in his (Dr Lipton's) own life:

> After decades of failure, that's what I finally manifested! Because so many people have asked how we did it, Margaret and I will explain in the epilogue how we have managed to create our happily-ever-after honeymoon effect for seventeen years and counting. We want to share our story because love is the most potent growth factor for human beings and love is contagious! As you will find when you create the honeymoon effect in your own life, you will attract similarly loving people to you – and the more, the merrier. Let us revel in our love for each other, so this planet can finally evolve into a better place where all organisms can live their own Heaven on Earth. I hope that this book will launch you on a journey – as

that instant in the Caribbean launched me – to create The Honeymoon Effect each day of your life.

(Lipton, 2011)

In his book *Biology of Belief*, Lipton discusses the interaction of the endocrine, immune, and nervous systems with the culture medium of the body and mind (Figure 10.1), or gut-brain, heart-brain, and head-brain, as I have discussed earlier. Exposure to toxic stress causes these body substrates to release stress hormones into the bloodstream. Hormones such as adrenaline prime our muscles so that we can escape from impending danger. The human cell contains mitochondrial and nuclear DNA and is surrounded by the cell membrane.

Lipton performed experiments to locate the cell's brain, concluding that it was not DNA, as, when the DNA was extracted, the cell survived. Eventually, he discovered that the protein receptors in the cell membrane acted as the cellular brain. Our sensory receptors are composed of protein and receive information via neuropeptides before transmitting a signal to the nucleus for encoding. This signal creates DNA to enable it to adapt to the environment. Dr Lipton concluded that "our perception of the environment directly controls the activity of our genes."

Thus, our beliefs directly affect the molecular structure of water in our body. This has relevance to the head-brain, which is ninety per cent water. This water is affected by emotions and changes in vibrational energy. It comes in many forms: the ocean bathing our cells, blood, lymph, cerebrospinal fluid, capillaries, and visceral organs. Stuck, unexpressed emotions can consolidate as belief systems, which directly influence our bodily fluids, resulting in chronic disease and illness. Recognising and reprocessing these stuck emotional states can be achieved with SF-EMDR psychotherapy.

In the case of the 9/11 attacks in New York, many survivors continued running for miles, well away from the danger zone, until their immune systems gave way and they collapsed from exhaustion. According to Dr Lipton, during the first six years of life, we "download" behaviour programmes from our parents, siblings, and from other experiences and social interactions. As well as the Darwinian "survival of the fittest" theory of natural selection, it is now believed that we also evolve via cooperation within communities and through collaboration for the greater good of society, not just regarding the success of the individual. It is also known that the epigenome is more powerful than the gene, in that it determines which genes are switched on or off. This can be expressed as shown in Figure 10.1.

This can be expressed as follows (Figure 10.2):

• Environmental signal: the frequency of love or fear;
• Wave interaction with DNA codons;
• Regulatory protein changes shape;
• Protein sleeve comes off deoxynucleic acid DNA;

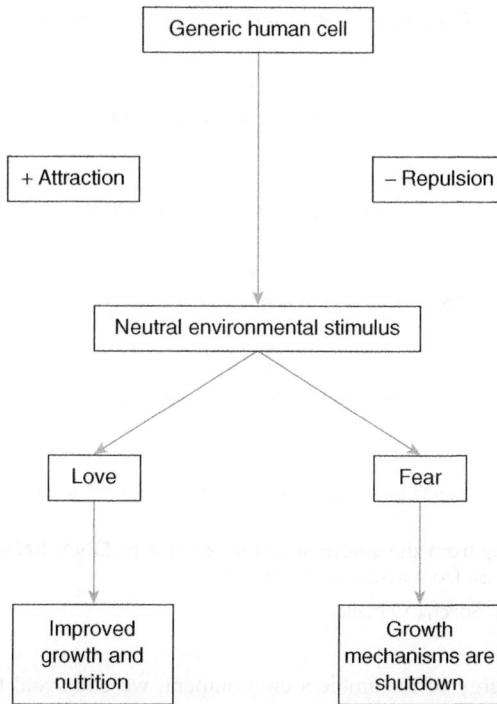

Figure 10.1 The concept of the biology of perception from environmental stimulus to growth of cell. This was conceived by Dr Bruce Lipton. This series of interactions leads to the growth of viscera centrally and the muscles of arms and legs in the periphery in the human subject.

- Messenger RNA molecule copied;
- New proteins go into production from component amino acids.

Thus, the signals in the environment drive epigenetic activity and switch on healthy or unhealthy gene activity. Each person, based on the scientific evidence, can ask themself the following: what are the environmental signals I perceive? Destructive emotions, such as fear, generate a waveform pattern that only interacts intermittently with the base-pair codons of DNA. This will lead to a limited range of instinctive or reactive responses. The associated stress has the possibility of coding for harmful proteins in the body's cellular nuclei. If, however, we perceive a loving atmosphere or environment, a completely different waveform is expressed. This emotion has an increased frequency and, therefore, interacts with all codons in the DNA double helix. This gives us the potential to activate all sixty-four codons possible within the known DNA double-helix structure. This means that by being better attuned to

Environmental signal - Frequency of love or fear

↓

Wave interaction with DNA codons

↓

Regulatory protein changes shape

↓

Protein sleeve comes off deoxynucleic acid DNA

↓ ↑

Messenger RNA molecule copied

↓ ↑

New proteins go into production from component amino acids

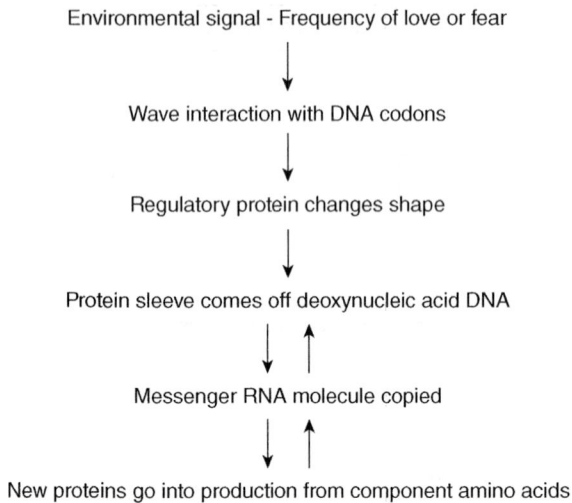

Figure 10.2 Pathway from the emotions of love or fear to DNA, RNA, and new protein formation from essential amino acids.
Source: Sorcha O'Malley.

the emotional energy of the ambient environment, we can avoid fear and access a more loving emotional experience. When the human genome project was completed in 2000, scientists were surprised that only around 30,000 genes were decoded, accounting for ten per cent of cellular DNA. The remaining ninety per cent of DNA did not appear to code meaningfully for proteins and was perceived to be genetically redundant – or "junk" – DNA. Given the knowledge we now have of epigenetics in switching genes on or off, one hypothesis is that this remaining ninety per cent of DNA has yet to be activated epigenetically. The question to pose is: what energetic genetic frequency of emotional energy will interact sufficiently to trigger a mRNA response in the remaining forty-four codons?

The human brain project

This was launched in August 2013 with a seventy-eight-page vision statement: www.humanbrainproject.eu. The goal is to map out the million billion synaptic connections of the brain over the next decade. This will be a multi-disciplinary effort led by Professor Markham from EPFL in Lausanne, Switzerland. The work will be divided into three strands:

1. Future neuroscience;
2. Future medicine; and
3. Future computing.

Six strategic objectives have been set:

1. Design, develop, deploy, and operate computers for researchers in the above fields;
2. Stimulate research into the brain's structure and function including the causes for and diagnosis of brain disease;
3. Generate and collect strategic neuroscience data, which can inform objective 1;
4. Implement and analyse any innovation and its results for its social and philosophical implications, involving citizens and researchers in a far-reaching conversation about future directions of research;
5. Train scientists in Europe across disciplines to enable convergence of information and computer technology and neuroscience, creating an enhanced capability for academia and industry across the European continent;
6. Provide a coherent approach to leadership and project management so that regional, national, and European research programmes are effectively aligned.

This ambitious project is analogous to building a human brain with input from the periphery (European countries) to the centre (Project Headquarters in Lausanne, Switzerland). Crucial to its success will be a two-way flow of information, as happens between neurons in the human brain. At the nerve centre will be someone with sufficient synaptic capacity to hold the big picture in mind, and to focus on the end goal of the key six strategic objectives for the full flagship (SOFF). In mythological terms, this is reminiscent of the voyage to a new land taken by Noah, by his chosen people and animals in the Ark of the Covenant. This is a good analogy, as when the ship sets sail we can all climb aboard and journey across the ocean waves to our new destination.

The power resources for this project are enormous. Whereas the human brain uses about thirty watts, the output of many power stations will be needed to generate sufficient computer capacity to build realistic models of the brain's phenomenal computing power and its thought output.

How can humanity reactivate its double-stranded DNA to take maximum advantage of what scientists have referred to as the ninety per cent junk DNA?

From the research I have done, a sea-change in the earth's planetary orbit is required for sunlight of a higher frequency to reach humanity from the star system. It has been suggested that the most likely time for this to happen was after the winter solstice of 21 December 2012. This date has long been flagged as the moment when our solar system aligns with the galactic centre. This epoch comes around once every 26,000 years. Humanity has no record of historical events from that time. Indeed, the oldest scientifically dated monument is that of Gobekli Tepe ("Belly Hill" in Turkish), near Istanbul. These megalithic stones predate Stonehenge by over 6,000 years. It is believed to be the site of the world's oldest temple: a cathedral on a hill situated thirty minutes from Urfa, an ancient city in south-eastern Turkey. Layers of stone carvings have been built up, leaving the hilltop covered in sand as it stands today. It is now believed that building this temple led to the development of complex civilisations. German archaeologist Klaus Schmidt has been excavating this site for the past ten years, and we await his theories on the purpose of these mysterious structures from this ancient Turkish civilisation. Ninety-five per cent of the site has yet to be revealed.

Even though only five per cent of this site has been excavated, the detailed stone carvings found to date make this the most important archaeological site currently being excavated anywhere on earth. The structure of the stones uncovered so far dates from 12,000 BC. The location was used for "religious purposes," but no stone tools have been recovered on the site.

The creators of this monument went to great lengths to bury it in sand and debris; this fortuitous act preserved it from destruction. The collective wisdom of the researchers is that this civilisation intended to leave a message for their descendants. In the above view, I am struck by the similarity to the triple spiral symbols central to the Newgrange monument in County Meath, Republic of Ireland. It is believed that Stone Age beings communicated using the Ogham language, based on knowledge of the frequencies of underground structures, such as the location of reservoirs of water, which could be divined by dousing. In addition, the "Om" mantra from India has similarities to this triple spiral. The spiral is the basic expression of three-dimensional energy progressions and can be measured with a pendulum. The K52 entrance stone to the Newgrange Megalithic site in the Boyne Valley (County Meath, Republic of Ireland) is adorned with carvings of spirals and the triple spiral. The significance of these is not fully understood.

One striking characteristic is the variation in and significance given to the triple-spiral symbol across different cultures. From listening to Michael Poynder give a presentation based on his book *Pi in the Sky*, I think this might relate to a previous capability humanity had concerning the double helix of DNA.

This might be represented by the various symbols for the caduceus through-out history. The engravings at Newgrange, on both stones K1 and K52 and in the inner chamber itself, most beautifully illustrate this. If indeed, humankind had a genetic structure composed of fully activated double-stranded DNA, this would allow for the vastly increased range of codon possibilities and could explain how we were once able to utilise what is now called junk DNA.

This term was first introduced by Ohno. Now, genetic science describes this section of DNA as "introns." It is part of our common ancestry with other species of life on planet earth. Wan and colleagues (2014) reported that the second layer of information was embedded in all RNA transcripts in the form of an RNA secondary structure. This RNA structure was found to influence almost every step in the process of gene expression. The extent of this influence is unknown at present. There are both coding and non-coding RNAs in the human genome. In conclusion, the broad contribution of RNA structure and its variants to the regulation of our human genes was reported. This scientific finding shows that we are more than a double-stranded DNA helix, as first thought when Crick and Watson discovered DNA in 1952. We have the potential, through epigenetics, to activate these additional RNA structures.

According to the myth of Atlantis, before its fall, humanity had reached a state of "God-like evolution." Man risked self-destruction and – to prevent this – a catastrophic fall, perhaps of water, occurred. Many creation myths from different cultures around the world attest to a catastrophic deluge enveloping the earth. Few survived what has been described as a worldwide tsunami. Even today, several descriptions exist of dreams where people are swept away by waves higher than a mountain. This would explain a vessel floating on the spherical surface of the ocean, as in Noah's Ark. As described in the Old Testament, it was only when the rains subsided, and the raven came back with a leaf from an exposed branch that landfall could occur on Mount Arafat. This is one of the highest peaks in Turkey.

Assuming ninety per cent of the world's population was wiped out, man then might have regressed to a more primitive species and hypothetically lost his advanced form of genetic DNA. The earliest known resurrection of civilisation myth in the post-diluvian era was in Sumeria and Mesopotamia. The monument covered up in Gobekli Tepe could relate to the structure of the DNA as it replicates from the double strand of DNA to a third strand, via messenger ribonucleic acid (mRNA). This statement is speculative on my part and is not backed up by scientific evidence. Instead, I am responding to my intuition or gut instinct. This is a good example of how the left and right hemispheres evaluate evidence. When undergoing SF-EMDR psychotherapy, clients and patients have the best of both worlds: an integrated, holistic perspective.

The "Om" sound may be used to open the third-eye chakra or pineal gland and has been used in India since before 3,500 BC. The frequency of this sound might represent the copying of double-stranded DNA by messenger ribonucleic acid (mRNA) to make a new strand of DNA.

The symbol for "Om," documented in India around 3,500 BC, is said to represent the universal void of creation. In addition, it is possible that the purpose of the chants of Om before, during, and after meditation was to increase the energy of the chakras, perhaps to assist with DNA replication and protein synthesis.

This would fit in with the model I have proposed for SF-EMDR psychotherapy. Perhaps the way to evaluate the impact of SF-EMDR psychotherapy scientifically is to measure its impact on telomere shortening. I would hypothesise that exposure to the gamma frequency of bilateral cerebellar stimulation would increase the enzyme telomerase, thereby diminishing the deleterious effect of telomere shortening on DNA replication. This is explained in the seven-element relaxation exercise on p. 193.

Biology of perception and natural selection

According to Lipton's book *Biology of Belief*, our new perception controls our genes and selects what genes are expressed. By looking at the historical achievements in monuments such as Newgrange and Gobekli Tepe, we can surmise that these peoples had access to more of the genetic DNA potential than humankind does today.

Cairns, Overbaugh, and Miller (1988) discussed the origin of mutants in their article on "adaptive" mutations (i.e. mutations that are not random). They found that some forms of bacterial mutation occurred spontaneously before there was any outward sign of the utility of the mutation. The conclusion was that bacteria have some choice over the mutation they produce. The human corollary is that an individual human genome may profit by experience. Thus, it is possible that genetic instability (leading to a greater risk of mutation) can be switched on by living in a stressful environment but switched off when that stress has been treated successfully.

This could be a cellular representation of the last universal common ancestor (LUCA). All seven billion inhabitants of the earth can trace their ancestry back to LUCA, which first appeared on earth 3.8 billion years ago, according to Professor Brian Cox (2013). We now exist as leaves derived from different branches of the tree of life. Mitochondria and nuclei have combined in the above cellular representation to form the diversity of life known today. This can help to put any conflicts or difficulties with others in perspective as they are ultimately part of the main – that is, ourselves.

Contribution of Dr Marcus Raichle to the field of research into the neurobiology of trauma

Raichle defined the default mode network (DMN) in 2001 as an area of the brain, which is active when the brain is at rest. It consists of the following areas:

- Post cingulate cortex (PCC);
- Ante cingulate cortex (ACC);
- Medial prefrontal cortex (mPFC);
- Parietal lobe;
- Temporal lobe (middle temporal gyrus).

Over different ages, the default mode network architecture matures from a "local" organisation to a "distributed" organisation. There is a dynamic development between the two-task control networks, the default network, and cerebellar networks. Initially, there is segregation of local, anatomically clustered regions. In children, regions are largely organised by their anatomical location, but anatomically clustered regions segregate over time. The cluster of frontal regions best demonstrates this segregation. In children, the more distributed adult functional networks are, in many ways, disconnected. In time, the functional networks integrate. The isolated regions of the default mode network in childhood that coalesce into a highly-correlated network best illustrate this integration. Organisation of the DMN shifts from the "local" arrangement in children to the "distributed" organisation commonly observed in adults.

The DMN functions less well under high-working memory load. An intact DMN is necessary for:

- Theory of mind (TOM). This is the capacity to attribute mental states, desires, beliefs, and attributes of another person;
- Autobiographical (episodic and semantic) memory; and
- The ability to look forward and plan for the future.

Patients with PTSD often re-experience traumatic events by reliving their worst sensory fragments. Their working memory becomes overloaded, and these fragments are stored in a disorganised way. They are usually completely unable to think about the future, are preoccupied with reliving their traumas in the present, and have a fragmented sense of self. This affects how they think about themselves.

They tend to expect the worst, have symptoms of dissociation, and feelings of shame and self-loathing. The research points to a disturbance in the DMN as a biological substrate for PTSD. SF-EMDR psychotherapy can help traumatised patients with the above symptoms. It is known that, in PTSD, the DMN shows little connectivity between the post cingulate cortex and the medial prefrontal cortex. I would hypothesise that after five two-hour sessions of SF-EMDR psychotherapy, the patient with PTSD would start to display the connectivity at rest consistent with a healthy DMN. Thus, the PCC would be able to recognise objects and salient past events, the medial PFC would enact self-referential awareness, the lateral parietal lobes would embody the self, and the temporal lobes would sub-serve all aspects of memory. Under fMRI, these four brain areas would be fully interconnected post-treatment if this hypothesis is correct.

In a child aged between seven and nine, the DMN is like that of a patient under chronic stress. Thus, developmentally, the adult traumatised patient only can respond at rest with the DMN of a child of that age. My goal in this book, and in the explanations underlying the neurobiology of SF-EMDR psychotherapy, is to prove that the DMN can be restored and brought back online so that it can start functioning like the DMN of a healthy adult. It is this question that research into trauma-informed care is set to answer. I believe the therapist will be able to answer this question by applying the practice any theory of SF-EMDR as a new paradigm for both psychotherapy and peak performance.

Northern and southern neural pathways of Professor James Austin

Austin (1999) has described an upper, or northern, pathway, which is egocentric and involves the upper occipital cortex. It is specialised for action and pays attention to what is above the visual horizon. This includes your lucky stars, blue skies, clouds, and mountains. The immediate environment might include a sabre-toothed tiger; this pathway processes visual-image, colour processing, and

hearing. The lower, or southern, path is allocentric. It processes the propriocep-
tive and parietal environment of what is within arm's reach. For women, their
fusiform gyrus processes the facial features of a newborn baby while their hands
provide afferent feedback to take care of their infant. Men can hold a tool such
as a hammer in their hand and accurately hit a nail on its head using this
pathway. Hence the saying "You've just hit the nail on the head," which means
to have represented something exactly.

Both pathways combine egocentric and allocentric awareness. The three hotspots
of the DMN are activated at rest, generating a sense of psychic self-identity and
helping us navigate safely through our environment. The hotspots are active when
we are involved in a self-related activity and cool down when an acute external task
is attempted. It is now known that these areas of high and low activity, as seen on
functional MRI, change every twenty seconds. This is the intrinsic cycle of human
brain activity. When there is a wish to go into a meditative state, a triggering
stimulus, such as a gong, shifts the allosteric pathway upwards in awareness and
lowers the attention paid by the egocentric one. Hence, referential reprocessing of
the other is increased while that of the self is decreased. These techniques can be
incorporated into SF-EMDR psychotherapy sessions.

Symptomatically, patients experience enhanced emotional awareness, improved
sense of self, greater affective regulation, and, finally, better social functioning.
Research into – and dissemination of – the techniques of SF-EMDR psychotherapy
for both trauma and peak performance will, I hope, allow this question to be
answered definitively over the next decade.

Crucially, patients and clients must be enabled to grieve unresolved traumatic
grief and losses. They must also be helped to reconnect their social, friendship,
work, and educationally related networks. As both patients and clients often
present with a distorted sense of their own self-worth, it is vital, via SF-EMDR
psychotherapy, that they become aware of their inner affective state.

Through affective reprocessing, they then experience both how to widen their
window of affect tolerance and hpw to develop a capacity for emotional regulation.
Once out of the disabling dissociative states of hyperarousal (RAPIDS) and
hypoarousal (FROZEN in FEAR) (see Figure 2.2), they are no longer hijacked by
emotions and will benefit from the later stages of SF-EMDR psychotherapy. The
patient can experience the present truthfully. The self-reflection during the last thirty
minutes of a session allows them to plan for the future and derive meaning from the
experience.

Milton H. Erickson, and Professor Ernest Rossi and Kathryn Rossi

I became aware of Milton Erickson after reading his 1982 book *My Voice Will
Go With You*. He viewed the unconscious mind as creative and able to solve
problems. He was a polymath and trained as a psychiatrist, a family therapist,
and in medical hypnosis. He influenced different schools of psychotherapy,

including brief solution-focused therapy and neuro-linguistic programming. Before Francine Shapiro developed EMDR, she consulted with Richard Bandler and John Grinder in California about a female friend who had severe cancer. They gave her advice about their understanding of eye movements, which I have outlined. Shapiro developed and built on these ideas through research lectures and experimentation. Since the 1970s, psychotherapies have continued to evolve, but the basic foundations of integrating science with psychotherapy evolved from the joint discussions and collaborations between Erickson and Rossi. Some of the techniques taught in Ericksonian therapy are:

- Encouraging resistance;
- Providing a worse alternative;
- Communicating by metaphor;
- Encouraging a relapse;
- Stimulating a response by frustrating it;
- Utilising space and position;
- Emphasising the positive;
- Prescribing the symptom and amplifying a deviation; and
- Seeding ideas.

Prof Rossi is widely published in the field of psychotherapy, and in my book *The Art of BART* I outlined how his model of genomic and proteomic change in the consultation fitted in with my therapeutic approach. Drawing from his latest research over the last few years, my SF-EMDR psychotherapy has the added dimension of integration with quantum field theory. I have discussed his ideas in more detail in Chapter 8.

What can the patient learn from their collective experiences?

Many patients see themselves as broken or damaged goods before referral to the therapist. However, the following tale will help to change that perspective.

> Two Africans lived in a village with no running water. Each day, they carried a ceramic pot down to the river, filled it up, and brought it back to the village. Each person arrived back at the village with their ceramic pots only half full of water. This was hard to understand as both ceramic pots on the surface seemed the same.Time passed, and different members of the village went to collect the water with new metal pots, which did not leak. They retraced the steps of their predecessors. To their surprise, they found that along the path back to the village, row upon row of beautiful flowers had sprung up where the old ceramic pots had cracked and leaked.

Thus, our patients and clients who might have seen themselves as broken and damaged can realise that an unbroken wholeness exists within them, which can coexist with the brokenness. They can be both messed up and very alright at the same time. By inviting our patients and clients to hold on to these thoughts, we can metaphorically water their souls and wait for their own flowers to bloom. My SF-EMDR psychotherapy has a crucial role to play in managing the response of the patient and client to their stressful environment. The aim could be to prevent the development of traumatic stress for such at-risk individuals.

A recent Danish study by Bernstein and colleagues followed a cohort of 746 soldiers before, during, and after deployment to Afghanistan. They found that the greatest risk for developing PTSD was linked to childhood adversity experiences (i.e. a stressful living environment) rather than the specific war experiences. Indeed, a less well-educated group with the most childhood adversity had reduced levels of PTSD in the theatre of war. They reported that the camaraderie of their fellow soldiers was something they had never experienced before. On returning to their troubled civilian lives, their PTSD levels increased. This finding had never been reported in the literature before. It confirms my thesis of how being in the loving, supportive environment of the army on active service can be sufficient to counteract the fear of attack by enemy combatants.

The Muslim mystic Rumi said in the twelfth century that "it is only through our wounds that light can enter to start the process of healing." I would suggest to our patients and clients that by allowing pure vibrational light energy to enter our physical and emotional wounds and scars, the path to healing could begin. This is the first step of their roadmap to the ultimate destination of recovery and peak performance.

Summary

In this chapter, I have looked at a new biology of perception and belief first espoused by Dr Bruce Lipton, a developmental cellular biologist. His latest book, *The Honeymoon Effect*, proposes that changing our beliefs and perceptions can prolong the state of wedded bliss that follows on from marriage. A flow diagram of the behaviour of the human cell shows the frequency of attraction as love and that of repulsion as fear. Dr Lipton proposes that environmental stimuli affect cell growth and that it is our perception of this environmental stimulus that switches gene activity on and off. There is a brief mention of the human genome project and the mammoth task of the human brain project, which is proposed for the next decade. Scientists have identified junk DNA in the human chromosome, and a description of monolithic sites at Gobekli Tepe and Newgrange is given. These sites are aligned with the orbit of the sun. In Newgrange, for 8,000 years or more, the sunlight has pierced the inner sanctum and is reflected upward by a polished stone shaped like a parabolic mirror. Approximately thirty-three modern-day humans can fit into this space and experience this natural illumination. This might have had religious significance for Stone Age man. I hypothesise that it might also reactivate "junk DNA," starting with accessing the increased vibratory frequency predicted to reach earth after the winter solstice, marking the end of the Mayan Calendar in December 2012. All the above mechanisms would explain how different genetic characteristics are expressed, both helpful and harmful. This allows for a recalibration of the nature–nurture paradigm of evolution.

A different perspective can inform the Darwinian theory of natural selection, survival of the fittest, and genetic determinism. This considers modern scientific enquiry and looks back in time at what was achieved by some of our earlier greatest civilisations. We can move to a state of attraction to positive environmental stimuli, such as living within a loving and supportive family, so that we can more rapidly activate our "lost DNA introns." The research related to the default mode network of the brain, proposed by Raichle and Snyder (2007), is presented. This has been subdivided into a northern–southern pathway by Professor James Austin (1999), which engages the person in different functions based on eye gaze (up or down), and the other somatosensory functions being used. The concept of an intrinsic rate of the brain's activity, which alternates between these pathways, was also suggested. This knowledge is fundamental to effective reprocessing, as the DMN is rendered ineffective by unprocessed significant life events. The work of Prof Ernest Rossi and Milton Erickson has been referred to, as over many decades they have compiled a body of work that has now been integrated with the latest studies from quantum field theory. Finally, a 2012 study of Danish troops in Afghanistan is mentioned, emphasising the role friendship networks play in overcoming adversity, and, using a parable, I explain how patients and clients can learn from their collective experiences. The chapter ends with a quotation from the mystic poet, Rumi. The research hypothesis is to perform functional MRI scans on patients with complex PTSD before treatment to assess the functionality and saliency of the associative brain networks. I hypothesise that the connectivity and maturity of the DMN will be confirmed by fMRI following approximately twelve hours of intensive SF-EMDR psychotherapy in the form of six two-hour sessions. This research remains to be quantified.

Chapter 11

Living in a hypothetical world dominated by the left hemisphere's perspective, and summary of the five stages of SF-EMDR psychotherapy

An introduction to our current worldview, which is dominated by the perspective of the left hemisphere

In the Western world, where the perspective of the left hemisphere dominates, the first aspect of life to suffer is its central coherence. The "bits" of something assumes greater importance than the whole picture. Gathering information "bit by bit" is a poor substitute for knowledge gained from experience. This allows the big picture to be seen. Expertise (Latin, "one who is experienced") is based on LH theory or abstraction. Quantity would take preference over quality: the principle of "what" over "how." People are reduced to the impersonal, that is, to mechanical perspective and number crunching: pure data without context. Societal cohesion is put at risk, with lack of trust and paranoia predominating among the populous. This worldview has cascaded from the political and financial elite since time immemorial. Indeed, this cabal has been called the Illuminati and has links to the Freemasons and other religious groups as well as bankers, industrialists, and financiers.

Previously, society demanded of its doctors, teachers, and priests a vocational and altruistic role. When we have only the left hemisphere perspective, these attributes may be viewed with suspicion. In many organisations today, this view predominates. Doctor–patient relationships, which are based on mutual respect, have been damaged by management in organisations that enable the hierarchical system to retain power and control. Certainty and security are sought out obsessively by management. This power structure cannot tolerate uncertainty or insecurity: anything that challenges the status quo is too risky. This idea of being in control is promulgated by the left-hemisphere perspective. Doctors, however, are taught to tolerate and embrace uncertainty, and this requires a whole-brain approach.

There is a scientific comparison with Heisenberg's uncertainty principle, which is a concept from quantum mechanics proposed in 1927. The image of concentric circles illustrates how we can never be sure of the exact location of any particle in space.

A common-sense view involves both hemispheres, is based on intuition, as mentioned in my introduction, and depends on interhemispheric collaboration. In a world dominated by LH thinking, this common-sense view breaks down. Behaviour associated with aggression and anger escalates as these emotions find expression in the LH. Insight is channelled via the RH and it, too, diminishes. There is a lack of autonomy and a tendency to act as if by rote, that is, without conscious awareness. The human mind becomes technocratic, with a distinct lack of its sense of uniqueness, awe, or wonder.

According to McGilchrist, increases in our material well-being do not correlate with happiness. Happiness levels in Britain were reported to be fifty-two per cent in 1957 and only thirty-six per cent today. Happiness depends on 'the breadth and depth of one's social connections" (www.livehappy.com). In so-called primitive societies, most interactions occurred face-to-face. Over the course of first-world development, globalisation and urbanisation, along with the fragmentation of communities, have increased the levels of unhappiness if correlated with the rising prevalence of mental illness. It has also been established that social integration counteracts the harmful effects of smoking, obesity, hypertension, and a sedentary lifestyle.

The Conservative Party's Manifesto announced the Big Society, as a policy objective. This may be a flawed concept in that, for the Big Society to exist, there must be feeder networks from the smaller social networks dotted all around the political landscape. If these are not joined up, then the goal of the Big Society is unlikely to happen. Currently, the Conservative Party (founded in 1834) has a membership of 134,000 and falling, whereas the Countryside Alliance (established only in 1997) has a membership of 100,000. The former currently has 303 MPs and uses top-down methods of recruitment, whereas the latter has grown exponentially, initially by amalgamating like-minded bodies and appealing directly to the grassroots. As I have already explained, this bottom-up approach is how our neural networks survive and thrive. The lesson for political parties is clear: adopt this approach or wither on the vine. The use of large-scale mass-media campaigns by political parties seems not to have encouraged increased membership among an increasingly disaffected public. Single-issue organisations and political parties, such as UKIP, seem to be able to mobilise and harness grassroots opinion.

The expression "I heard it on the grapevine" refers to the spreading of ideas through rumour or gossip, perhaps by people working in vineyards. This form of communication by word of mouth is a successful example of bottom-up reprocessing as used initially in SF-EMDR psychotherapy. This is later combined with top-down cognitive reprocessing for the most effective outcome.

Summary of five stages of BART (now termed SF-EMDR) for psychotherapy and peak performance

Stage one: Bilateral affective reprocessing of thoughts.

The bilateral and reprocessing phases remain constant throughout the five stages. Ideally, each stage can be completed in either one two-hour session or two one-hour sessions. In the first stage, the key goal is affective reprocessing. This can be illustrated by activation of the felt bodily sensations (primordial bodily feelings, gut reactions, or instinctive response to the traumatic event). Fight, flight, freeze, fright, feigned death, or fall reactions are reactivated safely within the window of affect tolerance.

Stage one involves engagement of emotions associated with the core or proto self. This stage promotes both cerebellar and cerebral activation of consciousness. It then leads to transformation and integration of somatic maps of the patient's viscera or bodily organs. This allows re-experiencing of the traumatic memory being processed by the patient.

Experience of the traumatic memory being processed

Thus, by the end of stage one, the autonomic nervous system of the patient has been activated from the periphery through the brainstem and cerebellar pathways. This allows the original traumatic event to be felt less intensely.

The patient will often place the zappers over their abdominal region when initially processing the traumatic event. This is usually accompanied by a feeling of sickness or nausea. They are encouraged to stay in touch with this feeling until it subsides and reprocessing moves to a higher vibratory level.

In stage one, the goal is to establish bilateral cerebellar stimulation and start the reprocessing of thoughts from the gut via the heart to the brain.

Stage two: The body's accelerated recognition of thoughts.

During the second stage of SF-EMDR psychotherapy, the patient's level of autonomic arousal in the aftermath of trauma has been further reprocessed. This occurs while preventing the patient from lapsing into the dissociative states of either hypo or hyperarousal.

The therapist maintains a focus on the patient's feelings, emotions, and sensations concerning their traumatic experiences. The patient's narrative is contained and transformed via their imagination. The events are reviewed repeatedly using the "Magic" remote until they are experienced factually with minimal distress and a low SUDS score (0–2). Patients are relieved that their memories are no longer associated with the previously unbearable, emotionally charged traumatic events.

The recognition of thoughts is a tautology, which emphasises the impact SF-EMDR psychotherapy has in the resolution of trauma. The scene is set for SF-EMDR psychotherapy to be used to identify specific unhelpful thoughts. It is at this stage that the most successful aspects of trauma-focused CBT can be employed, as the patient is better able to extract meaning from their traumatic experience.

At stage two, the goal is to establish the therapeutic relationship and, by mutual attunement between therapist and patient, they can start to re-think (recognition of) their previous thoughts.

Stage three: The brain's autonomic nervous system is resilient and together.

The patient's different brain systems (gut, heart, and head) and autonomic nervous system (immune, endocrine, and the chakra system) are given resources to enhance resilience during the third stage of SF-EMDR psychotherapy. Any fragmented personality parts of the dissociative identity disorder (DID) are pulled together. The DID patient may have the following parts: helper, lonely, parental, sexualised, school attendee, enraged, infantile, and promiscuous. The patient will be held in a safe mental state to come to terms with these different parts of their personality. Techniques such as ego-state therapy can be incorporated into SF-EMDR psychotherapy at this stage of the patient's treatment. Attention is paid to any triggers leading to an increased affective discharge by the patient. Sensory cues, such as smell, sound, movements, touch, sight, taste, and posture are identified and reprocessed. The technique of imagining an internal "padded" room helps to dissipate any negative affect experienced by the patient. The parts of the personality of the DID patient are brought together when they can hold the individual parts in conscious awareness. The patient is asked to check on the nature and function of each emotional personality (EP 1, 2, 3, etc.). It might be that their apparently normal personality (ANP) has become fragmented and requires integration. Colours are used to express different emotions associated with the different emotional personalities. Bilateral stimulation is applied during reprocessing of each EP until a new, more integrated aspect of the patient's personality emerges. Healthy emotional states associated with these EPs can be blended by getting the patient to imagine a "comfort" room, or, for adolescents, a "chill-out" room. Continual attention is paid to the patient's gestures during reprocessing, and these are fed back to the patient with suggested hypotheses to their potential meaning. The advantage of doing this during SF-EMDR psychotherapy is that these hypotheses can be tested for reliability and validity with the patient in real time.

By stage three, the patient has used their head-brain to integrate all the sensory and motor information from their visceral and enteric nervous systems. This helps to shield them from stress while any disintegrated personality parts are drawn resiliently together. This stage encourages the therapist to work with the client or patient to link or associate any dysfunctional emotional personalities. The parasympathetic and sympathetic nervous systems are optimally activated during this stage.

Stage four: The brain's axons are rewired for transmission.

As Hebb stated in 1949, neurons or cells that fire together, wire together. When a positive stimulus fires the cell neuron, it will go on to develop healthy synapses. A negative or abusive experience will tend to wire neuronal cells towards a development of an aggressive response. During adolescence, there is a spurt of brain development similar to that during the first few years of life. Axons lengthen, but some neuronal growth is stopped, especially from the ages of ten to fourteen. This can correlate with the "moodiness" of the teenager, when they are particularly unable to express themselves, and could be related to their underlying emotions. This is also a period when myelin from glial cells increases their transmission 100 times, especially in the prefrontal cortex. The process of myelination in the prefrontal cortex continues throughout adolescence. Synaptic pruning enables neural networks to become efficient, especially when categorising sounds. The growth of the corpus callosum continues until approximately the ages of twenty-five (women) or thirty (men). Earlier in the evolution of our Homo sapiens species, this was the expected lifespan. Thus, it was essential that pair bonding and procreation occurred early if the genes were to be passed on to the next generation.

Testosterone production slows synaptic pruning, making adolescent boys more awkward than adolescent girls. Their white matter continues to be myelinated in a linear manner throughout life. This is the normal state of brain development, provided that the patient has not suffered major adverse experiences in childhood. If so, then the SF-EMDR psychotherapist will be tuned in to the need to focus on this stage of the therapeutic process. By stage three, the patient will have experienced bilateral activation for approximately six hours. Following on from this, the goal of stage four is to have optimised the potential of the patient for axonal rewiring, enabling transmission across newly created neural networks.

Patients will have remained within their specific window of tolerance. Using the BOKA machine, the frequency of this bilateral activation will have been optimised to ensure transmission of their narrated experiences. The headphones and zappers can be set to resonate at different frequencies. I would suggest starting the headphones at a low rate of less than 10 Hertz. This will converge with the Schumann frequency mentioned earlier. I would further recommend beginning the zappers at a higher frequency of 15–20 Hertz. This equals the beta waves emitted by the conscious brain when our eyes are open. This frequency should be maintained while the zappers are reprocessing traumas located in the body.

As the patient continues reprocessing, they activate the solar chakra, then the heart chakra and the throat chakra. I would increase the frequency of stimulation until they can tolerate the maximum frequency of Hertz associated with the thalamocortical concordance. The sensory thalamus will forward its information, first to the cerebellum bilaterally, and then on to the cerebral cortex. This allows the patient both to digest and to reflect on the meaning of each traumatic experience. The last thirty minutes of the session allows for the bilateral stimulation of the zappers to be switched off and for the patient to recover from what has been experienced. I liken the course to having a brain workout.

Stages three and four of SF-EMDR psychotherapy are interchangeable, depending on the developmental age of the patient. This therapeutic engagement results in achieving neuronal potential where it has been arrested through traumatic experiences, or where the goal is to stretch the synapses to allow the client to reach peak performance.

Brain development during adolescence

Bilateral innervation starts from the peripheral nervous system (upper and lower limbs) and goes to the central nervous system (pons medulla and midbrain). At least ninety fibres of the lateral corticospinal tract cross the midline at the level of the brainstem. This provides a theoretical underpinning to the continuous bilateral cerebellar stimulation and the foot tapping as part of the figure-of-eight exercise, which is explained to the patient. The figure-of-eight represents the flow of information that I want the patient to achieve so that they overcome traumatic blocks to processing and, for the client seeking peak performance, to experience the flow, or being in the zone.

Stage five: Better, active, recovered, and triumphant. The patient is now ready to proceed to development of mental toughness, optimal functioning, and peak performance

As they receive high-frequency gamma waves (40–60 Hertz) at the level of the cerebellum, they resonate with increasing intensity throughout the brain and brainstem. The anterior cingulate cortex no longer must act as a brake mediating between the sympathetic HPA axis and the bidirectional vagal complex. Instead, the patient develops a mellow, whole-system integrated response. The patient's autobiographical self merges with their core self, as first described by Damasio.

This allows the patient to feel what is happening now. The patient can experience the depths of this ancient neuronal circuitry. They can activate their parietal lobes to integrate all past somatomotor experiences. The calm feeling-tone generated within the final stage of SF-EMDR psychotherapy enables the patient to experience the sense of dual awareness, where gut reactions related to a traumatic experience can be tolerated without generating an instinctive reaction.

By retraining the patient's response to threat, I explain how their amygdalae are now better inhibited by their frontal lobes. This allows for the impact of insight. This creative process by the patient activates new synaptic connections, allowing traumatic events to be seen or visualised differently. As the neurons are stimulated bilaterally at a gamma frequency of 40 Hertz, experiences are felt at both a brain and heart level. Hippocampal storage of new memories can change the previous traumatic memories permanently.

The following stages of development (shown in Figure 11.1), showing the path of continued progress from insight, wisdom, Samadhi, and non-dual awareness to elevated levels of consciousness is achievable with patients:

1. Insight;
2. Wisdom;
3. Samadhi;
4. Absence of conflict;
5. Knowledge of love, joy, and wonder;
6. Non-dual awareness;
7. Unity of consciousness (planetary mind at level of noosphere);
8. The increased vibrational frequency with interhemispheric integration and connection to the new 5D harmonic convergence.

Insight

↓

Wisdom

↓

Samadhi

↓

Absence of conflict

↓

Knowledge of love, joy, and wonder

↓

Non-dual awareness

↓

Unity of consciousness (planetary mind at level of noosphere)

↓

Increased vibrational frequency with interhemispheric integration

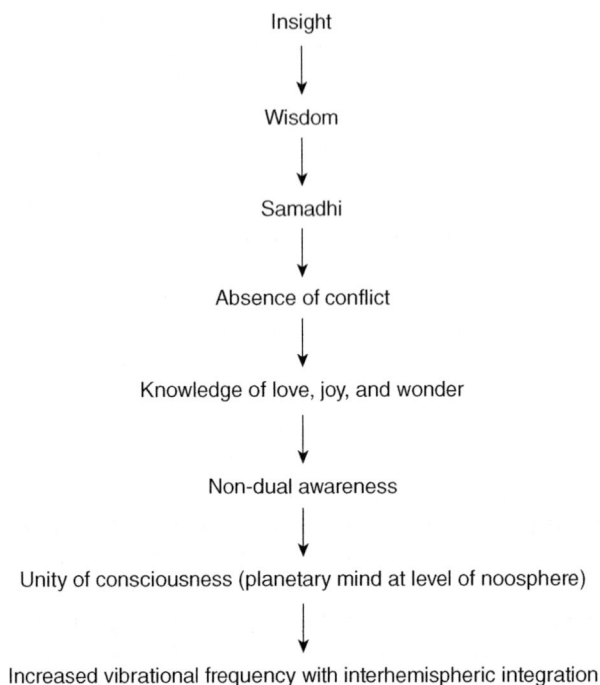

Figure 11.1 Illustration how from the development of insight, wisdom, Samadhi, and unitary consciousness can be achieved. The ultimate goal of SF-EMDR is peak performance by exposing the cortex to gamma-frequency brainwaves causing thalamocortical binding and interhemispheric integration.

As of 1 January 2018, it is believed that the vibrational energy of the universe has increased and that the toroidal magnetosphere is now resonating at a harmonic frequency of 432 Hertz. This means we have transitioned from 3D and 4D representational waveforms to a new 5D matrix complex fractal. The old certainties no longer apply as we complete a cycle of 250,000 years.

The goal of this final stage of SF-EMDR psychotherapy is for the patients, in conjunction with the therapist, to recognise when they are better able to be active, fully recovered, and triumphant.

Case example one

The patient's outcome is measured by improvements in the revised impact of events scale for patients with complex trauma, and by reduced scores in the Shut-D questionnaire for patients with dissociation. The patients report feeling lighter and having less weight on their shoulders. One patient could feel the tension and stress disappear from her body like water from a waterfall. It then dissipated on each side like the feathers of a peacock. She could feel her body solid, strong, and tall like an oak tree, and her feet were firmly connected to the earth via the roots. Nevertheless, her head could sway with the wind and she could experience the pink blossoms on the leaves. As she got up at the end of the session she put her hand one metre above her head and said, smiling, "I feel ten feet tall and am now strong enough for anything."

Case example two

A teenage boy had suffered a violent attack by a dog in which his arm was almost severed by the vice-like grip of an animal bred to be aggressive. He had held his arm over his face to protect it. His mother grabbed a brick and repeatedly hit the dog over the head to get it to release its grip on her son's arm. In a recent demonstration on "The Wonder of Dogs," a television programme on BBC Two, viewers were shown how terriers were employed as rat-catchers in the linen mills across England. The instructor offered the edge of a frisbee to the small terrier, and the dog started to shake its head vigorously from side to side without relinquishing the frisbee. If this had been a rat, the dog would have shaken the rat to death. In the same way, the crossbreed dog who attacked the boy held on to the boy's arm. He described to me how he heard the bones in his forearm snap as they shattered into multiple pieces. This animal was considered dangerous under the *Dangerous Dogs Act* as it was a crossbreed between a Rhodesian Ridgeback and a Pit Bull Terrier. Its owner made no effort to control his dog's aggression and, because of the attack, the boy underwent years of reconstructive surgery for shattered radius and ulna bones. The mother was terrified to leave the house due to her own traumatic stress symptoms. Both mother and son responded to several sessions of SF-EMDR psychotherapy. After two sessions, the boy's symptoms of PTSD had regressed, and he was no longer terrified by the sound of dogs barking. His impact of events scale had reduced from seventy to normal.

Moving on from SF-EMDR psychotherapy

The next step for insight is to develop wisdom. This occurs when the mind is in a quiet and reflective state. The patient can achieve affective regulation of thought at a body-and-soul level. In this state of Samadhi, conflict is absent, and knowledge of love, joy, and wonder abound.

Albert Einstein said in 1946 that 'the significant problems we face cannot be solved at the same level of awareness that created them." This is an apt metaphor for SF-EMDR psychotherapy. The initial trauma is experienced at a gut level, and this is gradually transcended at a higher level of consciousness. Non-dual awareness leads to a unity of consciousness at an individual level, the truth of what is awakened in the patient's mind. Change occurs as needed, as resistance is overcome. The potential for alchemical transformation exists when the patient achieves unity of consciousness. Behaviour based on previous trauma is addressed during this stage of SF-EMDR psychotherapy and peak performance and various types of future templates are used.

This last stage of SF-EMDR psychotherapy aims to integrate the functions of the LH and RH fully. These are somewhat artificially divided in Table 11.1, as both hemispheres are inextricably linked in structure and function. These functions will be further clarified by the six SOFF stated in the vision statement of the Human Brain Project as it undertakes its work over the next ten years.

Summary of final stage of SF-EMDR psychotherapy

The final stage of SF-EMDR psychotherapy brings the capabilities of both hemispheres together to resolve the patient's traumatic events. As Table 11.1 illustrates, each hemisphere is partially insulated from the other from a functional standpoint. Normally, performance is improved by decreasing interhemispheric interference. The stimulation of activity in one hemisphere tends to suppress activity in the other. Cooperation, however, occurs when there is reprocessing across hemispheres. This is especially important when task complexity increases. Spatial and verbal working memory is then fully engaged.

Epigenetic regulation of lateralised foetal spinal gene expression may underlie handedness

This research by Ocklenburg discusses lateralisation of the nervous system. Observation of the foetus in utero suggests that gene expressions in the spinal cord, and not the brain hemispheres, form the molecular basis for handedness. Hemispheric asymmetries have been shown in all major cognitive systems such as language, memory, attention, emotional processing, face perception, and executive functions.

The dominance of language in the left hemisphere is found in ninety-six per cent of right-handed subjects but only seventy-three per cent of left-handed subjects. To understand the origins of handedness fully, combining both genetic variation and epigenetic processes that modify gene expression is essential.

In utero coordinated hand movements begin as early as eight weeks post conception (PC). At thirteen weeks PC, ninety per cent of foetuses preferred to suck their right thumb. This has been found to be significantly correlated with subsequent handedness. Only after fifteen weeks PC do corticospinal tracts develop with projections to the anterior spinal cord. Thus, handedness is unlikely to be brain-determined, and hand movements come from activity patterns in the spinal cord. We can conclude that asymmetrical gene expression in the spinal cord is the molecular origin of handedness. Rostral cervical elements of the spinal cord (C2-C5) supply the head neck and shoulder; C6 innervates the thumb, C7 the middle finger, and C8 the little finger, with T1

Table 11.1 Functions of the right and left hemispheres

Right Hemisphere Master	Left Hemisphere Emissary
Noradrenergic neuronal transmission in ventrolateral thalamic nuclei	Dopaminergic neuronal transmission in corpus striatum
Overall how we come to understand the world	Increased ratio of grey to white matter
Spatial working memory	Verbal working memory
Global	Local
Perceives curves and circles (natural phenomena)	Perceives in straight lines (unnatural mechanistic phenomena)
Coordinator or unique	Categorical
Engagement	Alienation
Processes negative emotions	Processes positive emotions
Incarnation	Abstraction
Monitoring of environment	Production in environment
General	Particular
Episodic retrieval	Episodic encoding
Right prefrontal cortex active	Left prefrontal cortex active
Whole aspect and metaphor	Part aspect and literal
Verification and checking	Semantic processing
Sees things in the round	Cognitive sequential processing style
Processing of faces with a global perspective	Assimilation of information bit by bit into the whole picture
Appreciation of context and function	Linear processing and analysis
Processing of music, body movement, rhythm, and dance	Unidirectional, goal-bound, processing
Left Hand	**Right Hand**
Sinister, awkward, weaker	Dextrous, on God's side, stronger
Associated with mental ill-health	

innervating the antecubital fossa. The results show for the first time that at eight weeks PC there is a substantial increase compared to previous reports in gene expression asymmetries in CNS tissue, which correlates with the first onset of coordinated hand movements. Given that at eight weeks PC, there is no connection between the spinal cord and motor cortex, this implies that asymmetrical arm use is controlled by the spinal cord.

Implications of this study for SF-EMDR psychotherapy

This study lends support to the practice of continuous bilateral stimulation at the level of the peripheral nervous system. If the patient experienced any trauma in the first trimester, this might have delayed the functional connectivity between the spinal cord and motor cortex. Activation of the spinal cord peripherally could be hypothesised to optimise later hemispheric connectivity, which would then lead to the transfer of emotional symptoms stored in the right hemisphere to the language centres of the left centre, and then onto the frontal lobes for development of insight and meaning.

The corpus callosum has more than two hundred million white-matter neurons. These are only partly myelinated, and it takes between one and three hundred milliseconds (ms) for synapses across hemispheres to interconnect. This compares with other brain regions as follows:

Neuronal recruitment (ms)

- Brainstem 40;
- Cerebellum 120;
- Limbic system 240; and
- Frontal cortex 500.

This is the time it takes the initial stimulus to reach a point of conscious awareness where we are capable of thought. The advantage of SF-EMDR psychotherapy and peak performance is that continuous bilateral stimulation during the therapeutic session can enable the patient to access more efficient interhemispheric communication. It is widely recognised that during our waking moments, ninety-five per cent of our behaviour and thought patterns emanate from the unconscious. Only five per cent of our behavioural patterns are under conscious control. SF-EMDR psychotherapy aims to help the patient recover from their emotional "stuck points" related to their traumas. They can then live in harmony with the environment, rather than constantly reacting to it as if the trauma was still present.

The RH experiences the body through its spiritual and emotional resonance and aesthetic appreciation of the environment. Medicine is at its most effective when addressing these issues. Patients undergoing SF-EMDR psychotherapy and peak performance can restore these aspects of their life. The emphasis on the senses of smell, touch, taste, vision, hearing, balance, and proprioception enables patients to reconnect cerebrally with the specific somatosensory aspects of their traumatic events. The bilateral cerebellar stimulation that is integral and unique to SF-EMDR psychotherapy helps to connect thoughts, emotions, and embodied experiences of both hemispheres with the brainstem, motor, and sensory tracts supplying the limbs, skin surface, and deeper feelings and sensations registered at a visceral level. During reprocessing of the patient's trauma, they are asked to activate the associated gut reaction or instinct. Typically, this is felt in the region of the solar plexus before transferring to the chest and heart area. These heartfelt sensations and feelings usually relate to unresolved grief and loss, and enough time is taken to resolve any distress located here. During SF-EMDR psychotherapy, I have addressed concepts associated with Eastern medicine by focusing on energy levels within the body.

Typically, the seven chakras are located at points of maximal activity of the immune, nervous, and endocrine systems. Each chakra resonates at a specific frequency. This increases as we ascend towards the higher levels of consciousness. Frequently, the patient will have become overwhelmed by their trauma at an energetic level. Depending on the frequency of this emotion, it is likely to manifest as a blockage at any of the first five chakras. The flexibility of the process of SF-EMDR psychotherapy and peak performance encourages the therapist to locate this blockage through a process of patient observation and feedback, to determine the location of affective dysregulation. This affect is then activated using bilateral stimulation (preferably with tactile units) until the reprocessing has been transformed. The blocked information can then travel along pre-existing neural pathways. Invariably, patients report a lump in their throat. This indicates a block to information processing at the level of the thyroid gland, or throat chakra. Patients are relieved when this distressing sensation dissipates.

The information superhighway comes to the intersection, or sensory gateway, of the thalamus. The thalamus takes stock of the information and, if resonating at the correct frequency, allows this information to pass through to the cortex. If the patient is in a dysregulated state of arousal (RAPIDS or FROZEN in FEAR), then the thalamic gateway is closed, and the patient is only capable of reflex instinctive responses. The BOKA machine uniquely can apply the optimum thalamic frequency of 40 Hertz bilaterally. This, theoretically, allows the activation of thalamocortical pathways and frontal cerebellar pathways. The patient's corpus callosum facilitates these. This integrates the information with that of the Master (RH) and his Emissary (LH). The patient is in an ideal place to make meaning and learn from their reprocessed experiences. By the fifth or final stage of SF-EMDR psychotherapy, the patient is feeling better, they are physically active, on the road to recovery, and have a sense of triumph.

Philosophical aspects of SF-EMDR psychotherapy

My SF-EMDR psychotherapy adheres to the principle of dialectic growth espoused by Heraclitus, quoted by McGilchrist (2009, pp. 30–31): "Increscunt animi, virescit volnere virtus. The spirit grows, and strength is restored by wounding." In many ways, this links to the idea that the wounded healer is the best therapist. It also echoes the quote from Rumi mentioned earlier.

The worldview as seen from the perspective of the right hemisphere

The cultures from the East tend to see the world from the perspective of the RH. "Shizen" is the Japanese word for nature and means "of itself." Everything in nature has "kami," or spirit. All aspects of the biosphere are connected and can communicate with each other. Like Heraclitus's river, it is always changing but always itself. In the modern Western world, the predominant perspective is that of the LH. Currently, the global view of the RH from the East is starting to predominate, with the rise of Brazil, India, China, East Asia, and Japan. In the West, we must not usurp the role of the RH, so that once again it can become our master and the LH its emissary. SF-EMDR psychotherapy and peak performance seeks to draw together the mystery of life from the complementary perspectives of East and West. Awareness of non-duality, oneness, and integration of the information from the gut, heart, and head, sets us on a path that is free from suffering.

In my experience, SF-EMDR psychotherapy can help to reduce the patient's pain, conflicts, or crises to enable a deeper connection and allow the patient to come to the awareness of unity. The patient or client's body and mind are brought into balance and stability. SF-EMDR psychotherapy can help the patient achieve the combination of non-dual awareness and freedom from suffering.

In thermographic steps down, several stages are involved:

1. **Prakriti** universal creative energy steps down into our personal vision;
2. **Ether** steps down, bringing mental impulses into the physical body;
3. **Air** involves the attachments and aversions at the heart of our movement;
4. **Fire** – our personal power – directs energy into the world;
5. Through **water,** we give birth to our self-expression;
6. **Earth** involves the completion of the process and the release of stored energy.

The ouroboros is represented by two snakes coiled around a central staff. This is the universal symbol known as the caduceus. It comes from the Ancient Greeks, whose physician, Asclepius, used this to cure disease. It has always been associated with healing. The universal creative energy (Prakriti) steps down theomorphically into the personal vision of the patient. Through the ether, mental images step down into the physical body. Through breathing (air), the heart displays our loves and hates (attachments and aversions). Through generating warmth via the fire element, our personal power directs energy out into the world around us. Through the seventy per cent of our body that is water, we give birth to our self-expression. Finally, by connecting to the earth with our feet, we complete the cycle and release any trapped energy. This illustration uses some of the same components of my seven-element relaxation exercise. The order is reversed, which can be facilitated by the patient at the end of therapy.

By now, ideally, the chakras will be fully energised. The heart chakra gives off the most radiant energy. The electromagnetic, auric, and nervous system fields can reach all other chakra energy points to ensure maximal communication at all micro and macro levels for our patients and clients.

In SF-EMDR psychotherapy, a key goal is to integrate the Western ideas epitomised by the psychologist Maslow with Eastern ideas of energies radiating from key chakra energy points. For me, this resonates historically with the philosophy of the Greek iatric at the Delphic Oracle. Indeed, this is the origin of psychiatry (*iatros* and *psyche*). It comes from the Greek, meaning "healing of the soul." My goal is to reacquaint psychiatrists with the origins of their chosen discipline in the work of Heraclitus and Asclepius, who first used the caduceus for healing. The original rod of Asclepius had one serpent coiled around a staff. This originated from the following myth.

Asclepius was the god of medicine and noticed a serpent was badly injured. Another serpent came along and administered healing herbs, saving the wounded snake. I like the symbol of the eagle's wings as part of the caduceus on the cover of *The Art of BART* (O'Malley, 2015). The coiled serpents can represent the energy of the Kundalini, which, when activated, opens the third-eye chakra associated with the pineal gland and wisdom. The significance of the pineal gland is represented by the pinecone sculpture or Fontana della Pigna outside the Vatican (cf. *The Art of BART*, Figure 25, p. 47, illustrating two views of the sculpture). It is four metres tall and once spouted water from the top. It was originally in the Pantheon next to the Temple of Isis. It was moved to the Old St. Peter's Basilica during the Middle Ages before being moved to its current location in 1608. The fact that it was originally designed to spout water may relate to activation of the pineal gland during meditation on the intuitive aspects of the third eye.

This highlights how the chakras coincide with key endocrine structures in the body, suggesting that the Eastern mystics had a sophisticated knowledge of how the immune, nervous, and endocrine systems interact. They perceived health against the different-coloured light frequency emanating from the chakra energy systems. In Western thought, science tended to explore the cells microscopically, as illustrated by what follows.

Hypothalamic–pituitary–adrenocortical (HPA) axis

The hypothalamus secretes a corticotropin-releasing hormone, which induces the pituitary to secrete the adrenocorticotropic hormone, thereby influencing the adrenal cortex to secrete cortisol, which feeds back and regulates activity in the hypothalamus and pituitary. Cortisol also circulates systemically. I have shown earlier how activation of the endocrine glands along the HPA axis mimics closely the energy points associated with the chakras. This shows how Western and Eastern ideas are becoming harmonised.

Brain-immune system interactions

The brain regulates the immune system through the autonomic and neuroendocrine systems. The sympathetic innervation of the adrenal medulla secretes epinephrine, and there is both sympathetic and parasympathetic innervation of lymph nodes from synaptic connections in the hypothalamus. Glucocorticoids from the adrenal gland act on innate and adaptive immune cells. Neural relationships exist between the hypothalamus, brainstem nuclei, and autonomic ganglia. Neuroendocrine influences that alter immune function and that emanate from the hypothalamus consist of the hypothalamic–pituitary axis, prolactin, and growth hormone, which, together with epinephrine, influence innate and adaptive immune cells that secrete cytokines. In addition to autonomic feedback, several different types of cytokines and interleukins feed back to multiple sites in the head-brain. From here, the adrenocorticotropic hormone is released to act on the adrenal medulla. Prolactin and growth hormone are released into the peripheral blood.

The interaction of the immune, endocrine, and nervous systems is a key discovery of Western medicine. I have also shown how these interactions are compatible with Eastern traditions and the beliefs of the chakra energy systems. SF-EMDR psychotherapy capitalises on this architecture to get the best result for patients. It is the only therapeutic approach to combine the best in Western and Eastern medicine.

The activation of the body's immune system has been equated to the triumph of the human spirit in that it protects us from antigens and has our highest good at heart. These principles are consistent with SF-EMDR psychotherapy.

Summary

Life in a world according to the perspective of the left hemisphere starts this chapter, with the implications outlined. This does not happen due to the existence of the corpus callosum, which shares information between hemispheres.

The five stages of bilateral affective reprocessing of thoughts are explained. Each step is explained in images and then in words. This appeals to the strengths of the right and left hemispheres, respectively. The aim is for therapist, patient, and client to have a coherent overall view of the process, which will enhance their therapeutic gain.

A key reason for the success of SF-EMDR psychotherapy and peak performance is that it is entirely informed by affective neuroscience and neuroanatomy, especially given the fact that ninety per cent of neural information is homolateral up to the brainstem, before it becomes ipsilateral and crosses to the opposite cortical hemisphere. This flow of information is enhanced using figure-of-eight and ouroboros symbols.

The functions of the hemispheres are tabulated to provide a focus to boost areas of perceived weakness and augment areas of strength.

Philosophical aspects are mentioned with the discussion of the caduceus, the ancient symbol of healing. By now, the chakras are shown as fully energised and linked to optimised endocrine functioning. The newest research into the links with the HPA axis and the brain–immune axis are briefly discussed.

Chapter 12

Using SF-EMDR psychotherapy for peak performance in sport, business, academia, and any pursuit where anticipatory anxiety impairs results

How to become an expert in your chosen discipline

According to Ericsson and Lehmann at Florida State University in Tallahassee (1996), it normally takes 10,000 hours of practice to become an expert in any discipline. The skill-hungry years, from the perspective of neurological development, are from age eight to twelve. Thus, starting at age eight in your chosen discipline, one would require three hours of practice daily for fifty weeks per year until age eighteen. In Russia, China, Bulgaria, Ukraine, Romania, Poland, Hungary, and the Czech Republic, children as young as four are often exposed to this level of practice. Theoretically, they would then be at the level of "peak performance" at age fourteen. Their adolescent growth spurt and neurological improvements via synaptic pruning are yet to emerge, however. The long-term consequences for such an athlete could be long-term physical injury and psychological impairment.

"Flow" is being able to concentrate effortlessly in performing all types of skills appropriate to your chosen discipline, be it chess, football, hockey, or any other sport. Time slows as you concentrate on the activity at hand. Enjoyment in the pursuit is the key to success. There are four essential components to being in a state of flow:

1. Lack of awareness of time. In this state, participants lose all sense of time due to their intense, focused absorption in their chosen task. It is as if watching the clock would become a distraction and impair performance. In my experience, during a session of SF-EMDR psychotherapy, both the patient and I become jointly focused on achieving our reprocessing goals for the session. Sometimes, the 90–120 minutes are over in an instant. Conscious time appears to slow down as we enter the realm of reactivation and reprocessing of unconscious memories, feelings, emotions, and sensations. These principles would apply equally to an athlete seeking to improve their personal best, or to a team whose form had inexplicably dipped below its best.
2. Autotelicity. This is the conviction that your chosen activity is rewarding for its own sake. Following an intense session of SF-EMDR psychotherapy,

patients will confirm that they feel less burdened with worry. They also report feeling better mentally, emotionally, physically, and even spiritually. I can see evidence for these changes in the patient's posture, demeanour, and the different "vibe" emanating from them compared to the start of the session. I would expect a similar uplifting response to occur with anyone seeking to optimise their performance in school, university, the workplace, or in any world of sporting achievement.

3.   The "sweet spot." This is the point at which flow "flows." For example, the ability to hit the tennis ball on the part of the racquet where its response is true to the player's intent. Or, when the footballer strikes through the ball so that the imagined trajectory becomes a reality. In my clinical experience of using SF-EMDR psychotherapy, the narrative reciprocity that develops helps to alleviate the patient's distress. I remain alert and fully focused on the therapeutic process. In contrast, many of my patients report attending countless therapy sessions (including unmodified CBT) where they end up more frustrated due to the lack of progress in therapy. This might relate to the therapist not being tuned in to the patient. Thus, they are unable to "hit the sweet spot" with the patient and, consequently, there is no "flow" to the session. SF-EMDR psychotherapy offers a completely new potential in working with athletes across both time and distance.

4.   Automaticity. This is when the healing within the SF-EMDR session appears as if it is happening by itself. I believe this happens when the patient can resonate at a higher vibrational frequency, overcoming past traumas. They can tap into the heightened awareness of the therapist. Both patient and therapist then have the potential to tune into "source," "all there is," or "unitary consciousness." This invariably leads towards resolution of the patient's traumas and soul healing, or psychiatry. This is derived from the Greek words *psyche* and *iatros* (literally, healing of the mind).

All the above requirements can be achieved with the athlete, student, writer, worker, or sportsperson who wants to improve performance, minimise performance anxiety, enhance creativity, bring dreams to reality, recover fitness after illness, or implement the skills learnt in training in competitive matches.

The set-up to achieve flow is enhanced by my seven-element relaxation exercise. Breathing and heart rate slows down as the client reaches a state of relaxed concentration. Conscious thought takes a back seat as the client focuses on their body. The muscles that are attended to will depend on the client's requirements and the demands of the task. For example, improving hand–eye coordination and visualisation would be a key skill for sports such as golf, hockey, football, all racquet sports, archery, and most track and field events. SF-EMDR for peak performance uses the same template as SF-EMDR psychotherapy. The target will be a past performance that triggered anxiety or frustration. It could relate to being dropped from the team or being substituted when the client believed they were performing well. The highly trained client will have no difficulty tapping into their triune-brain, or neural network responses, that is, gut reaction, heartfelt response, and headwork. These will be accompanied by somatic sensations and movement impulses, as described previously. In this relaxed state, the client has an increased production of alpha waves and an initial suppression of activity in the prefrontal cortex as blood flow initially follows the flow of attention to the neural networks of the body, especially the enteric and cardiac plexi. It has been my experience, at the end of a SF-EMDR psychotherapy session, that patients experience a new tingling sensation in this most recently evolved part of the brain. I hypothesise that as experiences are resolved at lower energy or chakra levels, then interhemispheric resolution occurs. The pineal gland marks the point of the sixth chakra. This is also where the right and left prefrontal cortices meet. The tingling sensation might reflect new synaptic activity as the patient generates ideas consistent with recovery. The same response would be expected with clients seeking to improve performance.

Wulf and colleagues, kinesiologists at the University of Nevada in Las Vegas, also believe that the best learning occurs when you turn off conscious thought. The external focus of the body allows the client's flow of information to become automatic. Both client and therapist focus on a positive, goal-directed outcome for the session. If both can resonate at similar frequencies of attunement, an augmented and swifter response is possible.

Factors relevant to developing optimal functioning and peak performance

In an article discussing the performance of twelve Olympic gold medallists, Fletcher and Sarker (2012) develop a grounded theory of psychological resilience in Olympic champions. Resilience was defined as "a dynamic process encompassing positive adaptation within the context of significant adversity." As such, many factors impede the athletes' performance. These include:

1. **Stressors**, which were of three types:

    (a) loss of form;
    (b) organisational, for example, related to sports politics;
    (c) personal, e.g. related to family circumstances and relationships.

Exposure to stressors was found to be a prerequisite for future outstanding performance. Many of those interviewed said that without exposure to these stressors, they would not have become Olympic champions.

2. **Challenge appraisal**
    The best athletes in the world look at stressors as an opportunity for growth, personal development, and mastery of their technical discipline. They push themselves to train harder than the opposition in the expectation that this will give them a competitive edge.

3. **Metacognition**

A term coined by Flavell. It is described as an individual's knowledge of – and control over, their emotions – It is subdivided into three stages:

(a)   metacognitive knowledge;
(b)   metacognitive skills;
(c)   metacognitive experience.

Five psychological factors were found to exert influence on challenge appraisal and metacognition:

(i)   a positive personality;
(ii)   motivation;
(iii) confidence;
(iv)   focus;
(v)   perceived social support.

In this study, peak performance was described as fulfilling their athletic potential, rather than becoming Olympic champion. They have the higher mental faculties to reflect on their own initial reaction to stressors and to learn from this experience. The emotional reaction, such as disappointment in competition, is then used to spur achievement in the next competitive event. This harnessing of affect or emotion, rather than succumbing, is critical to the evaluative stages of SF-EMDR psychotherapy. I would propose tapping into the three major components of meta-cognition (knowledge, skills, and experience), using SF-EMDR psychotherapy and peak performance as a cornerstone in developing psychological resilience in athletes.

Being in the zone: use of SF-EMDR psychotherapy for optimal functioning and peak performance

When you are in the zone, you are barely aware of the world around you. Time seems to slow down as you focus on the task. Being in the zone can help to bring each person in touch with his or her element. Robinson has discussed this concept in detail in his 2009 book *The Element*.

SF-EMDR psychotherapy and peak performance can help the client prepare themselves to stay "in the zone." Imaginal re-experiencing of their chosen task while experiencing auditory and tactile bilateral stimulation can lead to future peak performance. Mind and body merge as one with gut instinct, heart feelings, and headwork all effortlessly synchronised. The last thirty minutes of the session is the opportune time for reflection. The neural networks associated with new learning are laid down. These can be put into practice at the next training session. Then, recalibration and feedback from training can occur at the next SF-EMDR peak performance appointment. A key element of SF-EMDR psychotherapy and peak performance is achieved by allowing the somatic sensations to synapse with the central nervous system (CNS). This is then reconnected with the peripheral nervous system (PNS), initially by rhythmically tapping first one foot and then the other. This allows a figure-of-eight wave impulse to be generated from head to foot. The latest research suggests that when this wave resonates throughout the body, a climate of joy, wonder, and love occurs, as the client's own DNA is stimulated maximally and the potential for replication of new codon combinations by messenger RNA exists. The opposite happens when the client is describing or experiencing a climate of fear and cell growth shuts down.

The client feels that they are in the zone when a sense of authenticity and freedom emerges in the session. Their neural networks or synapses are freed to connect in novel patterns optimal for peak performance in their chosen discipline. Each client, when they have resolved past failures or difficulties with SF-EMDR psychotherapy and peak performance, has the potential to reach a higher plane of achievement. This might involve accessing an energy field normally out of reach. They can be assisted to be in harmonic convergence with this meta-state. Usain Bolt provides an example of tapping into higher energy fields, as he uses his signature thunderbolt pose to assert his conviction that he is the fastest man on the planet and "a bolt from the blue."

During the night, the individual goes through stages of non-REM and REM sleep with associated brainwave activity. In the awake state, the client produces beta and alpha waves. Non-REM – stage one – or light sleep produces irregular, shallow waves. Stage two has bursts of rhythmic brain activity characterised by sleep spindles and K complexes. Stage three produces regular deep brainwave activity, and stage four has delta waves. REM activity comes next and is present for increasing periods during the night in ninety-minute cycles. Each SF-EMDR psychotherapy and peak performance session is designed to mimic the ninety-minute sleep–wake cycle of circadian and ultradian rhythms to get the maximum benefit from reprocessing therapy. It is essential that athletes travelling to competitions across time zones optimise their sleep–wake cycle without resorting to hypnotics. This can be achieved through a process of psycho-education of athletes and other individuals seeking to optimise their performance on the benefits of the 90-min sleep–wake cycle involving both non-REM and REM sleep, and through SF-EMDR psychotherapeutic peak performance. Recently, a poor performance by the England football team was attributed to the widespread use of hypnotics as the players wanted to sleep after travelling across several time zones by plane.

When the patient is unable to produce a healthy sleep cycle with regular periods of REM, this is an early warning sign of unprocessed traumatic stress and is often a precursor to mental ill-health or burnout.

Applying SF-EMDR psychotherapy and peak performance for athletics, sports, business, stage performers, artists, and anyone keen to achieve their goals

According to Waters (2013), in his spiritual dynamics newsletter, life can get easier. He suggests that instead of working hard to complete a project, it all just flows together in one smoothly moving path towards perfect completion (Figure 12.1). This is the promise of the Eastern philosophy of Wu Wei. This promotes the idea of doing without doing or action without effort. Patients can experience a state of flow that enables them to move through the task with ease, grace, and efficiency. The message of Wu Wei is to develop deeper states of inner awareness. In a state of flow, an action is guided from within. The inner being of the client is fully attuned to the universe. Synchronicity and coincidences become commonplace. People, ideas, and materials appear at the right time and place. There is a time and place for everything to come together for effortless achievement. The realm of being manifests in the world of action.

Western scientific thinking has been applied to the principle of Wu Wei by an American-Hungarian professor, Dr Mihaly Csikszentmihalyi. According to Csikszentmihalyi (1990), goals should be set just outside their current performance range, but realistically matched to future expected performance based on strength conditioning, coaching, assessment of training, and learning from past performances.

Any negative feelings, sensations, emotions, or associations with previous injuries are reprocessed with SF-EMDR psychotherapy. The flow of information

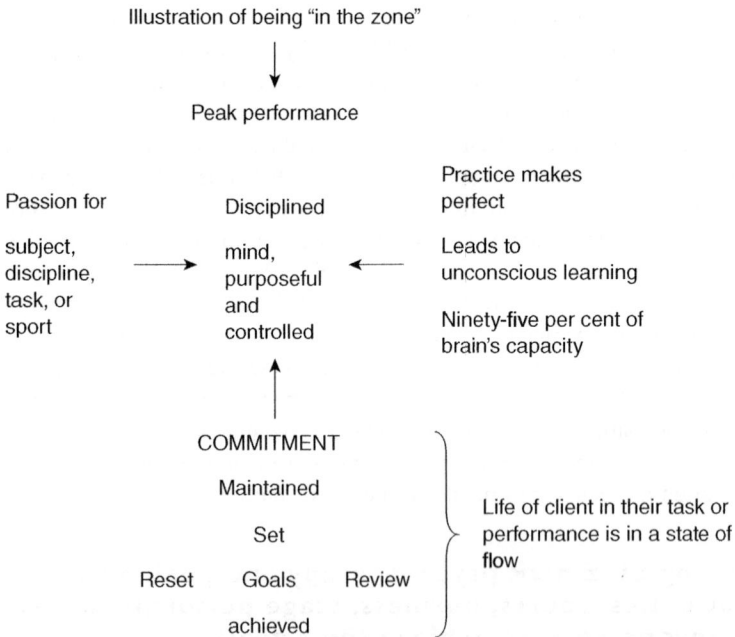

Illustration of being "in the zone"

↓

Peak performance

Passion for subject, discipline, task, or sport

→

Disciplined mind, purposeful and controlled

←

Practice makes perfect

Leads to unconscious learning

Ninety-five per cent of brain's capacity

↑

COMMITMENT

Maintained

Set

Reset   Goals   Review

achieved

Life of client in their task or performance is in a state of flow

Figure 12.1 Diagram showing how sports professionals and other artists can achieve a state of flow that allows them to perform at their optimum while "in the zone."

is activated from being stored in the body to the cerebral hemispheres. The client can activate the appropriate neural pathways, achieving enjoyment and success. Using guided visualisation, the chosen imaginal exercise stimulates mirror neurones and muscles as if they were performing live and the procedure becomes intrinsically rewarding. When the client or their team are performing well, the state of joyful feedback allows players to access higher energy levels, which help sustain peak performance. The five stages of SF-EMDR psychotherapy and peak performance are modified, focusing on the future template. An assessment is always made of recent and previous significant life events. Negatively charged events are reprocessed towards resolution, while positively charged ones are incorporated into the seven-element relaxation exercise.

Examples of successful sporting teams

I believe one of the reasons for the continued success of the New Zealand Rugby Team is their unity in embracing and performing the Haka. The instructions and actions of the Haka are outlined below.

Performance of the haka by New Zealand sports teams

The "Ka Mate" Haka generally opens with a set of five preparatory instructions shouted by the leader, before the whole team joins in. It has been criticised because its sole purpose is to intimidate the opposition. As an exercise in bilateral stimulation, it powerfully causes the blood to perfuse the blood vessels. The associated language (such as "stomp" the feet as hard as you can) mimics the gentler figure-of-eight stimulation of SF-EMDR psychotherapy and peak performance. I would suggest that my multi-user machine could replace the Haka in the dressing room for teams preparing to go out to the field of play.

Figure 12.2 shows schematically the postures and movements of the players during the haka. From observing the live performance, you notice the ferocity, energy, drive, and passion shown by native Maori and white New Zealanders alike. They are prepared to lay down their lives for their teammates, and the goal of rising to the top where the sun shines is articulated.

Anyone watching the All Blacks will notice the ferocity of the Haka, which is designed to strike terror into the hearts of their opponents. The lyrics suggest activation of the chakras from stamping their feet, thighs, and chest, to climbing up to the top of the ladder where the sun shines as they rise and emerge victoriously. This evolved as a "thank you" from a Maori chief, who hid in a food storage hole and eventually climbed out to be met by a friendly chief. This Maori tradition has been adopted by New Zealand and used with success for more than one hundred years. This was spectacularly demonstrated during 2013 when the All Blacks won all fourteen games they played during the calendar year. They were the first rugby team to achieve this during the professional era.

"Ka Mate"

Leader: *Ringa pakia!*   Slap the hands against the thighs!

     Uma tiraha!   Puff out the chest

     Turi whatia!   Bend the kness!

     Hope whai ake!   Let the hip follow!

     Waewae takahia kia kino! Stomp the feet as hard as you can!

Leader: *Ka mate, ka mate*   I die, I die

Team: *Ka ora, Ka ora*   I live, I live

Leader: *Ka mate, Ka mate*   I die, I die

Team: *Ka ora Ka ora*   I live, I live

All: *Tēnei te tangata pūhuruhuru* This is the hairy man

   Nāna i tiki mai whakawhiti ... Who caused the sun to shine again
   te rā   for me

   A Upane! Ka Upane!   Up the ladder, Up the ladder

   Upane Kaupane   Up to the top

   Whiti te rā,   The sun shines!

   Hī!   Rise!

Figure 12.2 Text of the Haka used by New Zealand Rugby Team.

All Blacks from 2014–2017

The All Blacks won all three matches in the Steinlager series, four games out of six in the 2014 Investec rugby championship, and their remaining five matches that year. In 2015, they won all seven games to lift the Rugby world cup. They won two out of three matches in the Investec Rugby Championship and 2016, and they won all their games except the momentous one against Ireland at Soldier Field, Chicago. This was Ireland's first win in over 111 years of playing the All Blacks rugby team. On 6 November 2016, the score was Ireland 40, All Blacks 29. Before this game, the Ireland squad formed a figure-of-eight in memory of Anthony Foley, in response to the All Blacks' performance of the haka. This was even more remarkable as it ended New Zealand's eighteen-game winning streak. Anthony Foley was a legendary figure in Munster and Irish rugby, who a few weeks earlier had died suddenly from a heart attack. He wore the number eight jersey for Munster and Ireland. It was highly symbolic that the Irish team chose to honour him in this way. (In the manual for SF-EMDR psychotherapy, a repeating figure eight is used to represent the strands of DNA and the activation of the chakras.) They won all their remaining matches that year. On the 21 October 2017, they lost to Australia 23:18, but bounced back with a win against Barbarians 31–22. They are current world champions and expect to win every game. The haka is fundamental to their winning philosophy, and the dramatic self-induced bilateral stimulation exhibits many features of SF-EMDR psychotherapy.

European Champions League football 2012–2017

Another example of peak performance is the triumph of football artisans Chelsea against Barcelona, the artists of European football, in the Champions League semi-final of 2012. Barcelona was 2–0 up and coasting when Chelsea scored just before half-time. Chelsea gained self-belief and pressure started to mount on Barcelona. When their talisman Lionel Messi twice hit the woodwork, it appeared as if fate had decreed they would lose. Barcelona continued to exhibit their elegant style of play, but this was not sufficient to breach the determined Chelsea defence, which grew in confidence in the second half. In the end, Chelsea progressed against all the odds to the Champions League final by beating Barcelona 3–2. Barcelona was caught off guard; no longer in their "element," or in control of events on the pitch. Perhaps if the team had imagined a scenario where Chelsea could win using BOKA and SF-EMDR psychotherapy and peak performance, they could have changed tactics. Instead, they stuck to their tactics of slick passing with movement off the ball, and lost.

Further examples from the world of Champions League football include the battle between Real Madrid and Manchester United. The latter has won three Champions League trophies while Real Madrid is chasing la Decima, their tenth victory. They were managed by two of the most successful managers of their generation in José Mourinho, then aged fifty, and Alex Ferguson, then seventy-one.

The score from the first leg was 1–1, with all to play for in the second leg. With both teams evenly matched on the pitch, the key was in the psychological preparation of the players and the managers' mind games transmitted via the enthralled media and public. In the end, Real won 2–1, with their star Cristiano Ronaldo scoring in the sixty-ninth minute. He described the match as "an emotional night" for him. The critical difference might have been his drive, desire to win, and ability to keep his emotions in check. He could keep his cool and prevent the red mist from descending and impairing his razor-sharp performance.

The individual and team peak performance, from the neurological and mind–body standpoint outlined in SF-EMDR psychotherapy and peak performance, could give that team the cutting edge necessary to progress to the next round. It is interesting that Alex Ferguson has announced his retirement and that his replacement is fifty-year-old David Moyes, the current Everton manager. Whether he can repeat Sir Alex's success will be closely watched. He has been given a six-year contract, in a recognition by the board that victory is unlikely to be immediate.

Meanwhile, José Mourinho returned to manage Chelsea in September 2013. In a recent Champions League match against Romanian champions Steaua Bucharest, Chelsea demolished them 4–0 away from home. Commentators reported how Mourinho had infused his intense desire and passion for winning into each player. From the prodigal return of Juan Mata to the tireless running of Ramires to the enterprise of the German Andre Schurrle, there were heroic performances across the team. Mourinho embraced Schurrle for his assist in the third Chelsea goal, which shows how Mourinho has adopted the peak performance principles espoused in this book. He said:

> I put the players under a lot of pressure for this game and they coped well. They used that as a motivation. I don't want to play in the Europa league, but I also thought that was a way they can grow up faster, faced with that pressure.
>
> (Fifield, 2013)

With his own affective expression and movement stimulation, which is often bilateral, involving both arms, he engages in reprocessing his thoughts. These feelings are then effectively communicated to his players. The similarities to SF-EMDR psychotherapy and peak performance are evident.

This was recently highlighted in a Premier League match where Mourinho protested vigorously that the opposing team were wasting time. He was banished to the stands and had to celebrate Chelsea's victory alongside the spectators.

His passion for Chelsea was evident from his bilateral gesticulations, which no doubt helped him to process his visible anger. He was charged with misconduct by the Football Association and decided to refrain from commenting on the incident until he heard from the referee why he "was prevented from doing his work." This episode had no adverse impact on the team, and on 22 October 2013, Mourinho's team beat Schalke 3–0 away from home, with Fernando Torres scoring twice on his hundredth appearance for the club.

In Mourinho's second spell managing Chelsea, they won a league championship. Despite this, he was sacked on 17 December 2015 after a poor run of results left Chelsea just outside the relegation zone. He was confirmed as the new manager of Manchester United on 27 May 2016. As of January 2017, they are in the Europa League, in the semi-finals of the EFL Cup, in the FA Cup, and lie sixth in the Premier League after a string of impressive results. This shows that Mourinho is a powerful motivator for his teams. However, experience indicates that in his third year his players are so exhausted that they are unwilling to compete as well as they have done in the previous two years. He seems to see his appointment as Manchester United manager in a different light and hopes to emulate his hero Alex Ferguson and be there for the long term, building a winning team in his image.

In his first year at Manchester United, he won three cups, including the League Cup and Europa League. This latter guaranteed automatic entry into the Champions League. United won their first three Champions League games and now look certain to qualify for the group stages in 2018. Their league form was dramatic, apart from a 2–2 and 0–0 draws with Stoke and Liverpool. This was followed by a reported statement from Mourinho indicating that his ambition for management went beyond Manchester United. Although consistent with staying with a club for a maximum of three years, this risked alienating his players, who may have perceived this as Mourinho not fully committing himself to the club while demanding total application and commitment from his players. Human nature dictates that players may respond unconsciously with a bad performance. On 21 October 2017, United lost 2–1 to Huddersfield, who had just been promoted from the Championship. Mourinho was quick to criticise his players for their lack of commitment, and for playing with less effort than in a friendly. I wonder whether he considered how his earlier comments might have contributed to this poor performance. On 5 November, his team lost 1–0 away to his former club Chelsea. It appeared that the Chelsea manager Antonio Conte had inspired his players to desire victory more than Mourinho had his players. It remains to be seen if this signals a fatal blow to their attempts to regain the Premier League title.

My goal is to work with some of his players using SF-EMDR psychotherapy to optimise their performance. I have piloted this approach with some success with a player playing for the first team at Nottingham Trent University.

Getting accurate feedback on your past performance to improve future ones

Figure 12.3 shows how to gain accurate feedback from your performance.

Another example from the world of football is Luis Suarez who plays for Liverpool. Recently, he was given a ten-match ban for biting an opponent. Although he apologised, he was known to have bitten an opponent before and received a seven-match ban for racially abusing Patrice Evra. This suggests that his default mode network (DMN) is stuck at a pre-juvenile level. When his body and mind perceive a threat, he communicates either like a baby or toddler,

Feedback ———————▶ Predicted state of emotions
so that
future
predicted
states in   Experienced state of emotions
more
accurate
▲   Appraisal within a context

│   Feelings related to sensory
Uncertainty
▲   Modalities e.g. taste, pain, touch

Individual traits

Risk preferences or anxiety

Adaptive behaviour

Regulation of homeostasis
▲

Integrated subjective state
of patients or client's
emotions or feelings

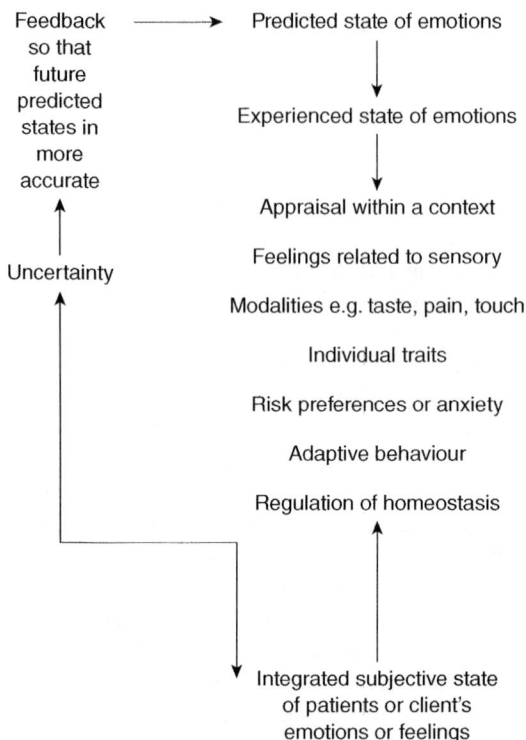

Figure 12.3 How to gain accurate feedback from your performance so that the prediction of performance in the future will become more accurate.

Source: Sorcha O'Malley.

who often bite due to frustration or by calling someone names as would happen in a playground. Suarez's undeniable talent on the pitch is sabotaged by these outbursts. I would suggest three sessions of SF-EMDR psychotherapy and peak performance would heal his traumatised DMN and allow him to manage any anger outbursts as they occur. To quote Dr Steve Peters, he would learn to box-in the frustrations and talk to the angry chimp – the part of his mind that is looking for instant gratification.

The five stages of SF-EMDR psychotherapy for both optimal functioning and peak performance

The process of moving towards peak performance following on from SF-EMDR psychotherapy can be broken down into five PARTS.

Part one: Practice activity review transition

The key goal of part one is to make the transition from the reprocessed thoughts developed from the five stages of SF-EMDR psychotherapy. Depending on the client's state, it may be possible to omit some of these stages. I would advise cataloguing any significant life events, however, as they may hijack performance at a later stage.

As stated by Robinson and Sayed, it will take 10,000 hours of practice to get one's neurons firing in a repeated pattern that can be replicated at will to reach the pinnacle in one's chosen sport or activity. The client is beginning the journey from conscious learning, involving the prefrontal cortex, to eventual unconscious learning, involving the deeper structures of the brain such as the cerebellum and cingulate cortex. The corpus callosum is essential for interhemispheric knowledge, and the bilateral stimulation described in SF-EMDR psychotherapy has a role to play in facilitating this process. The client is encouraged to review the achievements from the hours of practice in their chosen activity.

The role of deliberate practice in the acquisition of expert performance was initially studied by Ericsson, Krampe, and Tesch-Römer (1993, p. 363). They argued:

> The theoretical framework presented in this article explains expert performance as the result of an individual's prolonged efforts to improve performance while negotiating motivational and external constraints. In most domains of expertise, individuals begin in their childhood a regimen of effortful activities (deliberate practice) designed to optimise improvement. Individual differences even among elite performers are closely related to the assessed amounts of deliberate practice. Many characteristics once believed to reflect innate talent. These are the result of intense practice extended for a minimum of 10 years.

Practising for twenty hours per week for fifty weeks per year over a ten-year period equates to 10,000 hours. This is the figure quoted in Gladwell (2008) and Colvin (2008, pp. 39–42), and is known as the 10,000-hour rule. Following the years of practice, the client will have created a neural network, or pathway, that allows them to make the transition to improve performance in the actual event, competition, examination, presentation, or other chosen task.

Part two: Planning for action and revved-up for the trials

The key goal of part two is to become absorbed in the chosen task or activity. This allows the client to adapt so that they lose track of time when fully engaged in the performance. The action-plan, or planning for action, is also crucial, as this demands complete concentration. This state of absorption is a prerequisite to reaching a state of "flow." This is defined as that feeling of effortless concentration to those giving outstanding performances in different areas of skills and techniques. Working with the client by accumulating data from research on the relevant achievements of others, namely competitors in their chosen field or expertise, allows for gearing or revving up for the trials. This is a crucial stage where difficulties can be worked on, adjustments made, and any doubts or niggles ironed out. This sets the framework for the next parts of the process. Bilateral cerebellar stimulation during SF-EMDR peak performance facilitates interhemispheric learning, as well as optimisation of the functions of the right and left hemispheres.

Part three: Physical **a**utotelicity nerve **r**eflexes and **t**oned muscles

The critical goal of part three is to harness the previous psychological advantages with the physical emphasis. The word "physic" comes from the Greek, meaning the nature of healing, and, when combined with the suffix, incorporates the strength of the body as well as the mind. This part emphasises speed of thought and action, stamina, and drive to complete the project: a systematic approach to integrating gut-, heart-, and head-brains with immunological and endocrine organs. Again, the zappers can be used to provide bilateral stimulation to the key groups of muscles being used by the client. The hockey player will want to hone their hand–eye–

nerve reflexes and to strengthen and increase the flexibility of their leg muscles. We will also work visually on set plays and tactics: for example, those associated with the short corner. Staying focused with frequent substitutions during the game is also a key component in preparing for matches. Video analysis can provide useful feedback on past performance.

Autotelicity is defined as the client having the sense that the activity they are involved in is rewarding for its own sake. Through physical exercise, they will have developed the ability to perform with the flexibility of a baby moving all its limbs, but with the added control derived from the desire to achieve.

The final part of this stage involves the neurological reward from knowing that your nerves respond reflexively and, consequently, that the muscles needed are toned and effective. The final T can also represent the need for the client to be aware of tablets and toxins. These take the form of essential vitamins needed for muscle development and are listed in Table 12.1.

The recommended daily allowances (RDA), if exceeded, can be toxic, so knowledge of nutrition is essential for all performers. The world anti-doping agency (WADA) is in a constant battle to stay ahead of those seeking to boost their performance artificially. The athlete's biochemical passport has been introduced to prevent blood doping. Knowledge of the physiological systems outlined in this book will equip all clients to stay abreast of WADA requirements and testing policies.

Part four: Pinnacle of **a**utomaticity by **r**ehearsing **t**echniques

The key goal of part four is to embed the learning already achieved. The client can see the peak of Mount Everest ahead and is preparing to climb the summit. Essentially, they are marshalling their resources at base camp and getting ready for the challenge to perform on the next day or even within hours.

Automaticity means that the client can reproduce the necessary performance automatically, without having to think about it. This has been achieved by switching the location of the brain neurons that have been fired and wired

Table 12.1 List of thirteen essential vitamins with recommended daily allowances, effects of overdose, and original food source.

Vitamin	Chemical name	Recommended dietary allowance (RDA)	Overdose symptoms	Food source
A	Retinol beta carotene	900μg	Hypervitaminosis A	Orange, yellow fruits
B1	thiamine	1.2mg	Drowsiness	Pork, brown rice
B2	riboflavin	1.3mg		Dairy products
B3	niacin	16mg	Liver damage	Meat, eggs
B5	Pantothenic acid	5mg	Diarrhoea	Meat, avocados
B6	Pyridoxine	1.5mg	Nerve damage	Meat, vegetables
B7	Biotin	30μg		Egg yolk
B9	Folic acid	400μg		Bread
B12	Cobalamine	2.4μg	Rash	Meat
C	Ascorbic acid	90mg	Diarrhoea	Fruits and vegetables
D	Cholecalciferol	10μg		Fish, eggs
E	Tocopherols	15mg	Heart failure	Spinach, liver
K	Quinones	120μg	Clotting if patient is on warfarin	

together. Learning any new skill requires the processing power of the prefrontal cortex, which acts like an orchestra, bringing in the other neuronal networks of the brain according to need. Once these pathways have lit up, the respective associative cortices can forge a direct neural connection, obviating the need for orchestrated input from the prefrontal cortex. Now the activity is harmonious and plays to its own tune and rhythm. The prefrontal cortex takes a back seat. The neurons involved in the ninety-five per cent of unconscious processing take over. This unconscious learning, when reactivated, allows the client to be "in the zone." It has come about by the client's repeatedly rehearsing their technique so that nerves and overwhelming emotion are contained. This allows an opportunity to re-explain the RAPIDS, NARROW WATER, and FROZEN models of hyper and hypoarousal mentioned earlier.

Part five: Performance actually reaches target

The key goal of part five is the client reaching the desired target. To perform, the client must harness their mind and body architecture. This includes 213 bones, 500 muscles, and 7 miles of nerves. By dint of their vision, positivity, philosophy, and passion, they can now stand on the podium. They can realise their full potential. SF-EMDR peak performance via integration of top-down and bottom-up processing, with the information transferred between left and right cerebral hemispheres, can assist in this process.

Ideally, the performance of the client hits the target. During the performance, brain scans have shown that there is decreased activity in the prefrontal cortex. The client remains mentally focused and quiet. Any overthinking at this stage is likely to interfere with the automaticity of the flow process and impair performance.

Use of SF-EMDR peak performance in the world of golf

Rory McIlroy was the number one golfer in the world in 2012. He relinquished this accolade when he pulled out of the second round of the Honda Classic when seven over par. He later admitted that he was not in a great place mentally and that he had walked off the course impulsively. Prior attention to the detailed workings of the mind discussed here might have altered that fateful decision. By October 2013, he had slipped to sixth in the world and was without a victory in 2013 until his fortunes changed. This shows how even the most talented of athletes can succumb to external pressures and media expectations. Jack Nicklaus describes how he would imagine the trajectory of the golf ball before addressing the ball. He attributes much of his success to this disarmingly simple technique. By using his imagination, his mirror neurons were firing and, therefore, his unconsciously learnt nerve reflexes associated with each golf swing could be activated on demand. He had found a perfect way to counteract what golfers call the "yips." This is the loss of fine motor skills associated with any sport and is termed focal dystonia. It has ruined many golfers' careers. Recently, there have been reports in the literature of it being cured by emotional freedom technique (EFT). Given that this approach is designed to activate the body's meridians, I believe that SF-EMDR psychotherapy and peak performance can also affect a cure.

Normally, there is a surge of alpha waves produced just before the golf shot, the arrow release, or when about to deliver a speech or presentation. This allows the client to focus attention on the target. Other sensory inputs can be suppressed, such as the throbbing pain of a toothache. It is as if time stands still at that precise moment. Indeed, one of Rory McIlroy's explanations for his dip in form was a toothache.

When about to start the race, match, or presentation, the athlete enters a state of relaxed concentration accompanied by physiological changes. These include reduced respiratory rate, pulse rate, and blood pressure. This may be considered to represent the previously undescribed seventh, or hyper-focused, "F" state of the autonomic nervous system. This is "flow," where the client hits the "sweet spot" and everything flows towards the ultimate target. I hypothesise that this can be achieved by working through the five stages of peak performance illustrated above.

It would also be helpful to identify any unresolved traumatic stress in the golfer's life. In Rory McIlroy's case, he was forced to deny on his Twitter account rumours that he was about to separate from his girlfriend, tennis star Caroline Wozniacki, and that he was involved in legal action over a dispute with his management team. In recent press conferences, he has refused to talk about his private life.

Rory McIlroy has said "countless hours spent with lawyers this year" have been a "distraction" as he heads into this week's World Tour Championship in Dubai, still seeking his first win of 2013 (BBC Sports Online, 2013).

This implies that his current state of hyperarousal, indicated by the RAPIDS in Figure 12.2, will benefit from the calmer waters of the window of affect tolerance and emotional regulation.

By openly stating the pressures sportsmen and women face to succeed, he acknowledged the risk of stress-induced illness affecting performance. I saw this as a cathartic statement acting like a valve releasing the extraneous stuff in his head. As a result, he could focus on golf, winning the Australian Open in November, clinching victory with a birdie on the final hole. This was to give him his first victory of 2013. A victory in his first event of the year in Abu Dhabi was prevented by a two-stroke penalty for inadvertently putting his foot over a white line when taking a shot after a relief shot.

McIlroy has regained the number one spot in golf by winning the Open in Hoylake, Liverpool and the WGC Bridgestone event in Ohio in July and August 2014, respectively. This confirms his ability to produce peak performances under pressure. He then displayed his mental maturity by winning his fourth Major, the PGA Championship, or Wanamaker Trophy, 7–10 August, at Valhalla. McIlroy said that he "gutted it" down the back nine. This is a good example of his ability to control his gut feelings and instinct, which is the key aim of SF-EMDR psychotherapy.

In 2015, he won the Omega Dubai Desert Classic with a record score of 22 under par. However, he missed his first cut in 23 events at the next event the Honda Classic. Later that year he became the third player after Jack Nicklaus and Tiger Woods to win ten PGA tour events and four majors by age twenty-five. He was considered somewhat reckless to have become injured playing five-a-side football, which forced him to miss the Open championship. At the end of the year, Rory was awarded the European Tour Golfer of the Year. In 2016, he dropped down the world rankings to fourth but has now climbed to second behind the Australian Jason Day. Rory continued in this position midway through 2017 and made progress in catching Jason Day who had to pull out of the Masters following a freak injury where he slipped and fell down stairs while wearing socks. Rory finished the tournament in a tie for seventh place. Rory is an example of a sportsman at the peak of his powers who, barring injury, can continue to win majors and other golf tournaments for many years to come. This can happen by applying body, heart, and mind in the ways outlined in this book. Rory has decided to take an extended break after a trophyless season in 2017, which was marred by injury. He has now dropped to a world ranking of ninth, which he last achieved in 2009. He has set his sights on the Masters in 2018 which remains the only Major he has yet to win.

Rory injured his ankle playing football with friends prior to the Open. He was forced to withdraw from the Tournament

Clients and patients can be encouraged to set their own specific goals and objectives. Examples include:

- Scoring the winning goal in the match;
- Winning the race;
- Achieving their personal best performance;
- Completing the 5,000km race for charity;
- Completing a university dissertation (with honours);
- Success in running a business;
- Graduation with first or second-class honours;
- Getting a promotion at work;
- Publishing a book, either in print or electronically;
- Giving birth and bonding with the newborn baby.
- Becoming an airline pilot;
- Enjoying family life and the company of their children;
- Winning an Olympic gold medal in their chosen sport;
- Winning the world championships in their chosen discipline;
- Making a successful patent application, which leads to an
- important invention; or
- Success in giving a presentation, either in school, university, or work.

Think about what your chosen ambitions are and write them down. As the saying goes, the world is your oyster, or, as I like to say, your brains (gut, heart, and head) can become the centre of your universe.

Roy Keane, the retired captain of Manchester United Football Club, recently stated that when Darryl Southgate tried to chop him in half, he overreacted and was sent off. It is in cases like this, when the so-called red mist descends, that volatile players such as Wayne Rooney and, in the past, Eric Cantona, would have benefited from being able to instantly control their anger to prevent it turning into aggressive behaviour.

All three players have learnt from their experiences. Roy Keane was appointed as assistant manager to Martin O'Neill for the Republic of Ireland in November 2013. Wayne Rooney is arguably playing the best football of his career under new manager David Moyes. Eric Cantona has forged a career as an actor following his retirement from football.

Zappers used for optimal functioning and peak performance

The name I have coined for the tactile units attached to the BOKA machine and used for SF-EMDR peak performance is the "ZAPPERS." This stands for the

- Zone (i.e. being in the zone for optimal performance)
- Activating

- Peak
- Performance
- Excellent
- Results and
- Success.

It also implies applying determination and extra vibrational energy to achieve the desired outcome. This can be achieved by using the principles outlined in the five stages of SF-EMDR peak performance. These "Zappers" are still in the development stage, and I plan to have them manufactured according to my design and specification.

Use of SF-EMDR optimal performance in the world of musical rehearsal: peak performance session for Denis

Background to the SF-EMDR peak performance session

Saxophonist Denis was preparing for his final year performance, playing jazz. Denis had rehearsed the pieces he would be playing many times. This session is designed to identify any aspects of the performance that might be associated with anxiety, which could impair performance. We used the techniques outlined in this chapter to enhance his performance. The outcome was that Denis sailed through the performance without difficulty and passed with flying colours.

Exploration of any relevant trauma history

Before this peak performance session, Denis reprocessed an incident at a bus stop where a drug addict threatened him with a knife and demanded he hand over his mobile phone. Denis processed this memory very well and managed to get his SUDS rating down from eight to zero.

During the complete duration of the reprocessing session, Denis received bilateral cerebellar stimulation using headphones placed over each mastoid process, just behind the ear. Then, during reprocessing of the knife incident, the zappers were moved around the body, tracking the areas of maximal dysregulation.

When adhering to the SF-EMDR peak performance protocol, Denis held the zappers next to his throat until the sensation of using his laryngeal muscles to optimise the blowing of the notes on the saxophone was achieved. This is how the session went.

ART: Just imagine that you are playing or starting and what you are telling me is that you have done the chord changes and chord practices so much that you do not want to have to think about those.

DENIS: Yeah.

ART: Imagine that the part of your body that is reacting to . . . and it might be that you . . . so just hold your hands in whichever way they are going to be comfortable. There might even be a way of holding your hands here. [Here, Denis changed his posture.] You are going to be standing?

DENIS: I will be standing but . . . yeah . . .

ART: So, just imagine that.

DENIS: Yeah, I just want some . . . Because if I feel loose playing, I would feel like I'm like this. Just relaxed.

ART: So, if you just . . . you are feeling like that. Do you get a cue from the band? Do they say: one, two, three, four?

DENIS: I will be directing it all, yeah.

ART: Are you using . . . in front of you?

DENIS: No, not at all. It's memorised.

ART: Memorised. And do they have music?

DENIS: Depends if they've done their job. They can have music, so they don't have to memorise it, but I'd rather if they did because it looks better.

ART: And concerning the look of the group, do you need to dress in a certain way?

DENIS: Not at jazz . . . well . . . I think we might need to have to have suits on or something, but I'll check that. My drummer, I've never seen him in anything like that in my life.

ART: So, just let the music that you will be playing be heard in your head; notice how you are producing the sounds, just test out in your body and in your mind, so look for anything between now and then that needs to be fine-tuned.

DENIS: Yeah, intonation probably.

ART: So, think about the intonation and just hear it or sense it or feel it, just get into a position that is comfortable and the body position necessary to work on the intonation.

DENIS: That is all here. It is in my face.

ART: So just put it on your face.

DENIS: That will be on my cheeks.

ART: Yeah, on your cheeks. Yeah. So, the saxophone is on your cheeks. And what I want you to do now is just get relaxed while you are doing this and this is going to be all memory that your cheeks are going to remember and put the best intonation into practice. So, I want you to feel the intonation and the rhythm, and I want you to know if you can balance this intuitively with both parts of your brain. This is where you want to look at what you are doing here. It is the two sides of the experience you will have. I think music is very interesting because it is sort of taps into the functions of both right and left parts of the brain. So, as you think about that, let whatever intonation come to mind. Bring all elements of that music together. A part of it will be non-verbal. A part of it will be a sort of intuition. So, this is all on the right side [of the brain] still.

As I am saying these words, I want you to become aware of what your right hand is feeling. Do you notice how the emotions of the music and the sensations of your facial expressions are changing? Be aware both of your own and other people's reactions and the images that go with that. Images that maybe will come up as you play your music . . .

We know all about your survival responses [related to the knife incident] but, we doubt that they are involved here. What we are particularly linking to are your emotions and your sensory motor reactions and how you visualise the performance.

The left side [of the brain] is very much more analytical, but it takes full part in what the right side produces. It accesses information from the right cerebral hemisphere and breaks those images into linear pieces for analysis. It looks for the perceptions and the rationale behind things. So, I imagine, for you, it is always going to be one step ahead of what the right brain is producing, the left brain is always going to be thinking about the next note or musical phrase; there is that constant interaction.

And you know that the left brain is something that brings the divergent holistic right brain back down to the reality of the left-brain narrative. But, for the normal language functions of the left brain, you can substitute music as well. So, a link exists between the sensory information that you are feeling and that the rhythm is bringing to your experience with the language, which is the music that is linked to intonation.

I want you again to get the idea as you are seeing your brain in front of you and know the impact you will have by drawing on all the years of experience just for this forty minutes of jazz performance. All that intuitive information is brought to bear without effort because it is the lack of effort that the unconscious learning can be effectively utilised. This is ninety-five per cent of the brain's capacity for unconscious processing, while only five per cent relates to conscious learning.

DENIS: Yeah.

ART: Be aware of the continuous bilateral cerebellar stimulation as it helps the information to be shared between cerebral hemispheres.

DENIS: Yeah, I think my subconscious would . . . Because I don't see it. I wouldn't see it as left and right. But I'm kind of getting it now because when I'm improvising, I'll be thinking, when I'm thinking of the changes or when I'm not listening. When I am thinking rather than listening and then you'll be thinking, thinking, thinking and then you'll realise yourself: I'm not listening.

ART: Just what you did right then was very interesting. When you touched your left ear with your left hand – just do this again. [This is an example of a somatic experiment.] What does it tell you when you do that? As you are thinking, is it coming together? As that is the left side when you are saying that you are linking to that side of your brain in a way.

DENIS: Yeah, that is probably subconscious. Yeah.

ART: Yeah, exactly! So, it's just, again, part of it. So that's useful information, and the two sides of the brain are related. They are separated by a physical structure also. I mean it is not the way I see it, it's just that as the heart feels emotions, this can stop language being generated by the left side of the brain.

[When the window of affect tolerance and emotional regulation are exceeded.]

DENIS: Yeah, because I will start thinking: "right, I need to listen," then I will start listening, and then I will be subconscious. It might sound the same to someone else but in some way, it is different for me.

ART: What I want you to tell me, if you can, is what that felt like when you are sort of holding the intuition [in mind] and just noticing it, just following the intonation. Then you will fine-tune that intonation and we want it to be tuned to the right level. You want it to be there for just that forty minutes, so it is always a work in progress.

DENIS: Yeah.

ART: But as of now, where is it going to and where does it need to go?

DENIS: I just need to be able to perform without thinking. I just need my sax to start here and here. [Denis demonstrates his ideal position for the saxophone.]

ART: Hold it there, just hold one buzzer [zapper] there and link it to where the next one needs to go on the other hand.

DENIS: Yeah. It needs to be here. [Denis holds the zappers in the ideal position in each hand.]

ART: So, what I want you to do is imagine that the sax is now linking your body. Your throat is linking with the blower and the stomach, which is the sort of gut reaction or gut feeling, and just get a sense of how you can imagine the connections, the vocal connections, the music connections, the musical connections, the instrument connections, link those parts of your body. Some people visualise it like a waterfall or river connecting all the synaptic nerve connections.

Just see what makes sense with you and that it helps to make those elements of the music come together as you desire it for your sax performance.

DENIS: I like to think about it like a didgeridoo because when you blow, it is not just a blowing sound. You must make a noise in your throat. You must visualise the music in your throat. So, if you want to hit a high E, you must [Denis makes high-pitched sound with his throat], as your throat goes like that when you sing a high E, so your throat must be closed, or you will not be singing it. But, if you are doing a low one, it's like I need to widen my windpipe.

ART: So, if you just imagine that you are widening your windpipe and allow the air, the muscles, and the cricoid cartilage in the throat to produce the right sounds. It's very much like what is coming to mind as you imagine playing your instruments.

So, imagine that your windpipe is equally under that level of control and that you can create that didgeridoo sound.

DENIS: Yeah.

ART: How does that feel? [Locations reported by Denis have zappers applied bilaterally and are moved by the reported changes in sensation.]

DENIS: It makes me want to pick up my sax, to be fair.

ART: I've just noticed that it gives you the pleasure of playing the sax as I can see a smile on your face. Notice where that pleasure is and the feeling, as I want you to get in touch with that feeling.

So just follow that through and see that the music is being formed the way you want it to be.

DENIS: I can see my drummer smashing away. [Denis laughs.]

ART: And is the drummer in front or behind?

DENIS: No, he will be behind me, but he is the best drummer I have played with.

ART: So, just hold that in mind. So, it's a bit like there is a team behind you.

DENIS: Yeah, it was just like I'm bouncing off him because I do when I'm playing. I feed off him like mad.

ART: So, feed off him. So, imagine you are feeding off him, and his music is coming into your ears, as he is behind you, so it's coming directly to your ears.

DENIS: Yeah

ART: And notice the continuing bilateral cerebellar stimulation as a background rhythm as I turn up the frequency to maximum so that you can integrate this experience.

DENIS: Because I'm at the front, it's like, I'm only playing the sax but it's like, now, it's like I'm bass guitar, drums, piano it's all coming into the same direction, and I'll probably be loudest of all.

ART: Just stay in that moment. Bring the other members of the band in as much as they are in. You are the leader of the orchestra and chief executor here. The one that brings all the elements together and puts them into play, so you can imagine the orchestra components bringing players through jazz. Feel yourself getting into the rhythm of the stage performance. That said, imagine that you are halfway through the performance.

And know that you can do this and it's just the matter of how you can conserve your reserves of energy for the rest of the performance.

If you need to, see the audience supporting you. This is a good opportunity to look out for anything that could potentially crop up, for example, an alarm, a mobile phone ringing, or even a door slamming. You will stay in the zone, and nothing will have an adverse impact on your playing.

Just notice you are ready for any eventuality and then just follow it through. Take a couple of minutes with zappers in hand to play through the remaining numbers in your set.

DENIS: Yeah, I was just thinking of where there is one bit where it's just me and drum for ages going nuts and because he does so many mad rhythms like I can't get my head around a lot of them. So, if, I lose my four rhythms what will I do? Because he won't be on the four, he will be somewhere else, and no one else will know where he is. Then he'll come back. He'll always throw you off and throw you off and throw you off and you'll be like where am I, where am I, where am I? And just as you think you don't know where you are, he'll just come crashing in with a four, and it'll be the heaviest groove because he'll build the tension like it'll stretch the time and you'll be like Oh, what's going on, what's going on? And just as you say it, he'll be helping you to build the tension. But I was just thinking, if I manage to skip a beat on that, he'll always come back in.

ART: So, is there a word you can have with him beforehand, or a signal you can set up with him to anticipate when he is going to come in with this heaviest groove?

DENIS: He is such an intuitive drummer he doesn't need any signal. I tried talking to him.

ART: Because I thought the minute you do that you put your hand here so what I can suggest is repeating this movement. [Movement of index finger is referred to as somatic referencing point for Denis.] And this would get your thinking and intuition tuned in, so between the two you would be in complete harmony with the drummer.

DENIS: Yeah, I'll just play if he does throw you. You know that. You might be thrown, even if he throws you for four-eight bars he will always catch you back, and it won't just be a little subtle "I'm back here," it'll be the base player as well, and they will be on top of it.

ART: Good, good – so play it through and just notice how you want it to end. You are working up to the finale, and he's just coming up to your last piece. You are going through it in your mind, just fast-forward to the end and notice what feelings, sensations, or thoughts come up.

DENIS: Yeah, it will just be pure relief because the last two tunes are bloody tricky so it will be a matter of getting myself in the right place for that last tune or the last two tunes.

ART: So, just get yourself into the right place for those last two tunes and this is where you bring your resources to your aid, so you might think of any other good music teachers that you can imagine or that have helped you in the past. This is where you can imagine any support being there with you on the day. They don't have to be there, in reality, they can be there virtually, for example, by video link. Imagine how they can help you over the hurdle of those last two tricky tunes. Notice whatever image comes up. I often get people to imagine their favourite colour of light beaming down on the parts of their body necessary to get the best out of the instrument. This is the light stream exercise, and I can talk you through that later.

DENIS: Probably my piano teacher or my sax teacher from back home.

ART: Right. OK. So just imagine that they are there with you. Would you like them in the audience or on stage?

DENIS: Yeah, it would be nice to have them in the audience.

ART: OK. So just imagine that they are in the audience, OK? And that they are rooting for you. Remember how they nurtured your talent, brought you along and now, thanks to your talent, hard work, and determination, you are performing your jazz routine as they listen in the audience. We are concentrating on the last two tricky tunes that will bring your set to its grand finale.

DENIS: Yeah, no. The end because the last tune it's all it's just it's really off your head it's very "what's going on!" And the last bar is only four straight crotchets; it's just: baa, baa, baa, baa and that's the end. So, it will be nice, because it's just me and the drummer, me and the drummer build up for ages and then a whole band will come in with the beat, doh, doh, doh, doh, doh, doh, it's like it's all polyrhythms. So, it'll be nice just to get that last bar. Just have a big, simple baa daa daa daa done! That will just be the finale.

ART: Just notice the relief, just get yourself relaxed and feel the nervous energy dissipate as you realise the performance is over. Do a body scan from head to toe and notice any sensations.

DENIS: Just like an exhale of relief, which I can feel in my chest. [There is continued reprocessing of chest sensations with zappers.]

ART: So, what did you think of that?

DENIS: Yeah, it's good! It's nice because I have visualised this all the time, but I would never have gone into it in such detail. I would just be, like, I would lie in bed, and I think about it, get nervous and then try to relax.

ART: So, what was different about the way we simulated going through the actual performance?

DENIS: You know like, you wouldn't notice, but I was singing through the tunes all in my head the whole time. But I haven't even noticed – I know, I think it's just this beep.

ART: And does the beep help focus?

DENIS: Because when I had a steady beep, without even thinking of it, I'd be tapping in my head, or I'll be . . .

ART: I could see you tapping out the rhythm with your right and left feet at different times.

DENIS: Yeah, and I realise I can, as you're saying, how real that I was feeling as if I was visualising myself playing the solo during that whole time and playing tunes ahead of time. Yeah, that was useful! [Shy giggle.]

ART: So, do you think this could work with your other friends?

DENIS: Yeah, I'd love to see it with the band. I'd like to see if you got a similar response to the whole band playing together.

ART: I'd love to try this approach with a band!

DENIS: So, you could see what everyone else is worried about because everyone else is going to have different anxieties over different parts.

ART: Exactly, yeah. You could bring everyone's performance into harmony.

DENIS: The bit I find hard someone else might find easy.

ART: You could have the band set up. My machine would be set up perfectly for the band. It's essentially plugging everyone in at the same time, and then you could just let everyone do it in their head and go through it and then see what comes up for each band member.

DENIS: Yeah, the thing that I would like to find out is, could you do brain pictures?

ART: Yeah, yes.

DENIS: Can you see what parts of the brain are conscious and subconscious?

ART: Yes, you can certainly see that because this is all conscious here and this entire bit is conscious, OK? [I demonstrate conscious and unconscious processing with my model of the brain.]

DENIS: But, can you analyse it as it is happening?

ART: Oh, yes you can. I mean, it's hard because the scans normally have you lying down like that, but as we get better at it, there will be better ways to do it and tune into the brain's reprocessing.

DENIS: Because I would love to see it because the amount you internalise during the process we have been through is dramatic.

ART: Yes, it is mostly internalised.

DENIS: Because there is stuff that last year I would have had to think about when I'm playing, whereas now I just say that was the pattern I practised for six months.

ART: But, I'm glad now that we've managed to record this because I think I'd like to get this transcribed and I think it would work fantastically well with musicians. There is so much of it that is in your head, then it gets unconsciously internalised, and then when you start to think about it, it can become blocked from the process.

DENIS: Yeah, that is the thing when I was saying like you must read this to remind yourself to do stopping and listening. So, I am thinking: "Listen, listen, listen, listen!" Even if you forget the chord changes, you'd be better off not knowing when the chord changes and using your ear instead. Then knowing them and only thinking about it. Like I reckon, if I just had a groove going, and you just said "Jam over that groove," it's the one key you've got you can do what you want in it. Whether it's an intense chord change every two beats and you're like, aaaggrrrh, you're trying to get around them, up and in and out of them and I'm trying to get them smooth in and out and that second last tune it's literally, just chord changes every two beats [copying chord changing by clicking of fingers] that fast! I was like, deh, deh, deh, deh.

So, every chord, I must relate it to a mode. Every two beats [at] that speed I've got to think of a mode and a scale. The second one is going to be different from the first – if I hold a note from that over that one, a lot of the time it will sound horrible. But then, when you sit back and listen, you find all the notes that link together and you can make it sound as if it isn't just loads of unconnected notes.

ART: This language is new to me. I had no idea about music language or notation. However, you have now activated your prefrontal cortex and Broca's area in the left cerebral hemisphere. You have the reflective capacity for reprocessed thoughts related to your forthcoming performance in line with SF-EMDR peak performance.

ART: When you are doing the recital what is your happening in your mind?

DENIS: Hmmm, I see the music. What I mean is, with my eyes open, like, my eyes are open, but the music changes are going by my eyes. I can be looking because I can be playing and stare into someone's eyes and it would not even register with me.

ART: Are you hearing the notes or seeing them?

DENIS: Hearing them, and then visualising the musical chart. So, like, if I'm doing that tune, I'll be listening, and I'll be seeing the chords go by, or I'll be seeing that on a piano. Going around the changes in all their aspects. I know that is the thing that is different about sax. On piano, it's all visual. You can sing me a line, and I could just play it on the piano. Whereas if you sang me a line on sax, it would take me a minute to figure it out. Because none of it is visual on the sax, it's all ears, and you're like doh, dah, dah, whereas on the piano it's easy to see it.

ART: Taking it back to what we did, what do you think came out of the earlier bit that we need to reprocess? I think this would help as well by not having it interfere with your forthcoming recital.

DENIS: Yes, because I have not even talked about this with myself either. [Denis had never previously processed the knife attack.]

ART: What did you learn at the start of the session?

DENIS: It was interesting how it involved my throat for that memory [of the knife attack] as well as when I was imagining playing the sax.

ART: So now you can realise that that has naturally
healed. [The traumatic memory of the attack by the drug addict has been dealt with.]

DENIS: Yes, because if I get a lump in my throat as well, I won't just be able to talk, I won't be able to play the sax either, so I suddenly just can't afford to have this happen.

[This shows that, for Denis, reprocessing his memory of the previous knife attack helped him to perfect his blowing techniques essential to get a good sound from the saxophone.]

DENIS: I remember when I used to play the piano, never in my life had I had sweat in between my fingers, but every time before I performed, I would notice, "Why am I sweating there?" It's the weirdest place to sweat, nowhere else is sweating, and I'd be here rubbing it on a napkin. Some people had bottles or buckets of ice in which they dipped their hands before they went in. Why does it happen and how does my brain know to start panicking here? You know what I mean?

ART: That is very like the meridian response we were talking about earlier. That part of your finger is probably where the meridians are. They are the ones that relate to these fingers. They are the parts that get over-stimulated when you play the sax.

DENIS: Because nowhere else was sweating, so you just couldn't ignore it as you may miss some notes.

ART: So how is your whole body feeling now?

DENIS: I feel a little bit more relaxed now.

ART: A lot of people tell me that they feel sleepier.

DENIS: I want to have a rehearsal now, that's kind of what I feel like. Just want to get back and get them [the band] in a room and start. You know what I mean? Because I want to put all that I have learnt during this session ...

ART: ... into practice.

DENIS: Yes. Because I've been thinking about this so much while we are doing this; the more you think about it, the more you want to play.

ART: But I think this [SF-EMDR peak performance] has never been done before, so I think it will help and have a positive effect. Now that you have practised it in your head, it is as good as a performance.

The pursuit of happiness and fulfilling your life mission

Happiness is a mental or emotional state of well-being characterised by pleasant emotions ranging from contentment to intense joy. I will introduce readers to some recently developed models of happiness, which can be integrated with SF-EMDR psychotherapy. Practices such as yoga, Kirtan chanting, and Buddhist meditation can control levels of neurotransmitters resulting in pleasurable feelings. This is part of the lifestyle medicine change proposed by Dr Ranjan Chatterjee. His one-day course on 18 January 2018, was designed with GPs in mind.

Chronic stress is a by-product of modern society. It causes immune-system dysfunction and central-nervous-system inflammation. The levels of dopamine serotonin are reduced causing depression and anxiety. ACTH secretion is altered, affecting behaviour and the functioning of the peripheral nervous system.

Hormone and herbal supplements include canscors decussate, valeriana jatamansi, withania somnifera, bacopa mannieri, and panax ginseng (Bagchi et al., 2015; Bagchi & Hopper, 2011). Neuropsychiatric disorders are related to biopsychosocial, spiritual, and quantum-field-effect dysfunction. The body-mind is affected at the level of the whole person. Phytocompounds from ayurvedic herbs have been shown to interact with SNCE, APOE, and AMPA receptors. The pursuit of happiness can be considered to have been achieved by the people who achieve peak performance using the methods described in this chapter.

Happiness is a state of mind where mourning is absent according to Lester Levinson. He founded the release technique. In 1973 this was formalised into the Sedona Method. This is about choosing to let go. There are five steps:

Step 1: Focus on an issue that you would like to feel better about and allow yourself to feel whatever you are feeling now.
Step 2: Ask yourself, Could I

- Let this feeling go?
- Allow this feeling to be here?
- Welcome this feeling?

Step 3: No matter which question you started with, ask yourself this simple question: Would I? In other words: Am I willing to let go?

Step 4: Ask yourself this simpler question: When? This is an invitation to let it go NOW. This may happen easily and letting go can be a decision you can make any time you choose.

Step 5: Repeat steps 1 to 4 until you feel free of that feeling.

According to Maslow, happiness is associated with achieving something new. This includes material, spiritual, physical, or corporeal, e.g. the PERMA model:

Introducing a new theory of well-being

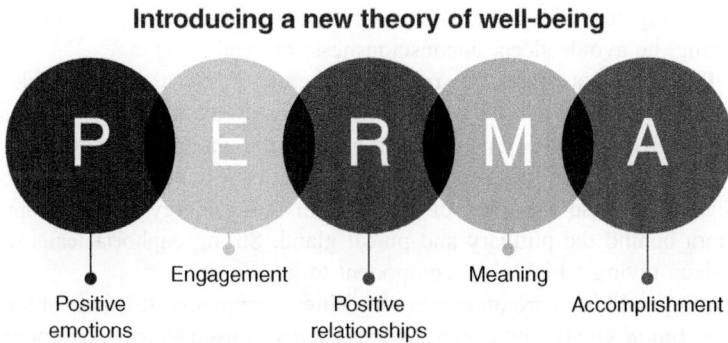

Engagement   Meaning

Positive emotions   Positive relationships   Accomplishment

Figure 12.4 Introducing the PERMA theory of well-being. This combines displaying positive emotions, engagement with positive relationships, meaning to life, and a sense of accomplishment.

Source: reproduced with permission from Ernest Rossi.

Role of yoga and meditation in achieving happiness

Yoga has been described as a pathway to God. Practitioners seek self-knowledge, enlightenment, freedom from desire, compulsion, fear, and unhappiness. Paramahamsa Yogananda brought his thinking and yogic practice to the United States. His self-realisation fellowship was founded in 1920 to preserve the purity and integrity of his teachings for future generations. *Autobiography of a Yogi* was first published in 1948 and my copy is in its thirteenth edition. He passed on in 1952 and has millions of devoted followers today worldwide.

Kriya Yoga can speed up human evolution.

The secret of cosmic consciousness is intimately linked with breath mastery. The Kriya Yogi mentally directs his life energy to revolve upward and downward around the six spinal centres or plexuses (medullary, cervical, lumbar, sacral and coccygeal), which correspond to the twelve astral signs of the zodiac.

(Paramahamsa Yogananda, 1955)

Cosmic man is believed to have twelve constellations revolving around the sun of the spiritual eye (cf. eye of Horus). Ancient belief stated that man's earthly and heavenly environment or inner and outer universe were built on twelve-year cycles like the twelve years named after animals in the Chinese calendar. It was stated that it would take a man one million years of evolution to achieve brain perfection and cosmic consciousness.

Kriyas can speed up this process by practising yoga many hours per day. It may take forty-eight years to achieve mastery. This ancient yogic technique converts the breath into the stuff of the mind. The breath becomes thought of as a mental concept, an act of mind, and a dream breath. The Kriya Yogi keeps his physical body fed with light. Breathing becomes unnecessary. While actively meditating, he avoids sleep, unconsciousness, or death.

As Paramahamsa states, cosmic life energy is on a par with the four fundamental forces – electromagnetism, gravity, weak interaction, and strong interaction. The chakras or wheels represent the ganglia or nerve plexuses mentioned above and correspond to different endocrine glands, see below. Happiness can raise the level of alertness in these energy centres, especially Sahasrara behind the pituitary and pineal gland. Strong euphoria leads to deep REM sleep giving a biological component to happiness.

Chanting and kirtan are other ways to achieve happiness. It is part of the yoga of sound (*naad* yoga) where sound-wave energy is used to raise consciousness. Chanting has been found in the West to make people feel better and better connected to themselves and the world in general.

Satsang involves singing, storytelling, and reading from holy books to enliven the connection with life in all its beauty. San-Kirtan was developed in 1486 by Sri Chaitanya Mahaprabhu who taught the divine consciousness of Godhead, which is mentioned by Ivan Tyrrell in his book about the human givens approach.

Buddhism embraced kirtan, involving chanting and performing plays about the Buddha's life. These practices can alleviate symptoms of psychosomatic illness like fibromyalgia, anxiety, depression, high blood pressure, and disorders associated with negative emotional states such as anger, hatred, selfishness, greed. The process involves observing the self-identifying cause going inward and generating self-love and compassion.

Biological components of happiness

Serotonin, dopamine, glutamate, and noradrenaline are all involved in happiness. Endorphins and enkephalins are neurohormones, which block the transmission of pain signals thereby contributing to happiness.

The Ayurvedic system of medicine and happiness

Gautama Buddha was born a prince before he rejected comforts and pleasures. At the age of twenty-nine he vowed to find the cause of and remedy for the burden of the sorrows and sufferings of humanity. Under the Bodhi tree in Bihar India, he became Buddha and found the eternal peace and bliss of enlightenment. Ayurveda means the science of life. It is used both to treat disease and to promote health and happiness. Western medicine has a lot to learn from its science and practice. Buddha taught the eightfold path:

1. Right understanding;
2. Right thought;
3. Right speech;
4. Right action;
5. Right livelihood;
6. Right effort;
7. Right mindfulness; and
8. Right concentration.

It is apparent how beneficial these behaviours would be in Western civilisation. Paritta chants are for protection from bad influences, which can be counteracted by wholesome states of mind. It is believed that the vibratory sounds produced by the recital of Paritta suttas in their Pali verses sooth nerves, induce peace and calm of mind, and bring harmony to the body-mind. Adherence to the noble eightfold path while listening can optimise the benefit on all levels – biopsychosocial, spiritual, and material.

The path to happiness according to Buddhism

This begins with understanding the root cause of human suffering (Dukkha). This can manifest as anxiety, distress, frustration, unease, and general dissatisfaction or malaise. This includes many of the complaints patients attend their GPs with within the NHS. Mental self-control and peace of mind is achieved by freedom from the needs and wants of life to enter a state of well-being and bliss. Lust, hate, and disharmony are sources of Dukkha. Health is our greatest possession and contentment the highest pleasure.

Summary

This chapter has discussed the role of SF-EMDR peak performance in helping clients to become expert in their chosen discipline. The key is to simulate being in the zone and can be summarised as lack of time awareness, autotelicity, the "sweet spot," and automaticity. Factors relevant in developing optimal or peak performance are stressors, challenge, and metacognition. There is a flow chart illustrating the concept of being in the zone. The role of normal and aberrant sleep architecture is explained. This can be activated via the imagery of mentally reperforming the chosen activity, for example, in sports such as golf, football, or rugby, and for those in business, on stage, or those in performing arts, where anxiety can impair performance.

Examples from the world of Champions League football are used to explain how SF-EMDR peak performance could improve results. The concept of being in the zone is illustrated.

I have described how SF-EMDR psychotherapy is applied in achieving peak performance alongside using feedback, so that future predicted states are more accurate. The task of achieving peak performance is broken down into five parts, somewhat analogous to the five stages of SF-EMDR psychotherapy.

Part one focuses on achieving the transition from psychotherapy to peak performance. There is recognition of the 10,000 hours of practice it takes to become world champion in your chosen field.

Part two focuses on the enjoyment needed in your chosen pursuit so that your complete absorption means losing track of time.

Part three deals with the motivational aspects of peak performance, so that the chosen activity is rewarding for its own sake.

Part four implies that the person has reached the state of unconscious learning and can rely on the firing of unconscious neurons and muscle fibres. Thus, learning has progressed from cognitive to associative to, finally, automatic.

The final part of SF-EMDR peak performance is when the performance hits the chosen target, and the cycle can begin again based on the next set of objectives. The problem of "yips" is discussed, with potential solutions, and the reader is encouraged to write down their own objectives. My model of using zappers is explained.

The chapter contains a transcript of a peak performance session with a jazz saxophonist preparing for a major performance.

The chapter concludes with an overview of happiness, which follows on from peak performance. Happiness is a state of well-being, of positive emotions, which are often disturbed by the chronic stress of everyday life. The role of neurotransmitters like serotonin and dopamine and hormones like endorphins are explained. Experimental herbal plants from Ayurvedic medicine were discussed concerning the alleviation of disease. Disease is a disturbance of mind, body, spirit, and consciousness both inner and cosmic. Various strategies to promote harmony and happiness are discussed, including yoga meditation, kirtan, along with a life free from attachments. The practice of these techniques combined with SF-EMDR psychotherapy and Ayurvedic medicine can both heal illness and disease and lead the person away from the mask of Dukkha to enjoyment of a state of happiness.

Chapter 13

Comprehensive mental health assessment questionnaire for children, adolescents, and adults

Assessment of brain functions related to functional attributes of Brodmann functional brain areas

Template for comprehensive assessment of the patient before SF-EMDR for psychotherapy or peak performance and use of the Herrmann brain dominance instrument

I have developed an assessment template, which is partly based on the attachment interview of the child by Dr Charles Zeanah and the Health of the Nation Outcome Scales for children, adolescents, and adults. In addition, I have added a chronology of stressful life experiences and traumas. This starts at conception and moves through pregnancy and all stages of the patient's life. It is critically important to identify an informant who can relate significant trauma up to age five. I have termed this schedule HoNOSCA-revised. In this revised edition, I have included aspects of the Human Givens psychotherapy approach including the RIGAAR method. Thus, preverbal traumas can be brought into conscious awareness during SF-EMDR psychotherapy (Chapter 13). The key point is to identify patients who were born premature, that is, at less than thirty-two weeks' gestation. A paper in *Archives of General Psychiatry* in 2012 describes how they have a much higher incidence of severe mental health problems in adulthood in comparison to those born at term. The lead author, Nosarti (2012), said that the increased risk of severe psychiatric disorder shown in the results was likely to be the result of "subtle alterations of brain development." This study indicates that of the one in thirteen children born prematurely in the UK, between one and six will go on to develop severe psychiatric disorders.

Nosarti recommends that all preterm children should be monitored at the age of five. To fulfil that role, clinicians can use this developmental questionnaire. Early identification of this cohort may lead to prevention of this level of comorbidity.

Template for taking history as a Human Givens and SF-EMDR psychotherapist

As in Maslow's hierarchy, physical needs are paramount. Our environment provides air for breathing, water to drink, adequate nutrition, and enough sleep. We also need to stimulate our senses and get sufficient exercise to strengthen the musculoskeletal system. A shelter is essential for protection and, in keeping with sexual desires and instinct, we are genetically programmed to reproduce and nurture our children until they have matured. This can be twenty-five in females and thirty in males. These are the "given" human physical needs. Human "given" emotional needs include:

- Secure attachment. This develops from six months to approximately age five. If the primary caregiver is the cause of emotional abuse and neglect, an insecure attachment results, which can be anxious, avoidant, ambivalent, or disorganised. The latter affects ten per cent of the population and is most likely to lead to adult psychopathology. At birth, babies have innate communication skills that they use to match the patterns of their parent's behaviour. An inconsistent caregiver who fails to meet basic infant needs increases the risk of insecure attachment.In the first eighteen months, the need for autonomy is paramount. If this fails to develop then shame and self-doubt take hold. Over time, with secure attachment, children gain an increasing amount of control and self-sufficiency over their lives.Children crave attention and like to give attention. In the parent–child relationship, positive attention is the fuel for future emotional development and the acquisition of social interaction skills. The need for attention is an essential human given. This has been dubbed the "Hawthorne effect." This found that paying attention to workers' needs improved their productivity. Without attention, children may die or suffer brain damage, as demonstrated by experiments ordered by German Emperor Frederick II and in the Romanian orphans' longitudinal study. Idries Shah (Griffin T and Tyrell I 2015 p115) studied Sufism and formulated an Eastern theory of attention. He proposed that attention is a constant in human interactions. The following principles apply:
  - Too much or too little attention can be detrimental;
  - Attention can be hostile or friendly;
  - The giving of attention by an organisation can be linked to undue influence;
  - Opinions may change depending on the source of attention;
  - If you are deprived of attention then anyone offering attention can quickly overstimulate;
  - Reflecting and learning develops the capacity to cope in an attention-deprived environment;
  - The need for attention starts in infancy and lasts into adulthood;
  - Many experiences in life are accounted for by attention theory which is a study of the giving, receiving and exchanging of attention;
  - The desire for attention is the fundamental imperative in human beings. Being aware of these principles can prevent you from undue influence;

- Forced attention or indoctrination is associated with emotional arousal. This can lead to obsessional behaviour and membership of cults;
- The need for attention allows unconscious factors to determine behaviours such as membership of political parties and religious groups; and
- Focused attention allows information to be absorbed unconsciously and once transferred to the cerebral cortex in stage four of the creative cycle, its full meaning and ramifications can be considered.

Patients who focus attention on their symptoms often maintain them. Withdrawing attention from dysfunctional beliefs can help to lessen their influence.

Thus, awareness of the extraction, extension, attraction, receiving, and interchange of attention is a fundamental prerequisite for brief, effective psychotherapy.

Professor Wall and Melzack (1999), pain specialists, drew attention to the relationship between fear, anxiety and pain:

> Fear generates anxiety and anxiety focuses the attention. The more the attention is locked, the worse the pain. There is, therefore, a marked correlation between pain and anxiety. The anxiety here is not the free-floating variety with a feeling of general disquiet that something is wrong but cannot be identified. The anxiety of pain is generated by the unknown and grows worse as the pain persists, and short-term expectations of relief fail to be fulfilled.

It is important in management to clarify the meaning of the pain to lessen its intensity.

- The need for intimacy. Connection to friends and the ability to have loving, intimate relationships. Being part of a wider community has evolved as a given need from our organisation into small groups of hunter-gatherers and farmers for survival purposes. Feeling loved has a beneficial effect on health especially the heart. Julian Gresser has developed the laughing heart initiative on www.alliancesfordiscovery.org. The ten steps are divided into three sections.

1. Experiencing involves:

   - Quieting the heart;
   - Finding your power;
   - Discovering beauty; and
   - Connecting to nature.

2. Exploring involves:

   - Harvesting creative genius in music;
   - Connecting laughing heart with everything; and
   - Enhancing your immunity through love.

3.   Applying involves:

- Paying it forward;
- Creating your own luck; and
- Celebrating and laughing.

- The need for privacy. Privacy is an emotional need that fosters reflection and learning from experience. Overcrowding and inadequate housing adversely affect health and well-being. Open-plan offices are more stressful to work in than workplaces with private offices. Overcrowding is also a risk factor for riots in prison and aggression in psychiatric inpatients. Often seeking solace in a solitary activity is one way of meeting our privacy needs. The need for self-reflection and man's search for meaning have evolved with the increase in our frontal lobe size of forty per cent in only 50-100,000 years out of over 2 million years of evolution of the human species.
- The need to become competent and achieve. Developing a sense of achievement and competence builds self-esteem and self-confidence. In nature, cooperation leads to benefits for all parties concerned. We are at our most successful when mind and body and soul are integrated towards the same goal. Dopamine is released when new learning has been accomplished, activating the pleasure and reward centres centrally. Emotional well-being seems to correlate with the ARC (autonomy, relatedness, and competence). Job satisfaction as an NHS consultant is a protective factor against stress, battle fatigue, and burnout. The latter was highest where consultants lacked training in management and communication skills. Experiencing success in desired goals breeds confidence and a sense of belief and meaning in the proposed task.
- The need for meaning. It is the search for a higher meaning that will drive the patient forward. It is current to encourage the patient to feel stretched in work or at home to build a life full of purpose and meaning. Individual choices rather than genetic predisposition determine happiness. Boredom and life without meaning increase the risk of mental and physical health disorders.Each therapeutic session allows for meaning and learning to be consolidated. This is phase four of the creative cycle of Prof Ernest Rossi referred to earlier. When we connect to ideas bigger than ourselves we see the bigger picture of life, which fills us with purpose and direction.

These innate needs are a table rasa at birth and essentially unmet. Through the RIGAAR approach, we can assess the endowment of nature for any given patient. These are the ability to use long-term knowledge to learn, empathise, and connect with others. By activating the right hemisphere emotion by SF-EMDR bilateral stimulation, we unlock the ability to problem-solve imaginatively. We initiate an observing self by creating new neural networks in the frontal lobes at the level of pituitary and pineal gland, activate our dreaming brain during the 90-120 min basic rest–activity cycle so that PGO waves trigger ongoing REM processing of emotionally charged events for the next forty-eight to seventy-two hours. This is facilitated by continuous bilateral stimulation at the top of the skull and the peripheral nervous system.

Factors perpetuating unmet needs:

- Toxic environment. This includes an abusive or neglectful home, a bullying school, or a stressful workplace. Context-blind or straight-line thinking by governments and large organisations increases the stress on the population. It is only with the development of more flexible organisations that we are better equipped to improve patients' physical and emotional health. The NHS is set up to diagnose and treat acute medical disorders. However, chronic conditions such as diabetes, obesity, and hypertension require a lifestyle change and adequate form of nutritional input. This new form of functional medicine is being introduced to the UK by Dr Ranjan Chatterjee (TED talk, 2105). Lack of social stability and austerity have added to the financial and social pressures on today's society. There is a need to move away from a symptom-reduction approach. My belief is that body and mind are intimately connected, and all clinicians must seek to get to the root cause of the problem in their assessment and management. This template for comprehensive health assessment is a step towards achieving this goal.
- Transgenerational transmission of disorders. This can vary from autism to ADHD to traumatic stress and insults during pregnancy. We are also conditioned by the culture we live in to treat symptoms as harmful and to seek a pill for every ill. The medicine of the twenty-first century will encourage a dialogue between body and mind, collaborating to solve the presenting problems. A good example of this is a chronic and enduring pain. Initially, post injury, the main factors contributing to pain are physical ones such as muscle damage and nerve injury. The body has self-repair mechanisms which kick in over the twelve months post injury. However, many patients report the same or increased levels of pain. Here the main factors are unresolved emotional ones. There is compelling evidence that physical and emotional pain sensations are transmitted via spinothalamic tracts to the limbic system. From here the cingulate gyrus and insular cortex process the emotional components of pain. Unresolved trauma may block this reprocessing. The limbic system also has projections to the hypothalamus, which initiates physical responses to pain, i.e. at an organ level in the body. The frontal cortex is involved in interpreting the meaning and attribution of the pain components. The oldest or spinothalamic arch tract receives painful stimuli from the dorsal root ganglion. These nerve fibres travel up and

down the spinal cord mediating visceral, emotional, and autonomic pain responses. The critical brain components involved are limbic system nuclei, the periaqueductal grey, and the hypothalamus. Electrical stimulation of the PAG releases endorphins. While stimulation of the raphe nucleus releases serotonin. This can relieve pain and lift mood respectively. Continuous BLS in SF-EMDR psychotherapy may help to alleviate the multiple symptoms associated with complex and enduring pain.

- Lack of coping skills. Environmental learning from caregivers and society may be insufficient to provide adaptive learning and skills to thrive in society. Misuse of imagination can exacerbate worrying and trigger a depressive episode.

We can help our patients find meaning by encouraging them to be involved with helping others, learning new skills, and being connected with something bigger than themselves. My discussion on quantum consciousness (Chapter 8) is one such example of peering into a future bigger than ourselves. This can aid the search for meaning and purpose in our lives.

The following template has been designed to provide a comprehensive assessment of emotional, mental, physical, and psychological needs and to document symptoms that are indicative of ill health from this holistic perspective. Patients who have experienced traumas that are unresolved have symptoms instead of memories. These include in no particular order; depression, irritability, loss of interest, numbing, decreased concentration, difficulty staying asleep or falling asleep, early morning waking, nightmares, flashbacks, being emotionally overwhelmed (RAPIDS or FROZEN in FEAR), loss of a sense of the future, hopelessness, helplessness, shame and worthlessness, blanked-out childhood memories, hypervigilance, relentless self-doubt, mistrust, generalised anxiety, panic attacks, chronic pain, headaches, substance abuse, eating disorders, voyeurism, sex addiction, dissociation, feeling unreal or out of body experiences, self-destructive behaviour, and the loss of the sense of "who I am."

The standard approach to treatment in the medical and psychiatric fields is to cluster these symptoms according to either the nomenclature of ICD 10 or DSM 5. However, Bessel van der Kolk, who was involved in the field trials of DSM 3 in 1978, stated that only two questions were asked of patients in the social domain and the majority of the traumatic history was omitted.

There is now clear evidence from the ACE study commissioned by Kaiser Permanente that childhood adversity predisposes to pathology in adulthood.

The approach adopted by Judith Hermann in 1992 divides trauma recovery into three stages:

1. Safety and stabilisation: overcoming dysregulation;
2. Coming to terms with traumatic memories; and

3. Integration of self and moving further away from the traumas. I would add a fourth and final stage:
4. Finding your life purpose for happiness, optimal functioning, and peak performance.

I wrote the following template to achieve exactly that. It is designed to be printed off and used for intake or initial assessment.

I would recommend you set aside a two-hour appointment to complete this form.

PATIENT COUNSELLING or PSYCHOTHERAPY DECLARATION GDPR COMPLIANCE

I, THE UNDERSIGNED

_____

HEREBY DECLARE

1. I accept that Dr Art O'Malley will provide EMDR to assist resolving my trauma, difficulties and/or post-traumatic stress disorder. Dr Art O'Malley is a qualified EMDR psychotherapist and I accept that his training and qualifications are bone fide in the field for online and face-to-face counselling.
2. For the purposes of the above, I hereby give my informed consent for Dr Art O'Malley to collect, obtain, write down, store, process, and use my personal data. I understand that doing so would help Dr Art O'Malley to provide as accurate as possible, full-scope advice on the issues raised. I recognise and accept that such personal data may include my name, date and place of birth, address, email, as well as any health data relating to my foregoing and current mental health status quo.
3. I am made aware that such data is only to be collected for the purposes of counselling and will be kept, read, used, and accessed by Dr Art O'Malley only.
4. I confirm that I have been informed of the relevance and purpose of any treatment procedures that my practitioner, Dr Art O'Malley, may undertake, and that I hereby give my consent thereto.

PRINT NAME: SIGNATURE:

_____   _____

DATE: _____

Address . . . .
. . . .
. . . .
Postcode . . . .

Landline

Work number

Mobile number

Email

Date of Birth

Referred by Address

Tel number

Present at assessment

Details of involvement with other services. Please ask patient to clarify any involvement with these services encompassing health social care education and the voluntary sector

GP practice Name . . . . Tel no	YOS/Forensic team Contact . . . . *Tel No*	Social Worker/ Family support *Name*	Services Contact . . . . Tel No . . . .
Child Protection register Safeguarding referral Social Services Police Protection Unit NHS Trust Safeguarding	**Ever accommodated or adopted LAC** . . . . **Foster care Residential care**	**Housing benefits PIP Universal Credit** *Yes/No*	**Home-based assessment Inpatient referral Consultation service**
Health visitor involved *Yes/No*	**Young carers** Name	**CAMHS worker/ clinician Names**	**Crisis intervention Adult Mental Health Team/EIP team**

Name	Tel No		**IAPT (Primary/ Secondary)** Contact . . . . Tel No . . . .
School . . . . Contact . . . . **Learning mentor** . . . . **SENCo Head of year**	**Police referral** *Yes/No*	**Sure Start or Child development clinic Keyworker** . . . . *Tel No*	**Paediatric Hospitals** Contacts . . . .
Educational Psychologist Name . . . . **Statemented Yes/No/In Process**		**Substance misuse referral** *Yes/No*	**Job-centre personal advisor Well-being** Contact . . . . **No**
Specialist hospital refer- rals (Specify)	**Learning disability service Challenging behaviour service** . . . . **Child development centre** . . . . Contact . . . . Tel No	**Support services Parenting** . . . . **Autism** . . . . **ADHD** . . . . **Other**	**Voluntary Sector – e.g. Domestic violence service Women's refuge Youth and community services** Contact . . . . **Tel No**

PROBLEM HISTORY

(a) List presenting complaints in child's/adolescent's own words

In order of severity

SUDS   0   1   2   3   4   5   6   7   8   9   10
    Neutral   Bad   Worst
Doesn't   bother   Bothers a bit   bothers a lot

Complete SUDS rating for each presenting complaint

(b) History of presenting complaints (background to referral)

Nature of symptoms

Onset

Frequency

Situations, places, times in which symptoms occur

Severity

Precipitating

Alleviating

Factors

Impact on work-life balance

Personal

Family

Friends

School

Work

Developmental history: Ask questions here if attachment disorder suspected.

1(a) Pregnancy

Planned/Unplanned

Feelings on finding out about pregnancy

Physical Health

Emotional well-being

Complications, drugs, alcohol

What were you doing during pregnancy e.g. working?

How much was baby wanted?

Were you ever pregnant before?

When did the pregnancy seem real to you?

What were your impressions about the baby during pregnancy kicks etc?

What did you sense the baby might be like (gender, temperament, personality)?

Any traumatic experiences during pregnancy (outline later)

1(b) Tell me about the labour and delivery

How did you feel and react at the time?

What was your first reaction when you saw (name of baby)?

What was your reaction to having a boy/girl?

How did your family react (husband partner siblings others)?

1(c) Were there any problems in the first few days after birth?

How quickly were you discharged from hospital?

How did you decide to feed your baby?

Breast-fed for any period?

Breast–crawl reflex present?

What was the experience of feeding like for you?

1(d) What was first month at home like – feeding, sleeping, crying?

Impact of baby's entrance into the family

1(e) Tell me about your baby's developmental milestones – smiling, sitting up, crawling, walking, talking

Motor

Social

Language

Was this different i.e. ahead or behind other children?

What did you think of your baby's intelligence in first few years?

1(f) Did your baby have a regular routine?

What happened if this routine was changed?

1(g) How has.............. reacted to being separated from you?

Dates and times if > 1 day in years 0-3

How did .... react to being apart from you?

How did you feel and what did you do?

1(h) How and when did you choose name?

2.   Does .... get upset often?

How do you feel and react? What do you do?

(a) When he/she became upset what did they do?

When sad

When frightened

When angry

What did you feel like doing?

(b) Tell me when .... was physically hurt e.g. cuts, scrapes, bumps, bleeding?

How did you feel?

What did you do?

(c) Tell me when .... was ill e.g. ear infection, cold/flu, illnesses, etc.

What was this like for you?

How did you respond emotionally and behaviourally?

3.   (a) Thinking about what you know about your first two years, describe the words that your parents used to describe you as a baby. If they are agreeable you can ask them. Examples include:

A joy. Fussy. Difficult. No trouble. Never slept. Sickly. Angry. Easily tired. Smiled a lot. Difficult to feed. Don't remember. Early walker. Brought up by caregivers. Fearful. Shy. Happiest alone. Always into things.

What is the characteristic phrase they would use i,e. the one they would put on your gravestone.

How have these labels affected you now? Write down patient's words

. . . .
. . . .
. . . .

(b) Pick five adjectives to describe your or your child's personality?

(i) Word

Describe a specific incident

(ii) Word

Incident

(iii) Word

Incident

(iv) Word

Incident

(v) Word

Incident

4. **Who does .... remind you of and in what ways?**

How does .... remind you of self and father?

How is .... different to mother and father?

What are the family characteristics on your side you see in ....
personality?

Other parent's side

5. **What is unique about .... compared to other children you know?**

6. **What is hardest to handle about .... behaviour? Give example?**

(a) How often does this happen

7. **Five words to describe your relationship with ....?**

Describe with incident or memory

8. **What aspect of your relationship with your baby is most pleasing?**

What would you like to change?

9. **How has your relationship with .... affected their personality?**

Has this relationship changed over time?

If so in what ways?

What is your own feeling about that change?

10. Which parent is closest to . . . .? How can you tell?

Has it always been that way?

As . . . . gets older do you expect this to change? If so how?

11. Tell a favourite story about . . . .

What do you like about this story?

12. Any regrets about how you have brought . . . . up?

In hindsight would you do anything differently?

13. Favourite age so far?

14. Most difficult time looking ahead?

15. What will . . . . be like as an adolescent?

Why?

What will be good?

And what bad about this stage of development?

16. What are your hopes and fears as .... becomes an adult?

This completes the modified attachment interview of the child and it is possible to ascertain whether from six months to age three the patient or client experienced an attachment that was
  secure (60%) or
  insecure (40%).
(Please circle category that best fits historical description.)

The next thirteen sections comprise the modified Health of the Nation Outcome Scale for Children and Adolescents. The best practice is to complete the scores by circling the relevant number from 0 to 4 on the left-hand side of the page relevant to each of the thirteen sections.
  in the boxes at the end of the template on p. x

1. Problems with disruptive, antisocial or aggressive behaviour (conduct disorder/oppositional defiant disorder)

Oppositional defiance, lying, stealing, running away, truancy

Oppositional to authority

Fire-setting, aggressive, delinquency, contact with law.

Tantrums

If relevant, take forensic history and proceed to risk

Risk to self

Risk to property

Risk to others

Risk from others

GRIST/FACE overall risks, short, medium, and long-term

Inappropriate sexualised behaviour
Assessment. Sexual abuse of other children
Include behaviour associated with any disorder e.g., hyperkinesis,

depression, drugs, alcohol or autism. Include physical or verbal aggression (e.g., pushing, hitting, vandalism, teasing). If disruptive behaviour due to overactivity, rate on scale 2 (below). If due to truancy, rate on scale 13. If due to self-harm, rate on scale 3.

0   No problems of this kind during the period noted
1   Minor quarrelling, demanding behaviour, undue irritability, lying, stealing
2   Mild but definite disruptive or antisocial behaviour, lesser damage to property or aggression or defiant behaviour
3   Moderately severe aggressive or antisocial behaviour such as fighting or persistently
    Threatening or very oppositional or more serious destruction to property, or moderate delinquent acts
4   Disruptive in almost all activities, or at least one serious physical attack on
    others, or animals, or serious destruction to property.

2. Problems with over-activity, attention, or concentration (ADHD)

Home

School

Other

Concentration span

Distractibility

Passive

Self-imposed and imposed tasks

Impulsivity

Inattention

Energy

Anergia

Motor skills

Clumsiness

Over-activity, under-activity

Restless

Fidgety

Co-ordination e.g. feeding, dressing

Buttons, laces, writing

Include overactive behaviour associated with any disorder, e.g. hyperkinetic disorder, mania, or due to drug misuse

0   No problems of this kind during the period noted
1   Slight overactivity or minor restlessness
2   Mild but definite overactivity and/or attentional problems, but these can usually be controlled
3   Moderately severe overactivity and/or attentional problems that are sometimes uncontrollable
4   Severe overactivity.

3. Non-accidental self-injury

Suicidal ideation

Attempts

NSSI

Overdoses

Hanging

Drowning

Non-suicidal self-injury such as hitting self

Self-cutting

Frequency

Severity

Type

Meaning

Outcome

Treatment
If scratching or picking due to physical illness or due to SLD or physical disability, or due to drugs or alcohol misuse, rate on scale 6.

0   No problem of this kind during the period rated
1   Occasional thoughts about death or self-harm not leading to injury. No self-harm or suicidal thoughts
2   Non-hazardous self-harm, such as wrist-scratching, whether associated with suicidal thoughts
3   Moderately severe suicidal intent (including preparatory acts, e.g. collecting tablets) or moderate non-hazardous self-harm (e.g. small overdose)
4   Serious suicidal attempt (e.g. serious overdose), or serious deliberate self-injury.

4. Problems with alcohol, substance/solvent misuse

Smoking

Amounts

Types

Alcohol dependence

Physical

Psychological

Drugs, considering current age and societal norms

Solvent use by other members of the family.

Rate aggressive/disruptive behaviour due to drugs and alcohol on scale 1
Rate physical illness or disability due to drugs and alcohol on scale 6

0   No problems of this kind during the period rated
1   Minor alcohol or drug use, within age norms
2   Mildly excessive alcohol or drug use

3   Moderately severe drug or alcohol problems significantly out of keeping with age norms

4   Severe drug or alcohol problems leading to dependency or incapacity.

5. Problems with scholastic or language skills

Hearing

Comprehension
Reading
Spelling
Arithmetic

Speech or language impairment associated with specific development disorder or hearing impairment.

Social response and use

Empathy

Referral for speech and language therapy

Include decreased academic performance associated with emotional or behavioural problems.

0   No problems of this kind during the period rated
1   Minor impairment within the normal range of variation
2   Mild but definite impairment of clinical significance
3   Moderately severe problems, below the level expected based on mental age, past performance or physical disability
4   Severe impairment much below the level expected based on mental age, past performance or physical disability.

6. Physical illness and disability problems that limit or prevent movement, impair sight or hearing, or interfere with personal functioning

Health problems

Hospitalisations

Treatment, physical effects of drugs or alcohol.

Fits, convulsions

Meningitis

Current medication

Compliance

Side-effects

Allergies to drugs

Food

Physical complications of psychological disorders, e.g. loss of periods from severe weight loss

Sexual development, puberty, menarche

Include hearing or visual impairment

Rate somatising disorders on scale 8, i.e., on organic somatic symptoms.

Include movement disorder, medication side effects, and physical effects from drug/alcohol misuse, self-injury due to severe learning or physical disability or because of self-injury such as head banging.

0   No incapacity because of physical health problem during the period rated

1   Slight incapacity because of a health problem during the period (e.g. cold, non-serious fall, etc.)

2   Physical health problem imposes mild but definite functional restriction

3   Moderate degree of restriction on activity due to physical health problem

4   Complete or severe incapacity due to physical health problems.

7. Problems associated with hallucination, delusions, and abnormal perceptions (mental state examination)

Please include signs of delusions either primary or secondary, derealisation, depersonalisation, or dissociation.

Rate disruptive or aggressive behaviour associated with hallucinations or delusions on scale 1. Rate overactive behaviour associated with hallucinations or delusions at scale 2. Assess for presence of hallucinations in the following modalities: visual, auditory, tactile, gustatory, olfactory and those linked to bodily sensation.

Assess for presence of either hypnogogic, hypnopompic or pseudo-hallucinations/illusions. Assess for presence of over-valued ideas such as distorted body image. Include any odd and bizarre behaviour associated with hallucinations and delusions.

0   No evidence of abnormal thoughts or perceptions during the period rated

1   Somewhat odd or eccentric beliefs not in keeping with cultural norms

2   Abnormal thoughts or perceptions are present (e.g. paranoid ideas, illusions or body image disturbance) but there is little distress or manifestation in bizarre behaviour, i.e. clinically present but mild

3   Moderate preoccupation with abnormal thoughts or perceptions or delusions, hallucinations, causing much distress and/or manifested in obviously bizarre behaviour.

4   Mental state and behaviour is seriously and adversely affected by delusions or hallucinations or abnormal perceptions, with severe impact on child/adolescent or others.

Document any suspicious or paranoid thoughts

Assess for presence of formal thought disorder i.e.

Thought withdrawal

Thought Insertion

Thought Broadcasting

Assess for presence of:

Passivity of affects, impulse or volition

Somatic passivity

Overvalued ideas, e.g. distorted body image, obsessions, compulsions

Assessment of cognitive function

Attention span

Digit span   forwards   backwards

Draw a person,

write name,

Recite days of week or months of year

Test orientation in time, person, and place

Assess concentration:

memory of name and address Peter Hargreaves 10 Grange Street Birmingham

Ask patient to repeat this address. If any part is repeated incorrectly ask two further times to ensure registration of information.

Recall at three mins and at end of assessment

Refer to psychological assessment if available to estimate IQ if there are any concerns about memory function

Assess insight of the patient. Are they aware of any perceptual abnormalities?

8. **Problems with non-organic somatic symptoms (Medically unexplained physical symptoms, MUPS)**

Include problems with gastrointestinal symptoms, e.g. tummy ache or non-organic vomiting, diarrhoea

Cardiovascular symptoms, e.g. palpitations

Neurological symptoms, e.g. pain, dizziness, headaches

Bladder symptoms, non-organic enuresis,

Bowel problems e.g. encoporesis

Sleep problems, e.g. initial insomnia, nightmares, and night terrors

Chronic Fatigue Syndrome/ME

Rate movement disorders such as tics and physical illnesses that complicate MUPS on scale 6.

0   No problems of this kind during the period rated
1   Slight problems only; such as occasional enuresis, minor sleep problems, headaches or stomach aches without organic basis
2   Mild but definite problem with non-organic somatic symptoms
3   Moderately severe, symptoms produce a moderate degree of restriction in some activities
4   Very severe or symptoms persist into most activities. The child is seriously or adversely affected.

9. Problems with emotional and related worries

Emotions:

Happy

Sad, crying, irritable

Anxiety

Fears

Phobias

Depression

Obsessional ideas

Rituals and ruminations

Compulsions arising from any clinical condition including eating disorders

Include early morning waking and diurnal mood variation

Mood scale 0 – 10 (highest mood)

Thought content

Views of self

World

Future

If aggressive, destructive or overactive behaviours attributed to fears or phobias, rate at scale 1

Rate only the most severe clinical problem not considered previously.

Rate physical complications of psychological disorders such as severe weight loss at scale 6.

0   No evidence of depression, anxieties, fears or phobias during the
     period rated
1   Mildly anxious; gloomy; or transient mood changes
2   A mild but definite emotional symptom is clinically present but is
     not preoccupying
3   Moderately severe emotional symptoms, which are preoccupying,
     intrude into some activities and are uncontrollable at least sometimes
4   Severe emotional symptoms which intrude into all activities and are
     nearly always uncontrollable.

10(a). Problems with peer relationships

Friends

Frequency of interaction

Quality of relationships (close friends)

Popularity, ignored, lonely

Assessment of empathy and ability to make friends. Boy/girlfriend. Theory of mind.

Include problems with school friends and social network, active or passive withdrawal from social relationships, over-intrusiveness, and inability to form satisfying peer relationships.

Include social rejection due to aggressive behaviour or bullying.

If peer relationship problems due to bullying or aggressive behaviour, rate on scale 1, if problems with family or siblings, rate on scale 12.

0   No significant problems during the period rated
1   Either transient or slight problems, occasional social withdrawal
2   Mild but definite problems in making or sustaining peer relationships. Problems causing distress due to social withdrawal, over intrusiveness, rejection or being bullied
3   Moderate problems due to active or passive withdrawal from social relationships, over intrusiveness and/or to relationships that provide little or no comfort or support, e.g. because of being severely bullied
4   Severe social isolation with no friends due to inability to communicate socially and/or withdrawal from social relationships.

Self-esteem (how you see yourself?)

Temperament (how others see you)

Emotional expression, response to new situations and people, adaptability, affections.

Easy. Slow to warm up. Difficult.

10(b). Chronology of stresses and traumas (stones) and positive experiences flowers

Adverse Childhood Experience (ACE) Survey

While you were growing up, during your first eighteen years of life:

1. Did a parent or other adult in the household often • Swear at you, insult you, put you down, or humiliate you? or • Act in a way that made you afraid that you might be physically hurt?
If yes, enter 1 _____ _____

2. Did a parent or other adult in the household often • Push, grab, or slap you or throw something at you? or • Ever hit you so hard that you had marks or were injured?
If yes, enter 1 _____ _____

3. Did an adult or person at least five years older than you ever • Touch or fondle you or have you touch his/her body in a sexual way? or • Try to or actually have oral, anal, or vaginal sex with you?
If yes, enter 1 _____ _____

4. Did you often feel that • No one in your family loved you or thought you were important or special? or • Your family members didn't look out for one another, feel close to one another, or support one another?
If yes, enter 1 _____ _____

5. Did you often feel that • You didn't have enough to eat, had to wear dirty clothes, and had no one to protect you? or • Your parents were too drunk or high to take care of you or take you to the doctor if you needed it?
If yes, enter 1 _____ _____

6. Were your parents ever separated or divorced?
If yes, enter 1 _____ _____

7. Was your mother or stepmother • Often pushed, grabbed, or slapped or had something thrown at her? or • Sometimes or often kicked, bitten, hit with a fist, or hit with something hard? or • Ever repeatedly hit over at least a few minutes or threatened with a gun or knife?
If yes, enter 1 _____ _____

8. Did you live with anyone who was a problem drinker or alcoholic or who used street drugs?
If yes, enter 1 _____ _____

9. Was a household member depressed or mentally ill or did a household member attempt suicide?
If yes, enter 1 _____ _____

10. Did a household member go to prison?
If yes, enter 1 _____ _____

Now add up your "Yes" answers: _____ This is your ACE Score.

Has the patient had any hospitalisations, surgery, or general anaesthesia?

Has the patient been involved in any accidents or traffic collisions?

Timeline:

From conception to 0 (Birth) to current age, add in brief description of key life events.

What are your worst memories?

These are represented as stones and what are your best memories e,g, birthdays, Christmas, family occasions, successes – academic, business, sports, music.

These are represented as flowers and are placed chronologically on the following timeline. They are read back to the client as a life-story over four to ten sessions. The final document is presented to the patient so the exposure to this narrative can be integrated with sensorimotor-focused EMDR psychotherapy and peak performance. This helps to contextualise the network of cognitive, affective, sensorimotor, and energetic aspects of the patient's traumas. The patient can reflect on the positive and negative aspects of their entire life up to the present. By going over the biography they are enabled to enhance understanding of these experiences by tolerating the window of affect tolerance of associated emotional and behavioural responses. This allows integration of complex trauma and dissociation associated with my model of hyperarousal RAPIDS. Eudemonia, CALM WATERS, and hypoarousal, FROZEN in FEAR. Knowing that the patient will receive a written narrative at the end of treatment acts as an incentive to complete treatment and is similar to the narrative approaches of Dr Joan Lovett and Narrative Exposure Therapy.

Pregnancy Stage	Events
weeks	SUDS (0-10)
0-13	First trimester
14-27	Second trimester
28-40	Third trimester
	Developmental Stages (Erikson, 1994)
Birth to 18 months	Trust vs. Mistrust
18 months to 3 years	Autonomy vs. Shame and Doubt
3 to 5 years	Initiative vs. Guilt
5 to 13 years	Industry vs. Inferiority
13 to 21 years	Identity vs. Role confusion
21 to 39 years	Intimacy vs. Isolation

40 to 65 years   Generativity vs. Stagnation

66 years and older   Ego integrity vs. Despair

Please document significant positive and negative events in chronological order

11. Problems with self-care and independence

Feeding:

Loss of appetite, dieting, distorted body image, fads, over-eating, weight gain/loss

Rate the overall level of functioning, e.g. problems with basic activities of self-care, i.e. feeding, washing, dressing, toileting, and complex skills, e.g. managing money, travelling independently, shopping, etc. considering the norm for the child's chronological age

Include poor levels of functioning arising from lack of motivation, mood or any other disorder.

Rate lack of opportunities for exercising, intact abilities and skills, e.g. an over-restrictive family on scale 12.

If due to enuresis and encoporesis, rate at scale 8.

0   No problems during the period rated; good ability to function in all areas
1   Minor problems only, e.g. untidy, disorganised
2   Self-care adequate, but definite inability to perform one or more complex skills (see above)
3   Major problems in one or more areas of self-care (eating, washing, dressing) or inability to perform several complex skills
4   Severe disability in all or nearly all areas of self-care and/or complex skills.

12. Family life and relationships/structure

Family tree:
Including names, age, occupation, and health of parents, grandparents

Names, age of sibling's other important people.

Close attachments/patterns of conflict

Relationships with foster parents, social workers/teachers in residential placements

Assess for family history of psychiatric disorder including parental history of hyperactivity, personality problems, mental handicap and mental illness if they affect the child.

Document any medical condition, e.g. epilepsy, stoke, diabetes.

Assess reported patterns of interactions between adults and siblings.

Assess specific family rules, discipline, support, hostility, over involvement.

Enquire about drugs and alcohol misuse.

Ask about emotional, verbal, physical, sexual abuse and marital disharmony Assess parental care and management including rules and expectations.

Have parents attended training e.g. Webster-Stratton?

Are they developmentally appropriate consistent effective, flexible?

Assess for parental neglect/rejection, over restriction sibling jealousy, abuse by sibling, enmeshment or over protection

Assess any problems associated with family bereavement loss and subsequent family reorganisation

Document accommodation history, i.e. periods away from home in the care of the Local Authority and/or relatives.

0   No problems during the period rated
1   Slight or transient problems
2   Mild but definite problem, e.g., some episodes of neglect or hostility
     or enmeshment or overprotection
3   Moderate problems, e.g., neglect, abuse, hostility. Problems
     associated with family/carer breakdown or reorganisation
4   Serious problems with child feeling or being victimised abused or
     seriously neglected

13. School/Education

Dates and names of nursery, primary, and secondary schools, academic
progress, interaction with peers and teachers, school attendance, truancy,
school report, educational psychologist, SENCo statement, strengths, weak-
nesses, problems e.g. bullying, school refusal, school withdrawal or suspension. Poor school attendance – rate last weeks if school holiday, rate last
two weeks of previous term.

0   No problems of this kind during the period rated
1   Slight problems e.g. late for two or more lessons
2   Definite but mild problems, e.g. missed several lessons because of
     truancy or refusal to go to school
3   Marked problems, absent several days during the period rated
4   Severe problems absent most or all days. Any school suspension,
     exclusion or expulsion for any cause during the period rated.

Kindergarten

Nursery

Primary

University

The HoNOSCA is completed after the initial assessment to give the therapist an
indication of case complexity and the length of time, number of sessions, and
other resources needed for a successful outcome

SECTION A   RATE 0–4
HoNOSCA
a. Behavioural Problems Range of **H1**   **H2**   **Subscale**
                            Section
                            scores

1. Disruptive, antisocial or   ☐   ☐
   aggressive behaviour

2. Over activity, attention and ☐   ☐
   concentration

3. Non-accidental self-injury   ☐   ☐

4. Alcohol, substance or solvent ☐   ☐
   misuse

b. Impairment   ☐   Out of 16   ☐

5. Scholastic or language skills ☐   ☐

6. Physical illness or disability ☐   ☐
   problems

c. Symptomatic problems   ☐   Out of 8   ☐

7. Hallucination and delusions ☐   ☐

8. Non-organic somatic   ☐   ☐
   symptoms

9. Emotional and related   ☐   ☐
   symptoms

d. Social problems   ☐   Out of 12   ☐

10. Peer relationships   ☐   ☐

11. Self-care and independence ☐   ☐

12. Family life relationships and ☐   ☐
    Adverse life events

13. Poor school attendance   ☐   ☐

                               ☐   Out of 12   ☐

H1	☐
H2	☐
TOTAL HoNOSCA SCORE H1-H2	☐

Emotional needs or Human Givens that are core drivers of our behaviour (met or unmet)

1. Security: feeling safe with space to grow
2. Autonomy: sense of control and freedom to make our own decisions
3. Attention: from newborn baby to present, giving and receiving attention is important
4. Being emotionally connected to others
5. Intimacy: friendship and loving relationships
6. Community: evolutionary need to belong to a group
7. Sense of status: and feeling of belonging to a group
8. Achievement and competence: of our own knowledge, skills, and abilities. Leads to development of spare capacity resilience or being stretched. Opposite is low self-esteem
9. Privacy: space-time to reflect on, learn from, and build up or consolidate gains made from our experiences
10. Meaning and purpose: service to others, purposeful role in life. Having belief in greater purpose than self, e.g. quantum consciousness.

The RIGAAR approach in Human Givens psychotherapy

1. **Rapport-building looks for evidence of body matching during the consultation**
2. **Information-gathering with use of presuppositions creating a temporary element to the situation**
3. **Goal-setting**

- What do the family want to work on?
- How do they want to do it?
- How will they know when they have reached their goal?

SMARTER goals are:

a. Specific, and stepping stones in place
b. Measurable and meaningful

c. Achievable and affordable
d. Realistic within reach
e. Time limited
f. Excites emotions
g. Relevant to building of coping skills (Resilience)

Please document at least 3 goals that fulfil criteria a to g

4. Accessing or Audit of Resources

1. Emotions and instincts
2. Empathy and communication skills
3. Memory
4. Imagination
5. Intuition
6. Insight
7. Reason
8. Enhanced awareness
9. Dreaming to solve problems
10. Generosity
11. Patience
12. Understanding
13. Creativity

Sensitivity, strengths, interests, and resilience factors

Mental toughness (challenge, commitment, control; life and emotions, confidence)

MTQ48 score..............This is available from AQR Ltd as an online resource.

5. Agreeing strategy or strategies
Clear and concise language
All parties understand and agree to their role
Feedback before during and after the task has been completed

6. Rehearsing success using guided imagery and future template using SF-EMDR for psychotherapy in a new paradigm for peak performance

This includes use of the Flash Technique (Mansfield 2017–2018). The patient is asked to focus on positive imagery. Following bilateral stimulation with the patient tapping in time with the therapist they are given an instruction to blink on the count of three. The patient allows the most disturbing image of the specific traumatic memory to flash by in an instant. The patient instantly returns to focus on the positive imagery until the SUDS level is reduced. The process is then repeated only this time the patient is asked to blink three times in between focusing on their positive imagery. It may take twenty-four goes to bring the SUDS level down to zero. The process of sensorimotor-focused EMDR can then proceed in the normal way. It seems voluntary activation of the blink reflex stimulates the brainstem and consequently the orbicularis oculi muscle involved in eye movements. This integration of facilitatory and inhibitory brainstem mechanisms is similar to activation of the peripheral nervous system during tactile bilateral stimulation in sensorimotor-focused EMDR.

General observations of patient or client, appearance, and behaviour

a. Eye contact
b. Include activity levels
c. Restlessness
d. Fidgety, abnormal movements e.g. tics rituals
e. Disinhibition
f. Co-ordination
g. Social interaction
h. Rapport
i. Attention

House and neighbourhood

a. Type of house
b. Financial difficulties
c. Area
d. neighbours
e. Support

Physical examination

Height (cm)   weight (kg)
Weight (kg) $BMI = \dfrac{\text{weight (kg)}}{\text{Height (m)}^2}$

< 18.5 anorexia
> 25 obese
> 30 morbid obesity
Normal range = 20-25

Dysmorphic features
General examination including:
Cardiovascular
Respiratory
Gastrointestinal
Musculoskeletal
Neurological
Handedness
Coordination
Formulation. This is completed by the therapist after the assessment has been concluded and is an opportunity to analyse and synthesise the salient information in order to develop a comprehensive treatment plan

Main complaints

Differential diagnosis

Predisposing

Precipitating

Maintaining

Preventative

Consider following factors

Resilience

Individual

Family

Social

Environment

The European Union made a worldwide impact with the general data protection regulation. The GDPR became law on 25 May 2018. Failure to implement this regulation could lead to serious penalties in terms of fines to an organisation or individual health professional.

I get the patients or clients to sign the following document. This I believe is compatible with the requirements of the General Data Protection Regulation. Other regulations relate to consent for communication by email text phone or video. There is also a requirement to get consent for subscription to any website information.

Use of the Herrmann Brain Dominance instrument
Herrmann Brain Dominance instrument (HBDI)

The HBDI is a system claimed to measure and describe thinking preferences in people. In his brain dominance model, William 'Ned' Herrmann (1991) developed a cognitive-style measurement while leading management education at General Electric's Crontonville factory. He identifies four different modes of thinking:

- **A. Analytical thinking**
  Key words: auditive, logical, factual, critical, technical, and quantitative. Preferred activities: collecting data, analysis, understanding how things work, judging ideas based on facts, criteria, and logical reasoning.

- **B. Sequential thinking**
  Key words: safekeeping, structured, organised, complexity, or detailed, planned.Preferred activities: following directions, detail-oriented work, step-by-step problem solving, organisation, and implementation.

- **C. Interpersonal thinking**
  Key words: kinaesthetic, emotional, spiritual, sensory, feeling.Preferred activities: listening to and expressing ideas, looking for personal meaning, sensory input, and group interaction.

- **D. Imaginative thinking**
  Key words: visual, holistic, intuitive, innovative, and conceptual.Preferred activities: looking at the big picture, taking initiative, challenging assumptions, visuals, metaphoric thinking, creative problem solving, long-term thinking.

His theory was inspired by the research into left-right brain lateralisation by Roger Wolcott Sperry, Robert Ornstein, Henry Mintzberg, and Michael

Gazzaniga and further developed to reflect a metaphor for how individuals think and learn. Use of that metaphor brought later criticism by brain researchers such as Terence Hines for being overly simplistic. Herrmann also coined the concept of Whole Brain Thinking as a description of flexibility in using thinking styles that one may cultivate in individuals or in organisations allowing the situational use of all four styles of thinking. Use of all four thinking styles can be encouraged using the techniques outlined in this book.

The brain is divided into four quadrants each with their individual functionality. It is possible to calculate your score by completing the 240 questions online at www.hbdi.org

A   **Left cerebral hemisphere**
B   **Left limbic hemisphere**
C   **Right Limbic hemisphere**
D   **Right Cerebral hemisphere**

The HBDI can be completed online and used to find the points at which your brilliance meets what you are passionate about. These can gel to identify the unique talents, which will help you to both find your element and put you in the zone. The goal in colloquial terms is to find both what makes you "tick" and what "floats your boat."

The theory suggests that strengthening your weaker quadrants will improve your overall creative potential.

Strategies appropriate to each quadrant of the Herrmann Brain Dominance Instrument are outlined.

Knowledge of this can be combined with SF-EMDR psychotherapy for our clients seeking to optimise their performance in school, university, work, or sport settings.

The following twelve brain functions have key associations with different Brodmann (1909) functional brain areas

1. Visuospatial working memory involves activation of the ventrolateral frontal cortex 46 and parietal lobe 7
2. Spatial working memory involves activation of frontal lobe 10 and posterior parietal lobe 39
3. Focused attention engages the right prefrontal cortex 11. This occurs at the latter stages of BART psychotherapy.
4. The ability to rotate objects mentally involves the superior parietal cortex 5.
5. The brain's strategy for visuospatial working memory involves the coming together of 2 streams of neurological information.

  A Parietal lobe (where) 5 and 7.
  B Temporal lobe Perception and memory for objects (what) 20 21 and 37.

6. This is called paired associate learning and involves linking memories such as a person's name and their telephone number. It allows the person to learn connections between related concepts.
7. Deductive reasoning involves activity in the back and outer surface of the frontal lobes and in the middle of the parietal lobe.
8. Visuospatial processing involves parietal cortex and the higher visual areas of the occipital cortex 17 18 and 19.
9. Visual attention again involves activation of the visual centres at the base and back of the brain.
10. Verbal reasoning tests activate the dorsolateral frontal cortex 46 and 47, which lie on the outer surface of the frontal lobe midway between top and bottom.
11. Verbal working memory activates the ventrolateral frontal cortex of the left hemisphere speech area.
12. Planning an activity involves the frontal lobe caudate lobe, supplementary motor area, posterior parietal lobe and the cerebellum. All of these areas are activated at the end of BART sessions as the patient or client reviews the session and plans their next steps in either psychotherapy or peak performance.

Conclusion

This final chapter outlines the uses of the Herrmann Brain Dominance instrument. This is useful to combine with SF-EMDR psychotherapy to monitor those quadrants that need to be targeted for improvement. The HBDI can also be used to analyse, strategise, organise, and personalise the information for each patient. Further resources are available at www.hbdi.org. I have included my initial comprehensive health assessment for children, adolescents, and adults, which contains the modified attachment interview of the child and the ACE questionnaire as a measure of early childhood adversity. I have also added in aspects of the Human Givens Psychotherapy approaches such as RIGAAR which nicely complements SF-EMDR for psychotherapy and peak performance.

References

Ananthaswamy, A. (2013). The Knockout Enigma: How Your Mechanical Brain Works. New Scientist, 2932: 32–35.

Andersen, B. B., Korbo, L., Pakkenberg, B. A. (1992). Quantitative Study of the Human Cerebellum with Unbiased Stereological Techniques. The Journal of Compartive Neurology, 326: 549–560.

Arriaga, M. (2014). Rebooting Democracy: A Citizen's Guide to Reinventing Politics. London: Thistle Publishing.

Assagioli's, R. (1975). Psychosynthesis (p. 17). Winnipeg, Canada: Turnstone Press.

Austin, J. H. (1999). Zen and the Brain: Toward an Understanding of Meditation and Consciousness. Cambridge, MA: MIT Press.

Azevedo, F. A. C., Carvalho, L. R. B., Grinberg, L. T., Farfel, J. M., Ferretti, R. E. L., et al. (2009). Equal Numbers of Neuronal and Nonneuronal Cells Make the Human Brain an Isometrically Scaled-Up Primate Brain. The Journal of Comparative Neurology, 513: 532–541.

Bagchi P., & Hopper W. (2011). Virtual Screening of Compounds from Valerianajatamansi with a-Synuclein. IPCBEE, 5: 11–14: ISSN: 2010–4618.

Bagchi, P., Somashekhar, R. & Kar, A. (2015). Scope of Some Indian Medicinal Plants in the Management of a Few Neuro-degenerative Disorders in Silico: A Review. International Journal of Public Mental Health and Neurosciences, 2(1): 41–57: ISSN: 2394–4668.

Bandler, R., & Grinder, J. (1975a). The Structure of Magic Vol I: A Book about Language and Therapy. Palo Alto, CA: Science & Behaviour Books.

Bandler, R., & Grinder, J. (1975b). The Structure of Magic Vol II: A Book about Communication and Change. Palo Alto, CA: Science & Behaviour Books.

Bannister, L., Berry, M., Collins, P., Dussek, J., Dyson, M., et al. (Eds.) (1995). Gray's Anatomy: The Anatomical Basis of Medicine and Surgery. London: Churchill Livingstone.

Baron-Cohen, S., & Wheelwright, S. (2001). The "Reading the Mind in the Eyes" Test-Revised Version: A Study with Normal Adults and Adults with Asperger Syndrome or High-Functioning Autism. Journal of Child Psychology and Psychiatry, 42(2): 241–251.

BBC Sport Online. (2013). Rory McIlroy says management issues have been a "distraction". 12 November. Available at: www.bbc.co.uk/sport/0/golf/24914810 (accessed 18 March 2014).

Bauer, P. M., Hanson, J. L., Pierson, R. K., Davidson, R. J., & Pollak, S. D. (2009). Cerebellar Volume and Cognitive Functioning in Children Who Experienced Early Deprivation. Biological Psychiatry, 66: 1100–1106.

Benios, P., Wells, R., Sackey-Aboagye, B., Klavan, H., Reidy, J., et al. (2018). Scientific Reports, 8: Article number: 4947. 10.1038/s41598-018-23062-6.

Bernsten, D., Johannessen, K. B., Thomsen, Y. D., Bertelsen, M., Hoyle, R. H., et al. (2012). Peace and War. Trajectories of Posttraumatic Stress Disorder Before, During and After Military Deployment in Afghanistan. Psychological Science, 23(12): 1557–1565.

Blakemore, S., & Choudhury, S. (2006). Development of the Adolescent Brain: Implications for Executive Function and Social Cognition. Journal of Child Psychology and Psychiatry, 47(3): 296–312.

Blore, D. (2012). In Search of the Antonym to Trauma. Germany: Lambert Academic Publishing.

Briggs, D. (Producer and Director). (2012). Heart V. Mind: What Makes Us Human. [First Broadcast on BBC4 TV, 10 July 2012].

Brodmann, K. (2006). Brodmann's Localisation in the Cerebral Cortex [Translated by L. J. Garey]. New York, NY: Springer Science and Business Media.

Buczynski, R., & Lanius, R. (2012). The Neurobiology of Trauma: How the Brain Experiences Unresolved Trauma: A Webinar Session. [Online] Available At: <http://nicabm-stealthseminar.s3.amazonaws.com/trauma2012/lanius/nicabm-ianius2012.pPdf> [Accessed 4 April 2014].

Buczysnki, R., & Porges, S. W. (2012). The Polyvagal Theory of Trauma. A Webinar Session. [Online] Available At: www.nicabm.com, [Accessed 24 February 2014].

Bullmore, E. (2018). The Inflamed Mind. London: Short Books.

Cairns, J., Overbaugh, J., & Miller, S. (1988). The Origin of Mutants. Nature, 335: 142–145.

Calaprice, A. (2011). The Ultimate Quotable Einstein. Princeton, NJ: Princeton University Press.

Canli, T., Congdon, E., Constable, R. T., & Klaus, P. L. (2008). Additive Effects of Serotonin Transporter and Tryptophan Hydroxylase-2 Gene Variation on Neural Correlates of Affective Processing. Biological Psychology, 79(1): 118–125.

Carey, G. W., & Perry, I. E. (2013). God-Man: The Word Made Flesh [Facsimile reprint of 1920 edition]. Eastford, CT: Martino Fine Books.

Carey, S., Diamond, R., & Woods, B. (1980). Developmental Course of Facial Recognition: A Maturational Component. Developmental Psychology, 16(4): 257–269.

Carlyle, T. (1922). Hoyt's New Cyclopaedia of Practical Quotations. Death of Goethe. Love Is Ever the Beginning of Knowledge, As Fire Is of Light. (Quote Reported in Hoyt, J, & Roberts.. New York and London: Funk & Wagnall's.

Cavdar, S., Onat, F., Aker, R., Şehirli, U., Şan, T., et al. (2001). The Afferent Connections of the Posterior Hypothalamic Nucleus in the Rat Using Horseradish Peroxide. Journal of Anatomy, 198(4): 463–472.

Cechetto, D., & Saper, C. (1987). Role of the Cerebral Cortex in Autonomic Function. In: Loewy, A., & Spyer, K. (Eds.), Central Regulation of Autonomic Function (pp. 208–223). Oxford: Oxford University Press.

Cherkassky, V. (2007). Functional and Anatomical Cortical under Connectivity in Autism: Evidence from A fMRI Study of an Executive Function Task and Corpus Callosum Morphometry. Cerebral Cortex, 17(4): 951–961.

Cherry, N. (2002). Schumann Resonances, A Plausible Biophysical Mechanism for the Human Health Effects of Solar/Geomagnetic Activity. Natural Hazards, 26(3): 279–331.

Col, B. (2013). Wonders of Life. London: HarperCollins.

Colvin, G. (2008). Talent Is Overrated: What Really Separates World-Class Performers from Everybody Else. London: Nicholas Brealey Publishing.

The Conservative Party. (2010). Invitation to Join the Government of Britain: The Conservative Manifesto 2010 (pp. 36–40). London: Conservative Campaign Headquarters.

Cox, B. (2013). Wonders of Life. London: Harper Collins.

Cryan, J., & Dinan, T. (2012). Mind-Altering Microorganisms: The Impact of the Gut Microbiota on Brain and Behaviour. Nature Reviews Neuroscience, 13: 701–712.

Cryan, J. F., & Dinan, G. T. (2012). An Evaluation of Neuropsychological Performance in Irritable Bowel Syndrome (Ibis): Relationship between Altered Visuospatial Memory Function, Salivary Cortisol Levels and Tryptophan Metabolism along the Kynurenine Pathway. Neurogastroenterology & Motility, 24: 175. Special Issue: Abstracts of The Joint International Neurogastroenterology And Motility Meeting, 6–8 September 2012, Bologna, Italy.

Csikszentmihalyi, M. (1990). The Psychology of Optimal Experience. London and New York: HarperCollins.

Damasio, A. R. (1996). Somatic Motor Hypothesis and the Possible Functions of the Prefrontal Cortex. Philosophical Transactions of the Royal Society B, Biological Sciences, 351: 1413–1420.

Damasio, A. R. (2010). Self Comes to Mind: Constructing the Conscious Brain. London: William Heinemann.

Damasio, A. R. (2006). Descartes' Error: Emotion. Reason and the Human Brain. London: Vintage.

Darwin, C. (1872). The Expression of the Emotions in Man and Animals. London: John Murray.

Davidson, R. (2004). Well-Being and Affective Style: Neural Substrates and Biobehavioral Correlates. Philosophical Transactions of the Royal Society of London B: Biological Sciences, 359: 1395–1411.

Davies, J. (2014). Cracked: Why Psychiatry Is Doing MoreHharm Than Good. London: Icon Books.

De Bellis, M. D., Baum, A. S., Birmaher, B., Keshavan, M. S., Eccard, C. H., et al. (1999). Developmental Traumatology: Part I Biological Stress Systems. Biological Psychiatry, 45(10): 1259–1270.

Deardorff, D. (2005). An Exploratory Case Study of Leadership Influences on Innovative Culture: A Descriptive Study. Dissertation, University of Phoenix. [Online] Available at: <www.rockypeaklc.com/dissertation> [accessed 4 April 2014].

Donne, J. (1987). Devotions Upon Emergent Occasions [Edited, with commentary, By A. Raspa]. New York, NY: Oxford University Press.

Ekman, P. (2003). Unmasking the Face: A Guide to Recognizing Emotions from Facial Expressions. Los Altos, CA: Malor Books.

Ellis, J., Brandimonte, M., Einstein, G. O., & Mcdaniel, M. (Eds.) (1996). Prospective Memory: Theory And Applications. Mahwah, NJ: Lawrence Erlbaum Associates.

Ericsson, K. A., Krampe, R. T., & Tesch-Römer, C. (1993). The Role of Deliberate Practice in the Acquisition of Expert Performance. Psychological Review, 100(3): 363–406.

Ericsson, K. A., & Lehmann, A. (1996). Expert and Exceptional Performance: Evidence on Maximal Adaptations on Task Constraints. Annual Review of Psychology, 47: 273–305.

Erikson, E. H. (1994). Identity and the Life Cycle. New York: WW Norton and Company.

Erickson, M. (1958/1980). Naturalistic Techniques of Hypnosis. In Rossi, E. (Ed)., The Cllected Papers of Milton H. Erickson on Hypnosis: Vol 1 . The Nature of Hypnosis and Suggestion, p. 168–176. New York: Irvington.

Fifield, D. (2013). Chelsea Back in Old Routine Thanks to Ramires Double at Steaua Bucharest. [Online] Available at: <www.theguardian.com/football/2013/oct/01/steaua-bucharest-chelsea-champions-league> [Accessed 13 April 2014].

Filler, A. (2007). A Historical Hypothesis of the First Recorded Neurosurgical Operation: Isis, Osiris, Thoth, and the Origin of the Djed Cross. Neurosurgical Focus, 23(1): 1–6.

Fisher, M. P. A. (2015). Quantum Cognition: The Possibility of Processing with Nuclear Spins in the Brain. Annals of Physics, 362: 593–602. Doi: 10.1098/rsif.2013.0901

Fisher M. P. A. (2017). Are We Quantum Computers or Merely Clever Robots? International Journal of Modern Physics, 31: 7.

Flavell, J. (1979). Metacognition and Cognitive Monitoring: A New Area of Cognitive–Developmental Inquiry. American Psychologist, 34(10): 906–911.

Fletcher, D., & Sarker, M. (2012). A Grounded Theory of Psychological Resilience in Olympic Champions. Psychology of Sport and Exercise, 13: 669–678.

Fox, N. (1991). If It's Not Left, It's Right: Electroencephalograph Asymmetry and the Development of Emotion. American Psychologist, 46(8): 863–872.

Freud, S. (1900a). The Interpretation of Dreams. S.E, 4, 5. London: Hogarth.

Freud, S. (1905d). A Case of Hysteria, Three Essays on Sexuality and Other Works. S.E, 7. London: Hogarth.

Gardner, H. (1993). Frames of Mind: The Theory of Multiple Intelligences [10th-anniversary edition]. New York, NY: Basic Books.

Garfinkel, S. N., & Critchley, H. D. (2013). Interoception, Emotion and Brain: New Insights Link Internal Physiology to Social Behaviour. Commentary On: Anterior Insular Cortex Mediates Bodily Sensibility and Social Anxiety. Social Cognitive and Affective Neuroscience, 8(3): 231–234.

Gellius, A. (1984). The Attic Nights of Aulus Gellius [Translated by J. C. Rolfe]. London: Heinemann (Loeb Classical Library).

Ghosh, P. Science Correspondent BBC News. Earliest Footprints outside Africa Discovered in Norfolk. [Online] Available At: <http://www.bbc.co.uk/news/science-environment-26025763> [Accessed 7 April 2014].

Gilbert, P., & Choden. (2013). Mindful Compassion: Using the Power of Mindfulness and Compassion to Transform Our Lives. London: Constable & Robinson Ltd.

Gladwell, M. (2008). Outliers: The Story of Success. New York: Little, Brown and Co.

Glaser, R., & Kiecolt-Glaser, J. (2005). Stress-Induced Immune Dysfunction: Implications for Health. Nature Reviews Immunology, 5: 245–251.

Gogtay, M., & Jay, N. (2004). Dynamic Mapping of Human Cortical Development during Childhood through Early Adulthood. PNAS, 101(21): 8174–8179.

Gowers, S., Bailey-Rogers, S. J., Shore, A., & Levine, W. (2000). The Health of the Nation Outcome Scales for Child and Adolescent Mental Health (Honosca). Child Psychology & Psychiatry Review, 5(2): 50–56.

Gray, H. (1995). Gray's Anatomy: The Anatomical Basis of Medicine and Surgery. Thirty eighth edition: London: Churchill Livingstone.

Griffin, J., & Tyrell, I. (2015). Human Givens the New Approach to Emotional Health and Clear Thinking. Hailsham: HG Publishing.

Hanson, J. L., Suh, J. W., Nacewicz, B. M., Sutterer, M. J., Cayo, A. A., et al. (2012). Robust Automated Amygdala Segmentation Via Multi-Atlas Diffeomorphic Registration. Frontiers in Neuroscience, 6: 166.

Hebb, D. (1949). The Organisation of Behaviour. New York: Wiley & Sons.

Hering, H. (1910). A Functional Test of Heart Vagus in Man. Menschen München Medizinische Wochenschrift, 57: 1931–1933.

Herisson, F., Frodermann, V., Courties, G., Rohde, D., Sun, Y., et al. (2018). Direct Vascular Channels Connect Skull Bone Marrow and the Brain Surface Enabling Myeloid Cell Migration. Nature Neuroscience, 21: 1209–1217.

Herrmann, N. (1991). The Creative Brain. Journal of Creative Behaviour, 25(4): 275–295.

Hess, W. (1949). Nobel Prize Acceptance Speech: For Medicine/Physiology (1949). [Online] Available At: <http://www.nobelprize.org/nobel_prizes/medicine/laureates/1949/press.html> [Accessed 18 March 2014].

Hobson, R. F. (2013). Forms of Feeling: The Heart of Psychotherapy (p. 98). London and New York: Routledge.

Hogenboom, M. Science Reporter, BBC News. Blow to Multiple Human Species Idea. [Online] Available At: <http://www.bbc.co.uk/news/science-environment-24564375> [Accessed 7 April 2013].

Horovitz, L. A. (2002). Eureka! Scientific Breakthroughs that Changed the World. London: Wiley And Sons.

Jung, C. G. (1964). Civilisation in Transition [The Collected Works of Carl Gustav Jung, Vol. 10]. London: Routledge.

Kandel, E. R., & Squire, L. R. (1999). Memory: From Mind to Molecules. New York: W. H. Freeman and Company.

Keats, J. (1817). Letter to Benjamin Bailey, 22 November 1817. In: Gittings, R. (Ed.), (1970). Letters of John Keats. Oxford: Oxford University Press.

Kennedy, M. (2014). 850,000-Year Old Human Footprints Found in Norfolk. The Guardian, 7 Feb 2014 (accessed 19 Sept 2018).

Kennedy, P., Clarke, G., O'Neill, A., Groeger, J., Quigley, E., et al. (1962). Cognitive, Social, and Physiological Determinants of Emotional State. Psychological Review, 69: 379–399.

Keyes, K. (1984). The Hundredth Monkey. Camarillo, CA: Devorss & Co.

Kinsbourne, M. (1988). Hemisphere Interactions in Depression. In: Kinsbourne, M. (Ed.), Hemisphere Function in Depression (pp. 133–162). Washington, DC: American Psychiatric Association.

Koestler, A. (1964). The Act of Creation. London: Hutchinson & Co.

Lama, D. (2012). His Holiness the Dalai Lama UK Visit. [Teachings by His Holiness the Dalai Lama; Pamphlet Issued on The Dalai Lama's Talk at The Manchester Arena, UK, 18 June 2012].

Langley, J. (1921). The Autonomic Nervous System. Part 1. Cambridge: W. Heffer & Sons.

Lanius, R., Williamson, P., Hopper, J., Densmore, M., Boksmann, K., et al. (2003). Recall of Emotional States in Posttraumatic Stress Disorder: An fMRI Investigation. https://doi.org/10.1016/S0006-3223(02)01466-X

Laub, B., & Shapiro, E. (2008). Early EMDR Intervention (EEI); A Summary, A Theoretical Model and the Recent Traumatic Episode Protocol (RTEP). Journal of EMDR Research and Practice, 2(2): 79–96.

László, E. (2007). The Akashic Field. New York: Dutton.

Leadbeater, C. (2013). The Chakras, A Monograph. Wheaton, IL: Quest Books.

Leonard, P. (Producer and Director). (2010). What Happened before the Big Bang? [First Broadcast on BBC2 TV, 11 October 2010].

Lerner, E. L. (1991). The Big Bang Never Happened. New York, NY: Vintage Books.

Lipton, B. H. (2001). Nature, Nurture and Human Development. Journal of Prenatal and Perinatal Psychology and Health, 16(2): 167–180.

Lipton, B. H. (2011). The Biology of Belief: Unleashing the Power of Consciousness, Matter and Miracles. London: Hay House UK.

Lipton, B. H. (2013). The Honeymoon Effect: The Science of Creating Heaven on Earth. London: Hay House UK.

Littleton, K., & Mercer, N. (2013). Interthinking: Putting Talk to Work. Abingdon: Routledge.

Louveau, A., Smirnov, I., & Kipnis, J. (2018). Structural and Functional Features of Central Nervous System Lymphatics. Nature, 24; 533(7602): 278

Lovett, J. (1999). Small Wonders: Healing Childhood Trauma with EMDR. New York, NY: The Free Press.

Luthar, S. S., Cicchetti, D., & Becker, B. (2000). The Construct of Resilience: A Critical Evaluation and Guidelines for Future Work. Child Development, 71(3): 543–562.

Makin, S. (2017). Where Does the Brain Store Long-Ago Memories? An Internal Filing System Sorts Events for Short- or Long-term Use. Scientific American, 12 April.

Malone, D. F. (July 2012). Horizon. Heart Vs Mind: What Makes Us Human? BBC Four.

Mantyh, F. (1982). Forebrain Projections to the Periaqueductal Grey in the Monkey, with Observations in the Cat and Rat. Journal of Comparative Neurology, 206(2): 146–158.

Maslow, A. (1943). A Theory of Human Motivation. Psychological Review, 50(4): 370–396.

McCraty, R., Atkinson, M., & Tomasino, D. (2001). The Science of the Heart: Exploring the Role of the Heart in Human Performance. Boulder Creek, CA: Heartmath Research Center.

McLeod, J. (2017). Qualitative Methods for Routine Outcome Measurement. In T. G. Rousmaniere, R. Goodyear, S. D. Miller, & B. Wampold (Eds.), The Cycle of Excellence: Using Deliberate Practice to Improve Supervision and Training (pp. 85–107). London: Wiley.

McGilchrist, I. (2009). The Master and His Emissary: The Divided Brain and the Making of the Western World (p. 17). New Haven, CT: Yale University Press.

McGivern, R., Andersen, J., Byrd, D., Mutter, K. L., & Reilly, J. (2002). Cognitive Efficiency on a Match to Sample Task Decreases at the Onset of Puberty in Children. Brain and Cognition, 50(1): 73–89.

Mcilroy, R. (2013). Rory McIlroy Says Management Issues Have Been A "Distraction". [Online] Available At: <www.bbc.co.uk/sport/0/golf/24914810> [Accessed 18 March 2014].

Meer, F. (1990). Higher than Hope: The Authorised Biography of Nelson Mandela. London: Hamish Hamilton.

Mercer, N., & Littleton, K. (2007). Dialogue and the Development of Children's Thinking: A Sociocultural Approach. London: Routledge.

Mieder, W. (2010). Making A Way Out of No Way: Martin Luther King's Sermonic Proverbial Rhetoric. Index of Proverbs and Proverbial Phrases (p. 352). New York: Peter Lang Publishing Inc.

Molden, D., & Hutchinson, P. (2007). Brilliant Nap: What the Most Successful People Know, Do and Say. Harlow: Pearson Education.

Muir, E., Lojkasek, M., & Cohen, N. (1999). Watch, Wait and Wonder: A Manual Describing A Dyadic Infant-Led Approach to Problems in Infancy and Early Childhood. Toronto: Hincks-Dellcrest Institute.

National Research Council. (2000). From Neurons to Neighbourhoods: The Science of Early Childhood Development. Washington, DC: The National Academies Press.

Nelson, E. E., Leibenluft, E., McClure, E. B., & Pine, D. S. (2005). The Social Reorientation of Adolescence: A Neuroscience Perspective on the Process and Its Relation to Psychopathology. Psychological Medicine, 35(2): 163–174.

New Zealand Folk Song. (2011). Ka Mate. [Online] Available At: <http://folksong.org.nz/ka_mate/1chant.html> [Accessed 4 April 2014].

Newton, I. (1675) Letter to Robert Hooke, 5 February 1675. The Newton Project. From Memoirs of the Life, Writings and Discoveries of Sir Isaac Newton (1), Edinburgh 1855. Letter Written Cambridge, 5 February 1675. [Online] Available At: <www.newtownproject.sussex.uk/view/texts/normalised/othe00101> [Accessed 24 February 2014].

Noesselt, T., Driver, J., Heinze, H. J., & Dolan, R. (2005). Asymmetrical Activation in the Human Brain during Processing of Fearful Faces. Current Biology, 15(5): 424–429.

Nosarti, C., Reichenberg, A., Murray, R. M., Cnattingius, S., Lambe, M. P., et al. (2012). Preterm Birth and Psychiatric Disorders in Young Adult Life. Archives of General Psychiatry, 69: 610–617.

Ogden, P., Pain, C., & Minton, K. (2006). Trauma and the Body: An SF-EMDR Approach to Psychotherapy. New York, NY: W. W. Norton & Co.

Ohno, S. (1972). So Much Junk DNA in Our Genome. Brookhaven Symposia on Biology, 2: 366–370.

O'Malley, A. G. (2015). The Art of BART: Bilateral Affective Reprocessing of Thoughts as a Dynamic Model for Psychotherapy. London: Karnac.

Oppenheim, D., & Goldsmith, D. F. (Eds.) (2007). Attachment Theory in Clinical Work with Children: Bridging the Gap between Research and Practice. New York: The Guilford Press (Ch. 1 By Zeanah, C. Dry, pp. 3–30).

Paramahamsa Yogananda. (1955). Autobiography of a Yogi. London: Rider.

Panksepp, J. (1988). Affective Neuroscience: The Foundations of Human and Animal Emotions. New York, NY: Oxford University Press.

Panksepp, J., & Bernatsky, G. (2002). Emotional Sounds and the Brain: The Neuro-Affective Foundations of Musical Appreciation. Behavioural Processes, 60: 33–155.

Parnell, L. (2013). Attachment-Focused EMDR. Healing Relational Trauma. New York and London: W. W. Norton & Company.

Pascal, B. (1995). Penseés [Translated with an Introduction by A. Krailsheimer]. London: Penguin.

Pelvig, D. P., Pakkenberg, H., Stark, A. K., & Pakkenberg, B. (2008). Neocortical Glial Cell Numbers in Human Brains. Neurobiol. Aging 29, 1754–1762. 10.1016/jneurobiolaging.2007.04.013 [PubMed]

Peters, S. (2012). The Chimp Paradox: The Mind Management Programme for Confidence, Success and Happiness. London: Vermilion.

Poem Found at <http://answers.yahoo.com/question/index?qid=20100901201717aauqnei> [Accessed 13 April 2014].

Poincaré, H. (1905). Sur la dynamique de l'électron. Comptes rendus de l'Academie des Sciences, 140: 1504–1508.

Pollak, S. (2012). Lecture Presented at the University of Manchester at the Department of Speech and Language Therapy. Developmental Neuroscience Seminar Series. November 2012. London: UCL Great Ormond Street Institute of Child Health

Porges, S. W. (1995). Orienting in a Defensive World: Mammalian Modifications of Our Evolutionary Heritage. A Polyvagal Theory. Psychophysiology, 32: 301–318.

Porges, S. W. (2006). Social Engagement and Attachment: A Phylogenetic Perspective. Annals of the New York Academy of Sciences, 1008: 31–47.

Porges, S. W. (2009). The Polyvagal Theory: New Insights into Adaptive Reactions of the Autonomic Nervous System. Cleveland Clinic Journal of Medicine, 76(Suppl. 2): S86–S90.

Porges, S. W., & Doussard-Roosevelt, J. (1999). Sleep State and Vagal Regulation of Heart Period Patterns in the Human Newborn: An Extension of the Polyvagal Theory. Psychophysiology, 36(1): 14–21.

Poynder, M. (1992). Pi in the Sky: A Revelation of the Ancient Wisdom Tradition. London: Rider.

Pujol, J., Vendrell, P., Junqué, C., Martí-Vilalta, J. L., & Capdevila, A. (1993). When Does Human Brain Development End? Evidence of Corpus Callosum Growth up to Adulthood. Annals of Neurology, 34(1): 71–75.

Raichle, M. E., & Snyder, A. Z. (2007). A Default Mode of Brain Function: A Brief History of an Evolving Idea. Neuroimage, 37: 1083–1090.

Rizzolatti, G., Forgassi, L., & Gallese, V. (2001). Neurophysiological Mechanisms Underlying the Understanding and Imitation of Action. Nature Reviews: Neuroscience, 50: 661–670.

Roberts, R. M. (1989). Serendipity: Accidental Discoveries in Science. New York: Wiley.

Robinson, K. (2009). The Element: How Finding Your Passion Changes Everything. London: Penguin Books.

Rossi, E. L. (1996). The Symptom Path to Enlightenment: The New Dynamics of Self-Organisation in Hypnotherapy. New York: Zeig, Thucker & Theisen.

Rossi, E. L. (2002). The Psychobiology of Gene Expression: Neuroscience and Neurogenesis in Hypnosis and the Healing Arts. New York: W.W. Norton.

Rossi, E. L. (2004). The Genomic Science Foundation of Body Psychotherapy. The USA Body Psychotherapy Journal, 3(2): 30–49.

Rossi, E. & Rossi, K. (2015). Optimising the Human Condition with Psychosocial Genomic Star Maps: Implicit Processing Heuristics in the 4-Stage Creative Cycle. The International Journal of the Psychosocial Genomics: Consciousness and Health Research, 1 (2): 5–17 www.psychosocialgenomics.com

Rusbridger, A. (2014) Interview with Professor Ray Dolan. [Online] Available At: <http://alanrusbridger.com/playitagain/interviews/interview-professor-ray-dolan-frs> [Accessed 18 March 2014].

Russell, B. (1945). A History of Western Philosophy. New York, NY: Simon And Schuster.

Sayed, M. (2011). Bounce: The Myth of Talent and the Power of Practice. London: HarperCollins.

Schachter, S., & Singer, J. (1962). Cognitive, Social and Physiological Determinants of Emotional State. Psychological Review, 69(5): 379–399.

Schutter, D. J., & Van Honk, J. (2006). An Electrophysiological Link between the Cerebellum, Cognition and Emotion: Frontal Theta EEG Activity to Single-Pulse Cerebellar TMS. Neuroimage, 33(4): 1227–1231.

Schwaller De Lubicz, R. A. (1998). The Temple in Man. Rochester, VT: Inner Traditions, Bear & Co.

Searl, J. (1990). The Mystery of Consciousness. New York, NY: New York Review of Books.

Seung, S. (2012). Connectome: How the Brain's Wiring Makes Us Who We Are. London: Penguin Books.

Shakespeare, W. (1979). Macbeth. K. Muir (Ed.). London: Methuen.

Shapiro, F. (2001). Eye Movement Desensitisation and Reprocessing (EMDR): Basic Principles, Protocols, and Procedures [2nd Ed.]. New York, NY: Guilford Press.

Sheldrake, R. (1988). Extended Mind, Power and Prayer. Morphic Resonance and the Collective Unconscious – Part III. Psychological Perspectives, 19(1): 64–78.

Sherrington, C. (1906). The Integrative Action of the Nervous System. New Haven, CT: Yale University Press.

Siegel, D. J. (2010). The Mindful Therapist: A Clinician's Guide to Mindsight and Neural Integration. New York: W. W. Norton.

Siegel, I. (2017). The Sacred Path of the Therapist: Modern Healing, Ancient Wisdom, and Client Transformation. New York: W. W. Norton & Company.

Siegel, I. (2018). The Sacred Path of the Therapist: Modern Healing, Ancient Wisdom, and Client Transformation. Journal of EMDR Practice and Research, 12(2): 92–92.

Simon-Thomas, E. R., Role, K. O., & Knight, R. T. (2005). Behavioural and Electrophysiological Evidence of a Right Hemisphere Bias for the Influence of Negative Emotion on Higher Cognition. Journal of Cognitive Neuroscience, 17(3): 518–529.

Sitchin, Z. (1976). The 12th Planet. New York, NY: Stein and Day.

Smith, H. H. (1972). Evolution of Genetic Systems. New York, NY: Gordon & Breach.

Smyke, A., Dumitrescu, A., & Zeanah, C. (2002). Attachment Disturbances in Young Children I: The Continuum of Caretaking Casualty. Journal of the American Academy of Child and Adolescent Psychiatry, 41(8): 972–982.

Stefanov, M., Potroz, M., Kim, J., Lim, J., Cha, R., et al. (2013). The Primo Vascular System as a New Anatomical System. Journal of Acupuncture and Meridian Studies, 6 (Issue 6): 331–338. 10.1016/j.jams.10.001.

Stickgold, R. Prof. (2002). EMDR: A Putative Neurobiological Mechanism of Action. Journal of Clinical Psychology, 58(1): 61–75.

Stringer, C. (2011). The Origin of Our Species. London: Allen Lane.

Toga, A., & Thompson, P. (2003). Mapping Brain Asymmetry. Nature Reviews Neuroscience, 4: 37–48.

Torjesen, I. (2012). Preterm Babies Have a Greater Risk of Psychiatric Conditions as Adults. BMJ, 344: e3922.

Tsuchiya, N., & Adolphs, R. (2007). Emotion and Consciousness. Trends in Cognitive Sciences, 11(4): 158–167.

Verhoeven, J., Revesz, D., Epel, E. S., Lin, J., Wolfowitz, O. M., et al. (2013). Major Depressive Disorder and Accelerated Cellular Ageing: Results from a Large Psychiatric Cohort Study. Molecular Psychiatry. Advance Online Publication 12 November 2013. [Online] Available At: <http://www.nature.com/mp/journal/vaop/ncurrent/abs/mp2013151a.html>

Villa, P., Kajantie, E., Räikkönen, K., Pesonen, A., Hämäläinen, E., et al. (2013). Aspirin in the Prevention of Pre-Eclampsia in High-Risk Women: A Randomised Placebo-Controlled Predo Trial and a Meta-Analysis of Randomised Trials. Bjog, 120(1): 64–74.

Vogt, B. (2005). Pain and Emotion Interactions in Subregions of the Cingulate Gyrus. Nature Reviews Neuroscience, 6(7): 533–544.

Wall, P. D., & Melzack, R. (Eds.) (1999). *Textbook of Pain*, 4th edn. New York, NY: Churchill Livingstone.

Wan, Y., Qu, K., Zhang, Q. C., Flynn, R. A., Manor, O., et al. (2014). Landscape and Variation of RNA Secondary Structure across the Human Transcriptome. Nature, 505: 706–709.

Waters, O. (2013). Doing by Not Doing. Spiritual Dynamics Newsletter. [Online] Available at: <http://www.spiritualdynamics.net/articles/author/owen/> [Accessed 18 March 2014.]

Weinreb, O., & Youdim, M. B. H. (2007). A Model of MPTP-induced Parkinson's Disease in the Goldfish. Nature Protocols, 2: 3016–3021.

Whitaker, R., & Cosgrove, L. (2015). Psychiatry Under the Influence: Institutional Corruption, Social Injury, and Prescriptions for Reform. London: Palgrave Macmillan.

Williams, C. (2018) The Secret of You; an Overlooked Bulge at the Back of the Brain Could Be the Key to Making Us Who We Are. New Scientist July 7, 36–39.

Wimmer, H., & Perner, J. (1983). Beliefs about Beliefs: Representation and Constraining Function of Wrong Beliefs in Young Children's Understanding of Deception. Cognition, 13: 103–128.

Wittgenstein, L. (1973). Philosophical Investigations [Translated By G. E. M. Anscombe]. Oxford: Wiley-Blackwell.

Wulf, G., McConnell, N., Gärtner, M., & Schwarz, A. (2002). Enhancing the Learning of Sports Skills through External-Focus Feedback. Journal of Motor Behavior, 34(2): 171–182.

Wundt, W. (1902). Principles of Physiological Psychology. Morphological Development of the Central Organs [Translated from The Fifth German Edition by E. B. Titchener]. New York, NY: The Macmillan Co.

Zecevic, N., & Rakic, P. (2001). Development of Layer I Neurons in the Primate Cerebral Cortex. The Journal of Neuroscience, 21(15): 5607–5619.

Index